Modern Britain since 1979

TAURIS HISTORY READERS

British Imperial History, 1773–1960
edited by *Douglas M. Peers*
Hardback ISBN 1 86064 159 8
Paperback ISBN 1 86064 160 1

British Women's History to 1914
edited by *Alison Twells*
Hardback ISBN 1 86064 161 X
Paperback ISBN 1 86064 162 8

Modern Britain since 1906
edited by *Keith Laybourn*
Hardback ISBN 1 86064 298 5
Paperback ISBN 1 86064 237 3

Modern Britain since 1979
edited by *Christine Collette & Keith Laybourn*
Hardback ISBN 1 86064 596 8
Paperback ISBN 1 86064 597 6

Race and Nation
edited by *Clive Christie*
Hardback ISBN 1 86064 195 4
Paperback ISBN 1 86064 194 6

Twentieth Century International History
edited by *Stephen Chan & Jarrod Weiner*
Hardback ISBN 1 86064 301 9
Paperback ISBN 1 86064 302 7

Modern Britain since 1979
A Reader

Edited by
Christine Collette
& Keith Laybourn

I.B. TAURIS

LONDON · NEW YORK

Published in 2003 by I.B.Tauris & Co Ltd
6 Salem Road, London W2 4BU
175 Fifth Avenue, New York NY 10010
www.ibtauris.com

In the United States of America and in Canada distributed by
Palgrave Macmillan, a division of St Martin's Press
175 Fifth Avenue, New York NY 10010

ISBN 1 86064 596 8 hardback
ISBN 1 86064 597 6 paperback

A full CIP record for this book is available from the British Library
A full CIP record for this book is available from the Library of Congress

Library of Congress catalog card: available

Typeset in Caslon by Steve Tribe, Andover
Printed and bound in Great Britain by MPG Books Ltd, Bodmin

Contents

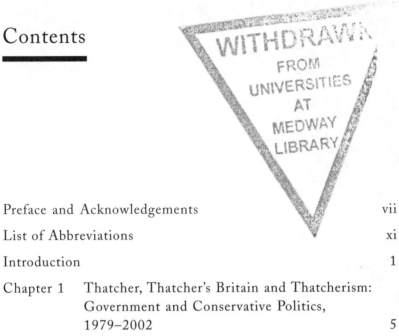

Preface and Acknowledgements

Many people have helped us in the production of this book. Most obviously Dr Lester Crook, of I.B.Tauris, has been an excellent and patient editor and also gave us permission to quote from the work of books produced by I.B.Tauris. Although there are about 50,000 words of introductory material in this book of about 116,000 words, the rest of the book is made up of both secondary and primary documents. Every publisher, and some individuals, connected with these sources has been contacted by us and we would particularly like to thank all those who have given permission for these documents to be published. They include Brendan Evans, for the use of extracts from his book on *Thatcherism and British Politics 1975-1999*; Beth Junor for material connected with the Greenham Common Women's Peace Camp, Mary Sharp for the Carlton Club Political Committee for the use of extracts from John Major's *Conservatism in the 1990s: Our Common Purpose* (Fifth Carlton Lecture, 1993), the Conservative Party, the Labour Party, Richard Grayson of the Liberal Democratic Party for the use of extracts from *Making the Difference: The Liberal Manifesto 1997*, the Minority Rights Group International for extracts from their report *The Rastafarians* by E. E. Cashman (1984); the Institute of Race Relations, and the Race Today Collective. Crown Copyright material, including extracts from *Hansard* is reproduced by the permission of Her Majesty's Stationary Office Ltd. The Stationary Office have also given permission to publish material. The Scottish Parliament has done likewise. The Equal Opportunities Commission has also given its permission for us to use some of their published material. The following individuals have also given us permission to use their material: Alice Brown, Lord Callaghan, Robert Hazell, Clare Farquar, Robert Hazell, Beth Junor (in connection with the Greenham Common Historic Site Fund) and Diane Richardson.

We would also like to thank Stephen Bird, archivist at the Labour History Study and Archive Centre of The John Rylands University Library, University of Manchester, for his help in locating some copyright owners. In connection with these enquiries, we would particularly like to thank Francis King for permission to use the extracts from the Communist Party Archive, located in the Labour History Archive of John Rylands Library, and to Ruth Frow for permission to use extracts from the privately published pamphlet *The Liquidation of the Communist Party of Great Britain* written by both Ruth and Eddie Frow.

Numerous institutions and publishers have given their permission to reproduce material. They include those listed hereafter: Addison Wesley Longman Ltd, Argyll Publishing, Blackwell Publishing, Edinburgh University Press, Ethnic Minority Group International, Family Policy Studies Centre, HarperCollins Publishers, Labour Research Department, Oxford University Press, Palgrave Macmillan, Pan Macmillan, Macmillan, Mainstream Publishing, Pearson Education, Pluto Press for extracts from Ron Ramdin, *Reimaging Britain*; Sheffield Hallam University Press, Sutton Publishing, I.B.Tauris Publishers, Routledge (part of the Taylor Francis group), the Taylor Francis, Thomson Publishing Services, the *Guardian* and the *Observer*.

Various journals have also given their permission for us to print extracts from their articles. These are *Critical Social Policy*, *Ethnic and Racial Studies*, *Ethnic Relations*, *Feminist Review*, *Parliamentary Affairs* (published by Oxford University Press), *Race and Class* and *Sexualities*.

Every efforts has been made to track down the copyright owners of the quoted documents. As previously indicated, every publisher whose work has been used has been contacted and, in the cases of self-published material and primary sources, the individuals or organisations concerned have also been contacted. Those who did not reply within about six weeks were also contacted by phone. Even then there has, in a number of cases, been no reply despite repeated efforts - letter and phone calls (of which a record has been kept). In particular, we were unable to obtain permission to quote from the writings of Margaret Thatcher. In the case of some publishers, such as John Donald, it has been impossible to contact them since they have gone out of existence. In the cases of sources that could not be located, as in cases where they could, the full sources have been quoted in the text. Nevertheless, the author and publisher would like to apologise for any inadvertent infringement of copyright and have, in any case, sought to keep within the Publishers' Fair Dealing Convention guidelines in the use of some recently published secondary sources, that is, books and articles. In every case the documents have been fully attributed on first citation.

Christine Collette and Keith Laybourn

Abbreviations

BBC	British Broadcasting Corporation
BDC	Brixton Defence Campaign
CPGB	Communist Party of Great Britain
DHSS	Department of Health and Social Security
DUP	Democratic Unionist Party
EC	European Community
EOC	Equal Opportunities Commission
HMSO	Her Majesty's Stationary Office
IRA	Irish Republican Army
LBBs	Liverpool Born Blacks
MSPs	Members of the Scottish Parliament
NUM	National Union of Mineworkers
OWAAD	Organisation of Women of Asian and African Descent
PIRA	Provisional IRA
PSBR	Public Sector Borrowing Requirement
RUC	Royal Ulster Constabulary
SDP	Social Democratic Party
SNP	Scottish Nationalist Party
TGWU	Transport and General Workers' Union
TUC	Trades Union Congress
UDM	Union of Democratic Mineworkers
VAT	Value Added Tax

Introduction

The years between 1979 and 2002 have seen a remarkable transformation in the social, political and economic life of Britain. The political consensus that once existed around the maintenance of the welfare state has gone; political attitudes within the Conservative and Labour parties have changed fundamentally; socialist and Marxist parties have collapsed or gone into decline; trade unions have diminished in power and influence; there have been tensions in creating a more equal society for women and minority groups; and there have been moves towards increasing democracy and regional self-determination within the United Kingdom. All of these issues are examined in *Modern Britain since 1979*.

From this multitude of changes, four major developments have been dominant. These are focused on the impact of 'Thatcherism' and the need to arrest Britain's economic decline, the redefining of the welfare state, the demand for women's rights, and the slow move towards a more multicultural and equality-based society in which all people have the right to increased self-determination – whether they be black, women, Welsh, Scottish or Irish.

Undoubtedly, the foremost issue for late twentieth-century Britain was the rise of Thatcherism. When Margaret Thatcher became Prime Minister of a Conservative government in 1979, she began to change the political climate of Britain. Committed to 'rolling back the state', reducing the burden of welfare and allowing

1

unfettered industry access to more funds to develop and expand to meet market requirements, she was committed to removing the impediments, as she saw them, to British economic growth. In shattering the old political and economic consensus, Thatcherism sought to destroy trade unionism and to assert Britain's economic and political independence in the face of what she came to see as an intrusive European Economic Community seeking to create a monolithic political and economic European state.

Thatcherism certainly achieved some of its objectives, above all in the undermining of trade union power, defeating the coal miners in 1984–5 and bringing about the collapse of trade union membership from about 13 million to eight million during her years in office (1979–1990). Her victories at the 1979, 1983 and 1987 general elections also forced other political parties to reassess their positions. As a result, the Labour Party moved from its old 'leftwing' policies of the 1983 general election, when its election manifesto was described by Gerald Kaufmann as 'the longest suicide note in history', to a situation where it regrouped under Neil Kinnock and dropped its old Labour and statist views under Tony Blair in the mid-1990s, re-emerging as 'New Labour' with its commitment to operating a partnership between the public and private sectors. Similarly, the Communist Party of Great Britain (CPGB) dropped its old commitments to Moscow, advocated Eurocommunism and its extension in Britain and gradually created its own 'pick-and-mix' form of Marxism in an attempt to staunch the flow and threat of Thatcherism. In the end, the CPGB dissolved and became the Democratic Left in November 1991.

The welfare state became one of the great battlegrounds for Thatcher, since she sought to reduce the financial burden of the state to release resources and lower interest rates for the expansion of private industry. Monetarism was to be the solution to Britain's economic decline, and the benefits of economic success would 'trickle down' from the top to the bottom of society. In reality, such a policy was thwarted by the fact that monetarist policies, and the reduction of some government spending, brought an enormous rise in unemployment which the state had to pay for. Nevertheless the movement from the demand-led approach to welfare, as envisaged by William Beveridge in the early 1940s, to the supply-led ideas of monetarism, brought change. By the 1990s, both John Major and Tony Blair had begun to reassess the future of the welfare state, anticipating a looser relationship between individual and government. Indeed, on 18 March 1999, Blair pledged the Government to a 20-year programme to eradicate child poverty, along with a new commitment that the new welfare state would be based upon a partnership between both private and public provision. However, Gordon Brown's 2002 Budget, with its emphasis upon enormously increasing the state contribution to the National Health Service, has, perhaps, modified New Labour's approach.

The last quarter of the twentieth century was also a time when women sought, and achieved, a measure of political and social change. The 1950s ideal of a two-parent nuclear family, headed by a male breadwinner, was challenged as being both oppressive in terms of social attitudes to women and an inaccurate portrayal of the lives of many working women. Legislation in the field of employment law improved women's position in the workforce and protected them to some extent against sexual harassment and discrimination, including that arising from time out for pregnancy and childcare. Feminism was a political force which demanded recognition from all political parties and trade unions. Single-issue feminist campaigns included a woman's right to choose abortion, the avowal of rights for lesbian women and resistance to the presence of nuclear weapons on British territory. Some feminists made alliances with the Labour Party, which returned an unprecedented number of women MPs in 1997. Feminism followed its own course of developments, in particular coming to accept the challenges from black and lesbian women to its perceived white, heterosexual, middle-class profile. Thus while feminist political practices changed, feminism remained a vibrant political philosophy. However, at the end of the century, while young women benefited from improvements to women's education and employment, older women still suffered from the after-effects of post-war gender discrimination, so that, overall, equality remained a goal, rather than an achievement.

Equality was also unrealised in terms of Britain's multi-culturalism. The longstanding presence of a variety of ethnic groupings did not prevent the racism suffered by colonial immigrants to post-war Britain. This discrimination, evident in the labour market and in housing and education services, survived to be faced by second and third-generation, British-born ethnic groupings. Indeed, racism was fostered by small but active neo-fascist groups such as the National Front. It was combated by action from minority groups themselves, including engagement in trade unions and the Labour Party; by legislation and by the activities of the various race equality and community relations bodies which developed. While the commonality of a black identity was perceived by some in the 1980s as empowering, official policy was to proclaim Britain's multiculturalism, while minority groupings turned to a celebration of diversity. The 1991 Census was the first to attempt a count of Britain's multiracial society, identifying three million people, 5.5 per cent of the population, as belonging to minority ethnic groupings. Of these, some groups and, again, young people, were more able to overcome discrimination than their seniors, by profiting from better education. For example, by the end of the century, Indian and African-Asian men were more likely to achieve a degree qualification than white men. Four black and five Asian MPs were elected in 1997, an unprecedented though woefully small number. Discrimination continued and the charge of 'institutional racism' was levelled at some British organisations, notably the police. Riots, partly motivated by racial tensions, were witnessed in several British inner cities from 1981 and were mirrored by those in certain Northern towns in 2001. The renewed perception of distinct Scottish and Welsh identities and the creation of the Scottish Parliament and Welsh Assembly complicated the pattern of multiculturalism, impelling some people to restate their British, or 'UK' identity. In Northern Ireland, after long experience of 'the Troubles', huge steps were taken to reconcile two distinct communities and the 'Good Friday Agreement' of 10 April 1998 has, so far, offered a considerable opportunity to reconcile conflict in Northern Ireland.

Essentially, then, this book seeks to examine the major trends and developments that shaped British domestic policy between 1979 and 2002. It examines various issues and debates that have emerged and, although events are still developing, suggests three main points. The first is that Thatcherism has changed the political landscape of Britain, despite moves away from her policies since the 1990s. Secondly, it suggests that the future welfare state will be a partnership between the public and private sectors, despite the 2002 Budget. Finally, that there is an increasing move towards equality and self-determination in British society – whether on issues of race, regional politics or women's rights – although there is still a long way to go.

Chapter 1

Thatcher, Thatcher's Britain and Thatcherism: Government and Conservative Politics, 1979–2002

In May 1979, Margaret Thatcher became Britain's first and, so far, only female Prime Minister. A powerful and determined politician, Thatcher gave her name to an ideology, Thatcherism, which stood for a limited but firm government, the rolling back of the welfare state, the end of consensus politics and a staunchly anti-European and independent attitude on many vital issues. As Prime Minister in three administrations between 1979 and 1990, she fundamentally transformed the nature and pattern of British politics. Indeed, she was one of the most combative of prime ministers in the twentieth century, challenging the post-war political consensus, in her attempt to restore what she described as 'Victorian values'. Her impact was clearly visible on the politics of John Major, her successor in 1990, and upon William Hague and Iain Duncan Smith, subsequent leaders of the Conservative Party (Documents 4–6).

Margaret Thatcher: The Early Years

Margaret Hilda Roberts was born on 13 October 1925, the younger daughter of Alfred Roberts and Beatrice Stephenson, in a family of lower-middle-class grocers, and she was raised as a Methodist. Her father was an ex-Liberal who became an Independent councillor and Mayor of Grantham, Lincolnshire, greatly influencing Margaret with his emphasis upon thriftiness and a belief in the free-market economy. She was educated at Kesteven and Grantham Grammar

School, where she was known as 'Snotty Roberts', and from there went on to Somerville College, Oxford, where she ended with a second-class honours degree in Chemistry. She worked for a period in commercial and industrial chemistry (1947–51) and then married a fellow Methodist, Denis Thatcher, in 1951. During these years, Thatcher read for the Bar and passed her exams to become a lawyer in 1953, practising for a few years in the field of tax law.

Thatcher's active interest in politics began at Oxford and she quickly became involved in parliamentary politics, losing in the Dartford parliamentary constituency at the general elections of 1950 and 1951. She eventually secured the Conservative candidature at Finchley in 1958 and represented that seat from 1959 to 1992 (when she was raised to the House of Lords). Initially, she was promoted to a minor post in October 1961 and was, successively, Conservative Party spokesman on pensions, housing, energy, transport, education and the environment between 1961 and 1970, entering the Shadow Cabinet in 1967. She then became Secretary of State at the Department of Education and Science in the government of Edward Heath, from June 1970 to February 1974. In this post, she campaigned for the extension of nursery education but also felt that the Ministry of Education was 'self-righteously socialist' and spending too much on education. Not surprisingly, she earned the reputation for being a 'cutting minister' when she transferred a small amount of money from the provision of school milk to science. The furore that resulted led to the catchy phrase 'Thatcher the milk snatcher'. At that point she appeared to be an unpopular political figure and with the defeat of the Conservatives in the general elections in 1974 it seemed that her political star was on the wane. Yet she stood against Edward Heath for the leadership of the Conservative Party in 1975 and won by 130 votes to 119, in what was effectively a backbench revolt against Heath. She then won the second ballot against William Whitelaw, who subsequently became Deputy Leader of the Conservative Party and Deputy Prime Minister and the subject of Thatcher's comment that 'Every prime minister needs a Willy'.

Thatcher as Opposition Leader

As Leader of the Opposition (1975–9), Thatcher moved to replace the old Heathite One-Nation and state-interventionist Tories with figures of the New Right, such as Sir Keith Joseph and Rhodes Boyson, who were favouring the free market of writers such as Milton

Friedman and Friedrich von Hayek. She had been influenced by such ideas through her father and had identified with these political figures when she became vice-chairman of the Centre for Policy Studies in June 1974. Her opportunity to introduce such ideas came when she won the 1979 general election, defeating a deeply unpopular Labour government led by James Callaghan, which had just faced its 'Winter of Discontent' of industrial disputes (see Chapter 4).

Thatcherism

Throughout the 1980s, British politics was dominated by Mrs Thatcher. She imposed upon her Conservative governments a monetarist policy which had been of marginal importance before she became Conservative leader. The basic philosophy was one of rolling back the state, reducing the burden of welfare and allowing unfettered industry access to more funds to develop and expand to meet the market's requirements. These views went back to the ideas of Friedrich von Hayek, whose book *The Road to Serfdom* (1944) argued that economic planning necessitated tyranny. Indeed socialism was the pathway to totalitarianism, for it offered economic and social security which held hidden dangers: when security is understood in too absolute a sense, the general striving for it, far from increasing the chances of freedom, becomes the gravest threat to it. These views were revived and revised by Rhodes Boyson in his collection of essays *Down with the Poor* (1971), and were given some support by the Heath Government of 1970–4. Boyson referred to the need to end paternalism and clearly stated that 'Not only is the present welfare state inefficient and destructive of personal liberty, individual responsibility and moral growth, but it saps the collective moral fibre of our people as a nation.' From the mid-1970s, Thatcher and Joseph promoted these views and the Conservative Party's 'conversion' to monetarism, free-market principles and a *laissez-faire* view of society. The philosophy of the New Right, which was of marginal importance in the 1960s, occupied the centre-stage of British politics in the 1980s and early 1990s. One central theme of the Thatcher administrations was the freeing of enterprise and initiative from the interference of the state. This meant that state expenditure on welfare had to be cut (Documents 7 and 9). As Keith Joseph once wrote, 'Cuts mean cuts'.

For more than a decade, the views of the New Right gathered strength. The promotion of the new philosophy of 'independence' was supposed to bring with it a whole array of benefits. It was to reinvigorate the economy, encourage competition, foster moral strength and character; remove the need for the welfare state (and the NHS), revitalise the family and regenerate self-discipline. Above all, it would emphasise that the 'nanny state' of Beveridge and the Labour Party must be swept away, that trade unions must be controlled more effectively and that collective rights must be removed (see Chapter 3).

Thatcherism was thus a major departure from the political consensus on welfare which some historians feel had dominated British politics since 1945; it was also a fundamental change of direction for the Conservatives. The new policies sought purpose and conviction rather than consensus, focused upon the destruction of trade union power and the changing of the balance of private and public assets in the nation by privatisation.

Thatcher's governments

Thatcher's first government (1979–83) lacked sureness of touch but displayed determination, particularly in seeing off the old Heathite Tories such as Jim Prior and Sir Ian Gilmour (Document 8). Faced with an annual inflation rate of well in excess of 20 per cent, Thatcher moved to redistribute income in favour of the rich in Geoffrey Howe's tax-cutting Budget of 1979 (Documents 1, 9). She then moved to control the supply of money, supporting Howe's 1981 Budget, which raised taxes during a recession – a monetarist action designed to reduce inflation – which ran contrary to accepted 'Keynesian' policy. The result was that unemployment, which was just over one million in May 1979, rose to more than three million by 1983, despite numerous changes that removed many claimants from the unemployment register. Thatcher's government became deeply unpopular and was soon falling behind the Labour and Liberal parties in the opinion polls, and struggling to keep ahead of the Social Democratic Party, formed in 1981 (see Chapter 6). However, Thatcher's government won the 1983 general election, largely because of the Falklands War, in which she sent off a British military expedition to repossess the Falklands Islands from Argentina in the spring and summer of 1982. This action culminated in Britain's recapture of the Islands on 14 June. As a result of Britain's military success, Thatcher's popularity rose to 80 per cent in some opinion polls. There were, however, other factors that helped Thatcher to secure her second general election success in 1983. The most obvious was that inflation fell from 21.8 per cent in April 1980 to 3.7 per cent in June 1983, revealing the success of her determined anti-inflationary policies, as well as the pitiable state of the Labour Party (see Chapter 5).

Thatcher's second administration (1983–7) was far more successful than the first. Insofar as it had direction, it became increasingly committed to the privatisation of public services and the reduction of public expenditure, particularly on the welfare state. Thatcher pressed forward with a whole range of legislation designed to reduce the power of the trade unions, which she felt buttressed a commitment to government control and intervention. Her governments introduced, between 1979 and 1990, eight acts (most obviously the Employment Acts of 1980, 1982, 1988, 1989 and 1990 and the Trade Union Act of 1984) designed to weaken trade union power, deregulate the economy and remove the checks on British employment which it was felt had been responsible for the relative economic decline of Britain since the Second World War. The 1980 Employment Act introduced a limited definition of legal picketing; the 1982 Act permitted trade union 'closed shops' only where 85 per cent of the workforce favoured them. The 1984 Trade Union Act forced trade unions to hold secret, and preferably postal, ballots, before legal industrial action could take place. These and other measures were a direct challenge to established trade union rights (Document 2 and Chapter 4). Indeed, the issue seemed to reach a defining moment with the coal miners' strike from 10 March 1984 to 5 March 1985. Fighting against the closure of pits, the miners were defeated partly because of the Conservative government's use of the law to restrict and punish the National Union of Mineworkers. Thatcher was determined that the miners would not bring down her government as they had done Heath's in February 1974. After the strike British trade unionism recognised the need to rethink its policies along a less confrontational route which took advantage of the new legislation.

Thatcher was lucky to defeat the miners, the lack of unity amongst the miners' unions helping her cause. Her luck held out when, on 12 October 1984, she narrowly escaped death when an IRA bomb exploded at the Grand Hotel, Brighton, during the Conservative Party Conference, killing five people and injuring 32 others. She helped to broker the Anglo-Irish Agreement of 1985 (see Chapter 11), which allowed the Irish Republic a role in the politics of Northern Ireland, and she was an active force at the time when Mikhail Gorbachov, the Russian President, was making moves towards ending the Cold War towards the end of 1984 and in early months of 1985. Thatcher's apparent invincibility and good fortune were, however, tested to their limits by the Westland Affair in 1985 and 1986. After a prolonged debate over the future of the Westland helicopter company, which Thatcher felt could only be saved by merging with the American firm of Sikorsky, Michael Heseltine, the Minister of Defence, resigned on 9 January 1986. Whilst this was itself damaging, the subsequent debate, in which Heseltine accused Thatcher of adopting a presidential style of government and of deliberately leaking information, led to a government defence which saw the resignation of the Home Secretary, Leon Brittan, for misleading the House of Commons (Document 3). The Westland affair could have damaged Thatcher's political future but, in the end, changed little. The improving economy, cuts in income tax and continued problems within the Labour Party ensured that Thatcher won the general election of 11 May 1987, with a majority of 102.

Thatcher began her third term (1987–90) in an almost unassailable position, with the economy doing well, higher levels of income tax down to 40 per cent by 1988, increased public spending and a revenue surplus. Yet in November 1990 she was replaced by John Major as Conservative leader and Prime Minister. Her resignation as Prime Minister was prompted by a number of events.

The economic situation of the country began to worsen from 1987 onwards and some sections of the Conservative Party began to question Thatcher's hostile policy towards Europe. On 20 September 1988, Thatcher made a speech in Bruges in which she declared her opposition to any diminution of the sovereignty of the United Kingdom, building up her reputation for toughness which had won Britain reductions in her financial contributions to Europe between 1984 and 1986 (Document 5). This put her in conflict with the sympathies of a section of her party in which Kenneth Clarke was a prominent figure and also with the many sections of industry that supported the European Economic Community. Also, Geoffrey Howe, her former Chancellor of the Exchequer and Foreign Secretary, who resigned as Deputy Prime Minister because of differences with her over Europe, delivered a dramatic resignation speech in the House of Commons on 13 November 1990, condemning her style and asking how Cabinet unity could be maintained 'when every step forward risked being subverted by some casual comment or impulsive answer' (Document 10).[1]

Howe's attack weakened Thatcher's position even further but was particularly damaging given her failure in connection with the Poll Tax in 1989 and 1990. Personally committed to abolishing the property-based rates, Thatcher advocated a system (the community charge, popularly known as the poll tax) whereby every adult paid the same local rates for the same local services. The scheme was first introduced into Scotland in 1989, where it was considered to be unjust since it required 'a widow in her flat to pay the same as a lord in his castle'. Yet the Conservative Party conferences insisted upon its introduction in England and Wales within one year rather than over a four-year period. The opposition to it was intense, both in terms of demonstrations (the most important being in London on 31 March 1990) and non-payment. Indeed, when John Major replaced Thatcher he quickly abandoned the poll tax and returned to a partially property-based system of raising money for local authorities.

Thatcher's resignation was a dramatic end to her political career (Document 6). Under Conservative Party rules at that time, the leadership could be contested every year. In November 1989, Sir Anthony Meyer, a backbench candidate, lost to her by 314 votes to 33. In November 1990, after the attack on Thatcher by Geoffrey Howe, Michael Heseltine decided to challenge for the leadership. She obtained 204 votes to Heseltine's 152, falling four votes short of the majority required for outright victory in the first round. Pressured to resign by various ministers, including Kenneth Clarke, she resigned on 22 November to make way for a new leader rather than face further political humiliation, but was dismayed by what she believed was the betrayal of her former followers. She remained in office until 28 November 1990, when she was replaced by John Major (Document 11). Her resignation resulted in a brief rise in support for the Conservative Party in the opinion polls. In 1992, she accepted a life peerage in the House of Lords as Baroness Thatcher of Kesteven and has remained a presence in Conservative politics ever since, particularly opposing Britain's closer involvement with the European Union and endorsing both William Hague and Iain Duncan Smith for the leadership of the Conservative Party in 1997 and 2001, respectively.

Thatcher's period as Prime Minister saw the undermining of a general consensus that had existed in parliamentary politics since 1945. In particular, it removed trade unions from close links with government, challenged the welfare state and promoted the privatisation of government-owned public services and industry. Above all, her period in office promoted a free-market attitude into British society and established in the minds of the British public that lower rates of taxation would allow individuals, not the government and public service institutions, to determine supply and demand conditions in the market. Thatcher's survival at the top of British politics owed much to fortunate events, such as the Falklands War and the miners' strike, which demonstrated her toughness and won her patriotic support. Yet there is still no doubting her impact upon the politics of both John Major, her Conservative successor, and Tony Blair, Labour's Prime Minister since 1997. Blair undoubtedly dropped the public ownership part of Labour's traditional Clause Four in 1994–5 because he felt that Thatcherism had made such a policy untenable (Document 6 and Chapter 5).

John Major, 1990–97

John Major is something of a political enigma. He emerged, with limited political experience, to become the Conservative leader and Prime Minister in 1990, successfully fought off many political challengers to his position throughout the early and mid-1990s, was heavily defeated in the 1997 general election, promptly resigning as Conservative leader, and immediately entered political obscurity. Indeed, Kenneth Baker has suggested Major published his autobiography in 1999 in order to avoid being ranked alongside Sir Anthony Eden, Neville Chamberlain and Arthur James Balfour as one of the Conservative Party's least successful twentieth-century premiers.[2] However, Baker, in generous mood, asserts that 'For a Brixton [in London] lad to spend longer in Number 10 than either Asquith or Lloyd George is no mean feat'.

John Major's political career began in 1965, when he helped form the Brixton branch of the Young Conservatives. In 1968 he was elected to Lambeth Borough Council. He became MP for Huntingdonshire in 1979, holding the seat until 1983 when he became MP for Huntingdon. He rose swiftly in the Conservative ranks, and was Private Secretary to the Minister of State at the Home Office by 1981. After holding some junior posts in government he became Minister of State at the Department of Health and Social Security (1986–7), and eventually Chief Secretary to the Treasury (1987–9). He then rose swiftly to the top of the political tree in little more than 16 months. During that period, he filled the post of Foreign Secretary (July to October 1989) and Chancellor of the Exchequer (October 1989 to November 1990), before becoming

Prime Minister (November 1990 to May 1997), defeating both Douglas Hurd and Michael Heseltine in the 1990 Conservative leadership contest. Although Major was a politically astute politician, and a good administrator, there was an element of political luck which saw him replace Geoffrey Howe, Nigel Lawson and Margaret Thatcher. Indeed, as Baker reflects, when Major opened his first Cabinet meeting in 1990, with a diffident smile, he asked the rhetorical question 'Well, who would have thought it?'[3]

Indeed, many were surprised at the ease with which Major moved through the Conservative Party and upwards through the Conservative government. Until he became Prime Minister, indeed even as Prime Minister, it was difficult to say what he stood for, except that he shared with Thatcher a loathing of inflation and a commitment to rolling back the welfare state. In other respects, he was more open to persuasion, more willing to seek consensus and less driven by any fixed ideology. His pragmatism led him to drop the Poll Tax, which Thatcher had introduced as a way of financing local government, and he was less confrontational towards Europe than Thatcher had tended to be. Yet he gained a reputation for toughness through his support for the Gulf War in 1991, when the USA, Britain and other nations drove Saddam Hussein's forces out of Kuwait. Major's determination was even more evident in the way in which he supported Boris Yeltsin in Russia in 1991. His victory in the 1992 general election also suggested that he was more than a caretaker Prime Minister.

Nevertheless, Major faced numerous problems within his party, particularly over Europe. His position on Europe was always one that stressed the need to protect British interests. However, within his party were a number of Eurosceptics, opposed to any measures that might lead to European integration. Major signed the Maastricht Treaty in December 1991, which edged Britain towards some measures of integration. However, it was blown off course in September 1992 when the sterling crisis led to Britain's withdrawal from the European Exchange Rate Mechanism. Major pressed ahead with the bill to ratify the treaty, but it was not pressed to conclusion until the end of 1994 and then only in the teeth of opposition from the Eurosceptics, eight of whom had the Conservative whip withdrawn (although they were restored to the party within four or five months) and one other who resigned it. They objected to the larger financial contribution that Britain would have to make to the European Union as well as to further moves towards integration. As a result the narrow Conservative majority in the House of Commons disappeared and, in December 1994, the government was defeated in the vote on increasing value added tax on domestic fuel. This proved an embarrassment for Major's government, which was already reeling from divisions, allegations of extra-marital affairs and the abuse of parliamentary privilege. With two Conservative MPs accused of accepting cash for tabling parliamentary questions Major had been forced to respond by setting up Lord Nolan at the head of the Committee for Standards in Public Life, which moved the government to ban paid advocacy by MPs and to require the disclosure of incomes earned from services offered as an MP. The findings of the Nolan report divided Conservative MPs and further scandals increased the perceptions of the widespread presence of 'sleaze' in British politics. In 1996, the publication of a report by Sir Richard Scott into the actions of junior ministers in deciding guidelines for the export of arms-related equipment to Iraq placed even more pressure upon Major's government.

Some of these pressures had forced Major to resign as Party Leader in the summer of 1995, and to provoke a Conservative leadership contest in which he was one of the candidates. The final straw had been his meeting, in June 1995, with more than 50 Eurosceptic Conservative MPs – the 'Fresh Start Group' – who seemed to have little respect for his position. In the event, John Redwood was Major's only opponent and Major won by 218 votes to 89 votes – the other 22 Conservative MPs failed to register a vote for a variety of reasons. Nevertheless, the Eurosceptics continued to pressure Major to take a tougher line on European integration and the single European currency, whilst Kenneth Clarke, the Chancellor of the Exchequer and a strong pro-European, reportedly threatened to resign if Major did so.

Despite the obvious difficulties faced by Major's governments there were achievements on other fronts. Major was praised for his handling of the Northern Ireland situation, in particular in his brokering of 'The Downing Street Declaration' in December 1993, whereby he and the Irish Prime Minister, Albert Reynolds, attempted to persuade the 'men of violence' on both sides to enter the democratic process (see Chapter 11). This led to the ceasefire in 1994 by the Irish Republican Army and loyalist paramilitary groups and the publication of a consultative document for future government in Northern Ireland in February 1995. So began the movement towards the power-sharing in Northern Ireland which has developed under Tony Blair (see Chapter 11).

Nevertheless, failures seemed to outnumber successes and the Conservative Party was trounced in the general election of 1 May 1997, which brought Tony Blair to power at the head of a Labour Party which had just won a landslide victory. The general election campaign had seen the Conservative Party split, with about two thirds of its 320 or so MPs declaring their firm opposition to the idea of a single currency for Europe. When the Conservative defeat occurred, Major resigned as Prime Minister and then as Conservative Party leader and was soon to disappear into political oblivion. However, Major's demise was not the end of Thatcher's influence; her political legacy can be seen in her impact upon Labour politics (see Chapter 5) and in the way in which she affected Conservative politics under William Hague (Document 6) and Iain Duncan Smith. Most obviously, in the case of the Conservative Party she has left the sharp division between pro-Marketers and anti-Marketers.

Documents

SECONDARY SOURCES AND INTERPRETATIONS

1. Edmund Dell, *The Chancellors: A History of the Chancellors of the Exchequer, 1945–90* (London, HarperCollins, 1996), pp.460–3

A Chancellor should not pretend more than he can achieve. Having won power there was no longer a need to pretend. In his first Budget in June 1979, Howe said that 'There is a definite limit to our capacity as politicians, to influence things for the better... The notion of demand management, expanding public spending, and "fine tuning" of the economy have now been tested almost to destruction.'[4] Judged by that modest and appropriate, philosophy, his Budget was both brave and politically farsighted.

If the transformation in economic management is intended, there is no point in delay. The government's majority was large enough to sustain it through a full Parliamentary term. The argument for prompt action was compelling. A key element in the Budget was a reduction in the PSBR (Public Sector Borrowing Requirement). Howe aimed to reduce the PSBR from £9.25 billion in 1978–9, or 5.25 per cent of the GDP (Gross Domestic Product), to £8.25 billion in 1979–80, or 4.25 per cent of the GDP. As the forecast for

1979–80 stood at £10 to £11 billion, this implied tax increases or public expenditure reductions of £2 to £3 billion. It was the beginning of the process whereby the PSBR would be reduced to between 1 and 2 per cent of output...

Part of the government's programme was to improve incentives. Thatcher believed in supply-side action to improve the performance of the economy. Monetarism, according to Keith Joseph, was not enough. Income tax cuts were regarded as an incentive which could be expected to improve the supply-side, though Lawson [Nigel Lawson, a later Chancellor of the Exchequer] considered that the principal justification was a moral one, the enlargement of individual freedom.[5] ... It was an incentive that Howe reduced the basic rate of income tax to 30p from 33p and the top rate to 60p from 83p. This would cost the revenue £4 billion. Asset sales and the first attack on public expenditure would help. But he would still need a major increase in indirect taxation, including VAT to 15 per cent, if he was to achieve his planned PSBR...

Other steps announced in the Budget included the decision to link pension increases simply to price increases rather than, as before, to price or income increases or whichever was the higher. This was, according to Lawson, necessary to regain control of public expenditure.[6] [Dell then discusses the control of prices through the Prices Commission.]

The Prices Commission had been first a Tory and then a Labour sop to the trade unions. It was probably more effective in deterring investment than prices. Its abolition was an heroic act. Nevertheless, its abolition was consistent with the conviction that inflation was a monetary phenomenon and that controlling the money supply, if ways could be found, would be more effective in the battle against inflation than any Prices Commission.

2. Keith Laybourn, *A History of British Trade Unionism, 1770–1990* (Stroud, Sutton, 1990; paperback edition 1997), pp.205–6, 208

[pp.205–6] Initially James Prior, the Secretary of Employment, was given the task of paving the way for the Conservative government's legislative programme on employment and trade unionism. In July 1979 he issued a consultative document which called for the limitation of picketing to the employees involved in the dispute and to their place of work. In addition, it advocated the extension of exemptions from the closed shop and declared an interest in providing public funds for secret ballots before strikes and for the election of full-time union officers. These recommendations formed the basis of the 1980 Employment Act which introduced a limited definition of lawful picketing, made secondary action illegal, required an 80 per cent ballot for a closed shop, offered union funds to hold ballots and allowed people to become members of trade unions and not to be unreasonably expelled from them. The trade unions were powerless to resist this Act when faced with rapidly rising unemployment and the patchy response to its 'Day of Action' on 14 May 1980.

Yet, the legislation did not go far enough for the Conservatives on the thorny question of the 'closed shop'. When Norman Tebbit replaced James Prior as Secretary of State for Employment in 1981, he extended the restrictions on trade unions through the 1982 Employment Act, which banned the pre-entry closed shops, only permitted closed shops if 85 per cent of those voting favoured them, provided compensation for dismissals due to a closed-shop arrangement operating, and gave employers the right to take action for damages against trade unions... The 1984 Trade Unions Act also made executive committee elections by ballot compulsory every five years, introduced ballots on political funds and before industrial action could be called.

[After discussing the introduction of other employment and trade union legislation, Laybourn continues, p.208] The 'Thatcherite' 'legislation has clearly reduced the protection given to trade unions and individuals operating within the industrial framework...

The first ten years of Conservative rule saw the dramatic decline of trade union membership. In 1979 there were almost thirteen and a half million trade union members, 12,172,505 being members of the TUC. By 1989 there were about ten million trade union members of whom about 8.6 million were members of the TUC. The decline has been rapid (and worrying,) although it may have more to do with the rise of mass unemployment than the failure of the trade union movement [see Chapter 3].

3. Hugo Young, *One of Us: A Biography of Margaret Thatcher* (London, Macmillan, 1988), pp.vii, 199–200

[p.vii] 'Is he one of us?' The question became one of those emblematic terms in the Thatcher years. Posed by Mrs Thatcher herself, it defined the test which politicians and other public officials aspiring to her favour were required to pass. It also epitomised in a single phrase how she saw an aspect of her mission. This was to gather a cadre of like-minded people who would, with her, change the face of the Conservative Party and at the same time launch the recovery of Britain. Those admitted to membership formed, in the beginning, an exclusive club. What they had in common was a willingness to repudiate the past, and detach themselves and their thinking from the consensus of the majority. 'One of us' in that sense had a subversive connotation. Those who passed the test belonged to a group of partisans intent on overthrowing many reigning orthodoxies...

[Referring to the 'Wets' in the Cabinet in 1979 and 1980, pp.199–200] To speak of the wets as a collective is, however, misleading. There were, among all the critics of the economic policy what may be termed inner wets and outer wets, although even that distinction conceals divergent tendencies within each category.

The inner wets, who after Howe's second budget had come to the conclusion by the summer of 1980 that the policy was fundamentally misguided, were Prior, Walker and Sir Ian Gilmour, supported by Lord Carrington, and, with increasing irreverence, by the leader of the House, Norman St. John Stevas. But they were by no means all of the same mind, or similar political purposes, Carrington's constant absence exonerated him from grappling with issues which, in any case, he did not really understand. Prior, while gloomy about the policy's chances of success, had his own preoccupations to consider. Too overt a challenge to the remorselessly deflationary Treasury could well have brought upon him demands for a far more stringent line with the unions, which it was naturally his highest priority to avoid.

The outer wets were still a fragmented class, Pym was one of them. He was experiencing his reservations, but also fighting to master the Ministry of Defence, and on rare occasions when an opportunity appeared to voice an economic opinion in cabinet he is not remembered, in the early years, for displays of forthright eloquence. Michael Heseltine, Secretary of State for the Environment, was another candidate-dissenter, but of quite different stripe from anyone else. Heseltine was an unrepentant Heathite, in that he believed passionately in an interventionist government exercising strategic industrial leadership; but he was the reverse of wet in that he considered the Thatcherite purge of extravagance and waste was proceeding far too slowly...

[The Westland affair of 1985 revealed splits in the Cabinet between Margaret Thatcher and Michael Heseltine over Thatcher's style of leadership. This led to Heseltine's resignation from the Cabinet and also accounted for Leon Brittan, the Home Secretary, in 1986.]

4. Nicholas Ridley, *My Style of Government* (London, Fontana, 1992), p.267

Margaret Thatcher was certainly a leader of the highest order. Political leadership has been described as the ability to stake out a radical agenda of action, to be able to succeed in mobilising public opinion behind it, and then to carry it through as well. On this basis she ranks alongside very few – perhaps only Gladstone.

5. Peter Riddell, *The Thatcher Era and its Legacy* (Oxford, Blackwell, 1991; first edition published in 1989), pp.219–20, 222, 230–1, 245

[p.219] 'Nothing lasts forever. Even the longest, most glittering reign must come to an end some day.'

Ian Richardson as Chief Whip Francis Urquhart in BBC television's 'House of Cards', November 1990, when looking at a photograph of Mrs Margaret Thatcher...

[p.220] Mrs Thatcher lost office because she had become a political and electoral liability in the eyes of a significant number of her Cabinet and parliamentary colleagues. They believed that it was necessary to modify some of the more unpopular aspects of Thatcherism. I see the events of November 1990 primarily as a change of personality and style, rather than a fundamental strategy. The Major government maintained the direction of the Conservative economic and industrial policy (the poll tax apart), even though the pace and method of implementation may alter with his less ideological tone. He also responded to a changing public agenda, such as increased concern with the quality of public services and the environment, which was already developing before her departure. These issues would require a different approach in the 1990s from whichever party was in power. Many of Thatcher's policies will none the less continue. Much of the shift from the post-war economic and industrial consensus has been accepted, consciously or otherwise by the opposition parties – perhaps her main achievement – even if neither they nor the British parties would go so far in a free market direction as she would like to have done.

[Riddell then discusses Thatcher's achievements, p.222] Lord Blake, foremost Conservative historian, was in no doubt. Writing in *The Times* just after she resigned, he argued that 'Margaret Thatcher's place in history is assured; the first women to be prime minister, the first since Palmerston to win three successive general elections, the longest continuous holder of office since Lord Liverpool... She was on the British political scene a giant amongst pygmies. She was one of the two greatest Conservative prime ministers in the 20th century and one of the half dozen prime ministers of all parties at all times.' A more centrist commentator, Robert Skidelsky, wrote in the *Guardian* that 'The historian will see the Thatcher premiership as a never-ending campaign, punctuated by set battles, sometimes broken off, but always resumed, against all those forces, which in her view, had brought, or were bringing, Britain low.'

[pp.230–1] Mrs Thatcher herself would list restoring Britain's place in the world as among her main achievements. She certainly banished the half-heartedness and implicit defeatism of much of British foreign policy in the 1970s. The voice of Britain, and Mrs Thatcher, was heard around the world. Her unabashed Atlanticism and hostility to closer European integration served her well politically for most of her premiership. In the first half of the 1980s her stand for Britain's money in the European Community outflanked Labour, which was eventually forced to come to terms with membership. But in time she lost touch both with changes in the community itself and with opinion inside her own Cabinet...

[p.245] Mrs Thatcher's record inevitably appears flawed both because of the forced manner of her departure and because of the serious economic problems at the time. Apart from her loyal band of followers, Mrs Thatcher may now become an unfashionable figure, as President Reagan did in the US after he left office in January 1989. Mrs Thatcher's Conservative successors, as much as the opposition parties, may want to distance themselves from her era as they attempt to change the agenda of British politics. The same has happened for previous prime ministers; it was many years after they left office before Lloyd George or Attlee received a favourable reappraisal. A balanced assessment of the Thatcher era will take at least a decade. For the moment, she stands as one of Britain's most remarkable prime ministers. She helped to shift the political debate in Britain. If she did not halt Britain's decline – and no one could do that – she did what a politician could do. She challenged and shook up British industry and society with effects which will last well into the 1990s.

6. Brendan Evans, *Thatcherism and British Politics, 1975–1999* (Stroud, Sutton, 1999), pp.223–4, 230, 233

[pp.223–4] Any evaluation of the impact of Thatcherism on British politics should primarily explore the extent to which it determined the policies of Blair's New Labour government... despite its marginality at the end of the decade, it is also necessary to analyse briefly the nature of the Conservative Party led by William Hague in the aftermath of eighteen years of governments led by Thatcher and Major. The Conservative Party continued to reel from its heavy defeat for two years after 1997. It was so suffused with Euro-scepticism that it proved impossible to elect such dominant and experienced figures as Kenneth Clarke to the party leadership, and in June 1997 Hague emerged as the candidate with the strongest support among Conservative MPs. Thatcher's continuing potency within the party was demonstrated by the fact that Hague considered it useful to secure her endorsement of his candidacy. To many in the party the day when Thatcher was deposed from the party leadership in November 1990 was a much bleaker day than the election of a Labour government in May 1997. Apart from continuing hostility to further European integration and to Britain's early membership of the single currency, it is unclear where the party stands in relationship to Thatcher's legacy. Hague has shown some tentative signs of endorsing a more libertarian style of politics than Thatcher in the area of social and personal morality, but reveals little sign of embarking upon the fundamental re-theorising of Conservatism which is now clearly required.

FROM OLD TO NEW LABOUR

Thatcherism's lasting impact on British politics is amply evident from the transition in the Labour Party to New Labour. This was an incremental process between 1983 and 1997. One of Thatcher's political goals had been to eliminate socialism in Britain whilst recognising that the Labour Party would survive as a political force, and to ensure that the main parts of her political projects remained intact after her departure from the political scene. This chapter demonstrates the considerable measure of success that she achieved through her party's role in the creation of New Labour. The policies of the Labour government since 1997 are indisputably closer to those of the Conservatives, however, than they are to traditional social democracy. The transition from Old to New Labour was a process which occurred very gradually between 1983 and 1992, stalled somewhat from 1992 to 1994 and then accelerated significantly after 1994.

[p.230] THE THIRD WAY

New Labour claims to have developed a new ideology, equidistant between traditional social democracy and Conservatism. This is the Third Way. It rejects undiluted capitalism and old-style social democracy. It is this desire to be at the centre of the spectrum which is its driving force...

[After discussing various examples of the convergence of Conservative and New Labour ideas, the book continues, p.233] A similar compromise between traditional Conservative and Labour views was patently implicit in the Blair 'tough on crime, tough on the causes of crime' soundbite. New Labour similarly offered both a communitarian resistance to Thatcherism, and a strong 'tendency to authoritarian social conservatism (curfews for kids, compulsory workfare, the appointment of a 'Drugs Czar'). Blair argues that the old left championed indiscriminate and often ineffective public spending, while the Third Way concentrates on ensuring that public spending delivers the required results. New Labour seeks the 'dynamic market' of America but also the 'social cohesion' of Western Europe.

PRIMARY EVIDENCE AND INFORMATION

7. Conservative Conference Annual Report, containing Mrs Thatcher's Political Centre Conference Lecture, Blackpool, 10 October 1968

We have now put so much emphasis on the control of incomes that we have too little regard for the essential role of government which is the control of money supply and the management of demand. Greater attention to this role and less to the outward detailed control would have achieved more for the economy. It would mean, of course, that the government had to exercise itself some of the disciplines on expenditure it is so keen to impose on others. It would mean that expenditure on the vast public sector would not have to be greater than the amount which could be financed out of taxation plus genuine savings. For a number of years some expenditure has been financed by what amounts to printing money.

8. Mrs Thatcher in an interview in the *Observer*, 25 February 1979

I do think I've got to have a Cabinet with equal unity of purpose and a sense of dedication to it. It must be a Cabinet that works on something much more than pragmatism or consensus. It must be a 'conviction' Cabinet... We've got to go in an agreed and clear direction. As Prime Minister I couldn't waste time having any internal arguments.

9. Geoffrey Howe's first Budget speech, 12 June 1979, *Parliamentary debates* (or *Hansard*), Fifth Series, Commons, 1979–1980, Vol. 998, Official Report, 11 June (London, HMSO), col. 240, 242 and 248–9

A NEW BEGINNING

It is our belief that many of these failures are themselves the result of action and intervention by the Government themselves. [Therefore there is a need to reduce taxation...]

That it why the British people are convinced – and we believe – that it is time for a new beginning. Our strategy to check Britain's long-term economic decline, which has gathered pace in the last five years, is based on four principles.

We need to strengthen incentives, by allowing people to keep more of what they earn, so that hard work, talent... are properly rewarded. We need to enlarge freedom of choice for the individual by reducing the role of the State. We need to reduce the burden of financing the public sector, so as to leave room for commerce and industry to prosper. We need to ensure, so far as possible, that those who take part in collective bargaining understand the consequences of their actions – for that is the way to promote a proper sense of responsibility...

The tax changes I shall propose today will be only the first step. They will take us a long way in the right direction.

INFLATION

But these changes will not themselves be enough unless we also squeeze inflation out of the system. It is crucially important to re-establish sound money. We intend to achieve this through firm monetary discipline and fiscal policies connected with that including strict control over expenditure...

We are committed to the progressive reduction of the growth of money supply...

Sales of state-owned assets to the private sector serves the immediate purpose of helping to reduce the excessive public sector borrowing requirement with which I was faced...

10. Sir Geoffrey Howe, speech attacking Margaret Thatcher in the House of Commons, 13 November 1990, *Parliamentary debates* (*Hansard*), Sixth Series, Vol. 180 (London, HMSO), 465

The tragedy is – and it is for me personally, for my party, for our whole people and for my Right Hon Friend herself – a real tragedy – that the Prime Minister's personal attitude towards Europe is running increasingly serious risks for the future of the nation. It risks minimising our influence and maximising our chances of being once again shut out. We have paid heavily in the past for late starts and squandered opportunities in Europe. We dare not let it happen again. If we detach ourselves completely, as a party or a nation, from the middle grounds of Europe, the effects of this will be incalculable and very hard ever to correct.

The conflict of loyalty, of loyalty to my Right Hon Friend the Prime Minister – and, after all, in two decades together that instinct of loyalty is still very real – and of loyalty to what I presume to be the true interests of the nation, has become all too great. I no longer believe it possible to resolve the conflict from within the Government. That is why I have resigned.

11. John Major, *Conservatism in the 1990s: Our Common Purpose* (London, Carlton Club Political Committee in conjunction with the Conservative Political Centre, 1993, The Fifth Carlton Lecture 1993 given by John Major), pp.11–14, 16, 25, 36

[p.11] When I first became Leader of the Party just over two years ago, I spoke of 'carrying forward the Conservative tradition', I spoke of Conservatism as 'a commonsense view of life from a tolerant perspective'. I set out the aim to create a 'classless society' and I spoke also of 'a nation at ease with itself'.

[p.12] THE CHARACTER OF CONSERVATISM

Dignity, security, independence, self-respect – those are the human aspirations we Conservatives understand and endorse. Conservatism in the 1990s has the ambition to bring them within the grasp of each and every citizen in our land... They are the instincts of a free people; an enterprising people; a generous people; and a tolerant people.

[p.13] We believe in fostering freedom by giving people more power to choose for themselves; by leaving people more of their own money to spend themselves on their own families and in their own interests. They will spend it better than any government, however benevolent.

We believe in fostering enterprise by keeping personal and business taxes low; by cutting down on the jungle of regulation; by creating a level playing field in which businesses can compete freely and fairly.

[p.14] OUR FOUR GREAT PRINCIPLES

We have no responsibility of doctrine that we set on an altar above common sense and instinct. We have nothing that will become irrelevant in a decade of change. There is no Clause Four in the Conservative Party – and there must never be. But what we do have are four cardinal principles: the principles of choice, ownership, responsibility and opportunity for all. They formed the core of our manifesto at the election – and they guide us in Government, as we put the Manifesto into effect.

As a Party, we have always worked to meet the people's aspirations to own their own homes; to have greater opportunity for themselves and their children; to enjoy the respect that follows from the exercise of choice; to build up wealth and then to be free in due course to pass that wealth on to the next generation.

Now that has always been a great Tory tradition – a continuous thread in our thinking. When Disraeli spoke many years ago of the 'elevation of the condition of the people' he made it clear, even then, that he meant all the people: 'all the numerous classes in the realm, classes alike and equal before the law'. That was not exactly 'a classless society' but it certainly expressed many of the aspirations of one: the equal treatment of all citizens by the State and the chance of advancement for all.

The second important and continuous thread of Conservative thought, from the time of Burke onwards, has been an awareness of the dangers of over-government. As Conservatives we do not like big government. We know the State can destroy, as surely as it can preserve – and more conclusively than it can create. We know the danger that unless it is reined back by constant and vigorous effort, it will grow inexorably. It can be a parasite that can destroy its host.

Now we reject utterly the idea that the State can manage economic and personal relations between people better than businesses and better than families.

The third great thread of thought is our understanding deep down in the marrow of our instincts of what binds a stable and a healthy democracy together. It is a sense of continuity that permits change without instability. Above all, perhaps, it is the little networks and small communities – Burke's 'little platoons', if you like – that are the tent pegs securing our wind-blown society to the ground. That we understand, not from books, not from experience but from deep instinct. It is one of the basic reasons why we are Conservatives.

[p.16] We the modern Conservative Party are heirs to both of the great nineteenth-century political traditions: to the Whigs, in our free market radicalism; to the Tories, in our belief in community and tradition. Unlike Socialists, we do not see the free market as a threat to communities; quite the reverse...

[p.18] So far I have been speaking mainly of the continuity in our philosophy. But I need hardly remind this audience that Conservatism has been a powerful force for change.

[He then argues for a balance between preserving the past and bringing about change and discusses many examples of what he means; p.25] So as we change and modernise – and we must do both – we must have an ear for history and an eye for place...

As we modernise the honours system – as, again, I believe we should – we must develop, and not destroy. It is time to get rid of old class-based distinctions; to make the system a little less automatic; to use it, in particular, to reward voluntary effort – but at the same time to maintain its historic value to a system of recognition and a reward for achievement.

[p.36] These are beliefs that would, in the different language of their time, have been familiar to Burke, Disraeli, or Salisbury. They link the ambitions of the child to be born in the year 2000 with the aspiration of previous centuries. It is, I believe, the genius of our Party that we fashion change in the images of our long traditions.

Notes

1. Sir Geoffrey Howe, speech in the House of Commons, *Hansard*, 13 November 1990.
2. *Observer*, 7 October 1999.
3. *Ibid.*
4. Quoting from Christopher Johnson, *The Economy Under Mrs. Thatcher* (Harmondsworth, Penguin), p.6.
5. Nigel Lawson, *The View from No. 10: Memoirs of a Tory Radical* (London, Corgi Books, 1991), p.693.
6. *Ibid.*, p.37.

Chapter 2

The Welfare State, 1979–2002

Introduction

By the 1950s, the British Welfare State had become an almost untouchable institution, the 'sacred cow' of British politics. This situation continued for more than 20 years, as successive governments, Conservative and Labour, maintained and developed the Welfare State as the central plank of the so-called post-war political consensus. But the survival and development of the Welfare State was based upon continued economic growth. In the 1950s, this link raised few concerns. Yet the relative economic decline of Britain, particularly since the mid-1960s, and the rising challenge of the monetarist policies that have become associated with Thatcherism have done much to challenge the continuance of (even) a (welfare capitalist) Welfare State. The Labour government's move to monetarism in 1975 saw the abandonment of full employment as a central plank of welfare policy. By 1979, the last vestiges of a dying Keynesian economic management approach were being laid to rest and with the return to government of a Conservative Party under the leadership of Margaret Thatcher, to whom consensus politics was anathema, it became clear that the whole relationship between the Welfare State and Britain's economic performance would be re-examined. The introduction of a supply-led, rather than demand-led, approach to competition and output meant that the 'Beveridge revolution', the initiatives of the post-war Attlee government and the 'post-war consensus' would be scrutinised and brought into line with more immediate economic monetarist directives (Document 1).

This change of approach became even more evident in the mid and late 1990s when both John Major's Conservative government and Tony Blair's Labour Party began to reassess the future of the Welfare State. Indeed, the *Guardian* of 8 May 1996 included an article on 'The End of the Welfare State', which stated that both the Labour and Conservative parties had 'declared an end to the welfare state as it had been known for the last fifty years foreshadowing a looser compact between the individual and government'. This comment, and the outlined objectives of Tony Blair's Labour governments (1997 to the present), suggest a future change in the relationship between both the individual and the state and the voluntary sector and the state. This became evident on 18 March 1999, when Blair announced a government pledge to a 20-year programme to eradicate child poverty, along with a commitment that the new welfare state would be based upon a partnership between both private and public provision (Document 5). This perceived need for change arises from the accumulated pressures emerging in the 1960s and 1970s.

Challenges to the Welfare State

Although there was a post-war consensus operating on welfare matters until the late 1970s, there were clearly tensions within the Welfare State which revealed dissatisfaction on all sides: criticisms came from Marxists, socialists, Fabians and feminists. However, the most critically destructive and influential have been those of the 'New Right'.

The New Right owe their ideas to the work of Freidrich von Hayek. To Hayek, liberty and individualism are in direct opposition to equality gained through collective measures. This view runs deep throughout his philosophy, which suggests that all governments that support equality and attempt to redress the 'natural' social balance of inequality only create imbalance and oppression. He maintains that all beings are competitive individuals and as such must live within the boundaries of 'natural' market forces. This situation, for him and his supporters, enhances wealth creation and safeguards liberty. Enoch Powell, and other Conservative statesmen, followed this line of argument, considering the Welfare State a burden and an institution of unfairness. Those that put the least in were considered to be those who took the most out. Powell raised the issue of controlling public expenditure in the 1960s and suggested that selective benefits might be the way forward, a solution to the conundrum of how to reduce the burden of welfare in a state that was facing economic decline.

Powell's views were endorsed by the Institute of Economic Affairs, the rightwing think tank, which produced a pamphlet entitled *Towards a Welfare State* (1967). The New Right emphasis was thus to be placed firmly upon the selective provision of benefits for the poor. Margaret Thatcher soon took up a similar stance. On 10 October 1968, she gave a Conservative Political Centre's Party Conference lecture in Blackpool and announced that a future Conservative government should not print money to finance expenditure and that future spending should come out of taxation and genuine savings. These views were further developed and applied to the Welfare State by Rhodes Boyson in a collection of essays entitled *Down with the Poor* (1971) (Document 17).

Not surprisingly, given the economic tribulations of the Labour government in the mid-1970s, James Callaghan came to similar views about the economic efficacy of the combination between Keynesian and Beveridge ideas. At the 1976 Labour Party Conference (Document 18), Callaghan's comments came relatively late into the debate and called into question the high level of commitment that the Labour Party was prepared to make to the Welfare State, as well as the maintenance of full employment in the future (see Chapter 4).

Nevertheless, it was Sir Keith Joseph who became the chief standard-bearer of the new philosophy of monetarism. Having been persuaded that Keynesianism was dead, he felt the need for a rethink on policy that looked towards a reduction in public expenditure, which would reduce the tax burden on industry and thus tackle poverty by encouraging industry to generate new work. The rise of Thatcher and her band of evangelicals transformed this new philosophy into action. The sheer force of authority made the idea legitimate under Thatcher.

The New Right believed that the Welfare State was failing. They maintained that the economic growth of the country was inextricably interlinked with the growth of the Welfare State. Economic growth had been held back by the demands of welfare, which had imposed an impossible economic burden. This had to be rolled back. In a version of the classical wage-fund theory they argued that governments fixed the rate of inflation through the control of the money supply, whilst trade unions fixed the corresponding rate of unemployment through the medium of their wage bargaining. Therefore, if trade-union wage demands were pitched too high, jobs would be lost. Conversely, the rate of unemployment could be lowered by labour market reforms removing controls on wages and conditions. Once government relinquished responsibility for unemployment, the *raison d'être* for budget deficits would disappear and the Public Sector Borrowing Requirement, seen as an important contributory factor in the excessive growth of the money supply, could be cut back. Traditionally, Conservatives have always disliked the public sector and such cutbacks, it was argued, would reduce both inflation and direct taxation. This in turn would improve the supply side of the economy through improved work incentives and the opportunity for higher personal savings – what Gladstone saw as allowing money to fructify in the pockets of the people. Finally, and of vital importance, a retreat from the Welfare State would remove the threat to liberty which liberal conservatives have always associated with the continuous expansion of the state. Once this 'rolling back of the frontiers of the state' had been accomplished, there would, it was hoped, be a return to the classical political and moral virtues of individual responsibility and prudent housekeeping.

The ideas of the New Right are, of course, enveloped within the philosophy of individualism. The Welfare State was, and still is, viewed with distrust by the New Right for several reasons. First, they argue that the Welfare State denies people a choice of service, exemplifying the coercion inherent in a system that dictates universal ideals of equality; in other words, it sets maximum standards.[1] Indeed, the British Welfare State has logically and ineluctably become the main instrument for the creation of equality by coercion.[2] Second, they feel that the Welfare State has diverted resources away from 'wealth-creating' sectors of the economy.[3] Third, they believe it has resulted in high taxation and government borrowing which led to a spiral of inflation. This is due to peoples' expectations, their reliance on a 'dependency culture' and government's unwillingness to put necessary unpopular policies into action. Fourth, they argue that welfare undermines the work ethic and culture; the unemployed have no incentive to work.[4] Fifth, that 'the [national] insurance principle is fraudulent, as a mechanism used to introduce back door socialism... [and] imposing higher taxation… In practice… contributions are a tax on employment'.[5] For these reasons, the New Right in general, and Sir Keith Joseph in particular, saw a situation in Britain that was described as 'dysfunctional democracy'.

If the New Right has been critical of the Welfare State so has the Left. Richard Titmuss had seen the Welfare State as a way of alleviating the worst conditions of poverty, a tool that would help to redistribute resources. The universality of benefits would break down class distinctions that discriminated against under-privileged groups. Yet, by the late 1960s and the early 1970s, Titmuss' attitude towards its development changed. He accepted that the Welfare State had not abolished poverty, and had not managed to reach the groups who needed assistance the most. The wealthiest groups had benefited the most, the poorest the least. Also, the Welfare State for Richard Titmuss, Tony Crosland and other socialists had become hierarchical, too centralised and bureaucratic. Moreover, the redistribution that they had so wanted had not taken place.

Marxists have also been sceptical about the Welfare State. To them, it is seen as an institution necessary to the survival of capitalism. If capitalism is concerned with accumulation, which is contrary to the benefits of the working class, it must legitimise this practice. The contradiction is explicitly clear; the capitalist state cannot function effectively with the Welfare State but, in a democracy, cannot function without it. In a capitalist society, then, welfare services and social services are seen as being accessible and accumulating forms of social control. Social harmony is maintained by alleviating the detrimental effects of capitalism.

Such political criticism of the traditional welfare state has been of major importance in reshaping the concept of how the future welfare state will develop. The New Right have set an agenda which New Labour has refined. In the end, the move is to continue with a minimalist Welfare State which will, increasingly, cooperate with the private sector in the 'Third Way' partnership, although it would appear to be avoiding the excesses of the market forces which Margaret Thatcher and John Major contemplated when they were prime ministers. Much of this direction, of course, cuts across the demands that feminists and women's groups present in their desire to remove inequalities of gender and poverty.

Women and Social Policy

(a) The family ideal and the feminist challenge

Much of the feminist critique of social policy was based on challenging the perceptions of policy-makers and service-providers that family households, where the male was the breadwinner and the woman undertook the caring, were universal. These perceptions carried with them multiple disadvantages to women. First, they were disadvantaged in the labour market by the expectation that they would take time off for childrearing and domestic duties. Second, they were disadvantaged in access to benefits, because the higher, national insurance-related benefits resulted from labour market participation. Third, they were expected to carry out domestic caring duties for no wage. Fourth, caring jobs, the prime example being nursing, were low paid because they related to the unpaid work women were expected to undertake in the home. Cuts in social services made by the incoming Conservative government in 1979 were protested as measures which would affect women by minimising professional care and maximising domestic caring. Links women made with trade unions (see Chapter 3) were helpful in this respect (Document 19). Further social service cuts were likewise protested. In addition, challenges were made to discrimination in particular areas of social policy, such as poverty, housing and health. The long-term feminist challenge to gender discrimination however, developing through the 1980s, lay in attacking stereotypical perceptions of the family household, by examining family structure and rendering women and their experience visible (Documents 1 and 6).

One way to cut through the multiple disadvantages that women faced was to value women's domestic labour. Feminists debated women's economic and social oppression within the household (see Chapter 8) and some argued that housework should be paid. As policy-makers turned to recommending care in the community for people who were chronically sick, mentally ill, disabled and elderly, so women's domestic burden increased. The desire to keep costs down meant that community care was poorly funded and effectively was family care: 'men, more often than women, have the power and resources to be in a position to choose not to be involved in the time-consuming and preoccupying aspects of care, or indeed domestic work of any kind.'[6] The General Household Survey of Informal Carers in 1988 was the first to provide a nationwide estimate of carers.[7] Neither the lack of real knowledge of the experience of caring nor its discriminatory nature prevented the shift in policy to care in the community being reinforced by the implementation of the NHS and Community Care Act 1990. While giving primacy to family care and self-help, this Act did go some way towards recognising carers' needs. It aimed to base service provision on a mix of family, voluntary, private and public provision, with local authority social services departments assisting access to and encouraging provision by the voluntary and private sectors and consumers having the power to choose. Public provision was subject to strict financial controls.

(b) Childcare and single-parent families

Childrearing was a prime caring role whose difficulties were obscured by reliance on the two-parent, male-breadwinner model that was no longer capable of universal application. There were 570,000 lone-parent families in 1971; 1,150,000 in 1989; lone parents were 12 per cent of all families in 1979, 21 per cent in 1992. Whereas parents' divorce was previously the cause of much single-parenting, increasing numbers of lone parents had never married.[8] The Child Benefit Act introduced by the Labour government in 1977 had provided financial assistance, payable to mothers, for each child on a non-contributory, flat-rate, tax-free basis, but was expensive. Means-testing of the benefit was debated, and its rate did not keep pace with inflation; in 1985, for instance, Child Benefit increased by only one third of the inflation rate.[9] From 1981, One Parent Benefit was made available to lone parents as well, at a sum which did not vary with the number of children. Family Income Supplement was payable to low-income families with at least one child on a non-contributory, means-tested basis and formed about 20 per cent of lone parents' disposable income.[10] The dependence of lone parents on these benefits was illustrated by employment figures; only 21 per cent of single mothers were in paid work by 1989. About 40 per cent of divorced mothers were in receipt of maintenance from former partners, but merely 14 per cent of single mothers.[11] The 1980s had seen the growth of the 'clean-break' divorce, whereby the parent who had day-to-day care of the child continued to occupy the family home, while the partner who renounced their share of the home paid little maintenance. This settlement of capital, rather than current income increased reliance on benefits.

Whilst Virginia Bottomley, Health Secretary and Minister responsible for family issues, adopted something of a benign stance towards lone parents, suggesting that there had never been a golden age of the family, Peter Lilley, the Social Security Secretary, felt that the growth of family disruption was 'deeply disturbing' and lead to divorce, violence and social breakdown on a vast scale.[12] Whilst Lilley felt that part of the reason for this might, regrettably, be the fact that wages levels for the unskilled are little more than benefits, Michael Portillo, the then Treasury Chief Secretary, waded in with the suggestion that 'over-generous benefits' were undermining the family.[13]

The Child Support Act of 1991 was an attempt to relieve the state of the financial burden of children in lone-parent families by transferring it to the former partner where, in the eyes of those who promoted traditional family values, it rightfully belonged. It also encouraged the lone parent to work by offsetting all benefit against maintenance but allowing working parents to keep some maintenance while topping up wages with Family Benefit (Document 7). The Child Support Act was much criticised, not least for the delays in the work of the Child Support Agency it had introduced. Research by the Family Policy Studies Centre in 1996 found a high level of dissatisfaction with delays and with getting information; that the formula for maintenance payments was considered unrealistically high; and that parents already paying maintenance were targeted for increased payments. Lone parents reported that their circumstances had either not changed for the better, or had worsened, sometimes causing much distress. Less informal help was received from the absent partner, for instance help with clothing. Benefits such as free school meals and mortgage interest payments had been lost. The relationship of the absent parent to the child suffered while the creation of new partnerships was more difficult for both the lone and the absent parent. There was more reluctance to admit paternity.[14] When the new agency was created in 1993 it was given the task of reducing benefits by £530 million. In the event the agency saved only about £400 million in its first year.[15] In the face of these criticisms, the Child Support Act 1995 amended the scheme to fix more realistic payments and to recognise past 'clean-break' settlements. The underlying premise of the legislation, that the two-parent family was the norm, remained unchallenged and was indeed reinforced by political rhetoric such as the 'back to basics' campaign of John Major's Conservative administration:

> [P]olicy responses towards lone parents, such as the creation of the Child Support Agency and the 'back to basics' campaign, have

been symptomatic of the way patriarchal institutions within British society have consistently reinforced women's dependency on men both inside and outside the home, and in relation to paid and unpaid work.[16]

(c) Child abuse

Undermining the traditionalists' view of the benefits of the two-parent family household were the cases of child abuse discovered in the 1980s: 'all the children who were the subjects of abuse and public enquiry were little girls and all the perpetrators of the actual physical abuse and violence, men, usually their fathers, step-fathers or men cohabiting with their mothers'.[17] Mothers, as well as their partners, received heavy sentences when court cases ensued and social workers were blamed for failing children. Fears that child sexual abuse was widespread led to much intervention by concerned medical and social work staff in Cleveland, investigated by Lord Justice Butler-Sloss. Indeed, 125 children were medically diagnosed as having been sexually abused from February to July 1987; various actions were taken by social workers but, by the time of the inquiry, 21 children remained in care while 98 had returned to their homes. In order to protect the children, 'the voices of the children were not heard', although the Official Solicitor interviewed 32 children over eight years old, reporting that the interviews revealed 'misunderstanding, mistrust, discomfort, anger, fear, praise, gratitude and sheer relief'. While pleading for greater recognition of child sexual abuse, the inquiry was concerned that possibly overconfident medical diagnoses had taken priority in dealing with the families and that poor communication between agencies had resulted in a crisis situation (Document 20). The use of drugs and alcohol, the absence of a parent and changes of partners by single parents were all seen to be contributing factors to the allegations; fathers were the most numerous abusers, followed by stepfathers, uncles and brothers. There was only one case of abuse by a woman.[18] However, boys as well as girls were the subject of alleged abuses and the inquiry emphasised inter-generational, rather than gender, relationships. The inquiry recommended acceptance of the White Paper on Child Care and Family Services published in 1987, whose provisions were enacted in the 1987 Children Act. This sought to protect children by emphasising parental responsibility, the role of the state being to assess risk and the need for support. Traditional perceptions of the family remained the basis of this legislation and it was criticised by feminist commentators for failing to combat the stress caused by insistence on this model and for failing to provide extra resources (Document 8).

(d) Poverty

From 1979 to 1991, the proportion of families in Britain with less than 50 per cent of average household income, an income below European Union decency thresholds, increased from 10 per cent to 31 per cent.[19] The difficulties faced by single parents were one aspect of the way rising poverty in Britain affected women who, raising children alone, as lone older women or one member of two-adult households formed the majority of the poor. This led some commentators to refer to the 'feminisation' of poverty. This was a contested thesis; while it was recognised that women as a whole were vulnerable to poverty because of their labour market disadvantage and time taken out of the workforce to raise children, this was not a new phenomenon. However, women's poverty was more visible because they more often lived in households without men and, moreover, was growing as cuts in social services affected women (Document 9). As well as carers, young unemployed women and pregnant women fared badly (Documents 5 and 10). From the great Booth and Rowntree pioneering poverty surveys at the turn of the nineteenth and twentieth centuries, poverty had been measured on a household basis. However, such measurement obscured women's experience within the household, which some feminists thus referred to as a 'black box', arguing for an individual, gender, ethnicity, age and physical ability sensitive measurement as a basis for social policy (Document 6).

(e) Health and housing

Poverty experienced by women was intimately related to their health and to the type of housing they occupied. Surveys since the Black report had shown the relationship between class and health; vulnerability to poverty, as well as actual experience of poverty, was stressful. Deprivation in housing was felt more keenly by the household member responsible for the chores and thus spending longer at home. More women than men were treated by general practitioners for mental illness in the 1970s and 1980s, outnumbering men three to one in depressive illnesses; while 40 per cent more women than men were admitted to mental hospitals. 'The fact that the health of women in paid work is better than women who are full-time housewives indicates perhaps the disadvantages in terms of health resources of staying at home, in a job which is unpaid, isolated and undervalued'.[20]

Feminist critiques of gender bias in health services developed more slowly in Britain than in the USA, partly because in Britain the major area of discussion was public versus private provision: 'most feminists, of whatever kind, accept that if one is going to have medical care, then it is probably best organised along the lines of the British NHS... available equally to all, irrespective of their sex, class, colour, creed'.[21] The feminist challenge eventually came to encompass both the way women were treated as service users and as service providers and the way that power was centred in the figures of the male consultants and administrators (Document 12). Women were major providers of unpaid health care and, as professional nurses were underpaid and overworked, 'the problem for nursing has been and continues to be the problem of gender'.[22] Attempts to overcome the shortage of nurses caused by their undervaluation included reform of nurse education. There was, however, some controversy over whether the traditional 'carative' aspect of nursing should be emphasised or whether a 'curative' role should be adopted, whereby nurses gave increased medical support. More fundamental challenges to health care provision were that health care had become an industry, causing harm to individual women and social harm to women as a group, by exploiting them as workers and providing misdiagnosis and inappropriate treatment, based on inadequate research, for women patients, denying them the information necessary for their participation in their treatment.[23] The lack of research into lesbian and bisexual women's health needs was protested. The 'medicalised model' of health care was challenged, whereby power of diagnosis and treatment resided with the specialist male to the detriment of the female individual. Ann Oakley's groundbreaking 1979 book, *From Here to Maternity*, describing her own experience of disempowerment during pregnancy and childbirth was important in critiquing the medicalised model of health care and influential in changing care during pregnancy (Document 13).[24]

The feminist challenge to gender bias in housing policy also encompassed women as consumers and providers of housing services. While traditionalists identified the houses as female space, architects, builders and estate agents, likely to be male, failed to appreciate women's housing needs.[25] As workers in housing services, women were concentrated at the low or unpaid end, as local authority clerks and administrators or contributing to tenants' associations.[26] The shift towards home ownership encouraged by the Conservative governments of the 1980s and 1990s was based on the ideal of the two-parent family: 'Houses are assumed to become homes because they provide and become the environment within which family relationships – close, private and intimate – are located'.[27] This policy failed to take into account the relative poverty of the growing number of single parents and of marriage breakdown and also the difficulty of meeting mortgage payments for women who took time out from paid work to raise children. By 1991, men were still overwhelmingly the majority of owner-occupiers, while married couples were more likely to own houses than single, divorced or widowed people (Document 14). Lesbian women were also disadvantaged in housing provision; a notorious 1984 judgement (Harrogate BC *v.* Simpson) ruled that a lesbian woman was not a member of the family of her deceased partner, despite 20 years cohabitation, and was thus unable to succeed to the tenancy of her partner's council house.

(f) Women and social policy today

By the 1990s, better education and careers improved life-chances for younger women (see Chapter 8). Girls were outperforming boys at GCSE and A level (Document 21) and more women were entering universities and colleges of further education. Women's hourly full-time earnings reached 80 per cent of men's and weekly earnings 72 per cent, rising from 73 per cent of hourly and 64 per cent of weekly earnings in 1978. The impact of these changes was limited: in 73 per cent of couples the man earned more than the woman (Document 22). While there were 686,000 child day-care and 384,000 playgroup places in 1998, there were seven children for each day-care place.[28] As this demand for places illustrates, mothers expect and are expected to work. However, social policy has yet to take account of the structure of women's lives. The 1997 Labour government cut the extra benefit payment to single parents, prompting a revolt by 47 Labour MPs, while including single parents in its 'Welfare to Work' campaign (Documents 15, 16).

Ethnicity and Social Policy

The male breadwinner-female carer family household model was not only gender-biased in that it disadvantaged women but was also ethnocentric, based on the perceived norm of the white majority ethnic group. As more work permits were offered to immigrant women than men from the Caribbean in the 1970s, Afro-Caribbean women built the tradition of being the breadwinner for their families, and were more likely to be in full-time work than white women; Asian women, however, were stereotyped as dependent on their families. Black women were more likely to be in low-paid work while a proportion of their paid labour was domestic work for other households.[29] There was a low take-up of social security benefits by people from minority ethnic groupings because of demands for documentation such as passports and proof of marriage.[30] People from minority ethnic groupings faced racism in society, racist assumptions about lifestyle, racism in provision of social services and institutional racism in police and social service institutions.[31] Chapter 9 deals with racism and ethnicity and Chapter 8 includes an account of black women's experience.

The Welfare State in Crisis?

If most sections of British society are demanding changes in the Welfare State does that mean that it is facing a crisis? Obviously, whether it is exaggerated or not, there is a crisis of types in the world related to the increasing burden of the Welfare State and the economic inability of nations to deliver the provisions and benefits in the face of poor economic conditions. It is certainly the case that rising unemployment, the ageing of society, the problem of immigration and social unrest, and the rising number of one-parent families are imposing, with other issues, burdens upon the British Welfare State and, indeed, on similar systems throughout the world.

Yet the British Welfare State is not feeling the same level of crisis as the more generously-based welfare systems adopted in other Western European and Scandinavian countries. The universally-based Beveridge/Labour Party model provides a national minimum for every citizen. The underlying principle is help according to need at a basic level. Its success against poverty has therefore been somewhat limited and, despite Conservative views to the contrary, expenditure levels are relatively low and for this reason British social policy can operate in a poor economic environment.

Despite, or perhaps because of, the British Welfare State system, poverty has continued to be a major problem in British society in the last 40 years. Indeed, David Piachaud makes the point that poverty rose in Britain over the years from 1953 to 1983 despite the attempts of social policy to provide relief. This detailed study also confirms the groups most vulnerable to poverty in British society: 'One-parent families and unemployed families were, in 1983, far the most likely to be poor with 53.2 per cent and 79.9 per cent below the constant relative poverty level respectively.' Ethnic minorities, already discussed, also come into that category as do the elderly (Document 4).

Structural and Policy Developments in the Welfare State since 1979

In 1979, Thatcherism signalled a very radical break in the pattern of post-war British political economy (see Chapter 1). What it set out to achieve was nothing less than a total restructuring of capital, labour, the state and relations between them and an attempt to undermine the old pluralism that had dominated the Welfare State. The assumption was that Britain declined because of the financial and social burdens of the Welfare State. Thatcherite policies were ones of strict monetary curbs, inroads into public spending, privatisation and legal constraint on trade unions (see Chapter 3).

The government's Medium Term Financial Strategy was vital to all this for it announced limits on the growth of the money supply. By making credit more difficult to obtain it would control inflation and bring about deflation. In other words, the tighter the policy the greater would be the liquidity problems and the higher the unemployment. In total what it amounted to was a reversal of Keynesianism in which competitiveness rather than demand was the operating criterion. Driving the less competitive to the wall would release resources in competitive areas. This strategy appeared almost immediately in Sir Geoffrey Howe's Budget speech of 12 June 1979, when he set the Public Sector Borrowing Requirement at £8.25 billion, £3 billion less than it had been, increased interest rates and pledged to slash public expenditure by £1.5 billion. The whole strategy was to have big implications for the Welfare State, the growth rate on social expenditure falling from an average of 5.4 per cent between 1965 and 1975 to 3 per cent in the Thatcher years (1979 to 1990).

Expenditure on council housing was reduced and the Housing Act of 1980 implemented the decision to sell council houses to occupiers at the market price plus a discount based upon the number of years of occupancy. The 1988 Housing Act also permitted landlords to purchase blocks of flats from the local authorities and allowed local authorities to transfer housing stock to housing associations (Document 2).

Social security also came under close scrutiny. The Conservatives were never able to reduce public expenditure as much as they would have liked. They introduced many measures, including a review of Supplementary Benefits, changes in housing benefit arrangements and reductions in the value of contributory benefits by altering the procedure for inflation-related increases and by extending the taxation of benefits. But this tinkering was considered to be limited. However, in 1983 Norman Fowler, the Secretary of State, decided that a more radical reform of social security was necessary. He set up a number of ministerially-dominated committees to explore the options and the outcome was a report published in 1985 (Secretary of State for Social Service, Cmnd. 9517, 1985) which declared that the social security system had 'lost its way.' Benefits needed to be better targeted and simpler. It suggested the need for a far simpler mean-tested benefits arrangement and expressed the view that the SERPS, the state pension scheme, would impose excessive burdens upon future generations. Yet he was unable to remove this scheme and simply reduced the benefit arrangements and introduced changes causing shorter-term contributors, such as women, to lose out. The 1986 Social Security Act therefore modified SERPS, replaced Supplementary Benefit with Income Support, and the Family Income Supplement with Family Credit. The maternity and death grants were also abolished and replaced by means-test-related benefits for the very poor. The biggest change was that the Supplementary Fund was replaced by a Social Fund, 70 per cent of the expenditure of which was to be in the form of loans.

Despite this pruning and simplifying, Conservative governments found it difficult to reduce social security expenditure in the way they would have liked largely because of rising unemployment (Document 1). Elsewhere, annual expenditure levels rose in real terms.

In education this has been largely due to the fact that high, catching-up wage settlements to teachers were honoured once the Conservatives came to power in May 1979 and as a result of the numerous educational experiments of the government which also cost money. The most important of these changes has been the 1988 Education Act which largely replaced the 1944 Education Act, set up the national curriculum, with its core and foundation subjects, required a religious education reflecting the dominance of Christianity and allowed the more widely-empowered governors of county and voluntary maintained schools, if they had the support of the parents, to apply to the Secretary of State for maintenance by grant from the government rather than from the local education authority. The opting out arrangement theoretically gave the parents more choice whilst in fact strengthening the hand of the state over education. Like many other areas of recent welfare policy, there was comparatively little prior discussion of the changes and the legislation could be considered to be a little too previous. As one commentator noted of the 1988 Act, it was 'action before words, decision before debate, the presumption of guilt exceeding all possibility of innocence in the previous way of doing things'.[32]

The only other major area of extension under Thatcher has been the provision of health care and personal services. In 1979, the Royal Commission on the National Health Service reported and endorsed the existing service whilst criticising its excessive bureaucracy. As a result the Conservative government took away one of the bureaucratic layers, the Area Health Authorities, in 1982 and left the planning to the Regional and District Health Authorities alone. To enable them to do this, general managers were appointed to balance the medical and administrative requirements of the service. Then, in 1990, new legislation set up National Health Trusts, semi-autonomous bodies answering to the Secretary of State and able to manage their own finances, appoint their own staff and offer a package of services that they can sell to the District Health Authorities. In addition, GPs were also allowed to become 'fund-holders', able to make independent arrangements with hospitals. The process has since been partly reversed and modified under Tony Blair's Labour governments since 1997.

In other areas, state resources have also been diverted into dealing with the increasing number of old people in the community. Throughout the 1980s there was an increase in private residential care especially as the Department of Social Security met part of the private charges in full, even though relatives were often called upon to 'top them up'. In addition, individuals in private residential care have been able to apply for Supplementary Benefit (Income Support after the 1986 Act). The potential cost of care was also increased by the fact that Sir Roy Griffiths' Report of 1988, which the government accepted and included in the new health structure in 1990, suggested that the local authority social services department should decide on social rather than income grounds that care was necessary and then have the responsibility to ensure that care, from either public or the private sector. If individuals could not pay for that care from their own income or from standard social security benefits then the local authority had to provide the subsidy. The local authorities could become the buyers of packages of care from private homes. The government obviously had to transfer resources from the social security budget to the local authority budget and the new system became effective from April 1993.

It is clear that the Welfare State has changed dramatically during the last 20 years. The problem remains how to match the needs of the deprived, poor and discriminated against with the limited resources of the state. As indicated later (Document 5 and Chapter 4), it is now clear that New Labour under Tony Blair is committed to the Third Way, a partnership between the private and public sectors which believes that it is possible to 'combine a free-market economy with social justice'.[33] This was evident in the child-poverty statement made by Tony Blair, on 18 March 1999, already referred to.[34]

Despite, or because of, the changes, and regardless of lofty and distant ambitions, the British Welfare State is still based upon gender (Documents 13, 14 and others) and class differences; it has not removed many social and gender differences (Document 22). It has changed and the voluntary sector has become more involved (Documents 1, 2), as first Thatcher and then Blair stressed the need for a measure of private and public participation and the encouragement of linking voluntary organisations. The Welfare State is changing rapidly and becoming increasingly focused, targeted and less state-dominated. Whether it will ever generate a more truly equal and balanced response to the needs of British society is another matter.

Documents

SECONDARY SOURCES AND INTERPRETATIONS

1. David Gladstone, *The Twentieth-Century Welfare State* (London, Macmillan, 1999), pp.87–9, 134, 141

[pp.87–9] There was a certain inevitability about the place accorded to voluntary action in the Thatcherite period. The government was committed to 'rolling back' the frontiers of the state and restoring Victorian values... The nineteenth century had been the age of self-help and mutual aid, of welfare activity predominately 'outside the state'. The Thatcherite project for slimming the state suggests a new (or a rediscovered) role for voluntary activity. But what was that role to be?

[There is an ambiguity in Conservative thinking.] This is made clear by a comparison of the statements about the voluntary sector in the 1979 and 1987 Conservative election manifestos. The first proposed that 'We must also encourage the voluntary movement and self-help groups working in partnership with the statutory services.' The latter argued that via tax relief on charitable giving, 'the scope of individual responsibility is widened, the family is strengthened and voluntary bodies flourish. State power is checked.' Whereas, in the earlier statement, the voluntary sector was seen as an addition to state provision – with partnership between them a policy objective – the latter offered a different view: the role of the voluntary sector not as a supplement to the state but as an alternative to it'.[35]

[Arguing that this was more rhetoric than a practical change, he contends that the pace of change did increase, that its impact was limited and that the voluntary sector was still dependent upon the state.]

[T]hroughout the 1980s public finance remained a major source of funding for the voluntary sector. Between 1979 and 1987 it doubled in real terms, fuelled mainly by the continued growth in special employment programmes and by the expansion of funding in housing associations, whose role in the supply of social housing the government wished to promote. The involvement of the voluntary sector in the Community Programme for unemployed people was especially significant. When it closed in 1988, voluntary agencies were supplying over half the projects of the Programme, whilst the Manpower Services Commission was providing 20 per cent of all government funding going to the voluntary sector.

[p.134] The gender perspective is a comparatively recent innovation in the analysis of welfare, and of the welfare state in particular. It played no part, for example, in Richard Titmuss's seminal discussion of the social division of welfare of the late 1950s. Its origins are usually traced to Elizabeth Wilson's *Women and Welfare* published in 1977, a book 'written particularly for women (and men) who work for the welfare state, and for women, housewives, mothers and workers who are subject to sexist ideology. It is intended as an exposure of that ideology. It is also a call to fight it...' Since that time the feminist perspectives have become increasingly sophisticated and diverse. Most contemporary studies tend to distinguish between liberal, socialist, radical and Black feminism... While such differences have produced different strategies for challenging male domination in social policy, in general 'feminists have made the issue of who controls welfare and how is it organised, questions of immediate concern and political priority'... Studies within this paradigm have thus documented 'the inequalities between women and men as recipients of welfare state services' as well as emphasising 'a different set of determinants shaping the nature of public policy provision and welfare'.[36] The result has been over the past 20 years feminist scholarship has challenged 'the universalist rhetoric employed by policy-makers and many earlier scholars [by] pointing out that the ostensible "universal" welfare states are often deeply structured along gender lines'.[37]

The literature on women and the welfare state is extensive. Within the genre, however, it is possible to identify three principal and often interrelated themes: women as producers, as consumers and as agents in the development of welfare states.

[Looking at the last of these, he continues, p.141] But that welfare state even further eroded the tradition of localism and made welfare issues the province of the central state. For women's agency this had two principal consequences. While women in the earlier twentieth century had made the transition from voluntary visitor to paid employee, they very rarely moved to paid policy-making positions in the civil service. As Lewis notes 'while British male settlers like William Beveridge moved into policy making positions as the balance of the mixed economy of welfare shifted in favour of the state, women did not'.[38] But furthermore 'the importance attached to the personal service work that was [women's] special provision diminished with the concomitant shift in the philosophy of social provision'. The agenda of universalism was one that encompassed the interests both of women and men.

2. Norman Ginsburg, 'Housing', in Robert M Page and Richard Silburn (eds), *British Social Welfare in the Twentieth Century* (London, Macmillan, 1999), pp.237–8

The two main planks of housing policy since have been, first, the drive to extend owner occupation as far as possible and, second, to retrench severely expenditure on council housing by raising rents, privatisation and cuts in bricks and mortar subsidies and investment. Housing policy has thus played a direct role in the growth of both homelessness and tenure polarisation by marginalising tenants and limiting the supply of social rented housing. The fall in house prices and hence confidence in owner occupation in the early 1990s produced a short-term policy reverse with increased investment in housing association provision and in refurbishment of council estates, but the fundamental policy of Conservative policy remained unchanged...

Since 1979, particularly in the early years of the Thatcher administration, the drive to extend home ownership has been less enthusiastically pursued. Hence between 1979 and 1989 the number of owner occupied dwellings in Britain increased by over 4.5 million, almost half a million a year on average. From 1989 to 1995, however, owner occupation has only increased by 1.1 million, around 180,000 a year on average... The two key elements were, first, the introduction of the right to buy with considerable discounts for tenants of social rented housing in the Housing Act 1980. By the end of 1995, almost 1.7 million dwellings had been sold to local authority and housing association tenants in Britain generating receipts of over £326 billion with discounts of a further £24 billion... making it by far the biggest of privatisation programmes...

The second policy element was the deregulation of mortgage finance achieved by a number of financial policy changes culminating in the Building Societies Act 1986... These measures allowed building societies to increase their borrowing and opened up the mortgage market to more competition. Mortgage rationing disappeared and lenders were willing to lend increasing proportions of properties' values, exposing themselves and borrowers to greater risks.

3. Extract from T Raison, *Tories and the Welfare State* (1990), pp.73–4, paraphrasing Sir Keith Joseph's view on poverty

First... family allowances gave no help to families with only one child – yet to bring in first children would take time and also add greatly to the cost of the scheme. Second, an increase in family allowance, whether or not taxes, could not be at a level which would give significant help to the poorest of wage-earning households. And, thirdly, the lowering of the standard rate of income tax threshold by Labour meant that certain people who should be seen in the category of family poverty were actually paying income tax and would therefore derive no benefit from family allowances after tax had been clawed back.

4. Alan Walker, 'The Persistence of Poverty among Older People', in *Research Highlights of Social Work*, 22

Despite the significant political commitment given to pensions in the 1970s – culminating in the State Earnings Related Pension Scheme (SERPS) in 1975 and a series of pledges to uprate pensions in line with earnings or prices, whichever was the greater – which resulted in some improvements in the relative position of elderly people in the income distribution... poverty is still the principal financial problem faced by elderly people.

5. Tony Blair's speech on child poverty and welfare of 18 March 1999, being quoted in the *Guardian*, 19 March 1999

[Tony Blair suggested that the modern welfare state should be 'active, not passive, genuinely providing people with a hand-up not a hand-out' and committed £6,000 million to tackling child poverty in the course of that Parliament. 'The Quiet Revolution' suggested that there are six characteristics of a modern welfare state. They are, he said:]
  * tackling social exclusion, from decayed communities to drugs and unemployment;
  * mutual responsibility, a hand-up, not a hand-out;
  * help focused upon those who need it most;
  * an end to fraud and abuse;
  * public/private partnership on welfare, schools and health, not just benefits;
  * a re-emphasis on active welfare, schools and health, not just benefits...

[He added that] The third way in welfare is clear: not to dismantle it or protect it unchanged but to reform it radically, taking its core values and applying them afresh to the modern world... Poverty should not be a birthright. Being poor should not be a life sentence. We need to break the cycle of disadvantage so that children born into poverty are not condemned to social exclusion and deprivation...

There will always be a mixture of universal and targeted help. But one is not superior or more principled than the other.

6. Miriam David, 'Putting on an Act for Children?', in Mavis Maclean and Dulcie Groves (eds), *Women's Issues in Social Policy* **(London, Routledge, 1991), p.99**

The picture that now emerges of the family is that the parents in the union are not necessarily any longer breadwinner father and housewife mother. In a substantial minority, the father may be unemployed. He may not be the biological father, but rather a step-parent. On the other hand, he may be forced to work long hours to make ends meet or to make a good household income. In a substantial minority, too, the mother may be a lone parent, rearing children alone, often in conditions of poverty... The vast majority of mothers are in paid employment, whether in two-parent or lone-parent households; albeit that employment is of a short, part-time variety and may involve a substantial number of changes. Mothers' chances of long-term, permanent paid employment, whether in lone-parent or two-parent households are quite slim, and the costs for women quite considerable... the apparent changes in family forms have had a major impact on women's working lives, despite the fact that their lives still do not mirror those of fathers.

7. Karen Clarke, Gary Craig and Caroline Glendinning, *Small Change: The Impact of the Child Support Act on Lone Mothers and Children* **(London, Family Policy Studies Centre, 1996), pp.8–9**

There was certainly justifiable concern over the efficiency and equity of the previous maintenance system. The 1980s saw a trend towards 'clean break' divorce, in which the parent with day-to-day responsibility for children was awarded full rights to the family home. This was offset by nominal or token cash payments towards the ongoing maintenance of children. As a consequence growing numbers of lone parents received little or no maintenance from former partners towards their children's care and increasingly relied on social security benefits for the whole of their day-to-day income. Considerable differences in the treatment of lone-parent families resulted from the adversarial nature of negotiations between former partners, the discretion which was widely used to determine maintenance awards, the absence of regular up-rating of main-tenance payments in line with inflation or improvements in a former partner's earnings, and the apparent ease with which some former partners avoided compliance with court maintenance orders. The courts also tended to protect the living standards of 'second' families of a former partner in assessing maintenance, whereas the majority of 'first families' – lone mothers and their children – lived on means-tested benefits. All these concerns added to arguments within and outside government, that action was needed to enforce the responsibilities of both parents to provide adequate financial support for their children.

These concerns shaped the two key aims of the Child Support Act: to increase the amount of maintenance paid by former partners and thus curb the rapid growth in public expenditure on lone parents; to tackle the differences in maintenance received by lone-parent families which bore little relationship to their needs. The Act also aimed to create greater equity between the living standards of 'first' and 'second' families.

A subsidiary aim of the legislation was to improve financial incentives to encourage more lone parents to enter paid employment. Under the rules for income support (the main means-tested benefit for those out of work), all maintenance is taken fully into account, so a lone parent is no better off. However, if she moves into paid employment and claims family credit to 'top up' wages from a low paid or part-time job, she can keep some of the maintenance; if her earnings increase so as to lift her off means-tested benefits altogether, she can keep all of the maintenance. It was therefore hoped that the prospect of being able to benefit from (higher) maintenance payments would encourage more lone mothers to derive their income from a combination of maintenance plus earnings (perhaps topped up by family credit). Changes to the definition of 'full-time' work and a disregard for some child care costs, both for family credit purposes, were therefore also introduced to complement the Child Support Act. However, little was done to tackle any of the other major barriers to employment experienced by lone mothers – lack of appropriate training, the availability of affordable child care and low pay. Indeed the implementation of other policies in these areas were actually making these barriers more difficult to overcome.

The Child Support Act was expected roughly to double the numbers regularly receiving maintenance – an increase of 200,000 lone parents. This included an estimated 50,000 lone parents (roughly 6 per cent of those on income support) who would no longer receive the benefit at all.

The key provisions of the 1991 Child Support Act were:

* The establishment of the Child Support Agency, which took over responsibility for assessing all child maintenance payments and for collecting them where requested. The Agency would provide a fair, consistent and efficient service.

* The introduction of a universally applicable, but complex, formula to calculate child maintenance liability. The formula was originally based on income support levels and disregarded the actual expenditure of an 'absent parent' other than some housing costs. Subsequent amendments to the formula have aimed to reduce the hardship reported by some 'absent parents' and their new families.

* All lone parents claiming income support, family credit or disability working allowance must agree to the recovery of maintenance from an 'absent parent' and must co-operate with the Child Support Agency in tracing him or her and assessing and collecting any maintenance due. This obligation is waived only when a lone parent has 'reasonable grounds' for believing it would cause him, her or any child to suffer 'harm or undue distress'.

* Lone parents refusing to co-operate without demonstrating a risk of 'harm or undue distress' risk having their benefit reduced by 20 per cent for six months and 10 per cent for a further 12 months.

* All the maintenance received by a lone parent is deducted, pound for pound, from payments of income support; £15 maintenance is 'disregarded' in calculating entitlement to family credit and disability working allowance.

* Lone parents receiving income support are guaranteed all their benefit entitlement, regardless of whether a former partner has paid the maintenance for which he or she is liable. Lone parents on family credit or who are not receiving any social security benefits at all are dependent on a former partner paying maintenance regularly, either directly or through the Child Support Agency, to ensure that they receive a regular income.

The Act thus removed virtually all discretion in the assessment and collection of child maintenance for lone parents receiving means-tested benefits (apart from cases of possible 'harm and undue distress'). Lone parents not receiving these benefits might choose between using the Child Support Agency or coming to an entirely private agreement. However, if they opted for the former, then the same complex formula was used to determine the level of an 'absent' parent's maintenance liability. Questions of contact between parent and children, spouse maintenance and all issues concerned with property and capital settlements were still to be dealt with by the courts.

8. Miriam David, 'Putting on an Act for Children', pp.107–8 (already fully cited in Document 6)

The specific pressure, however, came from those concerned about defining legally rights and duties for parents, children, local authorities and others involved in providing child care. In other words, it was pressure to ensure that those families which did not conform to the traditional nuclear family would as nearly as possible imitate or mirror it in their legal and consequent social responsibilities. Hence the centrality to the law reform of the concept of parental responsibilities whether for parents or those given responsibility in loco parentis. As a corollary, the other general principle in the Act is 'the child's welfare'. But this is defined in an incredibly narrow way to cover the child only in regard to care and contested family proceedings, when deciding any question of upbringing or property. The court, it is stated, may not make an order 'unless it considers that doing so would be better for the child than making no order at all'. A 'welfare check-list' of seven points is provided. These are:

 (a) the ascertainable wishes and feelings of the child concerned (considered in the light of his [sic] age and understanding);
 (b) his physical, emotional and educational needs;
 (c) the likely effect on him of any change in his circumstances;
 (d) his age, sex, background and any characteristics of his which the court considers relevant;
 (e) any harm which he has suffered or is at risk of suffering;
 (f) how capable each of his parents, and any other person in relation to whom the court considers the question to be relevant, is of meeting his needs;
 (g) the range of powers available to the courts under this Act in the proceedings in question.

These considerations will be used to determine which of four sorts of court orders to apply in family proceedings, namely, one a residence order (where children will live); two a contact order (who will have access); three a specific steps order (determining the exercise of parental responsibility, and four, a prohibited steps order (steps not to be taken without leave of the court). Local authorities, however, also retain other responsibilities for children in need and where consistent with this, to promote their upbringing by their families. To do this they have a duty to identify the children and publicise their services, to take reasonable steps to prevent neglect or abuse, to provide home help, holidays, family centres with counselling and other services to keep children in their families 'as they consider appropriate'. This latter term is also used for local authority provision of day care for the under-fives in need, facilities for child-minders and for older children. However, there are no resources associated with these provisions and, in general terms, local authorities are expected now to give assistance in kind, or, in exceptional circumstances, by a recoverable loan.

The emphasis, then, in the Act is on clarifying court proceedings for a child's welfare, not for providing generally for social welfare. There is a clear shift to legalising the procedures in courts and for social workers. Social workers will clearly become more involved in assessment of children at risk and defining the kinds of ways such children can be helped...

It is certainly the case that the Act emphasises the privacy of the family and the limited legalistic role that social work intervention should take. The emphasis is on parental and children's rights, in gender-neutral terms, rather than on the resources available to families. There is a clear shift from the social welfare model to a more justicial one.

9. Sarah Payne, *Women, Health and Poverty: An Introduction* (Brighton, Harvester Wheatsheaf, 1991. This was reprinted by permission of Pearson Education Limited), p.47

Similarly, women's earnings have remained low in comparison with those of men, despite the introduction of equal opportunities legislation in the latter half of this century. Thus in 1886 adult women in full-time employment were paid on average 52 per cent of male earnings; in 1988 women's earnings were on average 67 per cent of the figure for men. This represents a gain of a mere 15 per cent over the course of the century, whilst women continue to receive on average only two-thirds of male rates of pay.

The feminisation of poverty thesis, which argues that women's poverty has increased in this century and that women have formed a growing proportion of the poor, is therefore misplaced. What has happened however is that women's poverty has become more visible. Changing demography means that women are now more likely to be poor as a result of lone motherhood, marital and relationship break down, and old age, and less often poor within large family households... Women who are poor, as a result, are more easily counted and more readily observed, although the extent of the poverty women continue to experience within households remains obscured by both poverty research and government statistics. Further trends in recent years, however, suggest that women's risk of poverty, and the severity of that poverty, are growing as a result of changes in the labour market and in social policy. Changes in the payment of social security and the increasing privatisation of benefits such as maternity pay, sick pay and occupational pensions, have had a significant impact on women's risk of poverty. Similarly the restructuring of the labour market, and changes in the availability and cost of childcare, also carry specific implications for women. The increasing marginalisation of women's employment, poorer pay and conditions of employment, and cuts in real rates of social security, suggest that whilst paid work as a source of income for women is becoming more limited, social security benefits are increasingly unlikely to prevent serious poverty and deprivation.

10. Caroline Glendinning and Jane Millar (eds), *Women and Poverty in Britain* (Brighton, Harvester Wheatsheaf, 1987), pp.262–3

Certainly over the last few years women (and men) have expended a great deal of time and energy in defending what few rights women already have which might protect them against poverty, or in pressing for very small, piecemeal gains. For example the 1986 Social Security Act, the culmination of 'the most substantial examination of the social security system since the Beveridge report 40 years ago' (DHSS 1985a, vol. 1, para. 1.4) contains proposals which will have a severely detrimental effect on women's rights to income and on their consequent financial circumstances. As other contributors have already pointed out, young unemployed women, women in pregnancy and with young children, and, in particular, future generations of elderly women will be badly affected by the changes. In addition there has been no guarantee in the legislation that Child Benefit – often the only weekly income reliably available to non-earning women with children – will retain its real value. Indeed cuts in the value of Child Benefit have contributed towards the cost of the new means-tested Family Credit scheme, which has been designed to reduce wage demands from low paid men. In addition at least half a million children will lose their entitlement to free school meals, thereby both increasing the pressures on the household budget and also shifting the balance of their care further into the informal (domestic) sector. Nevertheless, the situation could have been much worse. The Green paper originally proposed the complete abolition of the state earnings related pension scheme, which would have been even more damaging for future generations of elderly women than the eventual modified retention of the scheme will be. An original proposal to pay Family Credit through the (male) wage-earner's pay packet rather than in the form of an order book to the (female) child carer was withdrawn during the final stages of the legislation's progress through Parliament. Child Benefit was not cut as dramatically as had originally been feared; and the threat of a defeat in the European Court finally pushed the government, in June 1986, to extend Invalid Care Allowance to married and cohabiting women, a measure which will direct some £55 millions (plus associated arrears of benefit) into the hands of an estimated 50,000 women carers of disabled or elderly people, who have no other source of independent income [*The Times*, 24 June 1986].

Real though these gains are, they are nevertheless minimal and may in the long run be far outweighed by other developments which will substantially increase women's poverty. For example, one of the main thrusts of present government policy (in line with a general commitment to privatisation) has been to shift responsibility for social security and income maintenance from the state to the private sector. Examples of this include the changes to SERPS and the moves to make employers responsible for paying benefits (unsuccessful in the case of family credit, but already in operation with statutory sick pay and due to be introduced in 1987 for maternity pay). The experience of statutory sick pay (Baloo, *et al.*, 1986) shows the extent to which low-paid and part-time workers are likely to be adversely affected by this shift to the private sector, which is in any case both inherently structured to women's disadvantage and difficult to regulate adequately. Any immediate strategy for change must therefore involve the protection of whatever rights women currently have; but it is also clear, in view of the evidence and arguments presented in this book, that far more radical structural changes are needed.

11. Sarah Payne, *Women, Health and Poverty: An Introduction* (Brighton, Harvester Wheatsheaf, 1991), p.5

Thus one sense in which the definition of poverty and deprivation fails to take account of the specific experience of women is through the focus on households as units of consumption, with no analysis of ways in which different members of a household have different access to the resources of that household, relating to the differential economic power of each sex, and of parents and children. This cannot be resolved simply through the incorporation of a measure of differential spending on behalf of different members of a household, as expenditure itself must be reclassified into necessity and luxury or leisure items, and as some responsibilities for expenditure bring stress and deprivation of other kinds rather than true economic power... For example, having control of the household's income during periods of shortage – as many women do – brings responsibility for making ends meet and providing for the needs of the household under difficult or impossible conditions, but it does not bring independence. This is an extremely complex scheme to unravel, the more so as the allocation of both purchasing power and resources within the household is not necessarily static or easily observed – women and men may take for granted the assumptions of how resources are to be divided, the going without by one or both partners, and so on. This question of how resources are allocated is complex and subtle: it is also one which has serious consequences for the health chances of different members of the household. Again, these are not straightforward to observe – it is not only the denial or allocation of material resources, but also the responsibility, stress, and threat of denial which complicates the picture of possible influences on the health of individual household members.

12. Lesley Doyal in Jonathan Gabe, et al (eds), *Challenging Medicine* (London, Routledge, 1994), p.144

Membership of the new Regional, District and Family Health Service Authorities also remains male-dominated. Only 10.8 per cent of general managers are women, as are 22.8 per cent of executive members of the authorities, 25 per cent of chairs and 30 per cent of non-executive members... Indeed, recent research suggests that the NHS reforms have reduced rather than increased the number of women on these bodies, with a decline from 35 per cent on Regional and District Health Authorities to a figure of 26.8 per cent following the NHS and Community Care Act, 1990... Ironically, then, the women's role in decision making may have been reduced still further at precisely the moment when the purchasing role could have been used to articulate their interests more clearly.

    The relative scarcity of women in senior positions in medicine and in the management structure of the NHS is in itself the object of feminist criticism. It is a result both of structural obstacles and also of more diffuse factors associated with 'male' occupational cultures. Hence medicine, like most of the other professions, is in need of major reform to ensure equal opportunities for all. But the implications are, of course, much wider than concern about the occupational advancement of a few women. Women's lack of authority and power also contributes to a situation where female users of the NHS continue to be constrained in the exercise of their own autonomy, as well as risking inappropriate diagnosis and treatment.

It is a central tenet of medical ethics that those receiving care should give their informed consent to it (Beauchamp and Faden, 1986). While most members of the profession respect this in theory, the practice varies markedly between doctors and institutions. Individual factors can inhibit the capacity of patients of both sexes to exercise their autonomy – lack of education, a paternalistic doctor, or one who lacks communication skills, for instance. However, research suggests that structural factors such as class, race and gender also affect the exercise of patient autonomy.

13. Ann Oakley, *Women Confined: Paradigms of Women as Reproducers* (Oxford, Martin Robinson, 1980), p.1

Having a baby is a biological and cultural act. In bearing a child, a woman reproduces the species and performs an 'animal function'. Yet human childbirth is accomplished in and shaped by culture, both in a general sense and in the particular sense of the varying definitions of reproduction offered by different cultures. How a society defines reproduction is closely linked with its articulation of women's position: the connections between female citizenship and the procreative role are social, not biological. Cultural attitudes both to women and to reproduction are marked by certain paradigmatic representations (OED 'pattern', 'example; 'paradigmatize' – 'to set forth as a model'). These abound in commonsense understandings of women and motherhood, but medical, psychological and social science are their main repository. It is from the 'scientific' representation of women as maternity cases that the character of mothers is deduced. 'Science' has hidden curricula of moral evaluations that masquerade as fact: it is these 'facts' that must be probed to expose the typical paradigms of women as reproducers that characterize the culture of the contemporary industrial world.

14. Rose Gilroy, 'Women and Owner Occupation in Britain', in Rose Gilroy and Roberta Woods (eds), *Housing Women* (London, Routledge, 1994), p.32

TENURE OF MALE AND FEMALE HEADS OF HOUSEHOLD

(as a percentage of each tenure category)	Women %	Men %
Owner occupation	23.81	76.19
Private rented	30.37	69.63
Housing association	53.78	46.22
Local authority	47.46	52.54
All tenures	30.54	69.46

Source: *Census*, 1991

HOME OWNERS BY SEX AND MARITAL STATUS		%
Married couples		77
Women	Single	44
	Widowed	51
	Divorced/separated	46
Men	Single	54
	Widowed	50
	Divorced/separated	54

Source: Table 3.33b, *General Household Survey*, 1991

15. Gill Scott, 'Child-care: The Changing Boundaries of Family, Economy and State', in *Critical Social Policy*, 57 18 (4) (1998), pp.520–1

Although it would be difficult to argue that the UK has seen a total transformation in its welfare regime over the last 10 years, it is indisputable that the nature of welfare, and the state's role within it, has experienced significant change. Not the least of these changes lies in the area of child-care policy, where changes, prior to and continuing with the change of government in May 1997, seem to highlight increasing discontent with the old boundaries of state and family. Debates now often involve a shift from discussion of the value of early childhood education and support for 'dis-advantaged' families to discussions which include, among other things, the relationship between child-care, economic change and economic dependence inside and outside the family...

There is little doubt that for many women in the 1990s the boundaries between work and family have changed. Work is no longer viewed as excluding mothers of children, and the use of child-care services is no longer seen by mothers as merely a valuable social or education service for their children but as a means of supporting their increasing employment. Evidence for this lies in the increasing numbers of women who are returning to work after having their children. From the mid-1980s the employment rates of mothers with children has risen sharply so that between 1983 and 1992 the figures changed from employment rates of 29 percent to 49 percent for mothers of children aged 0 to 4, and from 59 percent to 72 percent for those with 5 to 9 year olds... Furthermore, an even higher number report they would like to work if suitable child-care were available. The British Social Attitudes survey of 1990 reports that two-thirds of women with children under 12 would seek employment if child-care were available...

From the 1970s until the early 1990s child-care services used in the UK were those provided by local authorities, or those run largely by mothers themselves through the playgroup movement. The main boundaries of care were between the state and the family. However, as mothers became less 'available' for involvement in the playgroup movement, and the rate of working mothers increased beyond the level that other family members could provide the alternative care, so the market started to be used as a source of child-care, and child-care became seen as a partial alternative rather than the supplement to the care by mothers that was implied in most local authority and playgroup provision. Care by partners or other family members remains the main form of child-care for working mothers, but evidence from the fifth sweep of the National Child Development Study shows that in 1991 more than 20 percent of employed married mothers born in 1958, and 13 percent of employed lone parents, use paid, formal care for their children while they are at work...

16. Equal Opportunities Commission, *Women and Men in Britain: The Lifecycle of Inequality* (Manchester, EOC, 2001), pp.2–4

In the past the impact of child bearing has had a tremendous effect on economic status and income over women's lifetimes and this is generally still the case, particularly for the low-skilled and poorly qualified. The family structures of women and men at particular ages can appear quite different, because women tend to be younger than men at times of family change, for example when they first cohabit, marry, become parents or divorce.

In 1998, 25 per cent of all families with dependent children were headed by a lone parent, over 90 per cent of whom were mothers. During the past twenty-five years there has been an increase in the poverty of mothers, and lone mothers in particular. They are significantly more likely than mothers in couples to face ill-health. Young lone mothers and those who are poor or not working are especially vulnerable, with nearly half of women in these categories reporting less than good health in 1992–95. Teenage mothers tend to have a higher proportion of low birthweight babies, who also suffer from a higher infant mortality rate.

The ages at which women and men have children are strongly related to qualification levels. In the age group 25 to 34, 84 per cent of women without qualifications had dependent children compared with only 29 per cent of those with degrees or equivalent. The situation had reversed by the age of 45 to 54, so that 22 per cent of women with no qualifications had dependent children, compared with 42 per cent of women with degrees. For men, the pattern is not as extreme.

This is a clear indication that the lower the level of a woman's qualifications, the younger she is likely to be when she first has children.

PRIMARY EVIDENCE AND INFORMATION

17. Rhodes Boyson, *Down with the Poor* (1971), quoted in J Clarke, A Cochrane and C Smart, *Ideologies of Welfare: From Dreams to Disillusion* (1987), pp.133

Not only is the present welfare state inefficient and destructive of personal liberty, individual responsibility and moral growth, but it saps the collective moral fibre of our people as a nation.

18. James Callaghan, Prime Minister, Labour Party, *Report of the 75th Annual Conference* (London, Labour Party, 1976), p.188

We used to think that you could just spend your way out of a recession and increase employment by cutting taxes and boosting government spending. I tell you in all honestly that option no longer exists and that, insofar as it ever did exist, it worked by injecting inflation into the economy. And each time that happened, the average level of unemployment has risen. High inflation followed by higher unemployment. That is the history of the last twenty years.

19. NALGO Equal Opportunities Committee, Women and the Cuts, Discussion Paper, 11 January 1980

'If the Good Lord had intended us to have equal rights and to go out to work and to behave equally, he really wouldn't have created man and woman.'
Rt Hon Patrick Jenkin MP, Secretary of State for Social Services, speaking on a television programme on nurseries in November 1979.

This statement admirably sums up the essence of the theoretical underpinning which is part of the background to the Government's savage cuts in public expenditure. It was articulated even more clearly by Lord Spens in the House of Lords in July 1979 when he declared that married women should leave paid work and stay at home – 'I am not saying they should not be occupied,' he said, 'just that they should not compete in the market for paid jobs.'

After a decade of progress (and the Sex Discrimination Equal Pay and Employment Protection, Abortion and Divorce Reform Acts do represent progress, however slow at times) it is clearly necessary for the Government to provide a framework for its cuts which will minimise resistance from women who are beginning to get used to a degree of independence and choice in their lives.

Nevertheless, although women are challenging the assumption that their place is in the home it is conventional wisdom that women's primary role is their role as domestic labourers within the home and all else is secondary. This has led to a number of features in their participation in the labour market (features that make them very vulnerable to cuts in public expenditure):

– they tend to work part time

– their work is often in the 'caring' sphere, mirroring their domestic role, e.g. school meals workers, nursery nurses, hospital auxiliaries, teachers

– they rely heavily on 'support services' to enable them to go out to work, e.g. nurseries (even in the most enlightened homes, it is regarded as the woman's job to fix up a nursery place or find a childminder), home helps for elderly dependants etc.

In other words, women – both as workers in and consumers of the public services – will suffer unduly as a result of cuts in public expenditure.

Women will be affected as a result of the cuts in public expenditure, not only in the same way as men (general reductions in levels of services, early retirement for public service workers etc.), but also in a number of specific ways because of the position of women in society. It is essential that NALGO as a union recognises the extent of women's specific vulnerability to the cuts and maintains its pressure for equality of opportunity, better maternity rights, the provision of nursery facilities etc. Without this women as employees could easily become sitting targets for the cuts. At present it would appear that either the cuts are having no effect on staffing levels, conditions of service etc. for women, or that branches are unwilling to recognise the implications for their women members, since in a recent survey of branches, only 149 out of 1,200 replied and of these only three said their branches were encountering problems concerning women and the cuts (and two of these mentioned only nursery provision). The low response is somewhat worrying (especially with the Manpower Watch indicating a loss of part-time (women's) jobs which should perhaps have prompted a greater and more informative response from local government branches at least). NALGO has a good record on women's rights – it has not prioritised a male 'family wage' and underestimated the importance of women's employment (as trade unions have sometimes done). It must now face up to this latest challenge to women's participation in the labour market and recognise that unless we resist the attacks on women, both they and the union will be the losers.

20. Lord Justice Butler-Sloss, *Report of the Inquiry into Child Abuse in Cleveland 1987* (London, HMSO, 1988, Cmnd. 4/2), pp.243–5

FINAL CONCLUSIONS

1 We have learned during the Inquiry that sexual abuse occurs in children of all ages, including the very young, to boys as well as girls, in all classes of society and frequently within the privacy of the family. The sexual abuse can be very serious and on occasions includes vaginal, anal and oral intercourse. The problems of child sexual abuse have been recognised to an increasing extent over the past few years by professionals in different disciplines. This presents new and particularly difficult problems for the agencies concerned in child protection. In Cleveland an honest attempt was made to address these problems by the agencies. In Spring 1987 it went wrong.

2   The reasons for the crisis are complex. In essence they included: lack of a proper understanding by the main agencies of each others' functions in relation to child sexual abuse;

-a lack of communication between the agencies;

-differences of views at middle management level which were not recognised by senior staff. These eventually affected those working on the ground...

14 It is unacceptable that the disagreement and failure of communication of adults should be allowed to obscure the needs of children both long term and short term in so sensitive, difficult and important a field. The children had unhappy experiences which should not be allowed to happen again.

15 It is however important to bear in mind that those who have a responsibility to protect children at risk, such as social workers, health visitors, police and doctors have in the past been criticised for failure to act in sufficient time and to take adequate steps to protect children who are being damaged. In Cleveland the general criticism by the public has been of over-enthusiasm and zeal in the actions taken. It is difficult for professions to balance the conflicting interests and needs in the enormously important and delicate field of child sexual abuse. We hope that professionals will not as a result of the Cleveland experience stand back and hesitate to act to protect children.

21. Equal Opportunities Commission, *Facts about Women and Men in Great Britain, 2001* (Manchester, EOC, 2001), pp.3–4

Examination Achievements 1998/9
United Kingdom

	England	Wales	Scotland	% UK
Girls				
GCSEs and SCE Standard Grades *				
5 or more grades A*–C or 1–3	53.4	53.1	63.6	54.6
1–4 grades A*–D or 1–3	24.5	23.5	24.0	24.3
Grades D–G or 4–7 only	17.2	17.1	8.8	16.3
No graded GCSEs/SCEs	5.0	6.2	3.5	4.8
2 or more GCE A levels or 3 or more SCE Highers ^	33.1	30.1	32.3	33.2

Boys

GCSEs and SCE Standard
Grades *

5 or more grades A*-C or 1–3	42.8	42.1	52.1	43.8
1–4 grades A*-D or 1–3	24.8	24.2	29.6	25.2
Grades D-G or 4–7 only	25.4	24.0	13.8	24.1
No graded GCSEs/SCEs	7.0	9.8	4.4	6.9

2 or more GCE A levels or
or 3 or more SCE Highers   26.9   22.2   24.0   26.5

* examination achievements of pupils in their last year of compulsory education, England figures include GNVQ equivalents.

^ examination achievements of pupils in schools and students in FE aged 17–19 at the end of the academic year in England, Wales and Northern Ireland as a percentage of the 18 year old population; and of pupils in Years S5/S6 in Scotland as a percentage of the 17 year old population.

(Source: *Regional Trends 45*, Office for National Statistics)

Highest Qualification 2000

People of working age	Great Britain			
	Women		Men	
	thousands	%	thousands	%
Degree or equivalent	2,152	13	3,042	16
Higher education below degree	1,550	9	1,396	8
GCE A level or equivalent	2,805	17	5,550	30
GCSE grades A*-C or equivalent	4,579	27	3,215	17
Other qualifications	2,466	15	2,488	13
No qualifications	3,093	18	2,584	14
All people of working age*	16,799	100	18,496	100

* includes those whose highest qualification is unknown.

(Source: *EOC analysis of Labour Force Survey Spring 2000*, Office for National Statistics)

22. Equal Opportunities Commission, *Facts About Women and Men in Great Britain, 1999* (Manchester, EOC, 1999), p.13

Relative Earnings of Couples, 1996/97

Gross weekly earnings from employment or self-employment where both partners work 16 hours a week or more.

Great Britain	% of couples
Woman earns over 10 per cent more	16
Woman earns 5 to 10 per cent more	2
Earnings are within +/- 5 per cent	7
Man earns 5 to 10 per cent more	2
Man earns over 10 per cent more	73
All couples	100

(Source: *Social Focus on Women and Men*, Equal Opportunities Commission/ Office for National Statistics.)

Notes

1. George and P Wilding, *Ideology and Social Welfare* (London, Routledge and Kegan Paul, 1985), p.37.
2. *Ibid.*, pp.37–8.
3. Alan Sked, *Britain's Decline* (Oxford, Blackwell, 1988), p.77.
4. *Ibid.*, p.77.
5. George and Wilding, *Ideology*, p.41.
6. Hilary Land, 'Time to Care', in Mavis Maclean and Dulcie Groves (eds), *Women's Issues in Social Policy* (London, Routledge, 1991), pp.9, 13.
7. *Ibid.*, p.15.
8. Karen Clarke, Gary Craig and Caroline Glendinning, *Small Change: The Impact of the Child Support Act on Lone Mothers and Children* (London, Family Policy Studies Centre, 1996), p.7.
9. Melanie Henwood and Malcolm Wicks, *Benefit or Burden? The Objectives and Impact of Child Support* (London, Family Policy Studies Centre, 1986), p.1.
10. *Ibid.*, p.18.
11. Clarke, Craig and Glendinning, *Small Change*, p.7.
12. *The Times*, 21 June 1994.
13. *Ibid.*, 29 June 1994.
14. Clarke, Craig and Glendinning, *Small Change*, pp.38–40.
15. *Observer*, 2 July 1991.
16. Steven R Smith, 'Arguing Against Cuts in Lone Parent Benefits: Reclaiming the Desert Ground in the UK', in *Critical Social Policy*, 60, 19 (3) (1999), p.317.

17. Miriam David, 'Putting on an Act for the Children?', in Mavis Maclean and Dulcie Groves (eds), *Women's Issues in Social Policy* (London, Routledge, 1991), p.102.
18. Lord Justice Butler-Sloss, *Report of an Inquiry into Child Abuse in Cleveland, 1987* (London, HMSO, 1988), Cmnd. 4/2 cited p.25; causes, p.6; perpetrators, p.7.
19. Hilary Graham, 'Researching Women's Health Work: A Study of the Lifestyles of Mothers on Income Support', in Paul Bywaters and Eileen McLeod (eds), *Working for Equality in Health* (London, Routledge, 1996), p.11, cited p.128.
20. Sarah Payne, *Women, Health and Poverty: an Introduction* (Brighton, Harvester Wheatsheaf, 1991), p.11, cited p.128.
21. Clare Ungerson, *Women and Social Policy* (London, Macmillan, 1985), p.151.
22. Ann Witz, 'The Challenge of Nursing', in Jonathan Gabe et al. (eds), *Challenging Medicine* (London, Routledge, 1994), p.23.
23. Peggy Foster, *Women in the Health Care Industry* (Oxford, Oxford University Press, 1995), *passim*.
24. Ann Oakley, *From Here to Maternity: Becoming a Mother* (London, Penguin, 1979) and *Women Confined: Towards a Sociology of Childbirth* (Oxford, Martin Robertson, 1980).
25. S Bowlby, S Gregory and L McKie, '"Doing Home": Patriarchy, Caring and Space', in *Women's Studies International Forum*, 20 (3) (1997), p.344.
26. Marion Brion, 'Snakes or Ladders? Women and Equal Opportunities in Education and Training for Housing', in Rose Gilroy and Roberta Woods (eds), *Housing Women* (London, Routledge, 1994).
27. Bowlby, Gregory and McKie, '"Doing Home"', p.344.
28. Equal Opportunities Commission, *Facts about Women and Men in Great Britain, 1999* (Manchester, EOC, 1999), pp.6, 12.
29. Janet Cook and Shantu Watt, 'Racism, Women and Poverty' in Caroline Glendinning and Jane A Millar (eds), *Women and Poverty in Britain* (Brighton, Wheatsheaf, 1987), *passim*.
30. *Ibid.*, p.63.
31. *Ibid.*, and the Jenny Douglas article in Bywaters and McLeod, *Working for Equality in Health*.
32. Hugo Young, *One of Us* (London, Macmillan, 1988; taken from the 1990 edition), p.521.
33. Peter Mandelson and Roger Liddle, *The Blair Revolution: Can New Labour Deliver?* (London, Faber & Faber, 1996), p.17; updated and reprinted as Peter Mandelson, *The Blair Revolution Revisited* (London, Politicos, 2002).
34. *Guardian*, 19 March 1999.
35. Geoffrey Finlayson, *Citizen, State and Social Welfare in Britain, 1839–1990* (Oxford, Clarendon Press, 1994), p.359.
36. D Sainsbury, 'Introduction', in D Sainsbury (ed.), *Gendering Welfare States* (London, Sage, 1994), p.2.

37. John Stevenson, 'Engendering Welfare', in *Twentieth Century British History*, 6 (3), pp.381–6, particularly, p.382.
38. Jane Lewis, 'Gender, the Family and Women's Agency in the Building of "Welfare States": The British Case', in *Social History*, 19 (1) (1994), pp.37–55.

Chapter 3

The Attack upon Trade Unionism, 1979–2002

For the last 30 years, the trade union movement has been on the defensive. Throughout the 1970s it was taken aback by the determination of both Conservative and Labour governments to impose controls in industrial relations to reduce its freedom of action. Nevertheless, the trade union movement retained a degree of influence despite the fact that the 'Winter of Discontent' of 1979 turned much of the British public against its actions. But the movement was less effective in the 1980s and early 1990s when the declining position of Britain in world trade and consequent mass unemployment, eroded both its membership and economic muscle. These problems were compounded by the determination of the Thatcher administration to reduce the power of trade unions and to set them within a 'balanced' framework of rights and obligations framed in eight acts, six of them designed to deal specifically with trade unions on issues such as the closed shop and strike ballots (see Chapter 1). The conflict this engendered culminated in the Coal Miners' Strike of 1984/5, a year-long dispute which ended in the defeat of the miners and unemployment and social deprivation in many mining districts (Document 1).

The challenges of the 1980s and 1990s have undoubtedly altered the strength, position and attitudes of British trade unionism. They have forced unions to work with the new arrangements, in what has been referred to as the 'new realism', in an age in which the old post-war political consensus has disappeared. They have forced some modifications in the balance of power between trade unions and the Labour Party, and helped to change the relationship between the trade union centre and local branches. The end of the old post-war consensus has also brought into sharp focus the problems and issues concerning the organisation of women's trade unionism, which forms a substantial part of this introduction and provides the basis of many of the primary and secondary documents which appear later (Documents 3–7, 12–14). In addition, it has raised issues about the low pay and additional exploitation faced by many Asian workers, both male and female (Document 3).

The Thatcher Years, 1979–1990

Between 1979 and 1990 the Conservative governments introduced eight acts, including the Wages Act of 1986 and the Public Order Act of 1986, which brought about a radical change to the employment laws of Britain and forced trade unionism onto the defensive. The introduction of new legislation designed to make trade unions more accountable was central to the economic philosophy of the Thatcher government, which aimed to deregulate and 'free' the economy from constraints in order to achieve the economic renaissance of Britain. In other words, the attack upon trade union power was part of the process of rolling back the modern Welfare State and state control, which were perceived to be the cause of Britain's post-war economic decline. Such a sea change in government policies meant that the old tripartite relationship between government trade unions and employers, 'the old consensus', was dead. The origins of this change are to be found in the defeat of Edward Heath's Conservative government in early 1974, in the context of the Coal Miners' strike and the problems that strikes created in the 'Winter of Discontent' in 1979.

The Employment Acts of 1980, 1982, 1988, 1989 and 1990, and the Trade Union Act of 1984, imposed the new Conservative policies in a step-by-step approach. In their various ways they demanded greater accountability from the trade unions by demanding that they should seek approval for strike action through secret ballots, by making secondary strike action illegal, forcing ballots on the payment of political funds and a host of other changes (Document 9). In the course of this attack, membership of the Trade Union Congress fell from 12,172,508 in 1979 to about 8.6 million by 1989 (Document 8), a figure that was more or less maintained in the 1990s, although it excludes the 600,000 to 1,500,000 trade unionists who were, from year to year, not members of the TUC.

The trade union legislation permitted, almost encouraged, employers to break traditional union powers. This was most evident in the case of the very powerful printing unions who were confronted by Rupert Murdoch's News International Group, which insisted upon new working arrangements and no-strike arrangements for work on *The Times*, *Sun*, *News of the World* and *Sunday Times*. Murdoch dismissed 5,500 of his Fleet Street staff in January 1986, then had his newspapers written and manufactured at Wapping and distributed from the plant, using lorries owned by separate distribution agencies. This was in response to the print unions who were attempting to restrict the use of the new technology and the movement of the newspaper industry from Fleet Street to Wapping in the East End of London and at Murdoch's Kinning Park plant, as they had done in an earlier dispute in 1983. There was mass picketing and violence at the Wapping plant, with fines and threats of sequestration of union funds. The major event was the violent demonstration at Wapping on 24 January 1987, the anniversary of the beginning of the dispute. However, faced with a legal action against its funds, the Society of Graphical and Allied Trades (SOGAT) ended the dispute on 5 February 1987. The Amalgamated Engineering Union withdrew the same day and the National Graphical Association called off the dispute on 6 February. Government legislation, the action of the employer and conflicts between various unions and their members had contributed to the collapse of trade unions in a highly paid and trade-union dominated industry (Document 11). This type of event was not an unusual occurrence during the 1980s and contributed significantly to the erosion of trade union power, influence and membership and to trade unions changing their approach from direct conflict and militancy to the careful use of the law.

The Major and Blair Years and the Political Decline of the Trade Unions

The 1990 Employment Act, implemented under the Major – rather than the Thatcher – Conservative government challenged the trade union practice of operating a closed shop by making it an offence for employers not to employ non-union labour. It was the final plank in the Thatcherite attack upon trade union rights, although the Conservative governments of John Major also constantly refused to accept the need to establish a minimum wage level during the early and mid 1990s. The Labour governments of Tony Blair have, since 1997, accepted the minimum wage, albeit lower than the level demanded by trade unions. Nevertheless, the Labour governments (1997–2001, 2001–present) have steadfastly refused to remove the Thatcherite legislation, the vast majority of which still remains in place. Blair, in his capacity as Leader of the Parliamentary Labour Party, has also presided over the continued decline of trade union influence within the Labour Party. However, that process began in the early 1980s.

In the early 1980s, the trade unions still exercised their block vote powers at Labour conferences, using the vast affiliated trade union votes to get their way at conferences regardless of the wishes of individual members and constituency parties. At the beginning of the 1980s, they also gained 25 per cent of the vote for the selection of the Labour leader, although James Callaghan resigned as Labour leader in October 1980 forcing a vote for the new leader, Michael Foot, under the old system of a poll of MPs. The trade union proportion of the vote was later raised to 40 per cent. However, from then onwards, the trade unions began to lose influence. At the Labour Party conference in September 1992, it was decided that the strength of the trade-union delegates votes would be reduced from 90 per cent to 70 per cent. In February 1993, John Smith, who had replaced Neil Kinnock as Labour leader, pushed for the proposal to reduce the trade union vote in the Labour leadership contest from 40 per cent, and at the Labour conference in September 1993 agreed on one member one vote (OMOV), whereby trade unions and constituency party sections were forced to ballot members individually for the posts of Deputy Leader and Party Leader and to allocate the votes proportionally. The trade unions, MPs and the constituency parties were also given one third each of the vote in the electoral college. When Tony Blair became Leader of the Labour Party in 1994 he moved to exploit the weakened influence of the trade unions at the party conference and reduced the power of the trade unions on the National Executive of the Labour Party, creating his National Party Forum as an alternative power base (Document 2). In effect, the trade unions' power within the Labour Party has been greatly diminished, especially as Tony Blair has sought the so-called middle ground of British politics and created an almost presidential administrative structure to appeal directly to the people and bypass party politics.

Women and Ethnic Minority Groups

Surveys in the 1970s found high levels of union membership amongst ethnic minority workers.[1] However, working for low pay in bad conditions in jobs which the white population rejected meant that, on the one hand, many ethnic minority workers were outside the mainstream of trade unionism while, on the other, labour force disadvantage had a ghettoising effect (Document 3). Organisations such as the Indian Workers' Association could sometimes act as a bridge between workers and unions. The inevitable effect of continuing exploitation was a series of labour disputes; often outside the remit of formal bargaining machinery, these disputes were sporadic and characterised by *ad hoc* strikes, which were widely supported within the immigrant community.

The Grunwick photographic and print processing strike was a typical example in that the dispute became as much about finding a place in the union as in defying the management.[2] The predominantly female workers were largely from East African Asian backgrounds. In 1976, a small group, including Jayaben Desai, took action against enforced overtime, dismissal threats and poor working conditions and called on APEX to negotiate on their behalf; Grunwick's refused to recognise APEX, despite pressure for the government arbitration body ACAS. Frustrated at the lack of success, in 1977 the workers called a mass picket, which was widely supported and heavily policed. When the mass picket was called off in August 1977, Jayaben Desai and three other members of the strike committee began a hunger strike on the steps of the Trade Union Congress and were suspended by APEX. Although the strike was unsuccessful in achieving better pay and conditions, it won fame as an indication of the militancy of Asian women. Amrit Wilson wrote: 'That strike has proved that Asian women workers can be strong, resourceful and courageous, that they can stand up, face the world and demand their rights'.[3]

Even where there was a strong trade union presence, militancy was not, necessarily, supported. Ford's had plants near the centres of unrest in Toxteth (Halewood plant), Southall (Langley) and Brixton (Dagenham), where the street disturbances of 1981 were partly inspired by racial discrimination. The planned strike by Ford workers over pay and conditions was not supported by their union (TGWU) and the implicit issues of discrimination were not addressed.[4] Similarly, in 1982, when the government proposed the privatisation of health service ancillary organisations, which it was estimated would affect 70,000 mostly female black workers, the TUC took over the running of a nine-month strike which nurses supported; however, the Royal College of Nurses accepted the pay deal offered to nursing staff and the strike collapsed.[5]

The TUC prepared a *Black Workers' Charter* and a *Workbook on Racism*. However, to improve the representation of ethnic groupings and combat racism, black activists formed their own groups. In 1980, the Commission for Racial Equality found 59 such groups dealing with industrial relations and, in 1981, the Black Trade Unionist Solidarity Movement was formed.[6] Caucuses were created in some unions, including the National and Local Government Association (NALGO). The movement held its first conference in 1983. Some black leaders did emerge in the trade union movement, such as Bill Morris of the powerful TGWU. However, places such as Grunwick's remained outside the mainstream of British trade unionism. As Amina Mama wrote in 1984, despite black women's greater rate of employment compared to that of white women, 'we are to be found in the lower echelons of all the institutions where we are employed... where the work is often physically heavy... the pay is the lowest, and the hours are the longest and most anti-social.[7]

The Black Trade Unionist Solidarity Movement aimed to be non-sexist in its operations. Black and white feminists campaigned for changes within unions, drawing up a nine-point charter, 'Equality for Women in Trades Unions' (Documents 4, 5). However, these changes were slow to take effect until trade unions, suffering from a loss in subscriptions as male-dominated heavy industry declined, recruited with greater vigour in white-collar trades and the service sector, where women workers were comparatively well represented. Local and central government workers' unions and teaching unions paved the way in addressing issues such as reproductive rights and women's health and such issues also came to form part of the agenda of unions generally (Documents 6, 12, 13). Similarly, while some trade unionists recognised that better representation of all workers depended on improved representation for low-paid black workers, Asian and African-Asian men with higher education qualifications became just as likely as white men to gain professional jobs.[8]

In addition, women's support in the 1984/5 Coal Miners' strike was recognised as valuable. Miners' leaders Arthur Scargill and Mick McGahey had been amongst the Grunwick's pickets.[9] Women were active in Miners' Support Groups and formed their own organisation, Women Against Pit Closures (Document 10). The women's group at Barnsley was one of the first to be formed, partly by women from the mining community who were students at Northern College, a trade union college. Jean McCrindle, a lecturer at Northern College, who became treasurer of Women Against Pit Closures, recalled that hundreds of groups were formed in the first month of the strike; at a rally held in Barnsley on 12 May 1984: 'Ten thousand women suddenly arrived, from everywhere. Some came dressed in Welsh costume and they were singing... Then the majorettes, these girl drummers, turned up.'[10] By July 1984, Women Against Pit Closures had a national structure with groups at all coalfields. Close to a million pounds was raised in a year. Although the National Union of Mineworkers refused the Women Against Pit Closures' demand for associate membership, women's involvement affected the image of trade unionism. On the one hand, support group activities drew male trade unionists into the relief work, children's outings and family activities once seen as women's role and, on the other, women held welfare rights meetings and picketed the coalfields, traditionally seen as male activities. Prejudices were overcome and links were made with feminist groups.

An indication of the way trade unions came to foreground in what had once been seen as 'women's issues' was the TGWU 'Link-Up' campaign of 1987 when women-only recruitment campaigns involved community groups.[11] It became usual for unions to appoint equal opportunities officers and committees to deal with racial and sex discrimination. The Commission for Racial Equality argued for the monitoring of ethnic minority recruitment, training and promotion and some unions negotiated measures such as the inclusion of racism in disciplinary codes and the right for extended leave of absence to visit families abroad.[12] NALGO appointed an officer at national level to deal with race equality. These measures were successful in that Afro-Caribbean and Asian workers came to have higher rates of union membership than white workers, although Pakistani rates of membership were less high and Bangladeshi membership rates remained very low.[13] The equal pay and employment rights legislation of the 1970s and 1980s gave unions new powers to argue women's claims for maternity leave and pay, protection against unfair dismissal due to maternity or to sex discrimination and protection against sexual harassment. In 1993, Britain's largest union at that time, UNISON, was formed from the health and public sector workers' unions, COHSE, NALGO and NUPE. Women members predominated in UNISON, which carried forward the equal opportunities programmes of its constituent former unions, including the creation of a Lesbian and Gay group. The Trades Union Congress appointed an officer for Gay and Lesbian issues.[14]

Union membership declined overall in the last quarter of the twentieth century but the proportion of women to men members rose (Document 7). However, progress was not unchecked. The abolition of wages councils effectively removed collective bargaining from industries such as catering, where women and ethnic minority workers had been heavily represented. In 1998, 72 per cent of working-age women were economically active, compared to 84 per cent of working-age men, but, where both partners worked more than 16 hours a week, for 73 per cent of couples, the man earned over ten per cent more than the woman.[15] This continuing workplace discrimination was reflected in trade unions. The Labour Research Department, in March 2000, found that while women comprised 41 per cent of the membership of the top ten unions, they remained under-represented in the trade union élite and no women were general secretaries of the biggest unions with more than 7,500 members. The number of women full-time officers had increased, and GMB had appointed its first black national women's officer. TGWU and AEEU were amongst those unions reserving seats for women on their executive committees (Document 14).

Documents

SECONDARY SOURCES AND INTERPRETATIONS

1. Keith Laybourn, *A History of British Trade Unionism, c. 1770– 1990* (Stroud, Sutton, 1992), pp.210–11

Yet by far the biggest test of the new legislation... was the miners' strike of 1984/5. The immediate context of the dispute was the fact that Ian MacGregor and the National Coal Board offered the miners a 5.2 per cent wage increase in October 1983. The National Union of Mineworkers (NUM) rejected this and imposed an overtime ban from 30 October. Matters came to a head when MacGregor proposed to cut coal output and employment in the mines. There were spontaneous strikes such as at Cortonwood, where pits had been informed of their imminent closure. Effectively the coal strike began on 9 March 1984 at the pits in Scotland and Yorkshire, where notifications of closures had been made. However, there was to be no national ballot. Instead the NUM [National Union of Mineworkers] sent flying pickets from Yorkshire to Scotland and Kent to persuade the working miners, particularly those in Nottingham and the Midlands, to join the dispute, despite a High Court injunction forbidding such action. This led to mass picketing and violence, notably at Ollerton in Nottingham, where a Yorkshire striker on picket duty was crushed to death in the demonstration outside the pit, and later at the Orgreave coke plant. There were many twists and turns throughout the dispute. On 14 March 1984, the High Court gave the National Coal Board an injunction against the flying pickets, though the NCB chose not to use it. The government also maintained a police presence to stop the movement of flying pickets. At this stage, trade union support for the miners was mixed, although Arthur Scargill drew immense personal support at the 1984 TUC conference.

Yet as the strike ground on, court action began to take its effect. The South Wales Mineworkers were fined £50,000 for contempt over picketing and when this was not paid the sequestrators seized their funds of £707,000. The national union was also fined £200,000 on 10 October for breaking an order declaring their strike unofficial, and when it failed to pay its assets were seized – at least those assets which had not been salted away to Luxembourg, Dublin and other financial centres.

There was much violence and many incidents of high emotion during the strike. Arthur Scargill was much criticized for his refusal to hold a national ballot and there was much criticism by the NUM of the decision of a substantial proportion of the Nottingham miners to form the Union of Democratic Mineworkers (UDM), which sought to do business with the government. Snowden and the NUM were also intensely hostile to the decision of the National Coal Board to offer a Christmas bonus pay-packet to any miner who worked for four full weeks before Christmas. The violence which ensued included the much publicized incident when a concrete block was dropped from a motorway bridge on to a taxi taking a miner to work in South Wales, killing the driver and leading to two miners being sent to gaol for twenty years. Despite the NUM's opposition fifteen thousand miners did return to work under this offer.

Eventually the strike came to an end, in a ragged fashion and without any settlement, when a special delegate meeting of the mineworkers decided to return to work without agreement on 3 March 1985. The government had remained firm, the strike had not forced any power cuts throughout the winter and at the end of February 1985 the Welsh miners had returned without accepting an offer. There was no other outcome available, unless the NUM was willing to force the dispute through to another winter. After the ending of the dispute it was clear that the power of the NUM had been irrevocably destroyed and that it was unable to prevent the rapidly developing pattern of pit closures which reduced the number of miners by half over the next six years.

In many respects the mining dispute became the turning point in the attitude of trade unions and the TUC towards the government's industrial legislation. In 1986 the Electrical, Electronic, Telecommunications and Plumbing Unions (EETPU) and the Amalgamated Engineering Union (AEU) decided to accept funds for ballots as allowed under the 1980 Employment Act.

2. Keith Laybourn, *A Century of Labour: A History of the Labour Party* (Stroud, Sutton, 2000; pbk 2001), pp.151–2, 158

A year later Blair announced his intention to reject the old Clause Four at the 1994 Labour Party Conference, and praised the successes of capitalism. Soon afterwards, he presented his own Clause Four... It committed Labour 'to work for a dynamic economy serving the public interest, in which are joined the forces of partnership and co-operation... with a thriving sector and high quality public services...'

At first it appeared that constituencies and trade unions would be against the change and so, at the end of 1994, Blair held an intensive round of meetings where he personally appealed to 30,000 Party members to support his new Clause Four. There was stern trade union opposition to the new version, particularly from the Transport and General Workers' Union, but with more than two-thirds of the constituency Labour parties deciding to ballot their members, it was clear that about 85 per cent of their members would support Blair's new Clause Four.

At a special conference of the Labour Party held on 29 April 1995, which was seen as a test of Blair's ability to deal effectively with the trade unions, he won support for his Clause Four by just

under two-thirds of the vote. That revealed that 54.6 per cent of
the 70 per cent union vote and 90 per cent of the 30 per cent
constituency vote had supported Blair. Effectively, Blair had won
support for his reforming leadership of the Labour Party, and the
press and media recognized that this had been his personal triumph.
He had tackled and tamed trade-union opposition, buoyed up by
the recognition that he and the Labour Party would not be taken
seriously by the public if the proposal had been defeated. In the
end, the majority of trade unions and constituency parties dared
not vote against Blair if they wished the Party to have a significant
political future...

In order to press control further, Blair pressed the Labour Party
Conference of 1997 to adopt *Partnership in Power*, a document
which set out a radical programme to reform the Party's decision-
making process. By this, the Party Conference lost its control over
Party policy to a 175-strong national Party Forum which would
discuss policies, in a two-year rolling cycle, and the National
Executive Committee (NEC) of the Party was altered. The women's
section of the NEC was to be abolished and trade-union
representatives reduced from seventeen to twelve, although six were
to be women. Three places were to be reserved for members of the
Labour government (or Party) and appointed by Tony Blair... And
one for the leader of the Labour Group in the European Parliament.
Six were to be set aside for representatives elected by a postal ballot
of all members. These changes weakened the Labour Party
Conference, reduced the power of trade unions, and strengthened
the hand of Tony Blair, as Labour Leader.

3. The Race Today Collective, *The Struggle of Asian Workers in Britain* (London, Race Today Publications, 1983), pp.8, 10

At the Mansfield Hosiery mills, in Loughborough in 1972, at
Imperial Typewriters in Leicestershire in 1974 and at Grunwick in
1978, Asian workers, in these cases largely from African
backgrounds, rebelled and organised against the continuity of a
colonial relationship which is common and central.

... the ghettoisation of labour also meant that the school teacher
from Ludhiana, the mechanic from Hoshiapur, the graduate of
Punjab University, the illiterate middle peasant from a village in
Azad Kashmir, found themselves working on the same machines
on the same shop floor.

4. Anna Coote, 'Calling for Positive Action', *New Statesman*, 16 March 1979, p.35

A significant shift in policy took place at the TUC Women's Conference at Folkestone last week, when delegates voted for a programme of positive discrimination to increase the level of women's activity in trade unions. There are now nearly three and a half million women in TUC-affiliated unions, making 28.7 per cent of the total. Yet when it comes to making decisions they are absurdly under-represented. At last year's Congress, the ratio of female delegates to female members was 1:38,800, compared with a male ratio of 1:7,800.

Until recently, efforts to get women fairly represented have been hampered by a belief that if they are to become equal they must be treated as such from the start and should therefore not be allowed any 'privileges' such as special conferences or reserved seats on committees. Last week, however, the female activists in the union movement recognised that this approach would never get them anywhere.

The Conference endorsed a nine-point charter which advises unions with large female membership and no women on decision-making bodies 'to ensure that women's views are represented, either through the creation of additional seats or by co-option'. It suggests that each union should set up special women's committees at national and local level.

There was overwhelming support for a resolution calling for seven additional seats for women on the General Council (making a total of nine) and for doubling the number of elected members of the Women's Advisory Committee. In effect this last measure would mean doubling the Committee's strength. At present, ten out of 18 seats are filled by appointees of the General Council who are almost invariably male and who often cannot find time to attend meetings. The elected members, on the other hand, are chosen each year at the Women's Conference: they are almost invariably female, with a natural enthusiasm for the work in hand.

5. Polly Toynbee, 'Women in Trades Unions', *Guardian*, 10 March 1980

'Male trade unionists weep crocodile tears because few women want to take part in trade union affairs. Let them establish women's quotas in their top offices and see how many able women come forward to claim them.'

This week (10.3.80) the 50th TUC Women's Conference is on in Brighton. It is a small voice, with no power at all, attempting to remind the TUC that one third of the people it represents are women.

Almost every year someone puts up a motion suggesting that the TUC Women's Advisory Committee and its conference should be abolished, and there is another such motion this year. Most of the women agree that in an ideal world there would be no need for a separate women's section, but in the face of the colossal discrimination against women in trade unions, it's better than nothing. The 250 delegates to the conference will be greeted with banners and speeches, rallies and special historical exhibits honouring their 50th anniversary. But there is very little to celebrate.

Their greatest achievement was probably their success this year in getting the TUC out on a massive march against the Corrie abortion bill, the first time the TUC had actively demonstrated on a non-economic, non-industrial relations matter.

Otherwise, year after year, they pass resolutions to be passed on to Congress. Resolutions on equal rights, equal pay, protecting part-time workers and part-time jobs for women, nursery facilities at work, and holding union meetings at times suitable for women with children.

6. 'A Woman's Place is in her Union', *Landworker*, August 1986

The union negotiating team at Buxted Poultry's Sutton Benger plant has won the right to on-site cervical smear tests for women who want to use the facility.

Stewards had decided that the provision of cervical smears would be part of this year's pay claim.

About 60 per cent of the four-hundred strong workforce is female. They work in two shifts, either 7.00am to 3.00pm or 3.00pm to 11.00pm making it difficult to visit a doctor.

Enquiries round the site revealed that for many women visits to the doctors had to be fitted in with collecting the children, doing the shopping or other domestic chores.

General practitioners do not have to perform smear tests on women under the age of 35 years and then only once every five years, so in some instances women were obliged to look for alternative access to these facilities. This usually meant finding a health centre or well-woman clinic, not over common in rural areas.

The agreement provides for smear tests to be carried out on-site by the Women's National Cancer Control Campaign Unit.

The cost of testing is £1.45 per person, per year.

The test will be done by women doctors and nurses, which many of the Buxted women said they would prefer.

Les Collett, the district officer who assisted with the negotiations said, 'Many of the women here knew someone who had left it too late before going for a test and who suffered and in one case died because of it.

'The new agreement will allow women to have a smear test and breast examination as a matter of routine. The Unit will come to the site, it only takes a few minutes and will be much more convenient that having to take time off work or actually having to get round to making the appointment under your own steam.'

Following the success of the Sutton Benger agreement, which is one of the first in the whole of the poultry industry, TGWU officers in Swindon are approaching leading employers and union shop stewards in the area to attempt to set up similar agreements.

In small-scale businesses, the union is suggesting that employers get together with larger companies to pool resources.

'Credit must go to the stewards at Buxted who drew up the case,' said Les Collet. 'Without their hard work, and the support of the Sutton Benger workforce we would never have reached an agreement. I hope other stewards and branch secretaries will follow their example.'

7. Sylvia Walby, *Gender Transformations* (London, Routledge, 1997), p.40

By the 1970s most trade unions had made a very significant change in policy towards women workers, from one endorsing unequal treatment to one in favour of equal opportunities. During the 1980s many trade unions established new organisational forms to facilitate the articulation of the views of their women members, such as women's committees and women's officers. There are several reasons for this, ranging from the increasing presence of women as workers to the increased vocalisation of women's various political, social and economic interests. First, the growth in the number of women workers and the decline in the number of male workers has led to their increased significance as potential members of trade unions, both in terms of their subscriptions and their voting power. Second, there has been a significant growth in the number and proportion of women in trade unions... This has partly been due to the special recruitment of women workers, especially in non-traditional areas, such as part-time work. Since the 1980s there has been an overall decline in union membership, which has been much more pronounced among men than among women. This phenomenon is related to the demise of the heavily male areas of employment in manual work in manufacturing. This can be seen over even the short-time span of 1989 to 1992 when unions reported that male membership declined from 6,405,000 to 5,472,000 while female membership dipped only slightly from 3,753,000 to 3,577,000... There is a convergence in the gendered rates of union density as reported to the Labour Force Survey between 1989 and 1993 from 44 percent to 38 percent of men, and from 33 percent to 31 percent for women. Much of the gender difference is in fact made up of the difference between part-time and full-time workers with density rates of 39 percent for full-timers and 21 percent for part-timers in 1993, suggesting that density rates for full-time men and full-time women are quite close... Third, there has been a stronger articulation of women's political interests at diverse levels of society and polity from autonomous women's groups and sections in political parties, to professional associations and women's magazines. At the official national level, all major unions are now strong supporters of equal opportunities policies for women and men workers, although there is some variation at local level. Equal opportunities has become a 'normal' discourse; it has moved from being a feminist issue to one which has entered the mainstream.

PRIMARY EVIDENCE AND INFORMATION

8. Trades Union Congress Membership and Overall Trade Union Membership, 1978–1992, from various sources

1978	11.8 millions	1979	12.1 millions
1980	12.1 millions	1981	11.6 millions
1982	11.0 millions	1983	10.5 millions
1984	10.0 millions	1985	9.8 millions
1986	9.5 millions	1987	9.2 millions
1988	9.1 millions	1989	8.6 millions

Overall membership

1989　　　10.16 millions　　　1992　　　9.1 millions

9. The Employment Act, 1980 (1980 c 42)

An Act to provide payments out of public funds towards trade unions' expenditure in respect of ballots, for the use of employer's premises in connection with the ballot, and for the issue by the Secretary of State of Codes of Practice for the improvement of industrial relations; to make provisions in respect of exclusion or expulsion from trade unions and otherwise to amend the law relating to workers, employers and trade unions and employers' associations; to repeal section 1A of the Trade Union and Labour Relations Act of 1974; and for connected purposes.
[August 1980]

Trade union ballots and Codes of Practice

1 (1) The Secretary of State may by regulations make a scheme (below called 'the scheme') providing for payments by the Certification Officer toward expenditure incurred by independent trade unions in respect of such ballots to which this section applies as may be prescribed by the scheme.

(2) This section applies to a ballot if the purpose of the question to be voted upon (or if there is more than one such question, the purpose of any of them) falls within the purposes mentioned in subsection (3) below.

(3) The purpose referred to in subsection (2) above are –

(a) obtaining a decision or ascertaining the views of members of a trade union as to the calling or ending of a strike or other industrial action;

(b) carrying out an election provided for by the rules of a trade union; ...

Unreasonable exclusion or expulsion from trade unions ...

4 (1) This section applies to employment by an employer with respect to which it is practice, in accordance with the union membership agreement, for the employee to belong to a specified trade union or one of a number of specified trade unions.

(2) Every person who is, or is seeking to be, in employment to which this section applies still have the right –

(a) not to have an application for membership of a specified trade union unreasonably refused;

(b) not to be unreasonably expelled from a specified trade union.

Picketing

15 (1) It shall be lawful for a person in contemplation or furtherance
of a trade dispute to attend –
(a) at or near his place of work, or
(b) if he is an official of a trade union, at or near the place of
work or a member of that union whom he is accompanying and
whom he represents, for the purpose only of peacefully obtaining
or communicating information, or peacefully persuading any
person to work or abstain from working.

10. *The Valley's Star*, 6 March 1985

Strike Ends – Struggle Goes On

The decision to call off the strike on Tuesday by the NUM national
delegate conference last Sunday does not mean the struggle is over.
Arthur Scargill was right when he said the battle will now continue
but in another form. All those who have sacrificed so much this
last year are still determined and DEFIANT. The following
resolution passed unanimously by our Support Group last Sunday
night shows we have learnt from our struggles and are preparing
for the continuing battle:

'We, the members and supporters of the Neath, Dulais and
Swansea Valleys Miners' Support Group declare at this meeting on
March 3, 1985 that we will continue the struggle in defence of coal,
jobs, communities, democracy and world peace. The strike may end,
but the struggle goes on. We salute the women, men and children
of the British coalfields who have not been defeated at the end of
12 months. We pledge ourselves to use everything in our power to
reinstate every sacked miner. There will be no peace in the British
coalfields until that is achieved.'

11. 'News International, Wapping, Rupert Murdoch and the Print Unions', in the *Guardian*, 22 January 1986

Patrick Wintour reports on manoeuvres that have led to the next
bout of blood-letting in Fleet Street. Mr. Murdoch's bouquet of
barbed wire.

The growing concern over Rupert Murdoch's newspaper plant at
Wapping has the potential to develop into a trauma for the Labour
movement on the scale of the miners' strike. Fundamental issues
are involved – the right to strike, the rule of law in the workplace,

industrial relations, the authority of the TUC over its affiliates and finally the ability of the trade union movement to survive in the face of rapid technological change.

The immediate reason for the crisis is that for the first time in decades Fleet Street management are in the driving seat and finding life at the wheel quite exhilarating. Correspondingly the print unions are in retreat. In an attempt to prevent a rout the unions are edging towards an attempted shutdown of the Rupert Murdoch press in protest at News International demands for a legally binding no-strike deal as a precondition of the traditional print unions being represented at Wapping.

The difficulties facing the union in any such dispute are daunting. Few employers have prepared so long or as thoroughly for such an eventuality as has Murdoch. His £100 million Wapping plant has been turned from a white elephant left idle due to union opposition since 1983 into a technological time machine capable of seeing Murdoch's emergence from the Fleet Street production unions...

The workers on Murdoch's four national newspaper titles know that if they strike Murdoch is set to press his advantages. For instance, it is open to the company to respond to any strike by immediately sacking those in dispute without compensation on the grounds that they have repudiated their employment contracts. And one Times newspaper executive put it 'Once these people go out it will be the last time they do, they won't come back, never, never.'

Instead Murdoch will transfer his production to Wapping and its sister plant in Glasgow, relying on TNT hauliers to distribute the papers.

The success of the strategy is critically dependent upon the cooperation of the journalists and the printing capacity of the Wapping premises. The print unions are banking on Wapping being unable to churn out the 4.5 million copies of *The Sun* or *The Times* currently being produced each day...

No matter how much either party may wish to avoid it, the Wapping crisis is likely to become increasingly a re-run of the recent clashes between the electricians and the TUC over its affiliates. But unlike the clash over the state money for ballots – which electricians won – the TUC cannot afford to back down. The issue goes to the heart of the Bridlington procedure to organise Collective bargaining in union's sphere of influence.

The electricians may attempt to avoid outright flouting of the TUC by holding back from signing an agreement with Murdoch covering Wapping, but the decision to hold separate talks with the company and the very act of electricians printing papers at Wapping, is likely to be seen as sufficient grounds for disciplining the union.

12. Charter of the TGWU Region 6 Women's Advisory Committee, 1986

Annually the T & G organises a conference for women members. Every second year a Women's Regional Advisory Committee (WRAC) is elected to advise the Union on matters relating to women and their families.

This charter has been drawn up by the members of the WRAC. We hope that it will help you in your everyday struggle for better conditions, better wages and a better future for you and your families.

Attacks on the trade union movement and mass unemployment means attacks on women. For us this means low pay, poor working conditions, health and safety risks, cuts in jobs and hours of work and an increase in home work and casual work.

Legislation has not improved things for women. Women's pay is still only 73% of men's. Women are still in low paid, low status jobs. The Union exists to fight for our interests and is actively campaigning around the following Women's Advisory Charter.

Within the Workplace
1. An end to low pay.
2. Part time workers – full rights and benefits, same hourly rates as full timers.
3. Equal pay for work of equal value.
4. Fight discrimination and sexual harassment.
5. Trade Union monitoring of appointments and promotions.
6. Improved training facilities and educational opportunities for women.
7. Work place crèches [sic], child care facilities.
8. Home workers – trade union rates, health and safety conditions.
9. Shorter working week, flexible hours of work.
10. Extension of maternity and paternity rights to all workers.
11. Casual workers to be made permanent.

And within the TGWU
1. Branch meetings to be held in works time.
2. Child care facilities for either parents, for all meetings.
3. Women's items on all education courses.

4. No loss of pay for union activities.

5. Flexible hours for education courses.

6. Child care and crèche facilities available at our Education Centre at Eastbourne.

13. TGWU Region 3 Women's Advisory Committee, *Hersay*, Issue No. 3, October 1988

For many years the question asked by our women members has been, 'Why are we not allowed to take up a more positive role within the Union?' The answer is that there are no 'good' reasons why not, but many reasons why women should and must take up their rightful place as equal partners in our Union.

Of course, the reality is that throughout our history both sexes have accepted traditional 'Roles'. This has meant the development of basically male-dominated society.

However, circumstances have begun to change! More and more women are taking up employment, both in industry and commerce. Many have joined trade unions. Indeed, there are over 250,000 in the T&GWU.

In 1979 the Biennial Delegate Conference of our Union, directed by the General Executive Council to address the question of positively encouraging more than just words, the involvement of women in the Union. It introduced a wide ranging programme of education, training and research into the special difficulties facing women at work and women's involvement in the Union.

Since that time the General Executive Council have, and are, pursuing their commitment to equal opportunity in the most positive manner. To date, a number of actions have taken place, these being:

The setting up of a National Women's Advisory Committee, meeting on a quarterly basis and reporting direct to the General Executive Council through Sister Margaret Prosser, the National Officer for women. Also, 11 Regional Advisory Committees have been formed, reporting to both the Regional Committee and National Committee.

Our women have responded to these initiatives by giving not only advice, but also by active participation in such programmes as the Living Wage Campaign on recruitment directed at the low paid, most of which are women and the campaign on one of the most dreaded diseases, 'Cervical Cancer Smear Test.'

More recently, the General Executive Council decided to assist our women members to play an active role in the wider Labour and Trade Union Movement. Its decision was to allocate places to Labour Party Conference and the TUC Conference directly to our women members. This was allocated on the basis of 1 member from each Region to each Conference.

These significant and important changes have not been achieved without problems and frustration, as you are all aware. However, the difficulties we have had to overcome together simply derive from a lack of understanding as to precisely what it is that is being done and what we are trying hard to achieve.

The Advisory Committees are exactly what their name implies. They are a vehicle through which our members can help the constitutional committees; they do not have to replace them. We therefore reinforce our encouragement to women members to become more fully involved in our constitutional committees. Indeed, I have always argued, that if we are to move towards a better and more just society, we must utilise all the skills and attributes the working class possess. Our male membership will soon realise that in this struggle, to neglect over half of the team, can only at best maintain the status quo. But by working together we can and will win the battle for decency and equal opportunities for all – from cradle to grave.

The General Executive Council have shown the way forward, it's now up to all of us to continue and develop this initiative. They have provided the tools for the job, with which we can now help members to understand why equality in participation is the only decent and practical way forward.

I feel very proud by the initiatives taken by our Region's Women's Advisory Committee. In fact, this magazine is the first and only such publication within the Union and attracts much praise from General Executive Council members.

14. Labour Research Department, 'Women Everywhere but the Top', March 2000

Unions with WOMEN at the helm (membership)

Alliance and Leicester Group Union of Staff (3,068)	Clare Clark
The independent union for Abbey National Staff (7,468)	Linda Rolph
Association of Magisterial Officers (6,015)	Rosie Eagleson
British Orthoptic Society (1,011)	Sylvia Armour

Community and District Nursing Association (5,023)   Anne Duffy
National Association of Probation Officers (6,174)   Judy McKnight
Society of Chiropodists and Podiatrists (6,458)   Hilary De Lyon

Proportion of WOMEN in senior positions in largest 10 unions

	UNISON	T&G	AEEU	GMB	MSF	USDAW	CWU	NUT	GPMU	PCS
Total membership	260,000	1,290,549	874,927	725,000	712,010	420,000	309,811	287,732	228,438	201,296
WOMEN in membership	929,196	178,051	76,000	262,908	138,600	186,676	60,670	172,073	34,883	151,208
WOMEN as % of members										
1997–98	78	20	6	36	31	59	19	75	17	N/A
1999–00	72	20	10	37	33	60	21	75	17	58
WOMEN as % of NEC members										
1997–98	65	13	0	41	32	53	20	43	22	N/A
1999–00	62	32	10	41	33	53	18	41	17	44
WOMEN as % of TUC delegation										
1997–98	61	25	16	33	45	59	25	43	15	N/A
1999–00	58	30	19	35	39	39	31	39	17	48
WOMEN as % of national f.t. officers+										
1997–98	38	4	0	8	30	25	10	14	13	N/A
1999–00	21	0	0	17	38	57	14	20	13	38
WOMEN as % of regional f.t. officers+										
1997–98	24	8	2	13	16	24	N/A	11	5*	N/A
1999–00	30	8	4	20e	21	25	0	17	4*	19

N/A: not available or not applicable.

*: full-time branch officers.

+: excluding general secretaries, deputy general secretaries and dedicated Women's/equality officers.

e: estimate.

Notes

1. Ron Ramdin, *The Making of the Black Working Class in Britain* (Aldershot, Wildwood House, 1987), p.337.
2. *Ibid.*, pp.280–309.
3. Heidi Amrit Wilson, 'Finding a Voice: Asian Women in Britain', in Heidi Safia Mirza (ed.), *Black British Feminism: A Reader* (London, Routledge, 1997), p.31.
4. Ramdin, *The Making of the Black Working Class in Britain*, pp.319–321.

5. *Ibid.*, pp.317–18.
6. *Ibid.*, p.448; Beverley Bryan, Stella Dadzie and Suzanne Scafe, *The Heart of the Race: Black Women's Lives in Britain* (London, Virago, 1985), p.37.
7. Amima Mama, 'Black Women, the Economic Crisis and the British State', in Heidi Safia Mirza (ed.), *Black British Feminism: A Reader* (London, Routledge, 1997), p.37.
8. Ron Ramdin, *Reimaging Britain: 500 years of Black and Asian History* (London, Pluto Press, 1999), p.232.
9. Ramdin, *The Making of the Black Working Class in Britain*, pp.300–1.
10. 'More than Just a Memory: Some political implications of women's involvement in the miners' strike, 1984–85', Sheila Rowbotham interviews Jean McCrindle, *Feminist Review, Special Issue: Socialist Feminism 'Out of the Blue'*, 23, (Summer, 1986), p.113 and *passim*.
11. Robert Taylor, *The Future of Trade Unions* (London, Andre Deutsch, 1994), p.59.
12. Ramdin, *Reimaging Britain*, p.234.
13. *Ibid.*, pp.235–6.
14. Jill Humphrey, 'To Queer or not to Queer a Lesbian and Gay Group: Sexual and Gendered Perspectives at the Turn of the Century', *Sexualities*, 2 (2) (1999).
15. Equal Opportunities Commission, *Facts About Women and Men in Great Britain* (EOC, 1999), pp.7, 13.

Chapter 4

The Fall of the 'Old' and the Rise of 'New' Labour

Introduction

Tony Blair, perhaps more than any other Labour leader, has been the moderniser who has not been locked into the past. Most other Labour leaders – Attlee, Gaitskell, Wilson, Callaghan, Foot, Kinnock and even Smith – have had to assimilate the past culture of Labour, steeped in the trade union traditions and collectivism of the past. Blair, following through the ideas of his mentor Neil Kinnock, was determined not to be constricted by the old Labour culture. He felt that change was now more necessary than ever since the traditional mass industrial techniques had given way to a lighter more service-oriented type of industry. The traditional working-class workforce had changed enormously and declined. Blair accepted that the Conservative Party had been successful since it was seen as the party that opposed state control and that Labour was seen as the party linked with trade unionism, the state and ethnic minorities and social security claimants. Such perceptions, whether real or exaggerated, had to be changed. The 'New Labour' Party that Blair pressed for needed to cultivate the moderate image which Kinnock had been looking for in the 1980s and early 1990s (Document 1).[1] It needed to accept some of the changes that the Conservatives had introduced and to convince voters that it would not raise taxes, favour the trade unions, overspend and build up debts. In other words, it had to remove the demons of 'Old Labour'.

91

The 'Demons' of Old Labour

On 3 May 1979, Labour won 269 seats in the general election but was defeated by the Conservative Party, with its 339 seats. The Conservative victory inaugurated an era of Thatcherism which was to fundamentally change the direction of British politics, ending the post-war political consensus, undermining Keynesian management economics, and challenging the structure of the modern Welfare State (see Chapters 1 and 2). For Labour, the defeat was the starting point of 18 years in opposition, during which the fear was that Labour would never again be returned to government office.[2] With the erosion of the traditional working-class and trade-union base of Labour, it appeared that Labour was losing its political base at the same time as it was failing to capture the support of the skilled workers in the southern and south-eastern parts of England.

The years between 1979 and 1983 were particularly bleak ones for Labour. During this period, Labour moved to the left, with Michael Foot becoming leader in 1980 and the National Executive of the party falling increasingly under leftwing control. As a result, the party saw part of its right wing drift off, with Roy Jenkins, David Owen, Bill Rodgers and Shirley Williams, into the newly-formed Social Democratic Party in 1981 (see Chapter 6). The lines of demarcation had been drawn over issues of public ownership, which the left wanted and the right wished to move away from, and the electoral college arrangements for the selection of the Labour leader, which was being taken out of the hands of Labour MPs and being shared between trade unions (40 per cent), constituency parties (30 per cent) and MPs (30 per cent). In the end, 29 Labour MPs and, initially, nine Labour members of the House of Lords, joined the SDP.

The one redeeming feature for the right was that Denis Healey was Michael Foot's deputy, and the Solidarity group, led by Roy Hattersley, worked hard to ensure that Tony Benn's challenge for Healey's post, in September 1981, was narrowly defeated. From that point onwards, the right began to reassert its influence within the Labour Party. Nevertheless, Labour entered the 1983 general election against a background of declining trade union membership (see Chapter 3), the patriotic fervour of the Falklands War (see Chapter 2) and with a leftwing policy of reversing Thatcher's trade union legislation (see Chapter 4), renationalising privatised industries and committing Britain to unilateral nuclear disarmament. *New Hope for Britain*, Labour's manifesto, drawn up largely by the National Executive Committee (NEC) of the Labour Party, rather than the Shadow Cabinet, did not work – Labour won only 209 seats in the House of Commons as a result of gaining a mere 27.6 per cent of the vote. Gerald Kaufmann described Labour's manifesto as the 'longest suicide note in history'.

A radical rethink of party direction was urgently required, and this came when Neil Kinnock and Roy Hattersley became leader and deputy leader, respectively, in the autumn of 1983. Although Kinnock had begun his parliamentary career as a leftwinger, he was, by that time, drifting firmly to the right. As Labour leader, he immediately created a number of joint NEC-Shadow Cabinet committees which moved in the direction of moderation. He supported the introduction of one-member, one-vote (OMOV) in the mandatory reselection of Labour candidates, which the left wing had introduced under Foot's leadership, although this was at first rebuffed. Kinnock was also critical of Arthur Scargill's leadership during the miners' strike of 1984/5 (Document 1 and see Chapter 3) and the activities of Derek Hatton, whose Militant Tendency group was running Liverpool City Council in the mid-1980s and resisting the rate-capping of council expenditure imposed by the Thatcher government.

The test for Kinnock's modest moves towards moderation came at the 1987 general election and proved greatly disappointing. Kinnock entered the election with policies which were still seen to be leftwing and too extreme by the British voters. He recognised that Labour's defence policy commitment to unilateral nuclear disarmament was a vote loser but could do little to change it. Nevertheless, Labour fought the 1987 general election on unilateralism, a policy which was represented by the Conservative Party as meaning that British soldiers would have their hands in the air in any war. Labour was also attacked because of its intention to increase taxes on the rich.

Labour won 229 seats and 30.7 per cent of the vote in the general election of June 1987, an improvement on 1983 but a long way off forming a government. As a result, Kinnock began an enormous campaign of reform which saw Labour introduce a wide-ranging policy review between 1989 and 1991, which led to Labour abandoning state intervention and public ownership by 1992, the retention of some of Thatcher's trade-union legislation and, by 1990, to Labour's commitment to reducing her nuclear capacity by multilateral agreements (Documents 1, 3 and 6). Indeed, the 1992

Labour manifesto confirmed this position by claiming that as long as nuclear weapons still existed 'Labour will retain Britain's nuclear capability'.[3] In addition, it was made clear that the further expansion of the Welfare State would be tied to Britain's economic success.

Thus, between 1987 and 1992, Labour had removed every major symbol of its former leftwing policies (Document 6). In addition, by 1988 the Labour Party had accepted the principle of OMOV, using it in the leadership and deputy leadership contests of 1988.

Labour looked more electable during the March/April 1992 general election campaign and its manifesto, *It's Time to get Britain Working Again*, looked attractive in offering an extra £1,000 million for the National Health Service, £600 million for education and a variety of increases in child benefits and retirement pensions. Inevitably, the Conservatives and the press got involved in costing Labour's policies in terms of tax increases but Labour looked confident when it held a 'glitzy rally' at Sheffield Arena on 1 April 1992, which conveyed the impression that Labour was on the eve of victory. However, in the final analysis, it won only 271 seats on the 9 April 1992, a vast improvement on the 1983 and 1987 general elections but well short of the number required to form a government.

In the wake of this defeat, Kinnock and Hattersley were replaced by John Smith, as leader, and Margaret Beckett, as deputy leader. Under their management, the Labour Party moved further towards reducing trade union power and the full introduction of OMOV in leadership and deputy leadership contests (Document 4). However, Smith's death in May 1994, led to the election of Tony Blair as Labour leader, with John Prescott as his deputy. Labour had drifted a long way to the right since the early 1980s. Trade union power was being reduced, public ownership and unilateral disarmament were no longer on the agenda, and there was sensitivity about the vote-losing capacity of high taxation. The 'demons' of old Labour were being tamed. Tony Blair was to go further.

Broadening Membership: Feminist Issues and Race

The ethos of 'Old Labour' had been masculine. Broadening its appeal was one of the factors impelling the change to 'New Labour'.

The Labour Party's electoral decline from 1979 drove it to seek to broaden its membership base and relax its rules about links with other organisations. At the same time, some feminists perceived that the Labour Party might be effective in pursuing their demands (Document 7 and see Chapter 9). Women had formed about 50 per cent of Labour Party members since the 1930s but had been under-represented in the Party leadership.[4] In 1979, over a thousand Women's Sections of constituency Labour Parties were active, but women formed a mere 12 to 15 per cent of local election candidates and there were only 52 Labour women parliamentary candidates and 11 Labour women Members of Parliament.[5]

One of the impacts of feminism on the Labour Party was the promotion of equal opportunities programmes. These built on the legislation of the Wilson and Callaghan Labour governments of the 1960s and 1970s on sex and race discrimination, equal pay and employment protection, which gave women improved maternity pay and protection against unfair dismissal arising from pregnancy. Negotiations on equal opportunities policies aimed at ensuring that employers accepted the spirit of the legislation and were learning experiences both for feminist activists and Labour politicians. The Labour-controlled Metropolitan Authorities, including the Greater London Council, were to the forefront in constructing imaginative equal opportunities programmes and appointing equal opportunities officers and committees (Document 9).

The claim for equal opportunities extended into the Labour Party. Sarah Perrigo, historian and Labour Party activist, describes three phases of feminist involvement in the Labour Party. The initial period of attraction from 1979 to 1983 (Document 7) was followed by a second, more troubled phase from 1983 to 1987. In the third phase, from 1987, feminist and Labour Party modernisers shared similar goals.[6] The number of Labour women Members of Parliament went down to ten in 1983, while there were 13 Conservative women Members of Parliament, a rise from eight in 1979. Feminists within the Labour Party formed the Women's Action Group in 1983, aiming to increase women's representation on the party's National Executive Committee to five, from the four places set aside for women by the party's 1918 constitution. In addition, the Women's Action Group demanded that these women be elected by the Labour Party Women's Conference, instead of the Party Annual Conference, where women were greatly under-represented, and that the Women's Conference should have the right to submit five resolutions each year to the annual conference. Women-only shortlists for candidates in parliamentary elections were also demanded.

These demands aroused much controversy (Documents 8, 10).Women belonging to the Militant Tendency prioritised class issues and were, on the whole, opposed to the Women's Action Group

(Document 11). As a Militant profile was visible at Women's Conference for several years after its demise at Annual Conference, the former remained an arena for heated debate; in the uproar at the 1986 Isle of Bute Women's Conference, the Labour Party secretary, Larry (now Lord) Whitty was denied a hearing. While some feminists thought the Women's Action Group demands too limited, part of the backlash from the 1979–83 period was the rediscovery of the voice of the longstanding female Labour Party membership, suspicious of positive discrimination which might benefit a few high-flyers at the expense of the discomfort of the vast majority.

Nevertheless, the Women's Action Group was effective, distributed model resolutions and organised women's slates. At the same time, the leftwing Campaign for Labour Party Democracy, and modernisers within the Party, aimed at greater democracy in Labour Party decision-making, including an end to the unions' block vote at Annual Conference.[7] The unions, facing a loss in their traditional membership as heavy industry declined and seeking to attract the female labour force, moved towards favouring the reforms. The feminists' and modernisers' campaigns began to achieve notable successes, including the creation of electoral colleges within constituencies. Twenty-one Labour women Members of Parliament were elected in 1987, outnumbering the 17 Conservative women MPs. The 1989 Annual Conference voted for a 40 per cent quota of women officers at every level of the party. Clare Short, a leading Women's Action Group supporter and MP, was elected to chair the new women's committee of the National Executive and pioneered the 'W' list of potential women parliamentary candidates and exclusively female shortlists in half the constituencies. A Minister for Women with Cabinet status was proposed.[8] In 1992, the number of Labour women MPs rose to 37, and that of Conservative women to 20.

Action to end racism within the Labour Party and to extend its ethnic base was also evident in these years. In 1980, the Labour Party Race Action Group was formed to advise and lobby Labour MPs, local candidates and magistrates on issues such as citizenship and immigration law, ethnic minority monitoring, multicultural values, education, housing and the 'Sus' laws which gave police new powers to stop and search. Members of this group, including Russell Profitt, a London Labour councillor, were amongst those campaigning for the creation of Black and Asian sections at local and national level. In 1983, a National Executive Committee working party was formed to discuss this. The difficulties were the same as had faced feminist campaigners; some black activists thought the campaign misguided (Document 12); Militant was opposed, again seeing the measure as divisive of the workers' movement; some existing Labour Party black members were suspicious of the vested interests of the campaigners and were not in favour of separate black sections.[9] Whereas women had managed to win trade unions to their campaign, the only union which supported black sections was the National Union of Mineworkers, which had been radicalised during the 1984/5 miners' strike; black and Asian activists within the Labour Party were thus not able to achieve the positive discrimination which was given to women. Nevertheless, a Black and Asian Advisory Committee was formed in 1986 and became a full committee of the National Executive the following year. Ethnic minority officers were appointed in constituency Labour Parties. In 1987, four black Labour candidates were elected to parliament. Continued pressure at the annual conference eventually resulted in a National Executive recommendation that a Black and Asian Socialist Society, affiliated to the Labour Party, be created. This did not give black groups the power or status they had sought but was accepted, in 1991, as a compromise solution. An additional black candidate was elected in a 1991 by-election; in 1992 five black Labour MPs and in 1997 four black and five Asian Labour MPs were elected.

Clause Four and the Evolution of 'New Labour'

The symbol of the change from 'Old' to 'New Labour' was the removal of Clause Four of the Labour Party Constitution, which committed Labour to the common ownership of the means of production. Giles Radice and Steve Pollard, two modernisers, suggested that such an action was essential for Labour's political future.[10] A year later, Blair announced his intention to reject the old Clause Four at the 1994 Labour Party Conference, while praising the successes of capitalism. Soon afterwards, he presented his alternative Clause Four, which, after amendments, was accepted by the National Executive Committee of the Labour Party (Document 2). It committed Labour 'to work for a dynamic economy, serving the public interest, in which the enterprise of the market and the rigour of competition are joined with the forces of partnership and co-operation... with a thriving sector and high quality public services...' In addition, there were vague references to a just society, security against fear, equality of opportunity and other related issues. This new Clause Four was to replace the existing one, which had been the basis of Labour's commitment to social justice, equality and full employment. Effectively, the idea of redistribution of wealth and income within British society was being rejected. The race was now on to get this accepted by the party as a whole.

At first it appeared that constituencies and trade unions would be against the change and so, at the end of 1994, Blair held an intensive round of meetings where he personally appealed to 30,000 party members to support his new Clause Four. There was stern trade-union opposition to the new version, particularly from the Transport and General Workers' Union, but, with more than two thirds of the constituency Labour parties deciding to ballot their members, it was clear that about 85 per cent of the members would support Blair's new Clause Four.

At a special conference of the Labour Party held on 29 April 1995, which was seen by the press as a test of Blair's ability to deal effectively with the trade unions, he won support for his new Clause Four by just under two thirds of the vote. This revealed that 54.6 per cent of the 70 per cent union vote and about 90 per cent of the 30 per cent constituency vote had supported Blair.[11] Effectively, Blair had won support for his reforming leadership of the Labour Party, and the press and media recognised that this had been his personal triumph. He had tackled and tamed trade-union opposition, buoyed up by the recognition that he and the Labour Party would not be taken seriously by the public if the proposal had been defeated. In the end, the majority of trade unions and constituency parties dared not vote against Blair if they wished the party to have a significant political future. Their comfort was that Blair and the Labour Party moved in other directions to offset their doubts, most notably in moving the Labour Party Conference of October 1996 to vote in favour of the European Social Charter by 1 January 1998 (following through on Kinnock's support for it in 1989), supporting the introduction of the minimum wage and agreeing to end the internal competitive market in the National Health Service, which had been introduced by Thatcher and Major (Documents 1 and 5).

'New Labour' had now rejected the old Keynesian social democracy of the 'Old', which had suggested that the state could intervene to promote growth and thus ensure economic prosperity and employment. Instead, it was now committed to the pursuit of low inflation, through the increased powers of the Bank of England

and prepared to use interest rates in the same fashion as the Thatcher and Major governments had done.[12] This meant that increased tax rates were ruled out and that Labour's past commitment to redistributing income and wealth was at an end.

These views were confirmed in a book written by Peter Mandelson and Roger Liddle entitled *The Blair Revolution: Can New Labour Deliver*, published in 1996. It suggested that Labour was standing on the brink of power and outlined the type of society that New Labour wished to create. Mandelson had long been involved in the development of the New Labour strategy. He became MP for Hartlepool in 1992 and was Party Director of Campaigns and Communications between 1985 and 1990, when Neil Kinnock was Labour's leader; he had previously been a television producer from 1982 to 1985. Mandelson was steeped in the arts of the media and public relations. So was Roger Liddle, who was the Managing Director of PRIMA Europe, a body of public policy consultants. He had previously been an adviser in the Callaghan government, and had left Labour to join the SDP, before returning to the Labour Party and becoming one of Tony Blair's policy advisers. These were two of the so-called 'spin doctors' of 'New Labour'. Their lengthy and detailed book covered every aspect of New Labour's policy in building up a new society in Britain by 2005, from where Thatcher left off. It then suggested that New Labour's approach was based upon five insights: the need for people to feel secure; investment, partnership and top quality education for all; the recognition of the potential of government; and 'One Nation socialism' going beyond the battles of the past between private and public interests; and, further, the need to unite public and private activities in the ideal of social cooperation (Document 13).[13]

The commitment to partnership between public and private sectors, the 'Third Way', has been the fundamental characteristic of New Labour's general strategy. Despite repeated indications of this in policy, it would appear that Blair's willingness to cut across the political barriers for advice and help was not immediately evident. To the media and the public, Blair was more the man who had stood up to the unions and abandoned nationalisation. The more subtle points of his policy, particularly the rejection of Keynesian economic, large-scale government intervention and the maintenance of full employment, were not immediately detected. Instead, Blair's personality, charm and communication skills quickly endeared him to the British electorate.

The General Election of 1997

With Blair running high in the opinion polls it is hardly surprising that John Major delayed the general election to the last possible date, 1 May 1997, when Blair led Labour to a sweeping victory. With 44.4 per cent of the vote Labour won 419 seats to the Conservatives' 165 (336 in 1992), securing an overall majority of 179 seats. Labour's proportion of the vote was 10.8 per cent up on 1992. Also, most remarkably, 122 women MPs were returned, more than double the number returned in 1992. With this victory, and these changes, Blair had successfully presented the modernisation of the Labour Party as the precursor of the modernisation of Britain: 'New Labour, New Britain'.

The 1997 general election had returned the Labour Party to office after 18 years of opposition. The shift of support from the Conservatives to the Labour Party was the biggest this century, in what has generally been referred to as a landslide victory. Yet whilst it was partly achieved as a result of Labour's trans-formation, it was also a result of Conservative failings, which saw a decline in the Conservative vote from 42 to 31 per cent (see Chapter 1).

New Labour seemed fresh and innovative, with a populist leader. In the three years up to the election, as indicated, Labour was reducing its commitments to the trade unions (see Chapter 3) and to public ownership and widening its appeal to middle-class voters. In addition, in order not to be faced with a repeat of the financial fiasco of 1992, when the Shadow Budget discussion had been part of Labour's undoing, Gordon Brown, Labour's Shadow Chancellor of the Exchequer, made a speech in January 1996 promising not to increase VAT, the basic rate of income tax or the higher rate of income tax. He further declared Labour's intention to continue with the existing spending plans of the Conservative government for two years and that Labour's extra spending commitments would be paid for out of a 'windfall tax' imposed, as a one-off, upon the privatised industries which had been making massive profits and paying their bosses substantial increases, much to the annoyance of the British public. Brown's speech certainly helped Labour win the general election and Mandelson reflected that Labour could nail 'Tory lies about us on tax and spending'.[14]

Yet, there were also other factors at play. Rupert Murdoch, the owner of *The Times, Sunday Times, Sun* and *News of the World*, threw his support behind the Labour Party, which was reflected in the fact that the *Sun* and the *News of the World* supported the Labour Party. Only the *Sunday Times* was positively a Conservative paper.

Blair was particularly concerned about his party's image and its presentation to the media, to such an extent that Labour rented two floors of Millbank Tower, in Westminster, where Mandelson and about 80 staff operated to present the Labour message more effectively. Eventually, 250 staff were organised into 12 taskforces, specialising in particular issues, to respond to and rebut charges made by the Conservative Party. The 'political smart arses' at Millbank, as John Prescott referred to them, ensured that there were few political gaffes.

Labour's campaign went well and the manifesto, *New Labour: Because Britain Deserves Better*, issued on 3 April 1997, proved attractive by offering a ten-point personal contract with the British people, the central aim of which was to improve education. The manifesto emerged from the *New Labour: New Life for Britain* document, issued in 1996, which had promised to cut class sizes for young children; to halve the times between the arrest and punishment of young criminals; to cut the NHS waiting lists; to get 250,000 young unemployed back to work; and to set tough rules for future government spending and borrowing.

There were some problems, most obviously the Conservative suggestion that Labour's spending plans would cost £1,500 million more than government revenue. However, Labour responded to this perceived 'funding gap' by suggesting that it would also privatise in order to raise the necessary money.

In the end, Labour's campaign appealed to the upper working-class and middle-class voters throughout the South East of England, as well as traditional support. The failures of the Conservatives and the policies of the Labour Party were enough to win Labour its landslide victory.[15]

For women, the 1997 election was a breakthrough. Women-only shortlists in half the constituencies selecting candidates had operated from 1993 and, although deemed illegal in 1996, had been important in changing the attitudes of constituency selectorates. One hundred and twenty women were elected to the 1997 parliament, of whom 101 were Labour MPs; 35 of these were from constituencies which had adopted women-only shortlists.[16] However, while Clare Short was appointed minister in charge of aid to overseas countries and Margaret Beckett, Harriet Harman and Mo Mowlam to powerful ministerial positions, the latter were subject to Cabinet changes so that no women remained in charge of heavy spending departments. Mo Mowlam indicated, in September 2000, that she would withdraw from Parliament at the end of the first Blair government. The Ministry for Women failed to materialise although Tessa Jowell in the House of Commons and Margaret Jay in the House of Lords acted jointly as Ministers for Women.

The Early Years of the Blair Labour Government, 1997–2000

Once in office, Blair moved quickly to establish his New Labour credentials. In June 1997, he signed the European Social Charter on Workers' Rights. From the start, he also decided to strengthen the centre of government. Mandelson was appointed Minister without Portfolio inside the Cabinet Office to coordinate the work of government departments, and a strategy committee of the Cabinet was set up under Blair's own chairmanship. The Labour government also introduced a new ministerial code requiring that all media contacts and policy initiatives by ministers should be cleared in advance by Downing Street.

In order to strengthen control further, Blair pressed the Labour Party conference of 1997 to adopt *Partnership into Power*, a document which set out a radical programme to reform the party's decision-making processes. By this, the party conference lost its control over party policy to the 175-strong National Party Forum which would discuss policies, in a two-year rolling cycle, and the National Executive Committee (NEC) of the party was altered. The women's section of the NEC was to be abolished and trade-union representatives reduced from 17 to 12, although six were to be women. Three places were to be reserved for members of the Labour government (or party) and appointed by Tony Blair (party leader/ Prime Minister) and one for the leader of the Labour Group in the European Parliament. Six were to be set aside for representatives elected by a postal ballot of all members. These changes weakened the Labour Party conference, reduced the power of the trade unions, and strengthened of the hand of Blair, as Labour leader.

Riding upon huge popular support, Tony Blair responded by beginning a variety of initiatives, in a veritable rush of activity. In May, Robin Cook, the new Foreign Secretary announced that the United Kingdom would sign up to the European Social Charter; Blair offered Sinn Fein a meeting with officials on the Northern Ireland peace process without the preconditions of a renewed ceasefire; and, in the Queen's Speech to Parliament, the new Labour government set out its commitments to a minimum wage and to constitutional reform. Gordon Brown, the new Chancellor of the Exchequer, also announced that the Bank of England, rather than the Government, would take responsibility for setting interest rates through a new monetary policy committee. In June 1997, task forces were established on NHS efficiency and youth justice.

The 'New Labour' approach to the economy was also evident in Gordon Brown's first budget, in July 1997, with cuts in corporation taxes, on businesses, the reduction of VAT to five per cent on fuel, cuts in mortgage tax relief and the £5,200 million windfall tax on privatised utilities in order to finance the Welfare to Work programme and to reduce youth and long-term unemployment by 250,000. The 'New Labour' emphasis upon health and education was reflected in a commitment to further spending of £3,500 million. Shortly afterwards, however, it was announced that student grants would be replaced by student loans, as suggested in the (Ron) Dearing Report, the ideas being that money would flow into higher education. The overall New Labour formula was to be increased public spending without increased taxation: the best of both worlds.

New Labour, in applying its new philosophy, has focused upon five main areas. First, it has sought to communicate with the public and to present a better image of Labour policies than has previously occurred and suggested that there was a greater openness in government. Second, it has sought to apply market-led forces to its economic and social strategies, placing an emphasis upon the state acting as an enabler rather than simply as a provider. Third, its emphasis is essentially pro-European and pro-American. Fourth, it is committed to brokering a peace in Northern Ireland. Fifth, it has essentially stressed the need for constitutional reform in such areas as the electoral system, the devolution of government, and changes in the House of Lords.

Ostensibly, New Labour is about communication and more open government. Blair has emerged as the great communicator and as a populist leader. This was most evident on 31 August 1997 with the death of Diana, Princess of Wales. His style tapped into the popular mood of remorse throughout the nation at that time. In other areas, however, there has been less transparency than initially suggested. Indeed, David Clark was given the Cabinet post of Chancellor of the Duchy of Lancaster, with responsibility for brokering a Freedom of Information Act. The White Paper that indicated government thinking on the proposed Act, dealing with national and local government, quangos (non-elected bodies dealing with the distribution of government money), the NHS, and privatised utilities, was published in December 1997. The anticipated Freedom of Information Act was to signal a new relationship between the government and the people by which access to information would be improved and an era of accountability would begin. Nonetheless, since David Clark's removal from office, in the ministerial reshuffle of July 1998, the development of such an Act has slowed. Jack Straw, the Home Secretary, has taken responsibility for the Act, the first bill of which, in May 1999, revealed that the Government had withdrawn from its original position. Whilst schools, local authorities and hospitals are to be more accountable, it is clear that there will be exceptions where ministerial discretion will prevent unwarranted disclosure on the grounds that substantial harm might be done to the state. The Commissioner to administer the Act will not be independent and the government will not be forced to reveal how it arrives at policy.[17] In effect, the intended all-embracing act will not be implemented.

The market-led nature of New Labour's approach, the second feature of Labour policy, was, of course, blatantly obvious in Brown's 1997 Budget, particularly in the explicitly-titled programme of 'Welfare to Work'. It was also evident in the statement, in November 1998, that pledged that there would be a fundamental reform of the Welfare State and proposed a tax credit scheme for poor working families. In December, as part of that strategy, the government pressed forward with a reduction in benefits for lone parents, which led 47 Labour MPs to vote against the action, on a three-line whip, and 14 more to abstain. The Labour government in fact won by 457 votes to 107, with the support of the Conservatives.

Nevertheless, in January 1998 the government did announce its 'New Deal' for the unemployed of 18 to 24 years old, to work with subsidised private employers, education or training, self employment or a variety of other alternatives in its strategy to eliminate unemployment by early in the twenty-first century. In March 1998, Brown also announced a redistributive budget strategy which included the introduction of the Working Family Tax Credit, from October 1999, the Disabled Persons Tax Credit, increases in Child Benefit, subsidies for employers to take on the long-term unemployed and extra spending in many other areas. Therefore, it has not been entirely clear that New Labour has played down the redistribution of income element, although its great adherence to market forces suggests that social differences may be widened rather than narrowed. Indeed, the philosophy behind New Labour seems to have been to reduce social need through an alliance between the state and the private sector. This was outlined, in some detail, by Tony Blair on 18 March 1999 (Document 5 in Chapter 2).

As Peter Mandelson and Roger Liddle have stressed, the third priority for New Labour is its commitment to Europe. In government, it has followed through that commitment, recognising that the European Economic Community accounts for half of British exports and is responsible for guaranteeing about three million jobs in Britain. Despite the criticism of the Conservative Party, and some hesitation about a commitment to a single European currency, New Labour is committed to Europe. In October 1997, Gordon Brown announced that the government favoured eventual entry into the European Monetary Union but not in the lifetime of Blair's first Parliament and only if agreed in a referendum.

Fourth, beyond the domestic arena, the British political and military alliance with the United States is obvious. It was particularly evident in Blair's constant support for Bill Clinton, the then US President, in containing Saddam Hussein and Iraq from military expansion, and in the close relationship developed between Britain and the USA in dealing with the Yugoslavian government and the Kosovan refugee crisis throughout 1999. Indeed, in the Kosovan crisis Blair took the lead in the NATO action against the Serbian-dominated Yugoslavian state. In the case of Kosova, in particular, Blair carved out for himself the reputation of being a major political player on the world stage. In 2001, the war against Afghanistan projected him further forward in this role. Chapter 10 considers the Blair government's policy in Northern Ireland.

The fifth major commitment of New Labour has been to constitutional and electoral reform. Such a commitment was first announced in the Queen's Speech in May 1997. In June, it was also announced that the Liberal Democrats were being invited to take seats on a cabinet committee to discuss constitutional reform and other mutual interests. In December 1998, the Electoral Reform Commission was set up under Lord (Roy) Jenkins, the former Labour minister and co-founder of the SDP. Jenkins was set the task of devising a system of proportional representation for the Westminster elections in preparation for a referendum on the issue. In October 1998, Blair accepted its recommendation of an Alternative Vote Top-Up System of proportional representation for parliamentary elections and in June 1999 the elections for European MPs was based upon a system of proportional representation, with electors voting for parties not individuals. But since then, Jenkins' plans have been indefinitely shelved.

The Labour government also moved to create both a Scottish parliament and a Welsh assembly in 1999, allowing for a greater representation of national minority interest groups in an attempt to undermine the demands for political independence in both Scotland and Wales (see Chapter 7). And, in addition, there have been moves to modernise the monarchy and discussions about replacing the House of Lords with an assembly largely made up of life peers and a much reduced number of hereditary peers, en route to extinction, have been implemented.

The Blair government has certainly been hyperactive. Indeed, it is fair to argue that Blair has achieved the objective he set himself, at the 1997 Labour Party conference, of making his administration 'one of the great reforming governments in British history'. Certainly, there have been constitutional, economic and welfare reforms in abundance. Most certainly, the direction of British politics has been changed. Nevertheless, one might question the direction of some of these reforms. Whilst it is, perhaps, fair to suggest that the electoral and constitutional reforms will provide for wider participation in the politics of Britain, it is still evident that there has been some downgrading of the proposed Freedom of Information Act and some feeling that true decision-making is becoming increasingly concentrated in the hands of the spin-doctors.[18] In addition, there are many within Labour ranks who, while welcoming many of the reforms, are critical of the direction that they are taking and the Old Labour and socialist principles that they appear to be abandoning.

The resignation of Mandelson as Secretary of Trade and Industry, to which he had been promoted in July 1998, over the issue of his mortgage arrangement was a welcome sight to some party members and MPs. Nevertheless, rumblings about the style of government which, apparently, relies upon 'cronies' and sees the appointment of friends as advisers, still continues.[19]

The main siren voice has been Roy Hattersley, former deputy leader of the Labour Party, who, as early as July 1997, was declaring his lack of commitment to New Labour because of its desertion of policies to deal with the poor and its blatant ignoring of the need to redistribute wealth in order to move toward equality. The market-forces approach of both state and private enterprise is hardly going to redistribute wealth or create a fairer society.

Conclusion

Early in the twenty-first century, Britain is led by Tony Blair and a Labour government with a strong reforming zeal, with Blair becoming 'the great communicator' – a populist figure developing an almost presidential image to the people and bypassing party politics. It is offering a wider participation in politics, more regional and local decision-making, closer links with Europe, a modern political society and, above all, the Third Way in British politics – uniting the state and private industry in tackling the social and economic problems of the nation. The present Labour government is thus far removed from its predecessors, with less dependence upon the trade unions and less emphasis upon the state intervening in the economy on its own to ensure full employment. In capturing 'middle England' and the middle classes, Labour has loosened itself from its old traditional roots. Labour is no longer the class-based party of 1918 or even the more loosely based trade-union party of 1983. It is now the party of all classes which Ramsay MacDonald, one of its founding fathers, had hoped that it would be when he first helped to form the Labour Representation Committee in 1900. Blair's victory in the general election of 2001 has tended to confirm this impression, although there is much frustration within the old traditional working classes at the continued emphasis that New Labour has placed upon cooperation between the private and the public sector.

Documents

SECONDARY SOURCES AND INTERPRETATIONS

1. Andrew Thorpe, *A History of the British Labour Party* (London, Palgrave, 1997 and 2001 editions), pp.192, 205, 207–8, 212, 224

[Following the special conference of 24 January 1981 on the electoral college which committed Labour to electing its leader on a party-wide franchise; p.192]

On the same day, Jenkins finally returned to Britain. Within 24 hours, he, Owen, Williams and Rodgers – 'the Gang of Four' – issued their 'Limehouse Declaration' stating that the 'calamitous outcome' of the conference demand[ed] a new start, but it did establish a Council for Social Democracy, 'half in and half out of the Labour Party'... On 26 March, the Social Democratic party (SDP) was formally established... At first only 10 MPs followed Owen and Rodgers, but by the time of the dissolution of parliament in 1983 there were 30, 27 of whom were elected as Labour MPs in 1979...

[Having discussed factionalism within the party, the Militant Tendency and the general election defeat under the leadership of Michael Foot, the author goes on to discuss the move to the right within the party under Neil Kinnock. Faced with the miners' strike of 1984/5 and the Militant problem, it appeared that Labour had an uphill battle to strengthen its position, although Kinnock built up the leader's office into an alternative party structure and developed new policies; p.205]

These years also saw changes in party policy. The aim was essentially to make policy more 'popular', more credible (there had been widespread disbelief, for example, in Labour's 1983 promise to bring down unemployment below one million), and more congenial to the views of the shadow cabinet. The ensuing shift to the right was buttressed by, even predicted upon, the 'boom' conditions which were clearly prevailing at the end of 1985. At the same time, change was rather piecemeal, so that in 1987 the manifesto would be 'full of compromises and ambiguity'. Abolition of the House of Lords and plans to remove US nuclear bases from Britain were omitted, but the party remained committed to unilateralism. Withdrawal from the EC [European Community] was dropped, but this simply means that the party had little to say on Europe at all.

[Labour was defeated in the June 1987 general election; pp.207–8] The argument that Labour needed a more 'moderate' image fitted the leadership's agenda perfectly, and between 1987 and 1992, the party shifted further to the right. One side of this was policy. In July 1987 Neil Kinnock agreed the establishment of seven 'policy review' groups which would report to the 1989 party conference. The results were broadly as intended. On the economy, Labour moved still further away from nationalization, stressing the need for market disciplines and a government sympathetic to business... This meant in turn that Labour ruled out large increases in taxation...

In other areas, too, there was change. Occasionally, they were innovative, as with the pledge to introduce a national minimum wage and to create a Ministry for Women. But generally the trend was towards policy becoming more 'moderate'. First, the policy on the EC was modified. With withdrawal seemingly increasingly a lost cause... Labour became warmer towards Europe.

[Despite organisational and policy changes, Labour still lost the 1992 general election; p.212] The period from 1979 onwards was one of massive challenges for the Labour party. The election in that year of a Conservative government determined to undo much of what Labourites had achieved and held dear was a blow whose implications soon became clear. The 1980s were a decade of almost continual defeats. In the face of these defeats, Labour, after briefly and half-heartedly trying a 'leftish' approach, had first edged, and then rushed, rightwards to try to regain its electability. But in spite of all the policy changes, the organizational alterations, and the renewed faith in leaders, the party was unable to regain office. In 1992, and for some time thereafter, there were those who questioned whether it would ever do so again.

[The book then discusses the resignation of Kinnock, his replacement as leader by John Smith and, following Smith's death in 1994, the emergence of Tony Blair as leader with his 'New Labour' policies; p.224] Symbolic proof of 'New' Labour's success came shortly afterwards. In his 1994 conference speech, Blair had stated that Labour needed to change with a changing world in order to remain relevant; the party must not become 'a historical monument' and, in particular, it needed 'a clear, up-to-date statement of... objects and objectives'. It was clear from this that Blair was preparing an assault on Clause Four of the party's constitution... Although earlier in the year Blair had felt that the issue was not worth raising, he, and Mandelson, were now convinced by the party's private polling that 'fear of the unknown' was still hindering Labour's progress among its target voters. In March 1995 a new version of Clause Four was approved by the NEC, and at the end of the following month a special party conference approved it. The new clause gained the support of 65 per cent of the party's members, including 90 per cent of the CLPs and 54.6 per cent of trade unions. Those unions which opposed it, like the TGWU and Unison, had not balloted their members, as Blair's supporters were quick to point out. In 1959 Gaitskell's attack on Clause Four had come to grief and severely weakened his position; thirty-six years later, Blair's attempt to change it had received overwhelming support and made his position as leader more secure than ever.

2. Keith Laybourn, *A Century of Labour: A History of the Labour Party* **(Stroud, Sutton, 2000), pp.168–9**

The trade unions, by now diversifying into white-collar areas rather than declining at this point, were also responsible for the industrial unrest of the late 1970s, and the 'Winter of Discontent' of 1979, that led to the defeat of James Callaghan's Labour government in 1979. By the late 1980s, wedded to Clause Four, the trade unions, high taxation, unilateralism, an ever-expanding welfare state, it appeared that Labour was unelectable. The 1983 general election was its low point, its worst political performance since 1918 when it was still emerging as a political party.

The general election of 1983 was, however, a turning point. From that moment onwards, and through the successive leaderships of Neil Kinnock, John Smith and Tony Blair, the Labour Party moved to the right. Labour leaders acted to reduce the influence of the trade unions and effectively abandoned Clause Four, years before Tony Blair pushed for its formal abandonment in 1994 and 1995. Labour began to abandon the image of being a working-class party. It also abandoned the idea that the state could ensure that there was full employment, something foreshadowed by James Callaghan and Denis Healey at the time of the financial crisis in the mid 1970s. The unthinkable had happened, the Welfare State was no longer sacrosanct.

Since then Tony Blair has forced Labour to go the whole hog and reduce the power of trade unions, abandon public ownership, abandon unilateral disarmament, and create a new 'Third Way' in politics bringing both the state and private industry into a partnership for the future. In the year 2000, then, the Labour Party is fundamentally different from what it had been in 1918, 1945 or even 1983.

The Attlee governments had been about planning, social redistribution of wealth and income, and public ownership. The Blair Government has been about the 'Third Way' and about partnership between the public and private sectors of the nation, about enabling people to help themselves rather than simply providing public benefits out of high taxation. Blair's Government is committed to winning support from across the political spectrum. Even to the Gaitskellite revisionists of the 1950s the redistribution of income and wealth were essential in a society designed to ensure that there was social justice and full employment, although Clause Four was not seen as vital. In contrast, Blair has rejected the redistribution of income, nationalization and full employment in the search for policies of economic growth that will appeal to all sections of British society.

3. Martin Westlake, 'Neil Kinnock 1983–92', in Kevin Jefferys (ed.), *Leading Labour: From Keir Hardie to Tony Blair* (London, I.B.Tauris, 1999), p.171

A harsh case can be made out against Labour's longest-serving Leader in Opposition. After nine years of unremitting toil, Neil Gordon Kinnock succeeded in establishing root-and-branch reform of the party, involving both organisational and presentational change and the jettisoning of such policy shibboleths as unilateral disarmament, withdrawal from the EC [European Community], large-scale nationalisation and the whole go-it-alone concept of the Alternative Economic Strategy on which the disastrous 1983 general election was fought. In its place was erected a modern social democratic party. To achieve this, Kinnock turned his face on the left-wing positions he had espoused as a parliamentary rebel in the 1970s, did decisive battle with the entryist Militant Tendency and the Bennite left, professionalised Labour's approach towards the modern media and increasingly focused power in the Leader's office. All of this was controversial, winning him the hostility of the hard left, guarded approval on the right, and exposing him to charges of opportunism. Many of his enemies and some of his friends argued that he had been too ready to jettison policy in the search for electability.

4. Andy McSmith, 'John Smith 1992–94', in Kevin Jefferys (ed.), *Leading Labour: From Keir Hardie to Tony Blair* (London, I.B.Tauris, 1999), p.193

[John Smith was Labour leader from 1992 until his death on 12 May 1994.] The great hypothetical question is whether John Smith needed to die for Labour to end its long exile from government.

One school of thought dates Labour's recovery from the election of Tony Blair in July 1994, consigning Smith to the role of Old Labour's last leader, a decent man whose unwillingness to adapt to a drastically changed political environment would have led the party to its fifth successive election defeat. There were aspects of the Blair project which would not have been realised under Smith: the party's vote to abolish Clause IV, the promise to hold down income tax indefinitely. In general, Smith's politics were located somewhere to the 'left' of New Labour, a strange turnabout for someone who had been a pillar of the party's right all his life. This helps explain his enduring popularity in the Labour Party, where his death invoked a sense of loss unmatched by anyone since Aneurin Bevan.

5. John Rentoul, 'Tony Blair 1994–', in Kevin Jefferys (ed.), *Leading Labour: From Keir Hardie to Tony Blair* (London, I.B.Tauris, 1999), pp.208–9

He is regarded with distaste by traditionalists of both right and left within the Labour Party as an interloper whose only interest in the party's history is in junking it. Roy Hattersley and Arthur Scargill used identical analogies to explain their opposition to Blair. The miners' leader, explaining his decision to leave the Labour party, said, 'If the church to which you went decided to stop worshipping God and started worshipping the devil, you would have second thoughts'. The former Deputy Leader commented after a year of New Labour Government, 'If Christians sat down to invent a new religion and decided that the Sermon on the Mount was incompatible with the global economy we would conclude that they had ceased to be Christians'. Hattersley had been irritated by a seminar held in Downing Street in May 1998 to discuss the 'Third Way' and sarcastically welcomed it 'for the very good reason that, since the Prime Minister believes in the Third Way, it is important for him to find out what it is'. The seminar, said Hattersley, 'was another step towards the creation of a new party – cuckooing in the nest as we used to say about the Militants'.

Equally, Blair was hailed by many Conservatives, and by millions of former Conservative voters, as 'one of us'. In an unguarded moment before the 1997 election, even Margaret Thatcher said, 'he won't let Britain down'. Lord Rothermere, proprietor of the *Daily Mail*, who defected to the Labour Party, explained, 'I joined New Labour because that was obviously the New Conservative party'.

6. Eric Shaw, 'The Wilderness Years, 1979–1994', in Brian Brivati and Richard Heffernan (eds), *The Labour Party: A Centenary History* (London, Macmillan, 2000), p.127

Notwithstanding *Labour and Britain in the 1990s* was to permeate the so-called Policy Review, the comprehensive reappraisals of policy which the party undertook in the wake of the 1987 defeat. There were two phases to the Review. The first culminated in the presentation to the 1989 conference of the second report, *Meet the Challenge, Make the Change*. It included several substantial policy departures, but not the more ruthless expunging of existing policy that the leadership wanted. In the second phase the whole process was brought under much tighter leadership control. Kinnock used the third and fourth reports, *Looking to the Future* (1990) and *Opportunity Britain* (1991) – from which the 1992 Manifesto was largely drawn – to place their stamp more emphatically on the party's programme.

In most accounts the real significance of the Policy Review has been seen as the formal acceptance of the market as the best mechanisms [sic] for organising economic life. This – the argument runs – constituted an ideological transformation, the final vanquishing of the left and Labour's long-overdue adoption of continental social democracy. [Such a view is held by Martin Smith and Joanna Spear, *The Changing Labour Party* (London, Routledge, 1992).] This interpretation missed the real significance of the debates which took place within the party over the Policy Review. Firstly, the hard left – which with one or two exceptions, took little interest – was hardly engaged at all: the real contest was between the soft left and the right. Secondly, Labour governments had always accepted that the market should operate as a main coordinator of economic activity. In practical (if not rhetorical) terms [the] central question has always been the form and extent of market management not the market itself. [The article then goes on to suggest that the soft left was marginalised in this debate.]

7. Sarah Perrigo, 'Socialist-Feminism and the Labour Party: Some Experiences from Leeds', *Feminist Review, Special Issue: Socialist Feminism Out of the Blue*, 23 (Summer 1986), p.101

The past decade has seen an influx of socialist-feminists into the Labour Party, particularly in the larger towns and cities where the women's movement has succeeded in building a strong community network. Several factors were involved in women joining at this time. By the late 1970s a hostile political and economic climate was increasingly threatening the progress of the women's movement. For many feminists it seemed imperative that alliances be made with other movements similarly threatened if gains won were to be defended and the movement progress. Secondly, some socialist-feminists felt that the women's movement was itself in an impasse. Questions were raised about how to increase the constituency of the women's movement particularly amongst working-class women and women from ethnic minorities, and more generally about how to link class and gender issues and how to establish a significant dimension in the theory and practice of socialist and Labour movements. Many of us had gained enormous experience and confidence through our involvement in feminist politics and felt more able to enter (or in some cases re-enter) the more formal arena of Labour Party politics and make our voices heard. Thirdly, the Labour Party too appeared to be in the process of change.

8. Christine Collette, '"Taking the Lid Off" Socialist Feminism in Oxfordshire', *Feminist Review* 26 (Summer 1987), pp.76–7

The Labour Party is rich in the experience of women stalwarts who have given time and energy without reward to its cause; they are the focus of the work of the Labour Heritage Women's Research Committee, a group of women who conduct oral history, meeting around the country as occasion arises, and who publish an annual bulletin. Often in poverty, usually raising children, women were weavers of the fabric of the Labour Party and continue to nip and tuck the design. The tendency to disregard women who did not achieve high offices has perhaps been too readily reflected by a feminist historiography which stigmatises as victims even some women who were very sure and strong about choosing to stay in the grass roots.

One result may have been the concentration of the reformist Labour Women's Action Committee on achieving prominent positions for women activists – a rather uneasy 'me too' type of feminism which has failed to present to the unreconstructed Labour male an alternative to his chauvinist socialism. Split at the May 1986 Labour Women's Conference, separated by prejudices which need examining and are in part derived from the male-oriented labour historiography which has been too long dominant (that is, women in trade unions are non-existent/inactive/subordinate; women socialists are middle class do-gooders/ignorant of working-class lives), constituency and trade union women fudged the issue by uniting at the September 1986 Labour Party Conference behind oversimplified demands; a woman on every shortlist for selection of elected representatives; the introduction of the block vote at the women's conference in return for the possibility of more power.

PRIMARY EVIDENCE AND INFORMATION

9. GLC Industry and Employment Branch, *Danger! Heterosexism at Work: A Handbook on Equal Opportunities in the Workplace for Lesbians and Gay Men* (London, GLC London, *c.*1987), pp.85–6

Having an equal opportunities policy on the books does not necessarily mean that discrimination disappears, either in recruitment, hiring, training, day-to-day work, promotion, or firing. One way to help get work practices changed is to keep track of employer practices and employees' experiences through repeated survey questionnaires...

Management has to be queried regularly on its plans and practices. This does not necessarily take a very detailed form. The Equal Opportunities office of the GLC has asked London boroughs to respond to questions similar to these:

1. What is our policy regarding Equal Opportunities and employment of lesbians and gay men?
2. Are details on how to combat discrimination against lesbians and gay men included in your code of practice? If so, please give the details.
3. Do you provide any form of training to challenge heterosexism for personnel management or other staff? If you do, what form does it take?
4. Do you have any plans to change your policy statement, your code of practice, or training on heterosexism?

London boroughs could also be asked whether there were special posts for officers to address the issue of how to eliminate heterosexual employment practices.

10. Pam Tatlow, *Bristol East Red Rag* (Bristol East Labour Party, 1986)

The under-representation of women in the formal organisation of the Labour and Trade Union Movement is not a possibility but a certainty which you might think the Movement would strive hard to correct. In fact, almost the opposite has been true. From the TUC of the 1880s to the present the men who have dominated the 'public face' and offices of the Labour Movement by the acquiescence of capital, have not only ignored the struggles of women but also (and perhaps worse) assumed that they could equally well interpret, articulate and implement the aspirations and demands of Labour women...

The right of women to control their own bodies has always been misinterpreted within the context of 'family planning' and been regarded as a moral rather than a political issue – and Arthur Scargill, who had previously boasted of shouting down 'radical' women protesting at a May Day Rally at page 3 of the 'Yorkshire Miner' and in spite of years of work and education in the Labour Movement, was radicalised to recognise the extent to which women had been denied a voice in the Labour Movement and the latter had itself been deprived of socialist force, by the work of the Women's support groups during the 1984–85 Miners' strike. It was for these reasons that, for the first time, the NUM at Labour's 1985 Party Conference backed the demand of the Labour Women's Conference that the 5 places on the Party's National Executive Committee reserved for women should be elected at the Women's Conference itself rather than being voted upon as at present by the whole Conference. In fact this would only bring the Women's Section of the NEC into line with other sections – that is the Constituencies, trade unions, Young Socialists and Socialist Societies already elect their representatives either through the Conference (the LPYS) or by a vote of their own delegations at the Annual Conference itself. The demand for women to elect their own representatives and to achieve a direct political accountability between the 5 women members of the NEC and the women's organisation of the Party has met with bitter opposition. As a result, the National Labour Women's Committee at the request of the National Women's Conference is holding Shadow Elections for the 5 NEC places at this year's National Women's Conference. If the Movement is serious about giving women a collective and political voice then all Constituencies and Trade Union delegations should vote at the 1986 Annual Conference not only for the 5 women supp(o)rted by the Women's Conference but also for the rule change which would place the present 'shadow' elections on a proper constitutional footing – and Labour men, in particular in the Trade Unions, need to start arguing *now* that these important principles are supported.

To advocate equality for women but to do nothing to promote it is perhaps the worst form of opposition which Labour women face although the charge that it is all a diversion from the 'class struggle' given that the trade unions have consistently voted a majority of right-wing women into the Women's places and against the wishes of the women's organisations is also pretty hard to take! So this is the time brothers, it's not your tacit support which we want but an active campaign which will ensure that socialist women have a collective voice at all levels in the Party.

11. *Militant Broadsheet*, Labour Party's Women's Conference (1985), Labour Women's Organisation and Positive Discrimination

This year's Conference will yet again devote a considerable amount of time to the relationship of the LWO to the Party and the advancement of women as representatives at different levels. 'Militant' supporters would reject many of the ideas on which the document before conference on 'positive discrimination' is founded. Whilst wanting to see more women in leading positions and playing a greater role generally in the Party... the first and overriding consideration as far as we are concerned will always be the political ideas candidates put forward and the record of activity in the movement.

We also reject the analysis of the Party as a 'male Party'. Although this describes the majority of activists in many areas and of MPs and councillors the sex of the representatives does not determine the nature of the Party. The Labour Party is a CLASS party. The main battles taking place within it at present concern how the Labour Party can further the interests of the working class male and female. Women have had a vital interest in this as a doubly exploited section of the class.

12. Darcus Howe, 'Labour Party Conference '84, Defeat of Black Section', in *Darcus Howe on Black Sections in the Labour Party* (Race Today Publications, 1985), pp.6–10

The third day of the 1984 Labour Party Conference bristled with the debate on Black Sections.

Composite 51 required the conference to instruct the National Executive Committee

a. to submit to the 1985 Conference amendments to the rules for Constituency Labour Parties which will allow Black Sections to be formed, where Black members so desire, with the right to send delegates to general and executive committees in the same way as women's sections and young socialist branches;

b. following consultations throughout the Party, to submit to the 1985 Conference draft regulations on the organisation of Black Sections;

c. to allow existing Black Sections to continue recognising that they have a valuable contribution to make in the formulation of the Party's policy and campaign in relation to anti-racism and the wishes of Black people;

d. to take no disciplinary action in relation to the existing provisions of the Party's Constitution against those Constituency Labour Parties which have constituted Black Sections formally.

This resolution, the soft option, would be moved by the Tottenham CLP and seconded by the Birmingham Ladywood CLP.

Composite 52 required the NEC to submit to the 1985 Conference constitutional Amendments

a. to increase the composition of the NEC by five members to be elected at an Annual Conference of Black Sections;

b. mandatory inclusion of at least one black person, if any apply, on all parliamentary and local government shortlists;

c. promotion of a substantial extension of affiliation to the Party by suitable ethnic minority organisations at local regional and national levels.

This, the hardline position, would be moved by Westminster North CLP and seconded by Richmond & Barnes CLP.

The leadership was certain to win if it went to the vote. They had seen to that. Of the seven million votes at conference, six million belonged to the Trade Union barons and six hundred thousand to the CLPs. They had sewn up the Trade Union votes in the back rooms so the CLPs did not matter that much...

One entered the conference on the opening day and the Militant groups were organised to the hilt. 'Down with Black Sections' was the slogan which hit you at the front of the door and pursued delegates straight to the entrance. They were armed with a pamphlet which argued the case against Black Sections. The cadres were all black and the argument was a simple one: 'Black Sections divide the working class'.

The campaign made its first intervention at a conference fringe meeting on Monday 1 October. Russell Profitt, Parliamentary hopeful for Lewisham East, chaired the meeting. Also on the platform was Keith Vaz, prospective candidate for the European Parliament from Richmond and Barnes; Nurendra Makanjee and Bernie Grant, Haringey Councillors; Sharon Atkins former Militant supporter; Jo Richardson NEC member and Dianne Abbott, Westminster Councillor... Of the blacks, the majority were Militant supporters hostile to the platform.

Profitt declared himself a Marxist, Grant wanted white people off his back, Vaz was charming, Richardson was for Black Sections and Abbott reiterated the argument that the party was taking the black vote for granted and the only way to secure that vote (80% of blacks and Asians who vote, vote Labour) was to have Black Sections which would draw black people into the Labour Party. What was noticeable though was the high moral tone of the black speakers.

The highlight of the second day of the Conference was Neil Kinnock's speech... He wanted, he said, power so that 'at the earliest possible time we want to pass and enforce laws to punish race and sex prejudice.' And that was that.

He had stated his position in the pre-conference manoeuvring, providing a sort of manifesto against Black sections. It would create significant problems of racial definition which could lead to endless unproductive acrimony. Secondly, it would be racially segregationist. It is around both these points that those against the idea of Black Sections mobilise.

The debate proper was scheduled for Wednesday afternoon at 3.30 PM...

Bernie Grant, Haringey councillor representing Tottenham CLP and now leader of Haringey council, moved the motion...

Leaders of the Trade Union battalions, who sat directly in front of the speaker's rostrum, sat stony faced. They weren't impressed.

He added that blacks were not a priority in the labour movement; that the conference did not debate Grenada, Angola or Mozambique even though these were preoccupations of blacks in Britain.

This did not impress them either.

Should conference adopt black sections then these matters could be debated.

Stony stare.

Grant persisted: 'we are saying we're being used'.

They did not bat an eyelid.

And so the stage was set...

The opposition was cheap and less impressive but they drew

blood. If conference voted for the motion then we would be sent back on 'our banana boats' shouted a rather coarse delegate from the Post Office Engineers.

Hattersley's poodle from Birmingham said that blacks were doing quite well in the Labour Party and integration was the way forward.

Great applause.

Then came the vote. On Composite 51 – 5,927,000 against 500,000 for. On composite 52 – 5,427,000 against and 41,000 for. The vote was bad, but much worse was the fact that the campaign had confidently calculated two hours before that they would receive 2 million votes…

13. Peter Mandelson and Roger Liddle, *The Blair Revolution: Can New Labour Deliver?* (London, Faber and Faber, 1996), pp.1, 17

[p.1] New Labour has set itself a bold task: to modernise Britain socially, economically and politically. In doing so it aims to build on Britain's strengths. Its mission is to create not to destroy. Its strategy is to move forward from where Margaret Thatcher left off, rather than to dismantle every single thing she did…

[p.17] New Labour believes that it is possible to combine a free market economy with social justice; liberty of the individual with wider opportunities for all; One Nation security with efficiency and competitiveness; rights with responsibilities, personal self-fulfilment with strengthening the family; effective government and decisive political leadership with a new constitutional settlement and a new relationship of trust between politicians and the people; a love of Britain with a recognition that Britain's future has to lie in Europe.

Notes

1. Peter Mandelson and Roger Liddle, *The Blair Revolution: Can New Labour Deliver?* (London, Faber and Faber, 1996), Chapter 1.
2. Anthony Heath, Roger Jewell, John Curtice and Bridget Taylor (eds), *Labour's Last Chance: The 1992 Election and Beyond* (Aldershot, Dartmouth, 1994).
3. *It's Time to Get Britain Working Again* (London, Labour Party, 1992), p.11.
4. Christine Collette, 'Questions of Gender', in Brian Brivati and Richard Heffernan (eds), *The Labour Party: A Centenary History* (London, Macmillan, 2000).
5. Pippa Norris and Joni Lovenduski, *Political Recruitment: Gender, Race*

and Class in the British Parliament (Cambridge, Cambridge University Press, 1995), p.102; Jill Hills, 'Britain' in Joni Lovenduski and Jill Hills, *The Politics of the Second Electorate: Women and Public Participation* (London, Routledge and Kegan Paul, 1981), p.20.

6. Sarah Perrigo, 'Women and Change and the Labour Party, 1979–1995', *Parliamentary Affairs*, 49.1 (1996), *passim*.

7. Sarah Perrigo, 'Socialist Feminism and the Labour Party: Some Experiences from Leeds', *Feminist Review, Special Issue: Socialist Feminism Out of the Blue*, 23 (Summer 1986), p.101.

8. Clare Short, 'Women and the Labour Party', *Parliamentary Affairs*, 49.1 (1996).

9. Darcus Howe, 'Labour Party Conference '84: Defeat for Black Sections', in *Darcus Howe on Black Sections in the Labour Party* (London, Race Today Publications, 1985), pp.6–10.

10. Giles Radice and Sidney Pollard, *More Southern Discomfort* (London, Fabian Society, 1993), p.16.

11. *Observer*, 30 April 1999.

12. *Guardian*, 18 and 23 May 1995.

13. Mandelson and Liddle, *The Blair Revolution*, pp.3–4.

14. *New Statesman*, 24 January 1997.

15. S Fielding, 'Labour's path to power', in Andrew Geddes and Jonathan Tonge (eds), *Labour's Landslide* (Manchester University Press, Manchester, 1997), p.26.

16. Sarah Childs, 'The New Labour Women MPs in the 1997 British Parliament: Issues of Recruitment and Representation', *Women's History Review*, 9.1 (2000), pp.55–6.

17. *Guardian*, 25 May 1999.

18. Andy McSmith, 'Knives out for New Labour's sycophants and spinners: Blairite guru turns on toadies', *Observer*, 23 May 1999.

19. Martin Bright and Anthony Barnett, 'Blunkett accused over jobs for cronies. Plumb post of lobbyist friends fuels controversy over New Labour appointment', *Observer*, 23 May 1999, deals with the appointment of a man who worked with David Blunkett as a researcher, and worked as a lobbyist with Westminster Strategy for two years before being made a special adviser, the 66th such appointment by the Labour government.

Chapter 5

The Social Democratic Party, the Liberals and the Liberal Democrats

Introduction

The political history of Britain in the first half of the twentieth century was dominated by the debate about the political decline of the Liberal Party and the usurping of its role by the Labour Party as the progressive party in British politics. The history of Liberal decline has led to intense debate. Less controversial, however, is the fact that since 1951 the smaller parties in British politics, including those associated with the rise of nationalism in Scotland and Wales (see Chapter 6), have won an increasing proportion of the vote at general elections. In 1951 the two major political parties, the Conservatives and Labour, secured 96.6 per cent of the general election vote; the Liberal vote falling from 9 per cent to 2.6 per cent between 1950 and 1951; and the other political parties secured insignificant percentages. Thereafter the smaller political parties began to re-emerge. In the 1983 general election, they received 28.2 per cent of the vote and the Liberals, with 26 per cent of that vote, were only 2 per cent behind the Labour Party. Since then the support for the minority parties has been a little less. Yet the fact is that the less important political parties in British politics have captured a significant proportion of the general election vote and that the Liberals/ Alliance/Liberal Democrats have, and are, making an increasingly important impact upon British politics. Indeed, James

122

Callaghan's government relied upon the Liberal Party support during the late 1970s (Document 1).

The Liberal Party and the Social Democratic Party, formed in 1981, separately and together, have been the major challenges to both the Labour and Conservative parties at their moments of political weakness. Nevertheless, even the most ardent of Liberal supporters, such as Chris Cook, have been prepared to write off the seriousness of the Liberal challenge. Indeed, Cook wrote in 1993 that

> Since 1945 the Liberal Party has always found it difficult to establish an identity sufficiently distinctive from that of the two major parties. Even when its revival began in the late fifties it was easy to argue that it was no more than a 'protest' party and as recently as the 1987 general election one of the commonest complaints of electors was that they did not know what the Alliance 'stood for'.[1]

At the same time, the Liberal Party, in it various guises, has often influenced the wider political debate, and the other major political parties, by championing issues such as devolution and regional government, freedom of information and equal pay for women. Also, in the 1997 and 2001 general elections the Liberal Democrats secured 46 and 52 seats, respectively, and its support is closing in on the faltering Conservative Party led by Iain Duncan Smith (Document 9). Whether it will ever again become one of the two major political parties is open to question but what is certain is that it has dramatically improved its political position in Parliament and in local government since the 1970s.

David Steel and Pacts, 1976–1981

In the immediate post-war years the Liberal Party was led, in succession, by Clement Davis (August 1945 to November 1956), Jo Grimond (November 1956 to January 1967) and Jeremy Thorpe (January 1967 to July 1976). Throughout this period, and despite the occasional rise in fortunes encouraged by parliamentary by-election victories such as that at Orpington in May 1962, the much-vaunted Liberal revival never occurred. Indeed, the resignation of Thorpe, as a result of the allegations that he and Norman Scott had had a homosexual relationship, left the Liberal Party in turmoil. To steady political nerves, Jo Grimond acted as a temporary chairman until David Steel was appointed as Liberal Leader in July 1976.

From the start, Steel advocated and practised the politics of cooperation. With Jim Callaghan's Labour government facing possible defeat on a motion of no-confidence put forward by the Conservatives on 23 March 1977, its majority having slipped away as a result of parliamentary by-election defeats and the formation of the Scottish Labour Party by two Labour MPs, Steel joined with Callaghan in producing a joint statement which would become the basis of the 'Lib-Lab Pact' (Document 1). As a result, a joint consultative committee was set up between the two parties, chaired by Michael Foot, and there were to be regular meetings between Callaghan and Steel and between the Chancellor of the Exchequer and the Liberal economic spokesmen. Issues such as devolution were now on the agenda and the government agreed to introduce a bill for direct elections to the European Parliament which would consider the possibility of these elections being based upon the principle of proportional representation advocated by the Liberals. As a result of this deal the motion of no-confidence against the Labour government was defeated by 322 to 288 votes.

Not all Liberals were happy with this arrangement with Labour and there was some disquiet in Liberal ranks when the proportional representation aspects of the European Assembly Elections Bill were defeated. Nevertheless, a special Liberal Assembly endorsed the pact by 1,727 votes to 520 on 21 January 1978. Yet the deal came to an end when the referenda on devolution for Scotland and Wales (see Chapter 6) became embarrassing fiascos. The Labour government was defeated in the House of Commons and called an election in May 1979, which returned Margaret Thatcher and the Conservatives to power. For their troubles, the Liberals found that their proportion of the vote fell and that they lost 3 of their 14 seats (Document 9). The Liberals had been optimistic, especially with the success of their candidate, David Alton, in a parliamentary by-election on 29 March 1979, shortly before the general election. However, this success was misleading. The Liberals went into the election with a manifesto, *The Real Fight is for Britain*, a mixture of tax and ecological reforms and demands for electoral reforms – including a Freedom of Information Bill, the creation of a Second Chamber to replace the House of Lords, a Bill of Rights and devolution for English regions in addition to Scotland and Wales. This manifesto failed to win the Liberals much success in the general election and they faced further humiliation in June 1979 when, in a low turnout of only 32 per cent, they did badly in the first direct elections to the European Economic Community, gaining no seats and only 13 per cent (1,691,000 votes) of the vote. The Conservatives won 60 seats, Labour 17 seats, and the Scottish Nationalist Party the remaining one seat.

The Formation of the Social Democratic Party in 1981 and the Alliance

The formation of a Conservative government in 1979 seemed to offer little prospect for the Liberal Party to make any significant political gains. However, conflict within the Labour Party raised the prospect of the realignment of British political life which Roy Jenkins, a rightwing member of the Labour Party, had advocated in his Dimbleby Lecture in November 1979.

As already indicated (see Chapter 4), the Labour Party was facing serious internal conflict as the Labour right reacted badly to Labour conference decisions. The decisions to withdraw from the European Economic Community and to support unilateral nuclear disarmament produced some discontent. However, it was the holding of a Special Labour Conference at Wembley in January 1981, to establish an electoral college for the election of future leaders with a strong weighting towards the trade unions that was the final straw for the Labour right. A week after that decision was taken, four leading members of the Labour right – Shirley Williams, David Owen, William Rodgers and Roy Jenkins, known as the 'Gang of Four' – moved towards the creation of a new political party, publishing the Limehouse Declaration announcing the formation of a Council for Social Democracy. Soon afterwards, on 2 March 1981, 12 Labour MPs resigned from the Labour Party and on 26 March 1981 the new Social Democratic Party (SDP) was launched with, eventually, 13 Labour MPs and one Conservative. This new party announced immediately its intention to negotiate electoral arrangements with the Liberal Party and a new Alliance was formed after lengthy negotiations between David Steel and Roy Jenkins (Documents 1 and 2). This was ratified by the Liberals at their Llandudno Conference in September 1981 and by the SDP at its first conference in Perth in October 1981.

The Liberal and Social Democratic Party Alliance, 1981–87

The Liberals and the SDP were soon working together. Even before the Liberal Party conference, the Liberals had issued a policy statement, *A Fresh Start for Britain*, which reiterated the usual commitment to proportional representation, support for a Freedom of Information Act, continued membership of the EEC, and devolution (Document 1). The Liberals also supported Roy Jenkins' parliamentary by-election campaign in Warrington on 16 July 1981, which saw him come second to the Labour candidate but within 1,700 votes of victory. Soon afterwards, the SDP swelled to 21 MPs as a result of further Labour defections, and the Liberals and SDP won two spectacular parliamentary by-elections in Conservative strongholds. On 22 October 1981, William Pitt won Croydon North-West and shortly afterwards Shirley Williams won the Crosby by-election in Merseyside. On 13 October, the Alliance leaders agreed that each party would field half the candidates in the seats they contested at the next general election, with regional discussions deciding the precise allocation of seats.

The Alliance was thriving in the first blush of youth, with local municipal successes at the side of parliamentary achievements, most particularly Roy Jenkins' parliamentary by-election success at Glasgow Hillhead on 25 March 1982. At that time, the political polls indicated that Labour and the Alliance each had 33 per cent support throughout the country and that the Conservatives were trailing in third place. Alan Beith was optimistic about the Alliance and its place in a future government (Document 1). However, soon after Argentina invaded the Falklands on 2 March 1982, the political mood of the nation changed in favour of patriotic support for the Conservative government whose popularity rose to 46 per cent a month after the recapture of Port Stanley.

Not surprisingly, the Alliance, as well as Labour, did badly in the general election of 9 June 1983, winning only 23 seats with 25.4 per cent of the vote; Labour winning 209 seats with 27.7 per cent of the vote and the Conservatives 397 with 42.4 per cent. For the Liberals there was some comfort in raising the number of their MPs to 18 but for the SDP this was a disaster, with only 5 of their 21 MPs retaining their seats, losing Williams and Rodgers in the process.

Despite defeat, the Alliance percentage of the vote was the highest that the Liberals had gained since the general election of 1923. The SDP was, however, disillusioned with its failures and Jenkins stood down as its leader in favour of David Owen. Although the obvious successor to Jenkins, Owen did not work easily with David Steel. They were contrasting personalities, Owen being rather authoritarian in style whilst Steel was more relaxed. Owen's desire to gain power meant that he would never regard himself as deputy leader in the Alliance.

This tension was not helped by the fact that the Alliance, whilst polling well, continued to miss out on parliamentary by-elections and Euro-elections throughout 1983 and 1984, despite some successes at the local elections at that time and in 1986. The only dramatic success in 1984 was the return of Michael Hancock, of the SDP, as MP for Portsmouth South. In 1985, the Brecon and Radnor parliamentary by-election resulted in another Alliance (Liberal) victory. In 1986 the Alliance won the Ryedale parliamentary by-election by 5,000 votes in a traditional Conservative constituency. However, such victories were few and far between and the Alliance never gained the political momentum it needed. In addition, the Alliance began to face internal difficulties.

At the Liberal conference at Eastbourne in 1986, the Liberal leadership pressed for greater European unity in defence. This raised the prospect of the creation of a third major nuclear power and was rejected by Michael Meadowcroft, who asserted that the Liberal Party conference should make its policy, not the SDP and David Owen, and that a non-nuclear policy should be pursued. This was narrowly supported by the conference, by 652 votes to 625. In order to heal the damage for the Alliance, David Steel held a meeting of the key Liberal figures in this debate at Ettrick Bridge on 19 October 1986, at which a compromise policy was agreed. It particularly played down the importance of the European nuclear policy advocated by David Owen. The Liberal Party Council met in Bristol in December 1986 and came to an accord with the SDP over defence, accepting the need for a minimal nuclear deterrence that could be removed in the process of global arms reductions and a freeze on Britain's nuclear capacity. There were other peripheral agreements on the need to withdraw from President Reagan's 'Star Wars' policy and the removal of battlefield nuclear weapons.

The final agreement sealed the link between the Liberals and the SDP but the patching up of the Alliance was only temporary. The momentum of politics began to move against the Alliance in the following few months. In particular, one of the architects of the Alliance, the Liberal MP David Penhaligon, was killed in a car crash on 22 December 1986. However, there was a brief recovery in the Alliance's fortunes in early 1987, when it launched its document *Partnership in Progress*, and with its victory in the Greenwich parliamentary by-election in February 1987, a traditional Labour seat. It also retained Penhaligon's Truro seat in March 1987 and won more than 400 seats in the 7 May municipal elections. However, the June 1987 general election brought the Alliance back to reality.

The Alliance produced its manifesto, *Britain United: The time has come*, on 18 May, its main proposal being the creation of a great Reform Charter to strengthen both local and national democracy, but with the usual demands for electoral reform, freedom of information and devolution. Yet the appeal of this manifesto was limited and the Alliance added only 3 seats to its existing 18, and all those were won by the Liberals. The Alliance percentage of the vote fell to 22.6 down on the 25.4 of 1983 (Document 9). Thirteen of the seats were in rural areas of Scotland and Wales and three in the West Country. The fact was that the Alliance was still a Celtic fringe party with little influence in the English industrial heartland.

The Merger, 1987–88

After the general election, Steel pressed for 'democratic fusion' between the Liberals and the SDP at the national level since many local organisations were already merging. Williams (now President of the SDP), Jenkins and Rodgers, favoured a merger but David Owen, the SDP leader, vehemently opposed such a move. However, the ballot of the SDP's 58,509 members, announced on 6 August, revealed that 25,897 (57.4 per cent) favoured merger whilst 19,228 (42.6 per cent) were opposed in a 77 per cent vote of the membership. As a result, Owen resigned as SDP leader on 6 August, and on 29 August he was replaced by Robert Maclennan.

The SDP's annual conference at Portsmouth, beginning on 30 August, supported an amendment to begin merger negotiations (Documents 2 and 4). David Owen responded by moving to create an independent SDP, presenting the vision, or, as most would say, illusion, that a fourth party could be successful in British politics (Document 2).

The Liberals responded with overwhelming support at their annual conference at Harrogate, beginning 14 September 1987. The merger debate of 17 September produced a vote of 998 to 21, with nine abstentions, in favour of the merger. As a result, the merger negotiations began on 29 September. In the meantime, Owen began his Campaign for Social Democracy in September 1987 and became leader of the non-merger (or Continuing) SDP until its demise in 1989, although some of its activities continued until May 1990 when, in the Bootle parliamentary by-election, the SDP candidate obtained fewer votes than the Monster Raving Loony Party candidate.

The negotiations between the Liberals and the pro-merger SDP continued until December 1987 in an atmosphere of controversy within the SDP negotiating team, which saw a joint document, *Voices and Choices*, rejected by the parliamentary Liberal Party. In the end, however, the draft constitution was produced on 18 December, proposing that the new party be called The New Liberal and Social Democratic Party, or Alliance for short, that there be a federal structure for England, Scotland, Wales and Ireland, that the party be committed to NATO, and that the party decisions would be made by a federal party conference which would be limited in what it could decide. The draft proposals were well greeted by the press, particularly the *Guardian* (Document 5) but were not so well received by some sections of the Liberal Party and the Liberal Council meeting in December was unhappy at some of the proposals, including the name of the party and a full and clear commitment to NATO.

Nevertheless, at 4.00am on 13 January 1988, Steel agreed to the policy proposals of the new party with Maclennan, in what had proved an extraordinary night of negotiations during which four of the eight Liberal negotiators resigned; Michael Meadowcroft resigned over the commitment to NATO whilst Tony Greaves, Rachel Pitchford and Andy Millson resigned over the name of the party. There was even more reaction when the Steel-Maclennan 'mini-manifesto' emerged with its proposal to end tax mortgage relief, to end universal child benefit, to extend VAT to food, fuel, children's clothing and newspapers, and with a pledge of support for the Trident nuclear missile. The astonished reaction included a letter from Des Wilson, a former party president, who felt that the proposals were 'politically inept'. By the end of that day, Steel had retreated and the Liberal National Executive agreed, by 19 to 11, that the merger talks would continue but without controversial policy decisions and upon the basis of the Alliance's general election manifesto of 1987, *Britain United*. A new negotiating team was set up to save the day and to produce an agreement by the time of the Blackpool Assembly, which was just ten days away. The events of 13 January 1988 had been a fiasco (Document 2) and the *Observer* reflected upon the failings of the two party leaders in the events that had transpired (Document 6).

It was, therefore, with some relief that a new deal was struck, on 18 January 1988, that avoided the controversial aspects of the old one and avoided the definite policy on defence of Trident which Maclennan had sought. Whilst generally approved by the Liberals and the SDP, the new deal was criticised by SDP members opposed to the merger who felt that Maclennan had caved in, and by David Owen whom Maclennan had visited in an attempt at reconciliation. Liberal opponents of the merger, the self-proclaimed 'Grand Coalition', declared their opposition, suspected the hidden intentions behind the merger, and promised to oppose it at the Liberal Assembly in Blackpool.

That Assembly, on 23 January 1988, settled the matter by giving the merger its overwhelming support by 2,099 votes to 385, with 23 abstentions. There was also a commitment to review the inclusion of NATO in the preamble to the constitution at the first conference of the new party. The Social and Liberal Democratic Party formally came into existence in March 1988, its name being changed to the Liberal Democrats after a ballot of members in October 1989.

A New Agenda for the Liberal Party: Paddy Ashdown and Charles Kennedy

The new party elected Paddy Ashdown as its leader on 28 July 1988, in place of the joint leadership of Steel and Maclennnan (Document 3). Ashdown inherited a small party of around 58,000 members whose fortunes did not look good when they received only 6 per cent of the vote in the European elections of June 1989, in fourth place behind the Green Party. Indeed, by that time Michael Meadowcroft had already led a splinter group, sometimes referred to as the 'Continuing' Liberal Party, which contested local elections in the 1990s.

Yet the tide appeared to turn in October 1990 when the Liberal Democrats won the Eastbourne parliamentary by-election and followed this up with a similar victory at Ribble Valley in March 1991. Although the Party did not do particularly well in the 1992 general election, achieving less than it had in the 1987 general election (Document 9), it was on the way to recovery from the damaging days of 1987 and 1988.

Ashdown began to impose his own character and interests on the party (Document 3). It emerged as a clearer, more decisive party. It continued to be determinedly pro-European, supporting the Conservative government in the House of Commons on the ratification debate on the Maastricht Treaty in 1993 (Document 7). The party did well in municipal elections and there was even talk of Labour and the Liberal Democrats working together in the event of a 'hung' parliament emerging from the 1997 general election. In the end (see Chapter 4) there was a landslide victory for Labour and Ashdown was not offered a seat in the Cabinet. However, he had established the pro-European, pro-international, community-based, pre-devolution, more centrist, economically-focused party that emerged in *Make the Difference*, its 1997 general election manifesto (Document 7). The Liberal Democrats won 46 seats on 1 May 1997, which was seen a triumph for the work which Ashdown had done.

In the wake of this success, in September 1997, referenda on reform brought devolution to Scotland and Wales based upon proportional representation. Indeed, the Scotland and Wales Acts were passed in 1998. There were also other developments encouraging the development of proportional representation. With such measurable success it was, perhaps, surprising that Paddy Ashdown announced his resignation as Liberal Democrat leader on 20 January 1999, with effect from the end of July 1999. In the meantime, having secured only two Members of the European Parliament (MEPs) and 17 per cent of the vote in 1994, the Liberal Democrats now secured ten MEPs on the basis of the new proportional representation system introduced for the European election in June 1999.

Ashdown went out on a high note and was replaced by the less flamboyant Charles Kennedy, who was considered something of a political lightweight. Nevertheless, Kennedy pursued the established policies of the Liberal Democrats in the 2001 general election and secured a further increase in parliamentary seats (Documents 8 and 9). Effectively, then, the Liberal Party, in its various forms, is as strong as it has ever been since the early 1930s. Whether it succeeds in the twenty-first century will probably depend upon Iain Duncan Smith and his ability to revive the flagging fortunes of the Conservatives, just as much as the Liberal Democrats themselves.

Documents

SECONDARY SOURCES AND INTERPRETATIONS

1. Alan Beith, *The Case for the Liberal Party & the Alliance* (London, Longman, 1983), pp.vii, 113, 115, 118, 150–1, 153–4

[p.vii] The Alliance has not changed the nature of Liberalism and the Liberal Party: it has simply made the prospect of a government in which the Liberal Party is a major partner a real one for the first time in fifty years.

[p.113] The possibility of an Alliance between the Liberal Party and the Social Democrats was already a matter of public discussion even before the formal creation of the SDP in March 1981, and opinion both before and after that date indicated that public support for an Alliance of the two was considerably greater than the sum of support given separately to each of the parties. It was obvious from consistent opinion polls giving the Alliance over 40 per cent support while the Labour and Conservative parties found themselves well below 30 per cent, that the concept of an Alliance could do something which the Liberal Party had not so far managed to do: it could break the credibility barrier imposed by the electoral system. Here was a combination of forces capable of winning the number of parliamentary seats necessary to form a government.

[p.115] Modern Social Democrats were rejecting the Labour Party because of its plunge into Marxism, its violent anti-Europeanism and its attempt to make MPs the creatures of small left-wing cliques in the constituencies. Liberals share their revulsion at these things, but it is worth remembering that Liberals had themselves consciously rejected the Labour Party in its earlier less extreme form on the grounds... of its commitment to centralised State power through nationalisation, its authoritarian style, its subservience to trade unions, its refusal to accept the mixed economy and its deep innate conservatism.

[p.118] The next General Election Campaign will be unlike any other in the last half century. In past elections the Liberal Party has had to fight constantly to assert that it should be treated by the media as an equal contender for the government of the country... In the next General Election there will be no doubt in anyone's mind that there are three alternative governments; equally, there is no doubt in the mind of anyone who has studied the British electoral system that it will be at its most unpredictable when it attempts to digest a three-way split in the voters' choice fairly evenly spread throughout the country. The next Parliament, therefore, will probably be unlike any other in post-war years.

[pp.150–1] THE LIB-LAB PACT (1977)

[Agreement between David Steel and James Callaghan, dated 23 March 1977] We agreed today the basis on which the Liberal Party would work with the government in pursuit of economic recovery.

We will set up a joint consultative Committee under the Chairmanship of the Leader of the House, which will meet regularly. The Committee will examine government policy and other issues, prior to coming before the House, and Liberal policy proposals.

[It then goes on to discuss meetings with the Chancellor of the Exchequer, the need for legislation for direct election to the European Assembly and other legislation, adding that] We agree that progress must be made on legislation for devolution, and to this end consultations will begin on the detailed memorandum submitted by the Liberal Party today. In any future debate on proportional representation for the devolved Assemblies there will be a free vote...

[p.154] A FRESH START FOR BRITAIN (1981) [regarding the alliance of the Liberals and the SDP]

Our parties stem from different traditions and have their own identities. We share a common concern about Britain's political and economic future. The politics of contrived antagonism have undermined public confidence in our parliamentary institutions. Our class-based party system, in which the Conservatives favour the board rooms while the Labour Party favours the trade unions, has deepened the divisions between our people. Social Democrats and Liberals alike seek a Government which will put the national interest ahead of vested interests. Our two parties have therefore come together to surmount the deepening crisis now facing our country and to create again a sense of common purpose.

[It then attacks the four deep-seated evils of intolerance, class divisions, centralisation and increasing international insularity] Economic recovery will demand tough decisions and a national commitment to success... A lasting prosperity also demands the conservation of resources and the protection of the environment. We need a more balanced economy which encourages enterprise and innovation in both the private and the public sectors; effective industrial partnership; and a spirit of co-operation, which alone can provide the background for an added strategy for incomes...

We are committed to continued membership of the European Community which should be reformed from within. We believe in the proper defence of Britain through membership of NATO. We pledge ourselves to work within the wider international community for multi-lateral disarmament and for a more equitable distribution of the world's resources.

2. Geoffrey Lee Williams and Alan Lee Williams, *Labour's Decline and the Social Democrats' Fall* (London, Macmillan, 1989), pp.112–114, 134, 146, 148, 153–5, 156–7

[pp.112–14] At nine o'clock in the morning, in the Connaught Rooms, on Thursday, 26 March 1981, the 'Gang of Four' assembled to formally launch the Social Democratic Party. The official breakaway from the Labour Party had been made and reconciliation in the future did not look likely...

During the first few months of its existence the SDP attracted an enormous amount of support. Within ten days the Social Democratic Party numbered 43,588 members. The response was extraordinary... When asked at an interview what kind of strategy was used to lure the supporters, Vice-President William Rodgers quickly responded, 'We were pushing at an open door.'

The growing composition of the party was representative of a progressive, metropolitan middle-class liberalism (with a small l). The membership of the SDP was overwhelmingly middle-class – academics, journalists, civil servants, scientists, teachers, doctors, lawyers – all joined in great numbers.

[The book then goes on to discuss the disappointment of the 1983 general election and the replacement of Roy Jenkins with David Owen as SDP leader. The joint Alliance leadership of David Steel and David Owen was not an easy one, as is evident from the point of view of Alan Watson, President of the Liberal Party, interviewed on 23 April 1985; p.134] 'Personally, I am very optimistic about the way things are going with the Alliance. I would like to see a merger of the two parties after the last [1983] election... But those prospects were thwarted by the resignation of Jenkins as SDP leader and the illness of Liberal leader David Steel during that time. The merger was impossible without those two personalities. The SDP have been taken over by David Owen who makes no bones about it – he wants the SDP to have a separate identity.'

Indeed, David Owen stood as the major obstacle in the way of combining the two parties. Owen strongly argued, as do many others, that such a development would be welcomed by the two old parties. He explained that they would find it 'far easier to narrow an Alliance down into a small centrist band of opinion, but far harder with a two-party alliance to weaken both the distinctive traditional Liberal appeal and the distinctive new Social Democratic appeal which we have built up since our foundation'...

[After dealing with the problems of the Alliance and the disappointment of the 1987 general election, the book goes on to examine the problems connected with the talks merger; p.146] The two Davids were clearly not comfortable with each other; both felt constrained by the other's presence. They therefore came across in television appearances as Tweedledum and Tweedledee, united only by the lowest common denominator. This damaged David Steel less because that was expected of a Liberal leader, but damaged David Owen more because he had built up an extraordinary reputation in a short time from a narrow political base, and was then the most significant political figure apart from the Prime Minister herself. Clear, incisive, aggressive and with little humour, he had a cutting edge which the electors warmed to. He had also had the advantage of being able to arouse seething anger from his former Labour colleagues, which helped to define his position in exactly the way that was required. This terrific advantage was thrown away by the two-leader approach. It minimalised the effect of both of them. The election campaign was dogged throughout with differences of opinion between David Owen and his campaign advisers, particularly on the Liberal side where his appeal to Conservative voters created a deal of distrust and scepticism...

[p.147] David Owen's consistency of purpose as well as his personal resolve were largely obscured during the campaign by David Steel's ill-judged preference for a possible deal with Labour if the electorate opted for the delights of a hung parliament. The Alliance in fact could not decide whether it wanted to achieve outright power or seek to hold the balance in the new parliament. However, neither David actually appeared to know which outcome his party expected or preferred.

[The Alliance campaign of 1987 was in disarray; p.148] Therefore, before the election campaign was over, David Steel had resolved to face this problem by working for an early merger of the two disparate parties.

This idea was not mistaken in principle: it was an event badly executed, however. It resulted in the personal negation of David Owen, who was the one politician capable of providing the merged party with the kind of co-ordination it might well require. The merger proposal also appeared as a device to eliminate David Owen as a national politician; some old scores were settled... David Steel also came to regard Owen as a threat to the realignment of the centre. His conviction grew that a merger between the two parties would resolve both issues by removing Owen and the SDP from contention...

[Paddy Ashdown spoke in favour of the merger, and David Steel declared his support on 14 June 1986; p.149] On Saturday, Roy Jenkins came out in favour of a merger, which was entirely in line with his long-held belief that this was inevitable and desirable. Then on the Monday, both Shirley Williams and Bill Rodgers came out in favour of the merger, too.

[The book then discusses the presentation of the idea to the National Committee, the organisation of a ballot and David Owen's reluctance to lead the SDP unless there was grassroots support for the merger. Ultimately, Owen resigned and Robert Maclennan became leader of the SDP; p.153] The ballot, which took place in March 1988, was what really amounts to a sad end to the high hopes of 1981, as far as the SDP was concerned, and marked the ostensible end of the Liberal Party, as it had been for the last century. The original SDP was dead: the new SLDP was about to emerge into a hostile world.

[p.154] Of the 100,000 Liberals, only 52 per cent voted at all in the ballot; 87.9 per cent voted in favour, 12.1 per cent voted against, and there were 126 abstentions. Of the 59,000 members of the SDP, 55 per cent voted; 65.3 per cent voted in favour, while 34 per cent voted against; there were 125 abstentions and 132 spoilt papers.

[p.156] The Sheffield Conference of the Council of Social Democracy which met on 30 January marked the end of the original SDP...

[pp.156–7] The result of the vote was conclusive for the pro-mergerites: 273 voted for the merger, 28 voted against and 49 abstained.

3. Chris Cook, *A Short History of the Liberal Party, 1900–1992* (London, Macmillan, 1993 edition), pp.202–3, 210

[p.202] From the formation of the new party in March 1988 until the election of Paddy Ashdown in July, the Democrats made a somewhat faltering start...

[p.203] Ashdown faced major problems of party morale, low membership and financial problems – as well as the continuing existence of the Social Democratic Party under Owen. This SDP had been relaunched in March 1988 under the leadership of David Owen and the presidency of John Cartwright.

Paddy Ashdown's first challenge – and his first opportunity to shape the party in his own image – came with the initial conference of the SDLP in September 1988. Ashdown announced his allocation of the key portfolios – including foreign affairs to David Steel and the important Treasury and Economy posts to Alan Beith. Home Affairs went to Robert Maclennan. The Conference formally adopted the short title Democrats (although it was to reverse this decision a year later, settling on Liberal Democrats after much debate and wrangling). Paddy Ashdown's first major conference speech set out the policy priorities he was to develop over the coming years – with emphasis upon fair voting, Scottish and Welsh parliaments, industrial democracy, freedom of information, high-quality education, proper housing and an effective health service.

[The book then goes on to discuss the problems of the Liberal Democrats and the failures in the third direct elections for Europe in June 1989. Thereafter, there were municipal successes and some improvement in opinion poll ratings that gave the party some hope for the general election of April 1992; p.210] Nationally, the party had polled nearly six million votes, taking 17.8 per cent of the vote (down 4.8 per cent from the 22.6 per cent achieved by the Alliance in 1987). Considering the dark days of 1988 and 1989, this was a reasonable achievement. Nationally, the swing from Liberal Democrat to Conservative was 2.09 per cent, from Liberal Democrat to Labour a rather more marked 4.15 per cent (reflecting, no doubt, the collapse of the old SDP vote in constituencies such as Stevenage or Norfolk North-West which had no Liberal tradition).

The greatest disappointment, however, was in terms of seats gained and lost. The final tally of 20 reflected 4 gains and 6 losses.

PRIMARY EVIDENCE AND INFORMATION

4. Social Democratic Party Conference at Portsmouth, 30–31 August 1987. Amendments of Charles Kennedy of 31 August 1987, cited in Chris Cook, *A Short History of the Liberal Party 1900–1992* (London, Macmillan, 1993 edition), p.190

(i) that the objective of the negotiations shall be to create a new party incorporating the SDP and the Liberal Party; (ii) that there shall be one democratically elected leader; (iii) that there shall be one common set of principles and a single democratically elected policy-making machinery; (iv) that there shall be a constitution for this party based upon one member one vote and a national committee to set up a negotiating team that represents the views of the members as expressed in the ballot, and requests the national committee to put the negotiated terms before the CSD [Council of Social Democracy] and before the members in a second membership ballot.

5. *Guardian*, 19 December 1987

... on balance, the new order represents a sizeable shift towards the sort of political realism which most voters seem to respect.

The new federal conference, the constitution ordains, will be supreme, speaking in the end with greater effective authority than a Liberal Assembly (which its leaders were at liberty to ignore if they wished) ever did. Unlike the old Liberal assemblies, which had no set composition, opening their doors to those who will be strictly representative, with delegates chosen by constituency parties to represent them over a two-year period. And the familiar impetuous pattern of Liberal policy-making, where something which was no more than a gleam in the eyes of a few enthusiasts was chosen to turn up at a Liberal 'commission' became by the end of the week a consensual and cherished Assembly commitment – that, absolutely rightly, has gone. The new party has picked up the SDP system of policy-making by slow, deliberate stages: green papers first, white paper next, and enshrinement of the policy only after protracted thrashing-out. But there are Liberal successes, and SDP concessions here too: most of all, perhaps, in the commitment to decentralisation both at federal and constituency levels. And the Liberals' old insistence on a prominent role for councillors is perpetuated here alongside the SDPs stress on special treatment for women...

There is bound to be nostalgia, in this new professional world, for those old freewheeling improvisatory Liberal Party occasions when almost anything might happen. Some may find it all a little earnest and drab. Few would put their names to the lot of it without reservations. The Alliance negotiators look, even so, to have done a solid, sensible job. The necessary planks are in place. There's a platform to mount and to begin, after too long a silence, addressing the world again.

6. *Observer*, 17 January 1988

If the Liberals and the Social Democrats do finally reach the altar, it will be despite – rather than because of – the efforts of the two men who originally appointed themselves the marriage-brokers. Neither Mr. David Steel nor Mr. Robert Maclennan can escape responsibility for having done their unconscious best to inhibit the banns over the past few days. Even in retrospect, their joint performances over the so-called 'leaders' document seems so bizarre as to be almost unbelievable.

7. *Make the Difference: The Liberal Democrat Manifesto 1997* (London, Liberal Democrats, 1997), pp.6, 9–11, 16–17, 22–3, 28–9, 34–5, 37, 40–1, 43, 44, 56–7

[p.6] 'The Liberal Democrats exist to build and safeguard a fair, free and open society in which we seek to balance the fundamental values of liberty, equality and community, and in which no one shall be enslaved by poverty, ignorance and conformity.'
[p.11] Our first priority is to:
Give children the best start by providing high quality early years education for every 3 and 4 year-old child whose parents want it.
[p.16] Which party will be best for my job and our firm?
Our aim: To end the cycle of boom and bust and equip Britain's economy to compete in the market-place.
The problem: Despite the current pre-election mini-boom, the fundamentals of Britain's economy are weak. We continue to be held back by instability in economic management, an underskilled labour force and chronic under-investment. Britain continues to consume too much and invest too little.

Our commitment: Liberal Democrats will lock in economic stability, encourage saving and promote enterprise. We will raise the quality of Britain's workforce through additional investment in education and training...

[p.17] Investing in enterprise

Small business enterprise and self-employment are the engines of a modern dynamic economy and a vital source of new jobs and growth.

[p.22] Which party is serious about making our environment cleaner and safer?

[p.23] Our priorities are to:

Cut taxes on things we want to encourage, like jobs, by taxing pollution instead. This will not mean more tax, it will mean taxing differently.

Build environmental objectives into every government policy...

[p.28] Which party will make me feel safe on the streets and secure in my home?

[p.29] Our priorities are to:

Put 3,000 more police officers on the beat.

Build more affordable and secure housing.

End, by the year 2000, the scandal of people being forced to sleep rough on the streets.

Revive Britain's sense of community.

[pp.34–5] Which party will care for the NHS and put my patients first?

[p.37] Our priorities are to:

Halt all finance driven closures for 6 months, pending an independent audit of needs and facilities.

Invest £200 million each year to recruit more staff for front-line patient care. This will be enough, for example, for 10,000 extra nurses or 5,000 extra doctors.

Cut hospital waiting lists to a maximum of 6 months over 3 years.

End the two-tier system in the NHS

Restore free eye and dental checks.

[pp.40–1] Which party will clean up the mess in our politics?

[p.43] Our priorities are to:

Restore trust between people and government, by ending secrecy and guaranteeing people's rights and freedoms.

Renew Britain's democracy, by creating a fair voting system, reforming Parliament and setting higher standards for politicians' conduct.

Give government back to the people, by decentralising power to the nations, regions and communities of the United Kingdom...
Renewing democracy
Britain's political institutions are outdated and unrepresentative.
We will:
Modernise the House of Commons. We will reduce the number of MPs by 200 (one third) and introduce tougher rules for their conduct, behaviour and outside sources of income. We will improve drafting and consultation on legislation, and strengthen MPs' ability to hold the government to account.
Create an effective and democratic upper house. We will, over two Parliaments, transform the House of Lords into a predominantly elected second chamber capable of representing the nations and the regions of the UK and of playing a key role in scrutinising European legislation.
Introduce a fair system of voting. We will introduce proportional representation for all elections, to put more power into the hands of the voters and make government more representative.
Make politics more stable. We will establish a fixed Parliamentary term of four years.
Clean up party funding. We will reform the way political parties are funded and limit the amount they can spend on national election campaigns. We will make each party publish its accounts and lists large donors.
[p.44] Giving government back to the people
Far too much power has been concentrated in Westminster and Whitehall Democratic government should be close to the ordinary people.
We will:
Introduce Home Rule for Scotland, with the creation of a Scottish Parliament elected by proportional representation, and able to raise and reduce income tax.
Introduce Home Rule for Wales, with the creation of a Welsh Senedd, elected by proportional representation and able to raise and reduce income tax.
Create the framework to make existing regional decision-making in England democratically accountable, and enable the establishment of elected regional assemblies, where there is demonstrated public demand. We will create a strategic authority for London.
Strengthen local government. We will establish a 'power of general competence', giving Councils wider scope for action. We will allow

local authorities to raise more of their funds locally, giving them greater discretion over spending and allow them, within strict limits, to go directly to the markets to raise finance for capital projects. We will, in the long-term, replace Council Tax with Local Income Tax, and replace the Uniform Business rate with a fairer system of business rates, raised through local Councils and set in accordance with local priorities.

[p.44] We will:

Establish a power-sharing executive for Northern Ireland, elected under a fair and proportional system of voting...

[p.56] Which party has the vision to build the kind of world I want to live in?

... Our commitment: Liberal democrats will ensure that Britain plays a leading role in shaping Europe, democratising its institutions and strengthening its role as a framework for prosperity, peace and security. Britain, with its world experience, expert armed forces and permanent membership of the UN Security Council, has a unique role to play in reforming international institutions for the next century.

[p.57] Our priorities are to:

Make the European Union (EU) work more effectively and democratise its institutions.

Widen Europe to include the new democracies of central and eastern Europe.

Create a strong framework for Britain's defence and security through NATO and European co-operation.

Give Britain a leading role in reforming and strengthening the UN and other international institutions.

Promote an enforceable framework for international law, human rights and the protection of the environment.

8. Shares of the vote for general elections in Great Britain: 1951–1997

Year	Conservatives	Labour	Lib Alliance/Lib Dem	Others
1951	47.8	48.8	2.6	0.3
1955	49.3	47.3	2.8	0.6
1959	48.8	44.6	6.0	0.6
1964	42.9	44.8	11.4	0.9
1966	41.4	48.9	8.6	1.1

1970	46.2	43.9	7.6	2.3
1974 (Feb)	38.8	38.0	19.8	3.4
1974 (Oct)	36.7	40.2	18.8	4.3
1979	44.9	37.8	14.1	3.2
1983	43.5	28.3	26.0	2.2
1987	43.3	31.5	23.1	2.1
1992	42.8	35.2	18.3	3.8
1997	30.7	43.2	16.8	8.3

Source: Various books and newspapers.

9. The Liberal vote at general elections: 1970–2001

Election	Candidates	MPs elected	Forfeited deposits	Total Vote
1970	332	6	184	2,117,638
1974 (Feb)	517	14	23	6,063,470
1974 (Oct)	619	13	125	5,346,800
1979	577	11	284	4,313,804
1983	633	23	11	7,781,764
1987	633	22	25	7,339,912
1992	632	20	11	5,999,384
1997	639	46	0	5,242,947
2001	639	52	0	4,820,000

Source: Various books and newspapers.

Note

[1] Chris Cook, *A Short History of the Liberal Party, 1900–1992* (London, Macmillan, 1993), p.214.

Chapter 6

The Rise of Nationalism in Scotland and Wales

Introduction

Following the long sway of an Anglocentric outlook (Documents 1 and 2), devolution became a major issue in British politics in the late 1970s. In both Scotland and Wales there were cultural, economic and political motives for the growing demands that an ever-present sense of national identity be expressed in constitutional change. These demands were both influenced by and assisted in the rise of nationalist parties, the Scottish National Party (SNP, formed 1934) and Plaid Cymru (formed 1924). This sense of nationalism, underlying the constitutional changes, meant that the latter were more than a territorial reorganisation of British government. However, the absence of a comprehensive written constitution enabled wide-ranging debate, which, as James Mitchell has commented, was informed by an unexpressed but shared sense of United Kingdom nationality. From this perspective, Scottish, Welsh and Irish nationalism were regional phenomena (Document 3). To an extent, the Conservative government's undermining of local and regional government within Britain from 1979 made some sort of territorial reorganisation inevitable. The fact that English Metropolitan Councils were dismantled while Scottish regions were left intact indicated some recognition that excessive centralisation might affect the equilibrium of British government. In addition, relationships with the European Community, and in particular access to European funding, pointed to the necessity of establishing some sort of regional authority within Britain. The exact nature of the change wrought by the eventual formation of the Scottish Parliament and Welsh Assembly remains open to different interpretations.

The Devolution Debate in Britain in 1979

The issue of Scottish and Welsh devolution came to prominence when the 1974 minority Labour government found itself reliant on the support of the pro-devolution Liberal Party and on the small nationalist parties, the SNP and Plaid Cymru. Labour's longstanding anti-devolution policy was reversed at a special conference held at Glasgow in August 1974; the major transport and heavy industry unions were in favour, as were half of constituency Labour parties, overcoming the resistance of the traditionalist Labour Party in Scotland. The nationalist parties' reward for maintaining Labour in office was thus a consultative document on devolution, wherein the lack of firm proposals indicated how far the government was from action. This was quickly followed by a white paper, *Democracy and Devolution: Proposals for Scotland and Wales*. The commitment to devolution was maintained following the general election of October 1974, when the SNP won a third of the Scottish vote and returned 11 MPs to the House of Commons. Plaid Cymru returned three MPs. In 1976, a Devolution Bill for Scotland and Wales was unsuccessfully introduced. The pact between the Labour Party and the Liberals enabled the safe passage of subsequent separate Scotland and Wales Bills, which received Royal Assent on 31 July 1978.

In all of these measures the proposal was to maintain power at Westminster. Directly-elected assemblies for both provinces were proposed, but while the Scottish Assembly was to have some powers over Scottish Office functions, Welsh Assembly powers were to be extremely limited. Thus the Acts failed to meet nationalist demands but were resisted by those who did not wish for constitutional change. Moreover, inspired by political necessity, rather than the outcome of engaged debate, the principles of the legislation were not clear; Scottish historian James Kellas described the Scotland Act as proposing 'a Gothic structure which few understood or liked'.[1] In addition, membership of the European Community was a political issue; in both Scotland and Wales there both relatively keen advocates compared to Britain in general. How to characterise the moves towards devolution was not clear; pro-evolutionists' links with the Labour Party indicated that the issue belonged on the left of British politics; by contrast, the Conservative and Unionist Party was named after its commitment to a United Kingdom. Tom Nairn, a leftwing historian, wrote of 'The Break-Up of Britain' as a 'detour on the road to revolution'.[2] Yet, on the one hand, the socialist ethos which informed the Labour Party had the international solidarity of working people as one of its fundamental principles, while on the other, Labour Party organisation was highly centralised. In addition, Labour had long relied on its Celtic fringe for its British majority. Labour opponents to devolution included future party leader Neil Kinnock.

An amendment to the legislation successfully moved by George Cunningham, a Scot who represented a London constituency, demanded referenda that indicated 40 per cent of all recorded voters in favour before implementation of devolution. When the referenda were held, on St David's Day, 1 March 1979, Scottish voters were in favour of the proposals but a 40 per cent vote was not achieved; while in Wales only a quarter of voters were in favour (Document 4).[3] The outcome of the referenda confirmed the fears of their opponents. The SNP withdrew its support from the Labour government and introduced a motion of no-confidence. The Conservatives supported the motion, which was carried by one vote, and the Labour government fell. The Conservatives won the 1979 general election and for Mrs Thatcher, a confirmed anti-devolutionist, the long period of power had begun. In July 1979, the Scotland and Wales Acts were repealed, although Mrs Thatcher offered all-party talks on future progress.

Scottish and Welsh Nationalism

Culture

Cultural nationalism was strong in Wales, with its distinct music and literary traditions and longstanding campaigns to promote the Welsh language. The 1967 Welsh Language Act had proclaimed that Welsh and English had equal validity in administration and jurisdiction within Wales and made government funding conditional on bilingualism. A 1978 white paper on broadcasting promised a Welsh-language television channel from 1982. Activists who successfully campaigned against delay in this provision included Gwynfor Evans, who threatened a hunger strike if broadcasting did not begin as planned. The maintenance of Welsh culture was promoted by the Adfer society. In Scotland also there was a strong, and often underestimated, cultural base to nationalism. Music and literature formed part of Scottish tradition. Gaelic was preserved in the Highlands and Islands; as with Wales, the nearer the proximity to England, the greater the loss of the indigenous language. Scotland had its own press and television channels. The BBC also established Radio Scotland and Radio Wales. Both Wales and Scotland celebrated their histories and historical myths 'replete with heroes and villains and stirring adventures'.[4] Rugby in Wales and football in Scotland also contributed to cultural nationalism. The Church of Wales and the Church of Scotland maintained a Protestant tradition. In Scotland both the Protestant and Roman Catholic churches propounded a heterosexual and patriarchal outlook, opposing divorce and homosexuality.[5]

While in Wales many of the campaigns to preserve a distinct identity, especially the language campaign, were consciously anti-English, it is generally recognised that a sense of 'Scottishness' coexisted with a sense of Britishness. A 1979 survey showed that 52 per cent of respondents identified as Scots, 35 per cent as British, 2 per cent as English, 1 per cent Irish and 10 per cent other/not known.[6] In Scotland, with its Protestant and Roman Catholic communities, the dual sense of nationality overrode sectarian differences. Scottish unionism took a variety of forms, generally in favour of a union in which Scotland retained its distinct identity, and did not follow the same road as did Ulster unionism.[7] The Thistle group articulated Scottish unionism from the 1970s. The interweaving of the different perceptions of community can be illustrated by football loyalties; while Celtic supporters were Irish/Catholic and Rangers Scottish/Protestant, in matches against England all Scots were united in their loyalties.[8]

In both Wales and Scotland there was a longstanding tradition of militant working-class community action, linked to, but distinct from, the labour movement in England, indicated by the use of the terms 'Red Clyde' and 'Red Rhondda'. While these class warriors had often been an inconvenience, they were regarded with some pride within the British labour movement as a whole. O'Neill wrote that: 'As in Scotland, [in Wales] the dominant political narrative was rooted in class, rather than territorial politics'.[9] Partly due to this tradition, the culture of Scotland and Wales remained class-conscious. Working-class communities were sustained in Scotland by the reliance on council housing; in the mid-1980s, '63% of Glaswegians, 57% of Dundonians and 48% of Aberdonians' were in council housing and in Scotland in general there was more overcrowding and more substandard housing than in England.[10] This meant that the culture of home-ownership, on which much of the attractions of the Conservative governments of the 1980s and 1990s rested, was not experienced by large Scottish cultural communities. Finally, writing in 1977, Nairn was of the opinion that Scottish nationalism was more solitary, while Wales was more internationalist, preserving a distinct culture which looked to European and global terms of reference.[11]

Economics

As the figures for public housing indicate, people living in Scotland had a greater reliance on the Welfare State than did their counterparts in England. This was increased by high unemployment in Scotland, a situation also pertaining in Wales (Document 5). Wales suffered from underdevelopment and over-reliance on the coal and steel industries. While the steel industry contracted in the 1970s, production in coalmines was hampered by a labour shortage. Losses in the coal industry were heavy, amounting to £46 million in deep-mining in the year 1979–80. By the end of the 1970s, Wales' economic base was becoming broader, although North and rural Wales lay outside this development.[12] It was this rural decline which societies such as Adfer wished to halt. The Mineworkers' strike of 1984/5 was motivated by an attempt to maintain the coal industry and when it failed, pits throughout Wales closed in quick succession (see Chapter 3). However, the 'Valleys' Initiative' to reconstruct South Wales in the aftermath of the decline of the coal and steel industries had some success. Wales had 5 per cent of the UK population, but 22 per cent of inward investment. Unemployment was reduced by half.[13] Plaid Cymru's 1974 slogan, 'Rich Wales or Poor Britain' had thus been refuted, but this was not the perception in Wales, given the hostilities aroused by the miners' strike.

In Scotland, there was the same tale of the decline of heavy industry and with it the patriarchal workplace culture to which it had given rise. As WW Knox wrote: 'The year of 1979... marked the beginning of the end for the male, skilled, industrial, Protestant worker in Scotland'.[14] The final blow was the closure of the Ravenscraig steel plant in 1992. The effects were complex; sectarian loyalties were diminished, while, as young, skilled workers moved south to England, the profile of communities in Scotland remained more densely working class than was usual in the UK. As elsewhere, however, women joined trade unions in greater numbers, often meeting with hostility (Document 6). Scotland also attracted inward investment, much of it from the USA, which meant that manufacturing was controlled by companies outside Scotland, unimpressed by the Red Clydeside tradition and determined against trade unionism. As in Wales, the more remote from England, the less likely communities were to experience the benefits of this inward investment. That Scottish economic interests benefited from membership of the UK state, 'a wellspring of Scottish social and economic well being since 1945',[15] no longer seemed necessarily to be true. Moreover, North Sea oil brought jobs and was a boost to the British economy as a whole, but was exploited in the British interest, not the Scottish. Edinburgh, meanwhile, remained the fourth financial centre of importance after London, Frankfurt and Paris. New methods of communication in all industries, including the financial sector, also meant that there was less to be gained by the UK connection: 'Scotland's renascent nationalism coincided with market and information revolutions which shattered structures and hierarchies'.[16]

In fact, public expenditure was 20 per cent higher per capita in Scotland than in England: 'The minority nations were bound to the United Kingdom by a formula guaranteeing fiscal largesse greater than was justified merely by democracy'.[17] Nevertheless, on the one hand, Scotland seemed to be offering up resources which entitled it to a greater return, while on the other, it suffered from a perception that it was subsidised by Britain. The reliance on the Welfare State necessitated by unemployment was portrayed by the British government, keen to cut welfare spending, as indicative of moral turpitude and immaturity. Yet the Welfare State was part of the British heritage, a proud part of that dual sense of nationhood articulated by many Scots. Continued attacks on the Welfare State thus came to be seen as attacks on Britishness and the corollary was a greater sense of Scottish nationalism. Moreover, the labour movement was under attack in England and more likely to demand than to offer assistance. Indeed, as heavy industry declined, Scots, Welsh and English workers competed for jobs. Both Wales and Scotland had their own Trades Union Congresses with which to mount their own defences.

Politics

The existing arrangements for governing Scotland and Wales consisted of the Scottish Office (established 1885) and Welsh Office

(1964) and the Scottish and Welsh Select Committees (1979). In addition, Scotland, by virtue of the 1707 Act of Union, had its own system of local government and education and its own legal system (Document 1). While the long English domination of Welsh government had been commonly held to inspire rebellion, Scotland's distinct institutions were cited as aids to Scottish nationalism: 'the persistence of a Scottish political identity can be explained by the symbiotic relationship between the extant Scottish institutions and a distinct culture'.[18] Both Scotland and Wales were over-represented, per head of population, at Westminster. Scottish MPs were also over-represented in Cabinet.[19] The Conservative governments of the 1980s and 1990s supported a reduction in this over-representation and also wished to contain the spending powers of the Scottish and Welsh Offices. In 1992 a new formula was developed to reduce Scottish expenditure.

Nationalist sentiment built slowly but steadily after 1979 (Document 7). In Scotland, MORI polls indicated that support for an assembly as part of Britain but with separate powers grew slightly, from 47 per cent to 48 per cent from 1979 to 1983, while support for full independence grew from 14 per cent to 23 per cent in the same period.[20] The pro-independence SNP (Document 8), whose career has been described as 'a chronicle of "waves" of support, followed by troughs of decline',[21] however, was paying the price for its contribution to introducing the Conservative government and had to be content with 11.8 per cent of the vote in the 1983 general election, winning two seats. The SNP was divided between those who put nationalism first and those who wished to proclaim socialism also; its rising stars included nationalists Alex Salmond and Margaret Ewing but also Jim Sillars, formerly South Ayrshire MP, who had resigned from the Labour Party to found the pro-independence Scottish Labour Party and then moved onto the SNP's socialist '79 group in 1980. This group was suspended from the SNP. These controversies marked the low point of SNP fortunes, which thereafter began to revive. In Wales, Plaid Cymru suffered a setback in 1979, losing one of its three MPs (Gwynfor Evans), but retained the two seats held by Dafydd Wigley and Daffyd Elis Thomas. Plaid Cymru argued for an authority directly elected by Welsh people and responsible to them, located in Wales.

If men in Scotland and Wales were aggrieved that government was remote, women were even less well represented. Scotland sent only 24 women, and Wales a mere seven, to Westminster from 1918 to 1997. There were no Welsh women MPs from 1970 to 1984 and one only from 1984 to 1994, with no Welsh women Members of the European Parliament. Scotland's women MEPS dropped from two to one in 1994.[22] Women fared rather better in local government. In both Scotland and Wales, nonetheless, there was a lively women's movement which contributed to UK movements such as the Greenham Common protest against nuclear weapons and the 1984/5 Mineworkers' strike (Document 6 and see Chapter 9). The Red Clydeside/Rhondda image applied as much to women as to men in the labour movement.

These feminist and class politics did not necessarily translate into membership of and activity within nationalist movements. Women's inclusion in nationalist movements and their struggle for full citizenship have continued to be controversial issues, women often being perceived as repositories of national culture and bearers of the nation's children, rather than its 'Bravehearts'. Women's participation in the Welsh language movement, as educators of the nation's children, fitted easily with such typification, but feminism, challenging gender stereotyping, was seen as an alien import undermining the nationalist impetus and the unity of the nationalist parties.[23] By contrast, in Scotland, Alice Brown is of the opinion that including women in the movement for constitutional reform was an important political process, contributing to the agenda and strength of the broad-based reform coalition on the one hand, while empowering women on the other.[24] A reforming group does not need to draw on a sense of identity in the same way as an independence movement and, moreover, implicitly accepts the pre-existence of a state – James Mitchell's unarticulated UK nationhood. Plaid Cymru had women's sections and debated equal opportunities, eventually overcoming both male resistance and that of more traditionalist women, as well as agreeing to reserve five seats for women on its executive council for a five-year period from 1991. Women protested at the end of this experiment, but Plaid's leadership had been won over to supporting gender equality. Laura McAllister, who has traced the history of women in Plaid Cymru, is of the opinion that the change was due to the desire to benefit Plaid's public image: 'Plaid had traditionally enjoyed adopting the halo of radicalism'.[25]

In Scotland, Harvie was of the opinion that the cultural and political devolution movements were fusing from 1984.[26] The Labour Party which, like the Conservatives, had been content to appoint its provincial officers from London, in opposition moved to the left and was more willing to countenance devolved government. Scottish Labour conferences grew ever more favourable towards devolution and began to argue for greater powers for a Scottish Assembly; for instance, in 1983 demands included tax-raising powers, which had formerly been rejected. The following year, the Scottish Labour Party conference declared that the Conservative Party, whose electoral performance had been very poor, had no mandate to govern in Scotland. The Labour claim had much justice. The gap between the Labour and Tory vote grew from 21 per cent in 1979, to 26 per cent in 1983 and 35 per cent in 1987.[27] By then, the Conservatives held only ten of 71 parliamentary seats in Scotland. A *Glasgow Herald* poll in September 1987 showed that while 32 per cent of respondents thought Mrs Thatcher was good at her job as Prime Minister for the UK, only nine per cent thought she was good at her job in relation to Scotland, while 82 per cent thought she was poor.

In 1987, Donald Dewar introduced a bill for a Scottish parliament, which, while it had no hope of success, indicated Labour's growing commitment to devolution. The Liberal Democrats gave consistent support to devolution. In the same year, the Abolition of Domestic Rates (Scotland) Act introduced the hated poll tax to Scotland and bills started to arrive in 1988. The SNP backed non-payment and Jim Sillars, back in the fold, won the Govan by-election for the SNP with an anti-poll tax campaign. By 1989, Neil Kinnock had been won over to devolution. John Smith, who followed him as leader of the Labour Party, worked for devolution until his untimely death in 1994.

A *Scotsman* poll in March 1989 reported that 27 per cent of respondents thought Mrs Thatcher was good at her job, 70 per cent that she was not good, 19 per cent that the government was good at its job and 70 per cent that it was not.[28] Mrs Thatcher's anti-European stance enhanced the view that the Conservatives were the party of English nationalism.[29] Kenyon Wright, General Secretary of the Scottish Council of Churches, wrote that: 'Repeated overrulings of Scotland's vast majority of Scottish MPs by almost total conservative dominance in the South of England left feelings of national disenfranchisement' and had no compunction in naming Mrs Thatcher 'The wicked witch of the south'.[30] In Wright's opinion, it was not political policies alone which Mrs Thatcher sought to impose but an ideology that was alien to Scottish culture. Scottish Conservative conferences became 'extraordinary affairs dominated by the descent from the sky of the leader, ringed by men with guns'.[31] As Mrs Thatcher's policies hardened, appointments to the Welsh and Scottish offices were less successful; the comment that she perceived electoral failure 'was accounted for by the lack of Thatcherite rigour in the Scottish Office rather than its surplus'[32] could equally be applied to both offices.

Indeed, in the succeeding Major administration, the same view seemed to prevail when John Redwood, as Secretary of State for Wales, notoriously refused to sign documents in Welsh; his appointment 'served only to emphasise the deep lacuna in empathy, the lack of common ground, between central government and the provincial establishment'.[33] However, the appointment of Michael Forsyth to the Scottish Office under John Major seemed to herald a change of attitude, illustrated by Forsyth's attendance at the *Braveheart* film premiere wearing a kilt and by the return of the Stone of Destiny to Scotland on St Andrew's Day, 1996. This symbolic gesture was too little, too late, and was perceived as 'putting a kilt' on Scottish Conservatism. The Conservatives won no Scottish seats in the 1997 general election. The long period of Conservative government had helped to build nationalist sentiment in Scotland and Wales, as the rise of the SNP and Plaid Cymru illustrated. Paradoxically, the end of Conservative rule brought in a Labour government committed not to provincial independence, but to devolution.

The Creation of the Scottish Parliament

The Constitutional Convention

The road to devolution in Scotland was much assisted by the formation of the broad-based campaign to which Alice Brown referred, which harked back to previous occasions when Scots challenged alien absolute monarchy (Document 14). The Campaign for a Scottish Assembly was founded in 1980 by Jim Boyack, a University of Strathclyde lecturer and Labour Party activist, and aimed to combine the energies of political parties, trade unions, religious and other groups. From 1984, it started a campaign to launch a Scottish Constitutional Convention. The Convention set up a steering group, which drew up a document important in building consensus and stating principles for devolution, 'A Claim of Right for Scotland'. This document denounced the poll tax and adopted the line of 'no taxation without representation'. A more succinct 'Claim of Right' was signed at the Convention's inaugural meeting, held on 31 March 1989 (Documents 14, 15) by all Liberal Democrat and all Labour MPs in Scottish constituencies, save for the Labour maverick Tam Dalyell. Despite attending preparatory meetings, the SNP boycotted the Convention, which it viewed as a pre-emptive compromise, but support was given by the Labour, Liberal Democrat, Green and Communist parties, local authorities, churches, women's groups and the Gaelic community societies, An Comunn Gaidhealach and Comunn Na Gaidhlig, and a Women's Issues group was chaired by Labour MP Maria Fyfe (Document 9). These included representation; while Conservative women were unlikely to overcome voters' resistance, women found it hard to get selected for covetable, winnable Labour seats. The Convention favoured an alternative voting system with an obligation for parties to achieve a gender balance when selecting candidates.

The 1992 election illustrated the vitality of Scottish politics. Jim Sillars lost the Govan seat in 1992, but the SNP had 12,000 members to Labour's 16,000 and made substantial inroads into Labour's working-class constituency: the SNP's vote was 52 per cent working class, compared to Labour's 62 per cent.[34]

Labour, while remaining in the Convention, started to develop its own policies. Outside the Convention, Scotland United, Common Cause and Democracy for Scotland were founded; members of the latter maintained a vigil outside the Parliament building until the Scottish Parliament finally met. James Mitchell is of the opinion that: 'The period after the 1992 election was marked by far more sophisticated and serious thinking about Scottish devolution than in the preceding thirteen years'.[35] A final Scottish Convention report on St Andrew's Day 1995 recommended an alternative voting system, that parties should achieve 40 per cent of women representatives in their first five years, and limited financial powers for a Scottish parliament. From the various groups, the Coalition for Scottish Democracy was formed, leading to a Scottish civic assembly, operating under a policy of equal gender representation.

The Referendum

The Labour Party committed itself in June 1996 to holding a referendum with two questions, whether Scotland should have its own parliament and if so, whether that parliament should have tax-raising powers. The referendum was a controversial and divisive issue, which 'caused considerable disquiet in Labour ranks in Scotland and fury among Liberals there', while Kenyon Wright wrote that on publication of the proposals: 'I seemed to be almost constantly on the telephone trying either to find a solution, or to pacify angry and bewildered members of the Convention'.[36] The 'Think Twice' campaign against the referendum was headed by Donald Findlay, a prominent Conservative barrister, but also a Rangers' supporter, which limited his ability to appeal to all groups: 'Ultimately, "Think Twice" became a Conservative campaign'.[37] The campaign for a 'double yes' vote was run by Scotland Forward. This organisation, although equally broad-based, was separate from the Convention. Most importantly for its success, the SNP joined Scotland Forward after the publication of a government white paper in July 1997. The white paper proposals failed to justify the SNP's change of heart: they differed from those of the Convention, by focusing on the powers to be retained at Westminster – foreign affairs and defence, social security, railways, media – rather than those to be devolved. This compounded the controversy over the referendum. It seemed that Labour had regarded the Convention merely as a talking-shop and intended, when in power, to follow its own road. In addition, the number of Scottish MPs at Westminster was to be reduced, a sop to those exercised by the 'West Lothian question' (that while English MPs would be excluded from deciding Scottish local issues, the absence of an English parliament meant that Scottish MPs could decide English local issues).

In November 1997, a consultative steering group on the Scottish Parliament was established, on which parties and pressure groups were represented and which included several panels of experts. This eventually (1999) produced a report, *Shaping Scotland* (Document 16). The Scotland Bill passed its second reading in January 1998. The referendum was held in September 1998 (Document 11). The Scottish press was broadly supportive. Donald Dewar headed the Labour Party campaign, supported by the SNP and the Scottish Forward coalition, and the 'double yes' was supported by a majority of three to one. The Scotland Act, including limited tax-variation powers, received Royal Assent in November 1999 (Document 11). Major areas of expenditure were expected to be education and health, but precise details on finance, the West Lothian question and Scotland's relationship with Europe were left to be sorted out later. As Mitchell wrote: 'Scottish devolution, like its Welsh counterpart, looks set to be "a process rather than an event"'.[39] In both Scotland and Wales, civil servants remained answerable to the UK civil service, contrary to the proposals in the 'Claim of Right'. In both also there was cabinet-style government and the precedence of the First Minister. Both parliaments greatly increased female representation: in addition, both provinces had returned more women representatives to Westminster, Labour Party reforms (see Chapter 4) having empowered the selection of women candidates in both Scotland and Wales (Document 17). In both cases, power was ultimately retained by the UK: 'sovereignty clearly does reside at Westminster. The definitive statement... is Clause 33 (Scotland Act), which allows the Secretary of State to rescind any proposed legislation deemed to be constitutionally improper'.[39] The subsequent elections were held on a mix of constituency and party-list representation, one MSP being returned for each constituency and seven from party lists for each European Parliament constituency. Exactly how this system would operate was also left to develop; studies have shown that there is some confusion in the public mind about whom to approach.[40] The Labour Party won the largest number of seats, the SNP enough to form a credible opposition, but both achieved less than their targets (Documents 12, 17). The Liberals came just behind the Conservatives and took power with Labour.

The Creation of the Welsh Assembly

While the Labour Party began to form its proposals for both provinces after losing the 1992 election, in Wales there was not as vigorous nor as lengthy and broad-based a campaign as in Scotland and less extensive measures for devolution were proposed. The Campaign for a Welsh Assembly had been formed in 1987, changing its name to the Parliament for Wales Campaign to indicate its demand for a transfer of legislative power. However, the 1994 Labour Party policy document *Shaping the Vision*, whose measures fell short of the campaign's goals, was endorsed by a special Labour Party conference held in 1997. Plaid Cymru continued to campaign for 'a radical programme based on social justice, environmental sustainability, an elected national parliament and a voice in Europe' (Document 18).

After the 1997 election, a bilingual white paper, *A Voice for Wales*, was produced. A similar constituency and list system as in Scotland was to return 60 members of a Welsh assembly, which would have a smaller budget and less power than the Scottish Parliament, being able to suggest and amend, but not to introduce, legislation. As in Scotland, the proposal to hold a referendum was controversial. In Laura McAllister's opinion, the pro-devolution campaign suffered from being presented as part of the Labour Party's overall modernisation package. This enabled the English community to voice its opposition, while tying in a 'yes' vote to problematic party-political and, in particular, personal support for Mr Blair. Moreover, support for reform was cross party.[41] The 'Yes for Wales' campaign, launched in February 1997, had some success in mobilising cross-party and pressure-group support, notably winning Plaid Cymru to its side: '[Plaid Cymru's] National Council... recommended that its members became actively involved in the non-party Yes for Wales campaign. This was tantamount to a temporary ceasefire'.[42] The opposition 'Just Say No' campaign, was Conservative dominated but did draw support from across the political spectrum. In addition, some Welsh Labour MPs objected to the proposals as inadequate or misguided.

The referendum was held on 18 September 1997. Fifty per cent of the electorate voted, and the majority in favour was a mere 0.6 per cent (559,419 for, 552,698 against).[43] Support for devolution was lowest in those areas nearest England, where, as shown above, cultural and economic motives for reform were weaker. However, these figures were 30 per cent higher than pro-devolutionists had obtained in 1979: 'despite a campaign characterised by public indecision and voter apathy, the referendum result signals a significant shift in the political mood of Wales'.[44]

The Government of Wales Act was passed in 1998. Labour Party plans for the Assembly were somewhat affected by the need to replace Welsh Secretary Ron Davies, forced to resign after an obscure but potentially damaging 'moment of madness'.[45] Assembly elections were held on 6 May 1999. Plaid Cymru's campaign for greater powers for the Assembly fell short of demanding full independence, but Plaid succeeded in capturing 17 seats to Labour's 28. Liberal Democrats, who campaigned for a Senedd with increased power, won six seats and the Conservatives nine. Twenty days later, the National Assembly opened in Cardiff: 'The historic domination of Labour in Wales was replaced, perhaps permanently, by a multi-party system. Plaid Cymru (the Party of Wales) emerged as a clear second party'.[46] Women were well represented (Document 17). A 'Twinning' arrangement, agreed at the 1998 Welsh Labour Party conference, provided that where constituencies were geographically close and had the same potential for success, one man and one woman candidate should stand for the Assembly. Plaid Cymru also, while not going as far as Labour, had made some efforts to ensure women candidates were among those returned.[47]

Conclusion: The Debate on Devolution and Nationalism from 1979

In neither Wales nor Scotland had devolution brought the independence the nationalists desired. In both cases, a system had been imposed by a UK government which retained sovereignty and perceived devolution as territorial reorganisation, part of its modernisation programme for the UK as a whole. The nationalists have, however, benefited from the events of the last 20 years. As devolution came on to the political agenda, so did nationalism. Plaid Cymru, in particular, has raised its profile to become the main opposition party in the Welsh Assembly. Nevertheless, while James Mitchell wrote with justice of the extensive debate amongst the politically conscious, the extent of public engagement with the issues is in doubt. Kenyon Wright wrote that:

> it has to be accepted that even in the run-up to the 1997 general election the Scottish public still did not fully understand in detail what the Convention is all about. If there has been one single failure it has been to get across to the majority of the Scottish people... that Scotland's parliament... would effect (sic) the quality of life of every man, women and child in our nation.[48]

Iain MacWhirter was even more forthright: 'The popular view of the Scottish Parliament is that it has been an embarrassing shambles: at best a waste of public money, at worst a translation of "cooncil" sleaze into national politics.'[49]

Beyond Scotland and Wales, the debate on devolution and nationalism has been muted. The argument made by the former Conservative leader, William Hague, that all Britons should have voted in the referendum on Welsh devolution, would have had some merit had devolution been part of a UK modernisation package. Plans for the territorial reorganisation of the UK have not been debated by the UK as a whole. The West Lothian question remains unanswered. So do the fears of many ethnic groups that territorial reorganisation, allied to cultural identity by nationalist sentiment, is a regressive step in a multicultural UK. Some people feel excluded and fear disenfranchisement. Candidates from ethnic minority groups were selected for the Scottish Parliament and Welsh Assembly, but rarely in winnable seats. Moreover, in Scotland, the gay, lesbian and bisexual communities have faced an intolerant campaign by those sections of the press which opposed the repeal of Section 28/2A of the 1988 Act, which made promotion of homosexuality to minors an offence. This issue was prominent in the first year of the Scottish Parliament. A Scottish election survey in 1999 found that a quarter of respondents thought homosexual relations were 'always wrong', a figure admittedly down five per cent from a 1992 survey.[50]

The debate on English nationalism is now following in the wake of devolution:

> So far as there has been a real collective sense of English identity, it has rested for two centuries on the tacit assumption that Britain was an English run concern. Devolution has dropped the English into a disorienting limbo. If the Jocks and Taffys of the patronising English imagination slide away from the Union, there is little left to form a focus for a specifically English identity, except perhaps sport.[51]

Campaigns have begun for English regional authorities; three have established constitutional conventions. In London, the election of Ken Livingstone, standing as an independent, for the office of Mayor, has underlined the renaissance of regional politics.

The impact on Wales and Scotland and on the UK in general remains unclear, given the oft-repeated statement that devolution is a process rather than an event (Document 13). In the 2001 general election this was illustrated by the decision of some nationalist members of the Welsh Assembly and Scottish Parliament, who also sat as Westminster MPs, to stand down from the House of Commons in order to concentrate on their provincial responsibilities. However, both Plaid Cymru and the SNP fielded candidates for Westminster and made party political broadcasts to the UK as a whole. Some commentators perceive the future organisation of the UK as a federation, with a multi-party system. Plaid Cymru's position in Wales, the importance of the SNP in Scotland and growth of the Scottish Socialist and Green parties indicate a potential 'link into electoral trends across the Western world, which herald the end of neat, two part politics and one-part dominance'.[52] O'Neill concludes:

> If the strains between centre and perimeter accumulate without effective redress, then the sort of reimagination of the United Kingdom that is underway in the ethnically diverse politics of Canada, Spain, Belgium, and even in Italy, might be the next stage in the retreat from the Union state.[53]

Documents

SECONDARY SOURCES AND INTERPRETATIONS

1. Michael O'Neill, 'Great Britain: From Dicey to Devolution', *Parliamentary Affairs*, 53 (1) (January 2000), p.69

Nation-building and democracy in Britain grew within a unitary state administratively and politically managed from the centre. The Union of the kingdoms of Scotland and England (1707), the formal annexation of Wales (in 1536) and the colonising of Ireland (a Union of Parliaments occurred in 1801) consolidated the union state. Political legitimacy was vested in institutions whose writ ran throughout the kingdom. Political power, fiscal control and legal supremacy remained with Parliament, underpinned by indivisible sovereignty, famously captured in Blackstone's pronouncement (1765) that 'what the parliament doth, no authority upon earth can undo'. These arrangements were embedded in an all-embracing national identity, with regional élites assimilated into a metropolitan political culture.

The classical discourse on the British constitution reflects the political task of managing a plural polity – not by means of the federal architecture preferred by political élites in more fractured politics, but rather by acknowledging constituent nationalities within the fabric of the union state. Among the Victorian eminencies who addressed this issue Acton recommended moral equivalence between those 'different nations (residing) under the same sovereignty', precluding 'the servility which flourishes under the shadow of a single authority, by balancing interests (and) multiplying associations'... More influential by far was Dicey's summary dismissal of cultural diversity as a basis for efficient governance because it undermined parliamentary sovereignty and deprived 'English' institutions 'of their strength, and their life; it weakens the Executive at home and lessens the power of the country to resist foreign attack'. This Anglo-centric outlook, betraying a self-regarding account of history, and of governance as centralised authority, set the standard for succeeding generations.

2. Michael Keating and Arthur Midwinter, *The Government of Scotland* (Edinburgh, Mainstream, 1983), p.14

It has been generally recognised that regional and cultural diversity and territorial politics are not simply relics of history or characteristics of new states but a prominent feature of industrial and post-industrial societies. The nationalist upsurge of the 1970s in Scotland might have left little in the way of constitutional change but it dramatically highlighted the continuing heterogeneity of UK politics and profoundly altered perceptions of the nature of the state. In fact, managing diversity has long been one of the tasks of British government but the fact that the UK is a unitary state with a single Parliament and Cabinet has often blinded observers to the diversity of political activity within it.

3. James Mitchell, 'Contemporary Unionism', in Catriona MM MacDonald (ed.), *Unionist Scotland 1800–1997* (Edinburgh, John Donald, 1998), pp.118–119

[T]here is not even a collective noun for citizens of the UK... The absence of a collective noun, however, should not be confused with the absence of a United Kingdom national identity. It may be confused and at times be described as British when 'UK-ish' is meant, but identification with the state and, more importantly, with the people constituting the state exists... In political discourse in the UK, nationalism is generally taken to refer to 'regional nationalisms' challenging the state, to Scottish, Welsh or Irish nationalisms. However, the absence of references in academic texts to UK nationalism does not mean that it is weak. If anything, this signals its strength. UK nationalism is taken for granted to such an extent that it is often seen as part of the natural order. Only in times when the state is threatened – usually from outside rather than from within – do we tend to see the term nationalism used with reference to the UK as a whole. In recent years, the UK state nationalism has become increasingly recognised in dealings with the European Union.

4. Kenneth O Morgan, *Rebirth of a Nation: Wales, 1880–1980*
(Oxford, Oxford University Press, University of Wales Press,
1981), p.405

While the Scots that day (1 March) did produce a narrow majority
in favour of a Scottish assembly (amongst those who actually voted),
in Wales the results were overwhelmingly negative. In all, only
243,048 voted in favour of the assembly (11.8 per cent of the total
electorate) while 956,330 (46.5 per cent of the electorate) voted
against. Every one of the eight counties in Wales voted strongly
'No'. The 'forty per cent' rule was thus irrelevant. In Gwynedd, with
a preponderantly Welsh-speaking population and two Plaid Cymru
MPs, the proportion of the electorate in favour of the assembly was
the highest in Wales at 21.8 per cent. But even here there was a
two-to-one majority against the assembly (37,363 to 71,157).
Gwynedd voters evidently feared domination by a socialist body
far away in Cardiff. Elsewhere in Wales the majorities against
devolution were increasingly massive, most of all in the anglicized
south-east where only 7.7 per cent of the electors in South
Glamorgan and 6.7 per cent in Gwent voted in favour. At one level,
the entire devolution affair was a massive miscalculation of Welsh
opinion by the government, especially of the views of Labour grassroots party workers and trade unionists: it put the government's
entire position at risk and seemed to make defeat at the next general
election highly probable. At a more profound historical level, the
devolution debate, tepid though it was, did serve to confirm both
the cultural divisions within Wales, and the political and economic
factors which made the Welsh highly reluctant to embrace anything
that remotely resembled any form of separatism. Even a body as
modest as the proposed Welsh assembly could be made to appear
as the first step down the slippery slope to self-government; the
Welsh were as resolute against this in 1979 as in 1896. However
powerful their sense of cultural and historical identity, the Welsh
were, in political and economic terms, strictly unionist. Welsh
devolution was promptly wiped off the political agenda.

There were some possible by-products that could be salvaged,
perhaps stronger collective powers for the county councils, perhaps
a Welsh Select Committee in the House of Commons, perhaps
greater powers for the Secretary of State. Even the Conservatives
proposed, during the referendum campaign, that the Welsh Office
might be given its own independent budget, much as the abortive

assembly would have been, negotiated directly with the Treasury and free from the parameters of departmental financial control. But these reforms were unlikely to prove spectacular. The basic fact remained that, for the first time in the twentieth century, the Welsh had been offered a real prospect of power being transferred from Whitehall to themselves; when given the choice, they had thrown it out with contumely. Arguments about more democracy, more open government, and national identity cut little ice. The great devolution debate ended not with any kind of bang but with the most anti-climactic of whimpers.

5. WW Knox, *Industrial Nation: Work, Culture and Society in Scotland, 1800 – Present* (Edinburgh, Edinburgh University Press, 1999), p.261

There is, of course, a regional dimension to consider. Someone of working age in Strathclyde in 1980 was twice as likely to be out of work as someone in Grampian. However, the contrast is even more marked if we examine unemployment by parliamentary constituency. Glasgow Provan had an unemployment rate of 35 per cent for males aged 16–69, while Gordon in Grampian only had 3.8 per cent of males in this age group out of work. Many of the unemployed had been out of work for more than six months; indeed, three out of five men claiming benefit in May 1983 were in this category. Once unemployment grew to these proportions the effect was multi-deprivational as people's lives became blunted and restricted on a whole series of different levels. A report by Strathclyde Social Work Department in 1980 graphically showed the impact the closure of Singers' Springburn factory had on welfare services in Glasgow. Closure saw unemployment increase by 27 per cent in the city, rent arrears by 21 per cent, clothing grants by the DHSS by 23 per cent, reports to children's hearings by 38 per cent, as well as significant increases in the rent and rebate awards.

Thus, low pay and unemployment, as well as the increasingly age dependent structure of the population, has led to a greater reliance on social security. Between 1979 and 1982 the numbers claiming Supplementary Benefit (SB) in Scotland increased from 450,000 to 770,000 or by nearly 70 per cent. By 1991 just over a quarter of Scottish households had a gross weekly income of less than £100 a week to live on. Much of the increase can be accounted for by the growing numbers of OAPs and single parents on SB. In 1991 OAPs accounted for 18 per cent of total population compared to 6 per cent in 1901; indeed, female pensioners now outnumber girls under the age of sixteen. Pensioners constitute one-third of those in poverty, or around 240,000 people. Family breakdown has also increased the number of single parent families since 1945; in 1960 there were only 2,000 divorces in Scotland, but thirty years later the number had increased to 12,400. Kay Carmichael estimated that, in the early 1980s, 31 per cent of single parent families were living below the poverty line, and 50 per cent of them were on SB.

The upshot of all this is that one in five people in Scotland are living in poverty and the low income of many Scots has had a significant impact on the type and quality of housing available and their health.

6. WW Knox, *Industrial Nation: Work, Culture and Society in Scotland, 1800 – Present*, pp.287–8.

Thus, the ethos of the Scottish labour movement remains deeply patriarchal and shifts in the occupational profile of the labour market have done little to alter this. The idea that a woman's place is in the home, although less compelling than formerly, is still a strong and pervasive one in Scottish society. This was demonstrated during the miners' strike of 1984 in which women were supposedly accorded an important role in maintaining solidarity. However, oral accounts of the strike suggest that involvement in the dispute beyond 'running bingo nights' and working in 'the soup kitchen' was all that was acceptable to the men. As two wives of Dysart miners put it:

> Some jist didnae want women around – they had the attitude that it was OK for us to be in the strike centre washing dishes and making meals – but let them do the 'men's work'... a lot of them were happy to see women involved, as long as the women were doing things the men's way and for the men's benefit. But as soon as we started wanting to do things for ourselves... they didnae really like that very much... They didnae like us doing things without their permission... men [were]... wanting the women to become involved as long as it wasn't their wives because it was going to rock the domestic boat.

By marginalizing women's issues and keeping them, even in disputes that involved whole communities, in a subordinate position, the male dominated trade unions in Scotland were able to keep the focus of industrial relations on the narrow concerns of craft and related industrial workers.

7. Gillian Peele, 'Parties, Pressure Groups and Parliament', in P Dunleavy, Andrew Gamble and Gillian Peele (eds), *Developments in British Politics 3* (London, Macmillan, 1991), pp.86–88

In Scotland the Scottish National Party experienced a resurgence of support. The loss of the devolution referendum in 1979 had taken the edge off SNP support for a period but the experience of Conservative government encouraged a revival of nationalism, albeit in slightly different form than prior to 1979. There were two main reasons for the emergence of a distinctively Scottish reaction to government policies. The first was that, although the government had a United Kingdom majority, it was a minority party in Scotland. This was so in 1979 and became increasingly so as a result of the 1983 and 1987 general elections when the Conservatives were reduced to ten MPs out of seventy-one.

The second factor which proved conducive to Scottish nationalism was the ideological character of government policies. The free market thrust of Conservative economic policy, the centralising trend of welfare policy and the reduced autonomy accorded to local government all took on an added dimension of insensitivity in a Scottish context.

All the opposition parties in Scotland sought to capitalise on the unpopularity of the Conservative Party. Leading figures in the Alliance parties such as David Steel and Robert Maclennan had Scottish constituencies and their emphasis on constitutional reform fitted well with Scottish demands for greater autonomy. But the real contest was between the Scottish Labour Party and the Scottish National Party.

Labour had become more sympathetic to the idea of devolution after 1979 but it had to be careful not to support any proposals which might deprive it of the seats needed for governing the United Kingdom as a whole. The SNP for its part had identified a theme which it felt might make the idea of Scottish independence less cataclysmic for voters – the idea of an independent Scotland within the European Community. However, some of the SNP policies which restricted land ownership to Scottish residents seemed difficult to reconcile with an increasingly international European Community.

In some ways the SNP had acquired a new generation of leaders and a new agenda. Apart from the leader – Gordon Wilson – there were several prominent figures, notably Jim Sillars, Margaret Ewing and Alex Salmond. The party programme emphasised investment and planning and an industrial strategy calculated to restore the infrastructure of Scotland.

8. Michael Keating and Arthur Midwinter, *The Government of Scotland* (Edinburgh, Mainstream, 1983), pp.66–68

[T]he SNP is a purely Scottish body. While this makes its structure and functioning easier to explain, its internal organisation is nevertheless quite complex. It is also variable as, in recent years, the SNP had rarely stood still for long. It has always been either expanding or contracting and this has affected its structure and the relative power of the various elements.

Like the Labour Party's but unlike the Conservatives', the SNP's constitution places the ultimate power in the hands of the members and is founded on democratic principles. The basic unit is the branch, formed where there are sufficient activists and centring on communities and groups of members rather than, as in the other parties, on electoral divisions. This reflects the SNP's origins as a 'movement' rather than simply an electoral machine and the lack, until recently, of significant numbers of elected representatives. There are also constituency parties made up of branch delegates and, although the emphasis in recent years on elections has enhanced their importance, the branch remains the centre of activities. Regional and district parties also exist but are important mainly at election time...

At national level, the Annual Conference, made up of constituency delegates, is the supreme body in policy and other matters. In particular, it elects the officers of the party. There is also a National Council which meets quarterly and is largely chosen from the branches. It is concerned with policy between annual conferences and, while the division of labour between Conference and Council is not clearly laid down, the latter is more of a working body, while Conference is an occasion for social gatherings and creating an impression in the mass media.

The National Executive Committee, elected by National Council, is responsible for the month-to-month running of the party and for the supervision of the full-time staff. An unusual feature of the SNP is that policy matters are not generally handled by the NEC but by a body known as the National Assembly, elected from constituents, which receives reports from specialised policy committees, considers them and passes them on to National Council or Conference.

The officers of the party are elected at Conference. There is a president and three vice-presidents whose positions are largely honorific and a chairman who is effectively the head of the party. A number of executive vice-chairmen are responsible for specific matters such as Policy or Administration. These offices have in recent years been hotly contested among the various factions and tendencies in the party.

In 1974, with the election of seven, then eleven SNP MPs to Westminster, it was necessary to choose a parliamentary leader but he has never attained the status of the leaders of the other parties. Indeed, the SNP is almost unique among modern parties in having no clearly identifiable leader. Nor does the parliamentary party have the special position which its equivalents enjoy in other parties. This is explicable in a number of ways. The SNP has never had a major commitment to Westminster and, of course, has never sought to attain power there. So the Scottish end of its activities will inevitably be of more importance. Because of the small number of seats held by the party, some of its major figures do not sit in Parliament. However, in terms of finance and organisation, the SNP is fairly centralised. Candidate selection is a matter for constituency parties but, as in the other parties, a list of approved candidates is kept nationally.

As a political party, the SNP is, of course, a channel of influence in the policy process. However, its primary commitment is to changing the political system itself and this is bound to affect the manner of its participation in day-to-day politics before its goal of independence is achieved. Some nationalist purists hold that no other issues should be allowed to distract attention from the fight for independence and that the party should take no line on social and economic questions. Others believe that independence can only be 'sold' by relating it to bread-and-butter concerns and that the SNP should involve itself in government wherever possible to show its fitness for office. The latter strategy was tried in the 1960s when the party made considerable advances in local government but in many cases SNP councillors showed themselves politically divided. In the 1970s, the emphasis was on parliamentary activity, with eleven seats won in 1974 and the long saga of Labour's devolution legislation. The failure of this led to a bitter debate in the party and the formation of the '79 group', committed to independence and socialism by breaking Labour's control in industrial Scotland...

If the SNP were to decide not to be a one-issue party but to become simply a 'Scottish party' representing the territorial interest in the way other parties represent class or ideological interests, this might force the Labour, Conservative and Alliance parties in Scotland to compete more on distinctively Scottish issues. In turn, this would create more of a Scottish input into the party-political process which, as we have seen, is now tied closely to UK patterns. By emphasising the independence issue, however, the SNP excludes itself from widespread participation in the existing political system which thus retains its 'UK' character.

9. Alice Brown, 'Women and Politics in Scotland', *Parliamentary Affairs*, 49 (1) (1996), pp.33–4

One of the groups set up by the Convention was the Women's Issues Group, chaired by the Labour MP, Maria Fyfe. The agreement to have a group looking specifically at women's representation in a Scottish parliament was a significant step forward. It was made possible because of pressure from women representing political parties, the trade union movement, and women's groups, together with the support of some men within the Convention.

It was at this early stage that other women activists in Scotland entered the debate and formed the Woman's Claim of Right Group. This comprised women from different political parties, but predominantly the Scottish Green Party, in addition to women who were not formally involved in party politics. They came together mainly in protest at the small number of women, some 10%, who had been nominated for membership of the newly established Scottish Constitutional Convention: 'Once again, major proposals and decisions affecting the life and well-being of Scottish people would be made with women being significantly under-represented.' The group monitored the work of the Convention and submitted a separate document to the Women's Issues Group, later publishing a book of the same title.

The Women's Issues Group invited submissions from women in Scotland, and the question of representation within a new Scottish parliament was discussed amongst women in political parties, trade unions, local government, women's organisations, community groups and the voluntary sector...

Women activists across the party divide and outside party politics became increasingly aware that women's representation was extremely low and that it compared unfavourably with most other European countries. They began to ask why. The possibility of a new Scottish parliament which was to be run on a radically different basis from the Westminster Parliament added impetus to demand for change and provided a common focus for political action...

The aim of gender balance and fair representation of others traditionally excluded from elected office thus became intertwined with plans to build a more democratic new parliament. In its first report, Towards Scotland's Parliament, in 1990 the Scottish Constitutional Convention committed itself to the principle of equal representation. It set up two new groups to undertake more detailed work on the Procedures and Preparations for Scottish Parliament and the Electoral System for Scottish Parliament. The group examining the electoral system had to take into account the need for gender balance and fair representation of ethnic minority groups. Although there was general agreement that something had to be done to ensure that the Scottish parliament did not repeat the Westminster pattern, there was no consensus on the policies needed to ensure gender balance. In particular, the two main parties within the Convention divided along ideological lines, the Scottish Labour Party favouring positive discrimination, which the Scottish Liberal Democrats opposed. The Scottish Labour Party adopted a proposal for 'active intervention', first put forward by the Scottish TUC's Women's Committee, that there should be a statutory imposition on the political parties to select a man and a woman for each of Scotland's 72 constituencies – the 50:50 option. For their part, the Liberal Democrats were totally opposed to any form of statutory restriction on the freedom of parties to select and voters to elect their members of parliament. Instead they proposed electoral change on the basis of 'STV-plus', arguing that under a list system and with other 'promotional' policies the representation of women would improve.

While women were involved directly in the Constitutional Convention as representatives from the political parties or other organisations, they were also actively engaged in the debate within Scottish civil society and in organising women's conferences and other events. Their aim was to widen the debate to include women in parties not involved in the objective of maintaining pressure on the main parties. There was a broad consensus within and outside the parties that women should be more equally represented within a new Scottish parliament.

10. James Mitchell, David Denver, Charles Pattie and Hugh Bodel, 'The 1997 Devolution Referendum in Scotland', *Parliamentary Affairs*, 51 (2) (April 1998), pp.178–9

The main campaigning was done at national level though varying levels of local activity took place across Scotland. There, the parties for a 'double yes' campaigned on their own, with less than a quarter of local Labour, Liberal Democrat and SNP parties joining forces with Scotland Forward and fewer still combining with another party. The effort put in by the parties locally was less than in a general election; indeed over half put in less effort than they would have done in local elections. On the 'double yes' side, the parties were most active, while Scotland Forward provided a useful clearing house through which decisions made could be relayed to others and some discussion of tactics could take place. The 'double yes' umbrella group lacked people to make much of an impact itself on the ground. On the 'double no' side, Think Twice and the Conservatives were almost indistinguishable.

Devolution supporters appeared more united than in 1979 but, perhaps most important, the context in 1997 was wholly different from 1979. The Conservatives had been in power for 18 years, during which time they had become increasingly unpopular. Support for constitutional change had become associated with anti-Tory sentiments. Labour's honeymoon, following the election in May, was a wholly different context from the aftermath of the 1978–79 'winter of discontent' which had formed the backdrop to the referendum in 1979.

The 1997 Referendum results (%)

	Votes cast	Electorate
Q1 Support a Scottish parliament?		
Yes	74.3	44.7
No	25.7	15.5
Q2 Support tax-raising powers?		
Yes	63.3	36.4
No	38.1	21.9

Turnout 60.2

Polling day saw almost all of the main Scottish daily newspapers urging their readers to vote for the Parliament and tax-varying powers. The *Daily Record*, Scotland's largest selling daily, had a picture of children on its front page with the headline VOTE FOR US. The *Sun* carried a large cross with the headline X MARKS THE SCOT. Even the *Daily Express*, long a staunch critic of devolution, came out in favour, with a photograph of a book entitled 'Scottish History, 1997' and with the headline A NEW CHAPTER. Only the *Daily Mail* and the *Dundee Courier* urged their readers to vote against. This marked another change from 1979.

Scotland voted overwhelmingly for a Parliament and decisively for tax-varying powers (see table above). Counts were held in each of the 32 local authority areas. There was a majority for devolution in each area and a majority for tax-varying powers in all but two, Orkney and Dumfries and Galloway. Those areas which were most in favour of devolution in 1979 were the most enthusiastic in 1997. There was no 40% rule in 1997: had there been it would have been overcome on the first question and support for tax-varying would not have been far short of overcoming it.

11. Robert Hazell and David Sinclair, 'The British Constitution in 1997–98: Labour's Constitutional Revolution', *Parliamentary Affairs*, 52 (2) (April 1999), pp.163–4

The major difference from the devolution legislation of the 1970s is that the Scotland Act 1998 does not specify the powers devolved to the Scottish Parliament. The 1978 Act had a schedule defining the powers of the new parliament in the smallest detail; and gave extensive powers to the Secretary of State to intervene. The 1998 Act is a far more confident and generous measure. Following the model of the Government of Ireland Act 1920, it simply lists the powers reserved to Westminster, with all the remainder devolved to Edinburgh. The reserved powers are limited to the constitution, foreign policy, defence and national security, immigration and nationality, macro-economic, monetary and fiscal policy, regulation of markets, employment and social security, and transport safety and regulation. In the new quasi-federal system which is emerging these are the matters reserved to the centre. Devolved to Scotland will be health, education and training, local government, social work and housing, economic development and transport, civil law, criminal law, police and prisons, the environment, agriculture, forestry and fishing, sport and the arts. These are very significant devolved powers: a sphere of legislative action comparable to that enjoyed by a state or province in a federal system. The only difference is that the Scottish Parliament cannot amend its own constitution as laid down in the Scottish Act: it will continue to operate under the umbrella of Westminster sovereignty.

The government's large majority, and the authority it had gained through the referendum endorsement, meant that the bill emerged largely unscathed from the legislative process: another big difference from the 1970s. But there were a number of areas where MPs and peers expressed concern, which may foreshadow difficulties in the future. One was over the future reduction in the size of the Parliament. It will start with 129 members: 73 constituency members, based on the existing Westminster constituencies, and 56 additional members from eight regional lists to ensure proportionality. But in recognition of Scotland's current over-representation at Westminster, the Scotland Act provides for the number of Scottish MPs to be revised in line with the electoral quota for England at the time of the next Parliamentary Boundary Commission review. This will mean a reduction from 72 to around 57 MPs. What has not been generally noticed is the knock-on reduction of 15 constituency MSPs and a parallel reduction in the additional members. As a consequence the Scottish Parliament is set to shrink at the end of its second term in 2007 from 129 to just over 100 members. Liberal Democrat amendments in the Lords sought to avert this consequence but were reversed in the Commons.

A second area of concern was the electoral system. Critics objected to the principle of the Additional Member System (largely because it involves creating two classes of MSPs) and to the details of the government's version. The choice of closed lists for the additional members drawn from the regional lists was particularly controversial. The government was also criticised for its failure to make provision, as many had hoped it would, for the Scottish Parliament to be composed of equal numbers of men and women.

The financial settlement was also criticised as inadequate and unsustainable. The government proposes to maintain the Barnett formula, a hangover from the last Labour government's attempt at devolution, to determine changes in annual spending in Scotland. The operation of the formula has resulted in public expenditure in Scotland being around 25% higher than public spending in England. As Scotland is now the third wealthiest region in Great Britain,

English MPs in particular suggested that this could be a flashpoint for future conflict. Scottish MPs sought guarantees to protect future levels of public spending and complained that were the UK government unilaterally to revise the Barnett formula, Scotland would have little redress because the Scottish Parliament would lack the power to summon UK Treasury ministers to explain their decision.

No devolution debate would be complete without Tam Dalyell, now MP for Linlithgow, raising the West Lothian Question. Simply put, the question asks why Scottish MPs at Westminster should have the right to vote on English matters when English MPs will no longer be able to vote on Scottish matters. Tam Dalyell himself announced that he would no longer vote on English issues once the new Parliament was up and running, although the question was generally a less prominent feature of debate than it had been in the 1970s. But at the wider level the West Lothian Question will not go away, because it is essentially a question about fairness: fairness in representation, in the distribution of public spending, in the sharing of political power. If in time the English regions feel that they are losing out because of Scotland's louder political voice and more generous levels of public spending, there will be strong pressures to redress the balance.

A final area of concern was representation in Europe. This is bound to be a difficult issue, as it is in other European countries with a federal or regional system of government. Europe will loom large for the Scottish Parliament because it is precisely in those areas where power has been devolved that so much legislation now comes from Brussels: in economic development, agriculture and fisheries, the environment, training and enterprise. The government held to the line that it is the UK not Scotland that is the member state of the EU, and although Scottish ministers may be invited along as part of the UK delegation (e.g. on fishing), the role of Scottish ministers and officials will be to advance the single UK negotiating line.

12. William L Miller, 'Modified Rapture All Round: The First Elections to the Scottish Parliament', *Government and Opposition*, 34 (3) (1999), pp.299–301

As election day approached it seemed certain that Labour would come out on top and the Scottish National Party (SNP) would come second. Thanks to the new German-style electoral system it also seemed certain that Labour could not win an overall majority in the new Scottish Parliament and that the Conservatives would get some parliamentary representation however low their vote. But each of the parties had hopes and ambitions as well as expectations. Labour hoped to get over 60 seats in the new parliament of 129, enough at least to have the option of forming a minority government. The SNP hoped to get well over 40 seats, enough to let it assume the undisputed role of the opposition, and to mark a further step along the road to independence. The Liberal Democrats hoped to be more than a small but useful coalition partner in the new parliament. Out in the country they hoped the new electoral system would end the traditional handicap of a Liberal Democrat vote being dismissed as a 'wasted vote' and so let their votes rise to equal their underlying level of popular support. 'Other' parties and candidates hoped that the new electoral system and the new inclusive politics would somehow include them.

In the event it was modified rapture all round. Labour came top but with fewer seats – and far fewer votes – than it had hoped. The SNP got what its leader Alex Salmond still claimed was the basis for a 'strong opposition', but less than its minimum target of 40 seats. It won only one more constituency than in the 1997 British general election. The increased number of seats owed almost everything to the mechanics of the new electoral system. The SNP got fewer votes than at the British general election of October 1974. In terms of votes it had made no progress in a quarter of a century. Indeed, it had slipped back. The Liberal Democrats got enough seats to make them a useful coalition partner, and Labour's poor result made them a necessary one. But they came fourth, behind the Conservatives, and their party-list vote was lower even than their constituency vote. The new electoral system cruelly exposed their lack of underlying support and the disproportionality of their grasp on power. The Conservatives showed some signs of life, which was an achievement that should not be undervalued in the late 1990s, and got into third place in parliament. But they failed to win a single constituency seat and they got even fewer votes than in the disaster of 1997 when they lost all of the Scottish seats at Westminster.

'Other' parties and candidates also enjoyed a bitter-sweet mixture of success and failure. Collectively they won over 11 per cent of the party-list vote and three seats in parliament – one Green, plus Tommy Sheridan and Dennis Canavan. But their collective success masked many individual failures. Canon Kenyon Wright, the former Chair of the Constitutional Convention and principal architect of the devolution plan, was ignored by the public and won less than one per cent of the vote when he stood as an independent in West Scotland. The much-publicised Highlands and Islands Alliance with its radical plans for 'job-sharing' MSPs (Members of the Scottish Parliament), won only one per cent of the region's vote and got no parliamentary jobs to share. Arthur Scargill's Socialist Labour Party beat Tommy Sheridan's Scottish Socialist Party (SSP) in votes but won no seats. Dennis Canavan, Labour MP for Falkirk West, was not selected as his party's candidate for the Scottish Parliament. He stood anyway and scored a spectacular personal victory over the official Labour candidate. But that automatically expelled him from the party and his victory speech degenerated into a pathetic – and so far disregarded – plea to be readmitted. Since the election he has offered to postpone the threatened by-election for his Westminster seat in the hopes of doing a deal with Labour.

For the pollsters too, it was a mixture of success and failure. Their final polls correctly forecast that Labour would come out on top...

Even the electorate seems to have had mixed feelings. Turnout was lower than at the 1997 Devolution Referendum, midway between the levels typical for Scottish voting in British general elections and local council elections, perhaps a little closer to the latter. Canon Kenyon Wright described the voters as 'bored, cynical, and disillusioned'. Hopes had been raised for a new kind of democracy in a devolved Scotland but 'all the evidence from the way the parties have behaved has shown that they are not getting it'. No doubt that expressed a very personal view after his own defeat, but the sharp decline in turnout since the 1997 election for the British parliament implied that excitement over 'Scotland's first parliament in 300 years' did not extend far beyond the ranks of politicians and journalists.

13. Gerry Hassan and Chris Warhurst, 'A New Politics?', in Gerry Hassan and Chris Warhurst (eds), *The New Scottish Politics: The First Year of the Scottish Parliament and Beyond* (London, The Stationery Office, 2000), p.1

The institutions of the British state have been defined by their conservatism and their slow, evolutionary adapting to the times. By British standards then a constitutional revolution has occurred in the last few years which has radically changed and re-engineered the institutions of the British state. Within two years of a Labour government coming to power at a UK level, a Scottish parliament and Welsh Assembly were established, the process of real devolution to Northern Ireland begun and progress made on reform of regional and city representative assemblies in England. Moreover, devolution has taken on a life of its own. In Scotland, the Cubie Committee recommendations distinguished student funding from that of England and Wales – much to the consternation of the Department for Education and Employment: in Wales, Rhodri Morgan is now established as First Secretary, while in the London mayoral elections Ken Livingstone stood and won as an independent – both despite the blocking attempts of Downing Street.

PRIMARY EVIDENCE AND INFORMATION

14. Kenyon Wright, *The People Say Yes: The Making of Scotland's Parliament* (Argyll, Argyll Publishing, 1997), p.14

[Kenyon Wright, General Secretary of the Scottish Churches Council, was Chair of the Convention's Executive Committee.]

At the first meeting of the Convention in March 1989 in the historic setting of the General Assembly Hall of the Church of Scotland, I made that statement which was so widely reported as a gesture of defiance against the absolutism of the British State – "We say yes and we are the people". At the time I may not have been able to see where it was going to lead, but I did sense even then that it was the beginning of something significant that would change the face of Scotland and the United Kingdom for good.

In those uplifting moments, just before the Convention members lined up to sign that solemn *Claim of Right*, I remember... feelings that I have not dared to speak of publicly until now.

I had a strange sense that I was surrounded, not just by the many hundreds present in the Assembly Hall, but by a 'cloud of witnesses' from the past. On the one side I felt the guardian presence of those Scots who in the 1320 Declaration... told the King... that he ruled 'subject to the consent of the realm' and who pledged their lives 'not for honour, glory or riches but for freedom alone'.

I felt the presence of those who in the Claim of Right of 1698 had deposed the King for abusing his power and those who in 1842 had walked out of the General Assembly of the Church of Scotland in defiance of Westminster's right to impose patronage on Scotland.

15. Kenyon Wright, *The People Say Yes: The Making of Scotland's Parliament*, pp.52–3

The Claim of Right which was signed by all members of the Convention present and is held by the Constitutional Convention as guardians, reads:

'We, gathered as a Scottish Constitutional Convention, do hereby acknowledge the sovereign right of the Scottish people to determine the form of government best suited to their needs and do hereby declare and pledge that in all our actions and deliberations their interests shall be paramount.'

16. http://www.scottish.parliament.uk/welcoming_you/ff3.htm: The Scottish Parliament. Factfile 3

The working practices of the Parliament were devised through extensive discussion. An all-party Consultative Steering Group was set up in November 1997, under Henry McLeish, the then Scottish Devolution Minister. It conducted a wide public consultation exercise and commissioned expert evidence as well as holding meetings. A report, *Shaping Scotland's Parliament*, published in January 1999, contained the results of this process.

This report included comprehensive proposals for the working of the new Parliament. Four key principles were identified:

* Sharing the power: the Scottish Parliament should embody and reflect the sharing of power between the people of Scotland, the legislators and the Scottish Executive;
* Accountability: the Scottish Executive should be accountable to the Scottish Parliament and the Parliament and Executive should be accountable to the people of Scotland;
* Access and participation: the Scottish Parliament should be accessible, open, responsive and develop procedures which make possible a participative approach to the development, consideration and scrutiny of policy and legislation; and
* Equal opportunities: the Scottish Parliament in its operation and its appointments should recognise the need to promote equal opportunities for all.

17. Equal Opportunities Commission, *Facts about Men and Women in Scotland and Facts About Men and Women in Wales* (Manchester, EOC, 1999)

Members of The Scottish Parliament, 1999

Political Party	Women No of MSPs	% of MSPs in party	Men No of MSPs	% of MSPs in party
Conservative	3	17	15	83
Labour	28	50	28	50
Liberal Democrats	2	12	15	88
SNP	15	43	20	57
Other parties	0	0	3	100
All Parties	49	38	80	62

(Source: *Vacher's Parliamentary Companion*, June 1999)

Members of Parliament, 1999
Scotland Constituencies

Political Party	Women No of MPs	% of MPs in party	Men No of MPs	% of MPs in party
Labour	9	16	47	84
Liberal Democrats	1	10	9	90
SNP	2	33	4	67
All Parties	12	17	60	83

(Source: *Vacher's Parliamentary Companion*, March 1999)

Members of the National Assembly for Wales, 1999

Political Party	Women No of MWAs	% of MWAs in party	Men No of MWAs	% of MWAs in party
Conservative	0	0	9	100
Labour	15	54	13	46
Liberal Democrats	3	50	3	50
Plaid Cymru	6	35	11	65
All Parties	24	40	36	60

(Source: *Western Mail*, 10 May 1999)

Members of Parliament, 1999
Wales Constituencies

Political Party	Women		Men	
	No of MPs	% of MPs in party	No of MPs	% of MPs in party
Labour	4	12	30	88
Liberal Democrats	0	0	2	100
Plaid Cymru	0	0	4	100
All Parties	4	10	36	90

(Source: *Vacher's Parliamentary Companion*, March 1999)

18. Dafydd Wigley, 'Foreword', *The Best for Wales*, Plaid Cymru's programme for the New Millennium (Cardiff, Plaid Cymru, 1997)

This Election is the first in a new political era. The parties have changed and the options before the Welsh electors are different to those which have dominated our politics for over half a century. After 18 years of government the Tory party is split from top to bottom and looks like disintegrating. The Labour Party, as we have known it, has come to an end; New Labour has taken over with new faces, new policies and new principles – all geared to the politics of south-east England. The Liberal Democrats have thrown in their hand with Labour as far as Wales is concerned. So Plaid Cymru remains the only party which offers Wales a radical programme based on social justice, environmental sustainability, an elected national parliament and a voice in Europe. This manifesto defines these policies.

The constitutional future of Wales and Scotland is now a major issue. Little wonder: Wales is sick to death of rejecting selfish Tory values, election after election, yet still being forced to suffer right-wing policies imposed upon us by virtue of the Tory's London-veto. For it is not Wales which determines the policies that are administered by the Welsh Office and by the plethora of quangos which govern our country. Their remit is decided by London, and they are answerable to a Tory MP from Yorkshire who masquerades as a Secretary of State.

We need an elected Parliament in order to ensure policies implemented on the all-Wales level which corresponds to the needs of Wales, not London. We need priorities established in line with the values of the Welsh people. Simply, we need democracy.

Such an elected Welsh Parliament would take over full responsibility for education, housing, health care, jobs, agriculture, transport and environmental policy in Wales. We could then determine for ourselves what should be public policy in these areas, instead of having them thrust upon us by Tories in London. This Manifesto highlights the precise policies Plaid Cymru wants implemented in these and in other policy areas.

But in order to make a difference, a Welsh Parliament must have adequate powers. It must be able to make laws in these matters, laws appropriate to securing a socially just community in Wales. It must have adequate resources – the taxes raised in Wales must be channelled through a Welsh Treasury Department for this purpose. And it must be allowed to develop its own direct link with the European Union, where so many decisions are taken today which affect the vital interests of Welsh industry and agriculture.

Notes

1. James G Kellas, *The Scottish Political System* (Cambridge, Cambridge University Press, 3rd edition, 1984) p.154.
2. Tom Nairn, *The Break Up of Britain: Crisis and Neo-Nationalism* (London, NLB, 1977), p.90.
3. See http://www.llgc.org.uk/ymgyrchu/Datganoli/Referendum.
4. Arthur Midwinter, Michael Keating and James Mitchell, *Politics and Public Policy in Scotland* (London, Macmillan, 1991), p.5. Refers to Scotland only but may be applied to Wales.
5. Michael Keating and Arthur Midwinter, *The Government of Scotland* (Edinburgh, Mainstream Publishing, 1983), p.7.
6. Kellas, *The Scottish Political System*, p.124.
7. Catriona MM MacDonald, *Unionist Scotland, 1800–1997* (Edinburgh, John Donald, 1998), introduction, p.5. Events in Ireland did, however, have some impact; for instance, Scottish Conservatives lost votes after the implementation of the 1987 Anglo-Irish Agreement.
8. Kellas, *The Scottish Political System*, p.124.
9. Michael O'Neill, 'Great Britain: From Dicey to Devolution', *Parliamentary Affairs*, 53 (1) (January 2000), p.71.
10. WW Knox, *Industrial Nation: Work, Culture and Society in Scotland, 1800–Present* (Edinburgh, Edinburgh University Press, 1999), p.262.
11. Nairn, *Break Up of Britain*, p.158.
12. Kenneth O Morgan, *Rebirth of a Nation: Wales, 1880–1918* (Oxford, Oxford University Press, University of Wales Press, 1981).

13. Andrew Gamble, 'Territorial Politics', in Patrick Dunleavy, Andrew Gamble, Ian Holliday and Gillian Peele (eds), *Developments in British Politics 4* (London, Macmillan, 1993), p.83.

14. Knox, *Industrial Nation*, pp.252–269.

15. Richard Findlay, 'Unionism and the Dependency Culture: Politics and State Intervention in Scotland, 1918–1997', in Catriona MM MacDonald, *Unionist Scotland, 1800–1997* (Edinburgh, John Donald, 1998), p.113.

16. Christopher Harvie, *Scotland and Nationalism: Scottish Society and Politics, 1707 to the Present* (London, Routledge, 3rd edition 1998), p.221.

17. O'Neill, 'Great Britain: From Dicey to Devolution', p.70.

18. Midwinter, Keating and Mitchell, *Politics and Public Policy in Scotland*, p.4.

19. Harvie, *Scotland and Nationalism*, p.189. There were five Scots in John Major's 1993 Cabinet and one third of the members of Labour's 1997 Cabinet were Scots.

20. Kellas, *The Scottish Political System*, p.150.

21. *Ibid.*, p.128.

22. Alice Brown, 'Women and Politics in Scotland', *Parliamentary Affairs*, 49 (1) (January 1996), pp.27, 77; Laura McAllister, 'Gender, Nation and Party: An Uneasy Alliance for Wales', *Women's History Review* 10 (1) (2000), pp.53, 57.

23. See Chapter 9 for the debate on women's citizenship; McAllister, 'Gender, Nation and Party', pp.64–6.

24. Brown, 'Women and Politics in Scotland', p.26.

25. McAllister, Gender, Nation and Party', p.59 and *passim* for details of women in Plaid Cymru.

26. Harvie, *Scotland and Nationalism*, p.243.

27. Midwinter, Keating and Mitchell, *Politics and Public Policy in Scotland*, p.39.

28. *Ibid.*, p.209.

29. Knox, *Industrial Nation*, p.297.

30. Kenyon Wright, *The People Say Yes: The Making of Scotland's Parliament* (Argyll, Argyll Publishing, 1997), pp.39, 139.

31. Harvie, *Scotland and Nationalism*, p.202.

32. Midwinter, Keating and Mitchell, *Politics and Public Policy in Scotland*, p.25.

33. O'Neill, 'Great Britain: From Dicey to Devolution', p.76.

34. James Mitchell, 'Contemporary Unionism', in Catriona MM MacDonald, *Unionist Scotland, 1800–1997* (Edinburgh, John Donald, 1998), p.134.

35. James Mitchell, 'The Creation of the Scottish Parliament', *Parliamentary Affairs*, 52 (4) (October 1999), p.658.

36. James Mitchell, David Denver, Charles Pattie and Hugh Bodel, 'The 1997 Referendum in Scotland', *Parliamentary Affairs*, 51 (2) (April 1998), p.169; Wright, *The People Say Yes*, p.253.

37. Mitchell, Denver, Pattie and Bodel, 'The 1997 Referendum', p.176.
38. James Mitchell, 'The Creation of the Scottish Parliament', *Parliamentary Affairs*, p.664, citing Ron Davies, former Welsh Secretary of State.
39. O'Neill, 'Great Britain: From Dicey to Devolution', p.82.
40. http://website.lineone.net/scottishfreedom/polscotlandact.html; The Scotland Act 1998 Part One; Angela McCabe and James McCormick, 'Rethinking Representation: Some Evidence from the First Year', in Gerry Hassan and Chris Warhurst (eds), *The New Scottish Politics: The First Year of the Scottish Parliament and Beyond* (London, Stationery Office, 2000), p.42.
41. Laura McAllister, 'The Welsh Devolution Referendum: Definitely, Maybe?', *Parliamentary Affairs*, 51 (2) (April 1998), *passim*.
42. *Ibid.*, p.158.
43. http://www.llgc.org.uk/ymgyrchu/Datganoli/Refferendwm.
44. McAllister, 'The Welsh Devolution Referendum', p.149.
45. J Barry Jones, 'The First Welsh National Assembly election', *Government and Opposition*, 34 (3) (1999). Davies was replaced by Alun Michael, a controversial and unsuccessful appointment, and then Rhodri Morgan.
46. *Ibid*, p.332; http://www.wales.gov.uk/works/background_e.htm, How the Assembly Works.
47. McAllister, 'Gender, Nation and Party', pp.57, 59.
48. Wright, *The People Say Yes*, p.130.
49. Iain MacWhirter, 'Scotland Year Zero: The First Year at Holyrood', in Gerry Hassan and Chris Warhurst (eds), *The New Scottish Politics: The First Year of the Scottish Parliament and Beyond* (London, Stationery Office, 2000), p.16.
50. Hassan and Warhurst, 'Introduction: The New Scottish Politics', p.2.
51. Paul Smith, 'Whose Cup of Cocoa?', *Times Literary Supplement*, 16 March 2001.
52. Hassan and Warhurst, 'Introduction: The New Scottish Politics', p.6.
53. O'Neill, 'Great Britain: From Dicey to Devolution', p.93.

Chapter 7

Eurocommunism, the End of the Cold War and the Collapse of the Communist Party of Great Britain

Introduction

The Communist Party of Great Britain (CPGB) was formed in 1920, languished in the 1920s, emerged strongly in response to European fascism in the 1930s and peaked at 56,000 members in 1942, shortly after the Soviet Union joined the Allied war effort against Germany. After that, its membership declined, most rapidly in 1956 at the time of Soviet suppression of the Hungarian Uprising. By the 1970s, CPGB membership was declining dramatically, falling from 28,501 members in November 1975 to 20,638 in 1978, 12,711 in 1985, 7,616 in 1987 and a mere 4,742 in July 1991, four months before it went out of existence.

There are obviously many reasons for this decline of members, not least the collapse of many communist regimes in Eastern Europe in 1989 and the dissolution of the Soviet Union at the end of 1991. However, the membership of the CPGB was declining well before these events for it is evident that its lack of success in Britain, and in other Western capitalist nations, had led some communists to examine alternatives means to the Soviet model in order to create a communist state. In particular, Eurocommunism emerged in the 1970s as a response to the failures of Soviet communism but also caused further dissension and decline. It certainly accounted for considerable divisive conflict amongst the members of the CPGB in the 1980s and helped pave the way for its dissolution in November 1991.

Eurocommunism

The word 'Eurocommunism' was probably first used at the end of 1970.[1] At first, most leading European communists rejected it. Indeed, in June 1976, at the Berlin Conference of the Communist Parties of Europe, Santiago Carrillo, General Secretary of the PCE (Spanish Communist Party), declared that it was 'a most unfortunate term. There is no such thing as Eurocommunism.'[2] The General Secretary of the French Communist Party (PCF) also avoided the term at that meeting but his equivalent in the Italian Communist Party (PCI) accepted it and referred to the need for communists in Western Europe to 'seek new answers to the problem of transforming society in the direction of socialism' (Document 1).[3] In the wake of this conference, however, the term became more widely used. Indeed by the end of 1976, Santiago Carrillo had launched the formula of 'the Eurocommunist road to power' in *Mindo Orbrero*, on 16 December 1976,[4] and his views were further set out in his book *Eurocommunism and the State* (London, Lawrence & Wishart, 1977). In this book, Carrillo sought to produce a programme that was 'neither vote-catching nor revolutionary but based upon an assessment of modern capitalism'.[5]

The newly-emerging Eurocommunists stressed the need to extend democratic liberties and human rights and the winning of an electoral mandate to achieve socialism, thus relating their approach to the conditions of 'advanced capitalism' and, also, the need to diverge with the communism of Moscow.[6] They decided to delete 'dictatorship of the proletariat' from their phraseology, which had referred to Marx's democratic state ruled by the representatives of the working class based upon the principle of democratic centralism, bridging the interval between the overthrow of bourgeois rule and the establishment of a society of abundance which would have no need for a state of any sort: 'rule over men' would be replaced by the 'administration of things'. To Lenin, the dictatorship of the proletariat and democratic centralism were thus the twin principles of the state of society before the arrival of full communism. Eurocommunism emerged to challenge these Leninist ideas with the belief that a Communist party could define its own brand of socialism, participate with whichever capitalist enterprises it wished, work with whatever foreign groups it desired, and criticise other communist parties, including that in the Soviet Union.[7] Eurocommunism thus came to mean that any communist party could pursue whatever policies seemed appropriate for the creation of a communist state. The primacy of the Soviet Union, and the 'dictatorship of the proletariat' were no longer to be defining qualities for communism. Those who supported Eurocommunism often referred to the Gramscian ideas of gaining political hegemony through alliances, compromises and the gradual extension of communist ideals.[8]

The Communist Party of Great Britain and Eurocommunism

The CPGB had already worked out a programme, *The British Road to Socialism*, in the late 1940s and early 1950s, which envisaged a peaceful transition to socialism through parliamentary activity and pluralistic democratic socialism.[9] Nevertheless, the CPGB had closely followed the Soviet line and had identified itself with the Soviet invasion of Hungary in 1956, although it later formally distanced itself from the Soviet invasion of Czechoslovakia in 1968. However, the pro-Soviet elements within the CPGB began to lose control of the party during the late 1970s and throughout the 1980s, in such a way that the party split between the Eurocommunists and pro-Soviet factions, and numerous small Marxist groups who operated in their own spheres.

Many of the older members of the party, and faithful supporters of the Soviet Union, disagreed with the new Eurocommunist ideas which they saw as being unfairly critical of the Soviet Union. The *Morning Star*, and its editor Tony Chater, acted as a conduit for their criticism of the new Eurocommunist trends within the CPGB.[10] From 1977 onwards, then, the *Morning Star* led the Stalinist backlash to the Eurocommunism that was beginning to dominate the CPGB (Document 2), a Eurocommunism which was partly responsible for the defection of the pro-Moscow Sid French and the formation of his New Communist Party in 1977 (Document 4).

Clearly, the 'Eurocommunist' approach gathered pace within the party because of the disillusionment with the Soviet model of communism and with the move from an industrial base to the party to one increasingly dominated by intellectuals who had come through the student movement. It was partly encouraged by Martin Jacques, editor of *Marxism Today*. With some disdain for the working class, Jacques had commented that: 'Without the left intellectuals, the Labour movement cannot emerge as a leading force.'[11] Indeed, the domination by leftwing academics was particularly evident with the holding of a Communist University conference week in 1979. With up to 280 speakers attempting to broaden the appeal of the party, Sue Slipman suggested to the Executive Committee (EC) of the CPGB in March 1979 that industrial action, a feature of old Communist practices, was isolating workers from each other: 'The building of the Broad Democratic Alliance is the mechanics for democratic political change... At the moment we are tail-ending those involved in wage struggle, unable to intervene in a process which may be politically disastrous.'[12] The point was that the anti-monopoly alliances and strikes were leading the workers into conflict with their political allies in the Labour Party. In effect, the party's Eurocommunists were attempting to abandon the class approach to politics. No longer was the party geared to becoming the mass party of the working class, which it had sought to be since its founding convention in 1920. Only the old Stalinists clung to the 1920 goal, still orienting themselves towards the organised working class.

In the process of change, there was also discussion of the legitimacy of democratic centralism, in a 46-page report which justified the leadership and higher committees imposing their will upon the lower committees based upon the will of the majority of the higher committees.[13] However, the report's objective of greater discussions to end factionalism did not work and, indeed, party rules and democratic centralism were used by the Eurocommunists in the 1980s to root out the opposition of the old Stalinist and pro-Moscow type of communists, much as Stalinists had acted against the dissidents in the 1950s (Document 6).

The tensions between the Eurocommunists and the pro-Soviets began to mount in 1980, at the very moment when there were discussions about Inner Party Democracy. Indeed, there was an internal policy review in which, in a clear reference to Russian intervention in Afghanistan, it was stated that: 'The battle for peaceful co-existence and for the application of the principle of non-interference in the internal affairs of other countries is a base class position.'[14] Later, in the document, there was an explicit reference to the EC objecting to Soviet intervention in Afghanistan.[15] The Eurocommunist view was thus becoming dominant.

Stalinists versus Eurocommunists in the 1980s

In 1997, Edmund and Ruth Frow published a pamphlet entitled *The Liquidation of the Communist Party of Great Britain* (Document 2). Their main contention was that the CPGB was eventually liquidated because the leadership of the party colluded with *Marxism Today* in the 1980s to abandon scientific socialism, as outlined by Karl Marx and Frederick Engels in *The Communist Manifesto*, with more than a hint of influence from the hidden hand of MI5. In other words the Frows objected to the stripping away of revolutionary dialectics. In particular, they criticised an article by Tony Lane, in *Marxism Today*, which attacked the shop stewards and leaders of the working class as foremen and managers in waiting (Document 5).

The views of the Frows were foreshadowed by many others in the 1970s and 1980s, and particularly by the pro-Soviet *Morning Star*. Not surprisingly, the *Morning Star* came under the close scrutiny of an increasingly critical Eurocommunist-dominated party leadership who wished to control it. Since the *Morning Star* was run by a cooperative society registered as the People's Press Printing Society (PPPS), on which the CPGB had representatives, the PPPS was seen as one way in which to control its policy and actions. Yet the Eurocommunists were still not quite dominant in the CPGB for, when the Party Congress of 1977 criticised the *Morning Star*, a sub-committee set up to examine its contents advised against the paper being run by the King Street head-quarters of the party (Document 3).[16] There were subsequent charges and counter-charges about the precise relationship of the party and the *Morning Star*, and by 1981 relations between the party and the *Star* were incredibly tense.

The party leadership further criticised the *Morning Star* at the 1981 Party Congress. The conflict worsened in December 1981 when, in response, the *Morning Star* attacked the CPGB's Executive Committee condemnation of the Soviet-inspired takeover of Poland and the suppression of the Solidarity movement; it suggested that the Soviet actions were correct because the Polish people had forgotten their class destiny.

The Tony Lane article, produced in *Marxism Today* in 1982, and already referred to, created further tensions and led to a spate of correspondence, particularly from Mick Costello, the party's Industrial Organiser and one of the few pro-Soviet members of the leadership, who believed that Lane's article slandered the labour movement.[17] Lane responded by complaining about the Costello criticism in a letter written to the EC on 26 August.

Yet when the EC of the party met on 12 September, it gave only a mild rebuke to Martin Jacques, editor of *Marxism Today*,[18] for printing the Lane article without fuller consultation. It also stated that 'the Executive Committee does not accept that it was a gross slander on the labour movement', whilst accepting the importance and integrity of the shop-steward movement.[19] It was far more critical of Chater, Costello and the *Morning Star*'s deputy editor, David Whitfield, for forming a cabal to attack another party journal and to use the party's name without reference to the EC. It was thus clear that the party was dominated by the Eurocommunists and that those who opposed the dilution of 'class politics' had received a rebuff. Relations between the increasingly Euro-communist-dominated party and the pro-Soviet *Morning Star* worsened as the political committee of the party also attempted to secure Chater's removal as editor of the *Morning Star*.[20]

Gordon McLennan, the General Secretary of the party after John Gollan's departure in 1976, offered to meet Chater to resolve differences, but nothing happened. The party's problem was that it could not sack Chater, Whitfield or Costello, who had resigned as Industrial Organiser of the CPGB and joined the *Morning Star* as Industrial Correspondent, from their posts on the *Morning Star* because the PPPS was a self-governing body. Nevertheless, the CPGB bitterly complained that these individuals had been appointed to the *Morning Star* without the EC being in a position to express its opinion and decided to put forward a recommended list of candidates for the forthcoming election of six representatives to the management committee in 1983.[21] The *Morning Star* reacted by complaining that, in June 1983, a 'powerful outside body' was attempting to take over the paper. However, Chaterite candidates defeated the EC nominees in the Annual General Meeting elections for the *Morning Star*.

The movement was now even more deeply divided between the party and *Marxism Today*, on the one hand, and the *Morning Star*. The party was supported by Eurocommunists, pragmatic tradition-alists and the rank-and-file loyalists who resented Chater's action in hijacking the *Morning Star*. Chater and his supporters appealed to those on the left, including groups such as the Straight Leftists, who wished to protect the party's working-class heritage.

Chater and Costello attempted to present the Eurocommunists, the party leaders and *Marxism Today*, as both anti-trade union and anti-working class; claiming to represent working-class interests by defending the party against dangerous revisionism. It was this type of action that led Beatrix Campbell to write both a letter of criticism to the *Morning Star*, which appeared in *City Limits*, and to send a copy to the party's EC.[22]

The CPGB's leadership, in turn, emphasised that the development of political consciousness required compromise and realignments if the historic mission of the party, the securing of working-class power, was to be achieved. To underline this point, *Marxism Today* stressed the need for the Labour left to review its policies whilst the *Morning Star* contained articles admiring the achievements of the Soviet bloc.

The Straight Left faction, named after the *Straight Left* journal which appeared in 1979, also entered the fray with a 34-page pamphlet entitled *The Crisis in Our Communist Party: Cause, Effect and Cure*, allegedly written by Charlie Woods, an 83-year-old retired miner (Document 6). It attacked both the existing Eurocommunist leadership and the pro-Soviet *Morning Star* and called for a new leadership with new principles.

The conflict of opinion between all three factions spilled into the Communist press, including the monthly bulletin *Communist Focus*, where Mick Costello placed a critical article in anticipation of the 38th Congress, held in November 1983 (Documents 1 and 6). Despite the serious Chaterite challenge at the congress, the EC remained firmly in the hands of Eurocommunists. The Chaterites and the Straight Leftists, although antagonistic towards one another, produced a clandestine recommended list for the Executive Committee, and the Straight Leftists also produced a personalised bulletin called *Congress Truth*, which attacked both the EC and the Chaterites. In the end, the EC got congress to condemn the actions of the opposition groups (Documents 1 and 6). Congress also censured Chater and Whitfield and removed them, and most of their supporters, from the EC, including the four members of the Election Preparation Committee who had put forward a 'Political Alternative List' of candidates. These actions divided the party, some branches being most critical of the action taken by the EC (Document 7).

The EC of the CPGB moved quickly to discipline and remove members who broke the rules. Its May 1984 meeting adopted two statements attacking the events of the 38th Congress. One, 'Factional & other Unprincipled Activity at the 38th Congress', condemned the Woods' pamphlet for factionalism and expelled him from the party (Document 6). On 17 July 1984, three of the four members who had produced the 'Political Alternative List' were also expelled and another was suspended for three months,[23] an action which drew much criticism from within the party. The 'Executive Committee's

Statement' also noted that the PPPS was now facing an annual general meeting and declared that the party was putting forward five candidates – George Bolton, Tricia David, Ron Halverson, H Mitchell and Chris Myant. The disciplinary action of the EC drew widespread criticism within the party.

The conflicts proceeded at a pace. Even the Miners' Strike of 1984/5 brought no respite as *Marxism Today* appeared lukewarm on the dispute, printing only three articles, whilst the *Morning Star* was so generous in its praise of the miners that Arthur Scargill, their leader, stated that 'The *Morning Star* is guilty of one act, it supported working class politics and socialism.'[24]

Division within the party simply would not go away. The EC put forward candidates for election to the PPPS in opposition to the Chater-supported one and called for the removal of Chater and Whitfield at the 1984 AGM of the PPPS. That AGM was scarred with conflict and when the voting was counted only two party candidates – George Bolton (Mick McGahey's vice-president in the Scottish NUM) and Chris Myant – were returned.

The Chaterites then went on the offensive and attempted to work within the party districts, particularly in London, in an attempt to oust the Eurocommunists. This led to conflicts at the London District Congress on 24 November 1984 when Gordon McLennan, the party's General Secretary, ordered it not to appoint a new district executive committee, because ten of the delegates were considered to be Chaterites. But his advice was ignored and 22 of those who participated in the 'continued congress' were suspended from the party at a special EC meeting on 30 November 1984.[25] This meeting also issued a statement to *Unite the Party for the British Road: Defeat the Factionalists*. In January, the EC expelled Chater, Whitfield and other London dissidents from the CPGB, and also took action against dissident sections of the party in the North West of England (Document 3).

The party's Special Congress, in May 1985, was organised in such a way as to give the 'right revisionists', or Eurocommunists, a majority of two to one. The congress thus rejected the appeals of expelled London members, including the editor of the *Morning Star*, endorsing the expulsions that had taken place in both London and the North West. In November, 1985 the party also set up a North West provisional committee of 23 unelected members which ensured that the new Executive Committee of the North West was formed largely of 'right revisionists', or Eurocommunists (Document 2).[26]

In 1985 Mikhail Gorbachev rose to power in the Soviet Union. This forced the Straight Left and the Chaterites to support *perestroika* and *glasnost*, and an altogether more reformist type of communism, if only because they were still committed to the Soviet Union. Yet, despite this, membership continued its almost inexorable decline (Document 1). Given the prevailing mood amongst leading Eurocommunists, many members felt that there was no point continuing with the CPGB. The Political Committee (PC) therefore discussed the need for a fundamental realignment of the party in February 1987, but the meeting was deeply divided between those who wanted to preserve a party committed to social revolution and those who wished to widen the party into one of the broad radical democratic left.'[27]

Nina Temple, a future general secretary, although absent from the meeting, gave her views at this PC meeting through a set of notes she had sent. The previous year she had informed the EC that: 'First, of course, we are a Marxist Party. Not a Party of dogmatic, fossilised quotation-based Marxism, but a Party with a tradition of the creative development of the British Marxist tradition.'[28] The five pages of notes she now sent to the PC meeting indicated that she had moved further towards democratic reform and broad socialist alliances than the socialist revolution she once proclaimed, and were a pointer to the future (Document 8). She argued that the party had to go forward with this fundamental realignment particularly on issues such as unemployment, poverty, housing and health. She also maintained that the recent internal conflicts and the need for greater accountability were the reasons for the party's decline. In order to develop the party further, she felt that it had to have more relevance to British political life.[29] Yet there remained divisions between those demanding socialist revolution and those who wanted radical democratic reform. Temple, a rising figure in the party, was clearly veering to radical democratic reform and alliances with other labour and socialist groups.

Increasingly alarmed at its continuing membership decline, the party decided to hold a Special Emergency Executive Committee Meeting on 28 June 1987 to discuss the future of communism in Britain. At this meeting, Nina Temple, following up her advice to the PC, suggested that the party was still committed to removing social inequalities through *The British Road to Socialism* and the transformation of Parliament, and further stressed the importance of *Marxism Today* in countering Thatcherism, even as the party was 'consumed with inner divisions and disciplinary questions'.[30] She and others also discussed the need to establish a 'Broad Democratic Alliance' and to work with the Campaign for Nuclear Disarmament and similar protest organisations. At the same meeting, Dave Cook suggested that, even with changes made in 1977–8, *The British Road to Socialism* was now in need of an update. Others demanded more unity within the left.

There were few fundamental differences at this meeting for it was now generally accepted that Eurocommunism alone was no longer sufficient. The only real differences were of emphasis. Dave Cook attacked the EC, dominated by Eurocommunists since 1977, for not allowing 'a more thoroughgoing transformation of the party'. Yet what all the party agreed was that *The British Road to Socialism*, the policy of working for a socialist revolution through the parliamentary road, would be redrafted and that its approach would be to seek new alliances with the Greens, anti-racist bodies and students. The party was still committed to democratic centralism but stressed the need for more democratic participation by the membership in party life with an elected central leadership capable of directing the entire party. These measures did not impress the external opponents of the party leadership (Documents 2, 3).

The *Morning Star* continued to react against the party's approach and suggested that the 'Communist Party is being high-jacked [sic] by right-wing revisionists' aiming to destroy 'the Marxist basis and class approach of the Communist Party'.[31] The Communist Campaign Group was also formed at this time to oppose revisionism within the party and became particularly active in London, Brent being one of its major centres (Document 2).[32] When the *Morning Star* kept reporting how it was breaching CPGB rules, the party leadership became concerned and acted to meet and remove the challenge.[33]

In April 1988, many of those expelled from the party formed the Communist Party of Britain, as mirror image of the Communist Party of Great Britain that had existed before the rise of Eurocommunism. It held its first congress in November 1989, when it updated *The British Road to Socialism*, an admission of the fact that even this organisation was very much in line with the CPGB of the 1950s and 1960s.

Ignoring such opposition, the CPGB headed towards political oblivion. It had lost much of its trade-union support to Chater and the *Morning Star* faction, and it is to be remembered that Ken Gill, who left the party, was a trade-union general secretary, a member of the TUC General Council and Chair at the 1984 TUC Conference. Such a loss, and similar losses, could not be recovered easily. The CPGB lost out in municipal elections, with the number of councillors being down to single figures by the mid-1980s. In parliamentary politics the situation was even worse. Indeed, in March 1983 the party put forward a candidate against Labour's Peter Tatchell at the Bermondsey parliamentary by-election and received fewer votes than the Official Monster Raving Loony candidate.

The Communist right and the Eurocommunists won control of the party and their influence was expressed through 1989's redrafted version of *The British Road to Socialism* which became *Manifesto for New Times* at the November 1989 Congress. This *Manifesto* recognised the end of old forms of industrial and class conflict, addressed issues such as feminism, gay and green politics, and anticipated a remodelling of the party but, above all, was concerned to challenge and defeat Thatcherism, which was considered to have greatly undermined the appeal of communism (Documents 1 and 9 and Chapter 1).[34] Nevertheless, the congress was a bad-tempered affair. Two resolutions were passed against *Marxism Today*, and the *Manifesto for New Times* only gained a narrow vote in favour.

The 1989 Congress agreed a change of party leader, as from January 1990, when Nina Temple was elected unopposed as General Secretary. Temple assumed her duties in January 1990. With communism in the Soviet Union and Eastern Europe collapsing it was only a matter of time before, at the 43rd Congress of the CPGB, in November 1991, the party was dissolved by a majority of two to one (Document 10). The old Eurocommunist majority decided to reform itself as the Democratic Left, a party that attracted very little political attention in the 1990s, although there are some signs of its continued existence (Document 3).

Conclusion

Marxism in Britain exerted its greatest influence during the Second World War. After that it declined and became an increasingly marginal force in British politics. From the mid-1970s it became even more irrelevant as it fragmented into many feuding factions over the way to achieve communism in an increasingly Thatcherite Britain.

Documents

SECONDARY SOURCES AND INTERPRETATIONS

1. John Callaghan, *Socialism in Britain since 1884* (Oxford, Blackwell, 1990), pp.225, 228, 236–7

[p.225] As elsewhere on the Left the CPGB was now composed of a confused mixture of ideological currents which ranged from the advocates of decentralism and participatory democracy to old-fashioned Stalinists who looked to the socialist state as a provider of truth. The apparent successes of the Italian Communist Party in the 1970s strengthened the party's innovators, however, because of its obvious remove from the politics of 'Marxism-Leninism'. The rise of Thatcherism – even before the election of May 1979 – also illustrated the potency of a strategy which attached party ideology to popular beliefs and values in the construction of a new common sense...

[p.228] Within the CPGB, for example, ideological divisions were so deep that the 38th Congress in November 1983 was presented with an alternative recommended list of candidates for election to the Executive Committee. This challenge was defeated, but the proponents of traditional class struggle policies, centres on the industrial working class and support for the socialist bloc of countries, defied the party's decisions and used their control of the newspaper the *Morning Star* to organize factions against the leadership. Within a year of these events opposition majorities were elected to the district leaderships in London and the North-West of England. By now the *Morning Star* was more closely associated with non-party socialists such as Tony Benn, Arthur Scargill – the leader of the National Union of Miners – and other proponents of the policies of 1983. The CPGB leadership by contrast supported the positions taken by the party's theoretical journal *Marxism Today*, which was engaged in thoroughgoing revisionism. *Marxism Today* became the voice of the democratic pluralistic socialism partly inspired by the new socialist movement and the innovative local socialists such as Ken Livingstone, but also repelled by vanguardism as practised by groups such as Militant, as well as the bureaucratic paternalism with which the Labour Party and the trade unions were riddled. In January 1985 the CPGB began to expel or lose thousands of members opposed to the new thinking...

[p.236] A much more comprehensive *Manifesto for New Times* has been produced by the CPGB in response to the decision of its fortieth National Congress to prepare a new draft of the *British Road to Socialism*. According to the CPGB's analysis, 'society is in the midst of an epochal shift' characterized by fundamental changes in the structure of industry, the occupational composition of the workforce, and the configuration of class.

[It then goes on to discuss the decay of a structure based on large-scale units of production; p.237] If socialists are to work with the grain of the 'new times', as the CPGB analysis insists, they have to recognize the new aspirations generated since the 1960s by the new social movements and realize that 'the poles of the political map of the 1990s will be the politics of race and the underclass in the inner city and the growth of industrial regions' where the labour movement 'is not central to the spirit emerging in them'. The new segmentation of the workforce allegedly creates an underclass representing about one-third of the working class while the rest live in 'relative material prosperity'. This recomposition of the working class is held to have fractured traditional class identities and cultures at the same time as the new social movements began to emerge, with their stress on common identities other than those based on class. So while the CPGB continues to hold that 'class remains central to British politics', it has emphasized that a new class politics is required which can match the present diversity of the working class. Indeed, the emphasis of *Marxism Today* has been on the second part of the equation created by the 'new times' – that is, the need for a relationship between class politics and the social movements concerned with ecology, feminism, race, peace, and various forms of decentralized democracy. It was the CPGB's apparent retreat from class politics which contributed to the splits within the party... and which is regarded by its critics as all of a piece with the 'new revisionist spectrum' emerging after 1983.

2. Edmund and Ruth Frow, *The Liquidation of the Communist Party of Great Britain: A contribution to the discussion* (Salford, Jubilee House, 1996), pp.3, 12–14, 20–1, 23

[p.3] The process of stripping scientific socialism, as outlined by Karl Marx and Frederick Engels in the Communist Manifesto of 1848, of its revolutionary dialectics was promoted in the pages of *Marxism Today* under Martin Jacques editorship. Non-Party academics and journalists were invited to contribute. Their main line of attack was on the decline of the working class, the autonomy of the State and the need for Labour Party members to distance themselves from their traditional basis. The article which made the position abundantly clear was a vicious attack on shop stewards by Tony Lane in a September 1982 issue.

[pp.12–13] The Party and the *Morning Post*

If MI5 did aim to influence developments in the Communist Movement, what finer objective could they have than to provoke a clash between the Party leadership and the editorial staff of the *Morning Star* with the aim of liquidating both? This was only possible because the concept had grown up that the *Morning Star* was the organ of the Communist Party. When the *Daily Worker* was relaunched in 1946, it was as a Co-operative Society owned and controlled by its members. The registered name of the Society was *The People's Press Printing Society (PPPS)*.

The Communist Party had always indulged in sharp polemics and, on rare occasions, expulsions, but never on the scale of the 1980s. Long standing members of the Party who had spent many years struggling to establish democratic norms in their trade unions were appalled at the way in which their democratic rights within the Party were trampled on by the Eurocommunists. The outstanding feature of the liquidationist faction was the abandonment of democratic rights and the adoption of dictatorial decrees.

At the Party Congress in 1977 a resolution was passed critical of the contents of the *Morning Star*. The Executive Committee (EC) set up a Sub-Committee to examine the whole question. Although the Report of the Sub-Committee was critical of some aspects of reporting and use of space on the issues covered, basically it was agreed that the paper was doing a good job with limited resources despite declining circulation...

A sharp divergence of views developed and came to a head in September 1982 when the EC supported Tony Lane's attack on Shop Stewards in *Marxism Today* and dissociated itself from a critical article by Mick Costello in the *Morning Star*. The EC also demanded that Bea Campbell be given 1500 words to reply to Barbara Switzer who had supported Costello...

[There was resistance to the Eurocommunist attempt to dominate and liquidate the old party in the North West and London.]

The Executive Committee and the North West

[pp.20–21] The EC looked at the results of the election for the new District Committee which showed the Recommended List as having been largely ignored and gave the opinion that 'The result could only have been achieved as a result of organised effort that went against the principles of Inner Party Democracy.' They added that the current information was insufficient to show who had been indulging in factional activity.

Lacking that vital evidence, the EC never the less set out to make it impossible for the democratically elected District Committee to function properly, Gerry Pocock and David Priscott were appointed to attend District Committee meetings to report what happened.

Matters came to a head at the July 1985 meeting which was attended by Ann Pocock, Lou Lewis, Gerry Pocock, Dave Heywood, Arthur Adler, Roger O'Hara, Heather Malley, all of whom were appointed by the EC. In spite of such a show of force, the meeting rejected the Report and re-affirmed its plan which had been adopted at the June meeting. Having failed to cajole or intimidate the District Committee, the EC decided to dismiss it. They appointed Arthur Adler, Roger O'Hara and Heather Malley to be a Provisional Committee with Gerry Pocock to work with them.

The London District Congress

A week after the North West Congress the London comrades held their meeting. The Eurocommunists were uncertain of avoiding a severe defeat. The General Secretary refused to allow delegates to discuss a statement he had made from the EC as they were entitled to do under Rule 3. At the end of his speech he informed the delegates that had no right to elect a new District Committee and stormed off the platform amid scenes of uproar and confusion. Almost half the delegates left with the General Secretary but the proceedings continued and a resolution was unanimously adopted to adjourn the Congress for not more than three months. Blame was firmly put on the General Secretary and the EC for disruption. Full confidence was expressed in the existing District Committee and officers and a call was made for a Special National Congress...

Subsequent correspondence in the *Morning Star* expressed the view that the Rules of the Party had been flagrantly violated, delegates rights trampled underfoot and democracy and natural justice abandoned.

[The Frows indicate how the expulsions led to the formation of the Communist Campaign Group in 1985. There is also a discussion of the coalminers' strike of 1984/5, before they conclude with the end of the CPGB; p.23] At the 43rd Congress of the CPGB held in November 1991, the Eurocommunist majority formed the Democratic Left which abandoned the theoretical basis and principles on which the CPGB had been formed. It became a loose amorphous organisation functioning as a pressure group.

3. Keith Laybourn and Dylan Murphy, *Under the Red Flag: A History of Communism in Britain* (Stroud, Sutton, 1999), pp.183–5

The last forty years of the Party's history had been ones of decline. At first the Party had lost out in the Cold War atmosphere of the 1940s and 1950s. It had been slow to accept the implications of the 20th Congress of the CPSU [Communist Party of the Soviet Union] in 1956 and lost support as many of its members demanded a more democratic and representative structure. However, the Party still retained some vestige of influence and was still attracted to the Soviet system. By the 1970s and the 1980s the situation had changed dramatically. The Party leadership had lurched to the right, was dominated increasingly by the Eurocommunists, rejecting the old traditions based upon support for the Soviet Union, and hurtling towards a broader-based type of socialism, as a result of the apparent onslaught of Thatcherism, which owed less and less to the principles of Marxism and Leninism. This had seemed a necessary sacrifice for the CPGB leadership since they noted that the character of British society had changed, with the traditional industrial working class declining in numbers and influence at a time of increasing political diversification. In effect, the change from the CPGB to the Democratic Left, whether for good or ill, was a recognition that changes had occurred and that old-style Stalinism was now an anachronism which could not be saved even by the more moderate parliamentary approach towards achieving communism outlined in the various versions of *The British Road to Socialism*. In this respect the opening speech of Nina Temple to the 43rd Congress seem apposite:

> We must recognize that the era of Communist Parties is at an end. Our own party cannot be revived by nostalgia, discredited ideologies, rosy views of history or unaccountable command structures. Only an honest appraisal and a rupture with past undemocratic practices can take the best of our tradition forward with integrity.[35]

The Democratic Left therefore took up the mantle of the now defunct CPGB.

The Democratic Left has attracted little interest from the media and the public since it was formed in 1991. However, the old Marxist traditions and 'broad based socialism' still survive. In Scotland the Marxist Left and broad-based socialist tradition have come together in the Scottish Socialist Alliance, made up of Scottish Militant Labour and the Communist Party of Scotland, among others. In the elections to the new Scottish Parliament in May 1999, Tommy Sheridan was elected for the Scottish Socialist Party.

At the time of writing, in England and Wales, also, the Marxist/Socialist Left is coming together in socialist alliances which have resulted in electoral victories on a local scale, particularly the success of Dave Nellist, the ex-Militant MP in May 1998. Within the trade unions too the Marxist/Socialist Left is coming together to provide an alternative to the policies of New Labour. Indeed, in the UNISON election for General Secretary in 1996, the Broad Left candidate Roger Bannister came second to Rodney Bickerstaffe with over 60,000, or 20 per cent, of the vote. In May 1998, David Rix of the Socialist Labour Party, whose leader Arthur Scargill spent his youth in the CPGB, was elected General Secretary of the Amalgamated Society of Locomotive Engineers and Firemen.

There are signs that the Marxist-Leninist tradition and communism are not dead in Britain. Nevertheless, there is a long way to go before a meaningful and viable movement emerges again. At the present, like the CPGB for much of its history, Marxism is very marginal to British politics.

PRIMARY EVIDENCE AND INFORMATION

4. Letter from Reuban Falber, Assistant Secretary, to members of the Executive Committee of the Communist Party of Great Britain, CP/CENT/EC/15/14, dated 18 July 1977, dealing with the formation of the breakaway New Communist Party

Dear Comrade,

I am writing to put you in the picture regarding the formation of the breakaway organisation and the steps we are taking to protect the Party [formed on the previous Sunday].

It does seem from the information which has come in during the last few hours that the organisers of the breakaway party have over-estimated their likely support. Comrades from Sussex and Surrey, on seeing the report in the *Star*, have been phoning in asking for guidance and from other Districts indicate that even some of those who were contemplating joining the breakaway organisations are having second thoughts.

We have considered the question of calling an emergency meeting of the Executive Committee but at the moment feel that we should not take a decision as it does not seem that the E.C. is called upon to take disciplinary action, as those who are associating with the breakaway organisation have automatically put themselves outside the Party. We think that any statement issued by the E.C. would tend to be a repetition of what the Political Committee has already said. There is also the consideration that an Emergency E.C., and subsequent statement would elevate the importance of the issue and give the splitters more press publicity than they would otherwise obtain...

REUBAN FALBER

ASSISTANT SECRETARY

5. Tony Lane, 'The Unions caught on the Ebb tide', *Marxism Today*, September 1982, p.13

Growth of sectional influence
The move towards company bargaining with shop steward participation has gained a new clientele for the British Rail breakfast as shopfloor representatives have sat cheek by jowl with managers on their way back to London. Symbolic too has been the TGWU's purchase of a London hotel to reduce the expenses of shop stewards and other delegates on overnight stays in the capital. Here we are simply observing the creation of a new working class élite which has the opportunity (and too often takes it) of sharing in the expense account syndrome: the franchise of perks and fiddles has been widened.

Shop stewards and full time officers have had their opportunities. Some shop stewards have used their position as a stepping stone to promotion to charge-hand and foreman. A favoured few, usually convenors and full-time officers, have gone on to become personnel managers and even industrial relations directors. Such routes of progression, to say the very least, induce a mixture of cynicism and resentment among the rank and file. Other stewards have simply used the role as a means to an easy life, an opportunity to get off the job and out of the plant with spurious excuses of 'union business'. In the closed community of the workplace where words seemingly travel faster than the speed of sound and where union rhetoric proclaims altruism, such behaviour must inevitably have unfortunate repercussions for the way in which unionism is evaluated. And nor is this all...

In most workplaces of any sizes there are usually sections which, because of their strategic position in the process of production, are better able through the use of sanctions to gain advantage, than others. To that extent that sectional advantage which has been unilaterally pressed and shop-steward led, has upset differentials or caused loss of earnings to others then these actions have also helped to discredit trade unionism in the eyes of the membership.

The point of mentioning all of these things is to show that, one way or another, there is some substance to the implicit moral critique of trade unionism mounted by the rank and file and that this explains the crisis of legitimacy.

6. Factional & other Unprincipled Activity at the 38th Congress [November 1983], published in May 1984, CP/CENT/EC/1/01

Statement adopted by the May Executive Committee

OUR 38TH NATIONAL CONGRESS took place in a situation where various forms of unprincipled activity, including factional activity, reached levels unprecedented in our Party. They caused deep concern to the Majority of delegates, who referred these breaches of our dramatic proceedings to the Executive to deal with...

Pamphlet by C. Woods

Prior to the Congress a pamphlet with the title 'The Crisis in the Communist Party – Cause, Effect and Cure' was published in the name of a Party member, Charlie Woods and was widely circulated.

The political views in the pamphlet were not the reason that the EC took disciplinary action against the author of the pamphlet. They are views that have been fought and defeated at Congress. Its publication was a breach of EC decisions... that the pre-Congress discussions should take place in specified publications in which all comrades would have equal space and opportunity to expound their views...

The Political Alternative List

During Congress, prior to and during the election of the EC, a duplicated document headed 'Political Alternative List' was circulated, over the names of 4 members of the Election Preparations Committee.

[The issue was investigated and the members concerned interviewed.] One of the four (Barry Johnson) already at Congress realised that he had been wrong in this matter and he dissociated himself from the list, which he recognised was in breach of our procedures. The others (Brian Topping, Bruce Allen, Barbara O'Hare) continued to assert that they had done nothing wrong, and this was their position still when the EC discussed the matter with them.

The EC expelled the three who maintained that they had been in the right acting as they did. Not to have expelled them would have meant that, given the chance, they would have done the same again, and it would have encouraged others to do the same...

The EC wants to state clearly its deep concern at this situation. In our view *all* responsible comrades whatever their views on political differences within the Party should clearly and unambiguously dissociate themselves from this unprecedented and unprincipled behaviour.

7. Extract from a letter of the Carlisle Branch of the CPGB to the Executive Committee of the Communist Party of Great Britain, 17 January 1984, CP/CENT/EC/20/06

The expulsions were in fact an attempt at stifling the widespread criticism within the party of the present leadership and its policies, by administrative methods. [This was seen to be an example of] the retreat of the leadership of the party from the revolutionary Marxist-Leninist past and an open avowal of their revisionist socialist-democratic stance.

8. From notes sent by Nina Temple to the Political Committee Meeting of the Communist Party of Great Britain, 14 February 1987, CP/CENT/PC/16

In recent years we have embraced a wider political agenda, feminism, anti-racism, alliance politics, and largely through the success of *Marxism Today* have established ourselves as relevant to the thinking of the realigned left. But these developments have coincided with our glaring weakness in membership, electoral, activity, trade unions, youth, & loss of *Star* which have greatly hindered our ability to conduct struggle.

Are we going to accept as our new role being mentors of the Left – it seems in some way a return to the old vanguard. A small Party with the 'correct' line influencing the Labour [Party]? If we have accepted this role, which I think the Party being an engine of realignment might mean – then would we not be better in the Labour Party...

Personally, I still want to see the Communist Party developing as a campaigning Party able to generate struggle & ideas committed to empowering ordinary people – which means being out in the streets, markets, estates, neighbourhoods taking up fighting with people on issues of concern, including alliances, constructing a political movement committed to collective solutions & rejecting Thatcherism. We would need to overcome the Party's failure to campaign on unemployment, poverty, housing & health...

I think another problem we face is our policy or lack of it. I think many Party members don't know where the Party stands, the practise of not endorsing reports, printing pamphlets as personal documents etc. only makes matters worse...

9. *Manifesto for New Times: A Communist Party Strategy for the 1990s* (London, CPGB, 1991), pp.2, 7–8

This document is about how Britain can make progress in the 1990s. It is about how people can open up new possibilities for progressive change in the next decade. It is about creating a new popular politics for a new era, the new times. After a decade in which Thatcherism has been the dominant political force in British politics, this document is intended to offer new ideas, hope and purpose to all who want to see Britain develop in a more democratic, sustainable, egalitarian and open way.

Progressive change in the next decade is the essential first step towards putting socialism back on to the political agenda. The Communist Party is seeking to be part of a force in Britain which can create a new popular, political atmosphere: one in which there is hope and excitement about the future; where we can talk with confidence about striving towards socialism.

Thatcherism is the most immediate obstacle blocking the way to progressive change. Its defeat will be central to the renewal of popular, progressive politics. But Thatcherism will only be defeated electorally if it is defeated politically and ideologically. A movement to defeat Thatcherism must be underpinned by a common vision of the future – a society which moved to the rhythm of a popular humanism rather than a popular capitalism...

[p.7–8] *Politics and the New Times*

The 1990s will see a myriad political and social struggles. But in essence they will come down to a single question: on whose terms will the new era be moulded? Thatcherism's attempt to facilitate a 'conservative modernisation' will create privatisation, polarisation, fragmentation, public squalor and authoritarianism in the new times. Its grip will only be broken by a progressive movement gathered around the aspirations bred in the new times.

There are powerful social currents which offer an alternative path to modernisation which is more just, democratic, humane and sustainable. For on each of the central issues facing society in the new times, powerful progressive forces are developing. These movements do not necessarily share the same interests nor do they possess properties which unite them spontaneously. But they do move to a similar rhythm:

The green movement's response to the environmental crisis with a challenge to current economic priorities;

The optimism of internationalisation of the economy may be matched by a new era of more co-operative international relations, symbolised by the changes in Soviet foreign policy;

The mounting moral and political opposition to the savage inequalities Thatcherism is creating;

Nationalism's challenge to authoritarian centralism...

These are not formal policies or parties. They are moods, currents and forces in society. They can trace their lineage to discontent with the postwar settlement as clearly as Thatcherism. They could offer an alternative vision of modernisation which is credible and potentially more popular than Thatcherism.

For these forces are the grain of the new times. They stem from popular social aspirations. They offer the prospects of a new wave of progressive social and economic development in the 1990s...

[p.9] *Class Politics*

Class remains central to British politics. There is an enormous gulf between the increasingly concentrated, wealthy and internationalised ruling class... and the majority of working people who have to sell their labour to live – whether by hand or by brain, skilled or unskilled, black or white, men or women. But as capitalism has developed so the character of that class divide has changed. With society's passage into the new times in the 1990s the character of both the ruling class and the working class is changing. Thatcherism has coalesced a range of social support for its politics from these changes.

10. *New Times* (*the Journal of the Democratic Left*), No. 1, 30 November 1991, pp.2–3

[p.2] *Congress ditches PC rule book*

The first debate of Congress was the most divisive. Ending over 70 years of the Communist Party, it voted overwhelmingly to take the draft constitution for Democratic Left as the basis for debate throughout the weekend. Most delegates were keen to get quickly to the point of decision and only a handful backed a plea from Scottish councillor Willie Clark for a larger opening session.

When they did vote the result was clear. Some 72 delegates voted keeping the old Communist Party role back while 135 opted for the new draft. There were only three abstentions.

[p.3] *Opening Speech of Nina Temple*

I want to express my delight at that decisive vote which means the draft Democratic Left Constitution is the basis for amendment by the historic Congress. This confirms us on the course of transformation. We must recognise that the era of Communist Parties is at an end. Our own party cannot be revived by nostalgia, discredited ideologies, rosy views of history or unaccountable command structures. Only an honest appraisal, and a rupture with past undemocratic practices, can take the best of our tradition forward with integrity.

The debate we have conducted about transformation throughout this year was long overdue. It was resisted by previous leaderships. It should have been held years ago on the party's own terms, evolving alongside the party's developing commitment to democracy rather than dictated to us by the collapse of what was called communism. Instead, we have only faced up to it at the 11th hour. And this has been brought about as much by events and our own unremitting decades of decline, as by the implications of the empowering politics adopted in 1989 in our Manifesto for New Times.

This need not have been the case. As the Congress meets to discuss the transformation we must apologise to all those who fought within the party for years of radical democratic politics, and who were marginalised and often left the party in despair and frustration at its refusal to adapt and change. So many times, in the name of party unity, nettles were not grasped by the leadership who found it easier to accommodate the hard-liners rather than the radical demands for change.

The recent revelations carried first in our paper Changes, both about Stalin's role in writing the British Road to Socialism and about the secret massive funding of our Party by the CPSU explains much about these past compromises.

Notes

1. Ferdinand Claudin, *Eurocommunism and Socialism* (first published by Siglo Veintiuno, Madrid, 1977; this edition published in London by NLB, 1978), p.7. He suggests that the term was first used in 1970. However, HT Willetts, 'The USSR and Eurocommunism', in Richard Kindersley (ed.), *In Search of Communism* (London, Macmillan, 1981), pp.1 and 20, suggests that the term was first coined by France Barbieri in *Giornale Nuova*, 26 June 1975.
2. Claudin, *Eurocommunism and Socialism*, p.7.
3. *Ibid.*, p.7.
4. *Ibid.*, p.8.
5. *Ibid.*, p.8.
6. Fernando Claudin, *Eurocommunism and Socialism* (London, NLB, 1977).
7. *Ibid.*, p.7.
8. Willie Thompson, *The Communist Movement since 1945* (Oxford, Blackwell, 1998), pp.166–170.
9. Santiago Carillo (General Secretary of the Spanish Communist Party), *Eurocommunism and the State* (London, Lawrence & Wishart, 1977), chapter on 'The Historical Roots of Eurocommunism', p.111.
10. Communist Party of Great Britain archives in the National Museum of Labour History, 103 Princess Street, Manchester, recently renamed the Labour Party Archives and Study Centre, John Rylands Library, University of Manchester, CP/CENT/EC/15/16, referring to the *Morning Star*'s publications between February and July 1977.
11. Keith Laybourn and Dylan Murphy, *Under the Red Flag: A History of Communism in Britain* (Stroud, Sutton, 1999), p.167.
12. CP/CENT/EC/17/07, EC, 10–11 March 1979.
13. Internal Policy review, in CP/CENT/EC/17/10, July 1980, p.8.
14. *Ibid.*
15. *Ibid.*, p.11.
16. CPGB, Statement for the Executive Committee, Sub-Committee, *Morning Star*, 1978, p.14; CP/CENT/PC/14/15, Draft Report on the

Morning Star, 1 September 1978.

17. *Morning Star*, 26 August 1982.
18. CP/CENT/EC/15/14; Martin Jacques replaced James Klugmann, who had edited *Marxism Today* for 20 years, at the Executive Committee meeting, 12–13 March 1977.
19. CP/CENT/EC/11/01, Statement of EC, 12 September 1982.
20. E & R Frow, *Liquidation of the CPGB*, p.14; Thompson, *Good Old Cause*, p.185. Of course, the *Morning Star* did not have to consult the CPGB on appointments.
21. CP/CENT/EC/19/05, EC, 12–13 March 1983.
22. CP/CENT/EC/20/06, copy of letter from Beatrix Campbell.
23. CP/CENT/EC/1/01, 'Factional & other Unprincipled Activity at the 38th Congress'.
24. *Morning Star*, 11 June 1985.
25. CP/CENT/EC/21/06, Minutes of Special Executive Committee, 30 November 1984.
26. *Ibid*, 20 May 1985.
27. CP/CENT/PC/16/18, PC, 2 February 1987.
28. CP/CENT/EC/22/07, Report to EC, 11–12 January 1986.
29. *Ibid.*, PC, 14 February 1987.
30. CP/CENT/EC/13/05, minutes from a Special Emergency Executive Committee Meeting, 28 June 1987, 'Some points of discussion from Nina Temple'.
31. *Ibid.*, 18 July 1985.
32. CP/CENT/PC/16/18, letter from Graham Taylor, Secretary of Brent North branch, 8 February 1987.
33. *Morning Star*, 11 November 1985.
34. CP/CENT/EC/24/01, included the views of Nina Temple in this respect.
35. *Ibid.*, Nina Temple's opening speech.

Chapter 8

Feminist Debates and the Changing Position of Women in British Society

Introduction

The 'second-wave' feminism of the late 1970s and early 1980s, while emphasising its own message that 'the personal is political', made accommodations with other political philosophies. Accused of 'essentialising' the image and interests of white middle-class women, feminists accepted the need to celebrate diversity. Black feminism developed and gender stereotypes were challenged by a burgeoning gay, lesbian and bisexual movement. This is turn gave rise to Queer theory and 'third-wave', postmodernist feminism. Feminist activity ranged from single-issue campaigns, such as those on abortion and the Greenham Common protest against nuclear weapons, to involvement in party political activities. Glass walls/ceilings continued to inhibit women's access to equal pay and conditions at work; while younger women were able to benefit from the better education and career prospects for which feminists had fought, a generation gap developed as many older women were trapped in low-paid, part-time employment.

The first part of this chapter outlines feminist debates and campaigns from the last quarter of the twentieth century. The second part deals with women's engagement in the late-twentieth-century labour market. Chapters 3, 4 and 5, respectively, include an account of changing family structure and women's experience of the welfare systems of the period, women's involvement in trade unions, and in Labour Party politics. The emphasis on the latter is explained by second-wave feminism's interest in socialism and Marxism, as indicated in this chapter.

Feminist Debates and Campaigns

Second-Wave Feminism

Feminist theory and activity are commonly described as having three 'waves' of intensity and public visibility – first, second and third-wave feminism. First-wave feminist political philosophy had challenged the typification of women as irrational beings, confined to the domestic sphere, and their resultant exclusion from citizenship. First-wave political practice, at its peak at the beginning of the twentieth century, had therefore aimed at winning financial independence, education and enfranchisement for women. Second-wave political philosophy partly developed because, despite having won the vote, women did not reap the expected benefits. The political activity of the second wave was described by some as the Women's Liberation Movement and developed at conferences held from 1970, at Ruskin College, until 1978. The Ruskin College demands were for equality in employment and education, and for women's control over their own fertility, including free contraception and the right to choose abortion; in 1974 were added legal and financial independence, an end to sex oppression and to discrimination against lesbians, the right to a self-defined sexuality; an end to male violence was later added to these demands.[1] They indicate the feminist position that, despite the successes of the first wave, women's personal lives had not changed; politics did not seem to address questions of gender such as reproduction, domestic violence or sexuality. The second-wave slogan therefore became 'the personal is political'. Feminists perceived that the political sphere was broader than had been thought while the role of the state was smaller than had been envisaged (Document 1). Distrust of the state spelt women's autonomous political action. This demanded solidarity amongst women, 'sisterhood'.

Nevertheless, the last conference of the Women's Liberation Movement in 1978 had been marked by divisive and vehement debate between heterosexual and lesbian feminists. The late recognition of discrimination against lesbians had given the Movement a heterosexist profile; indeed, some feminists, for instance the Leeds Revolutionary Feminists' Collective, maintained that heterosexuality and feminism were incompatible.[2] Although, in practice, lesbians were represented in all strands of feminism,[3] these divisions meant that in the 1980s and 1990s it was no longer usual to refer to Women's Liberation/feminism as one movement.

Types of Second-Wave Feminism

While feminism was grounded in its own theory and engaged in its own activity, in the 1970s and 1980s feminists were often categorised as liberal, socialist, Marxist or Radical. This was both because some feminists professed such allegiances and because, for the traditional political theorists, it was easier to fit feminism into pre-existing traditions. It was inevitable, given the long Conservative rule from 1979, that accommodations were made particularly with the Labour Party which, defining its programme while in opposition, was both more accessible and more open to influence than the party of government (see Chapter 4). The Marxist outlook was appealing to feminists struggling to overcome women's economic oppression. Other feminists insisted on separatism, in order to claim and define a woman-only space. However, in practice, it was always difficult to fit one woman into one category; attempts to do so became less common in the later years of the twentieth century (Document 2).

Feminism continued to develop, taking a more theoretical turn, and was seen to be multifaceted. Women's Studies courses developed, growing from second-wave feminist activity within the community, rather than from universities, which showed hostility to the new discipline.[4] Feminist academics and students challenged both the content of the curriculum and traditional pedagogical methods, eventually succeeding in including modules within existing courses while arguing for a separate Women's Studies discipline (Document 17). The breakthrough was a Masters' level course at the University of Kent; other Masters and undergraduate courses followed. Journals such as *Feminist Review* (published from 1979) were prompted by the growth of the academic discipline of Women's Studies and the need to provide feminist interpretations of the curriculum. The editors' intention was also to 'intervene in political debate and activity within the women's liberation movement... The context then was, of course, one in which there existed a national movement with regular conferences'. By its eighth issue, *Feminist Review* was described as a socialist feminist journal, but by 1986, recognising that 'what is now called feminism is a much more diverse and scattered phenomenon', its editors were much less comfortable with this label (Document 18).[5]

Second-Wave Feminist Campaigns

Sexuality and housework were important areas of second-wave feminist debate (Document 3). The role of 'housewife' pointed not only to women's economic and social oppression by men, but also to their sexual oppression. Having established the social construction of gender roles, feminists perceived that sexual roles attributed on a gender basis were also socially constructed. American feminism was influential in this respect (Document 4). Women's refuges were established in major cities to give women protection from violent partners, inspired by Erin Pizzey, who remained a controversial figure in the women's movement, preferring to operate independently. Rape and pornography became issues central to feminist theorising. Rape Crisis Centres were set up and Reclaim the Night marches held. The group Women Against Violence Against Women was especially active in these campaigns. Sixteen Rape Crisis Centres had been formed by 1981.[6] The concern with male sexual violence, plus the need to escape a male-defined sexuality was the understanding of political lesbianism and its ethos that only by women loving women would full freedom be achieved (Document 5).

Some lesbian feminists, sharing the concerns of gay men, turned their attention to gay and lesbian campaigning. They particularly focused upon Section 28 of the Local Government Act 1988, which made the promotion of homosexuality to minors illegal and over health literature which implied that AIDS/HIV was exclusively a gay concern (Document 19).

Theorising about sexuality and emphasising a woman's rights over her own body impacted on one of the high-profile campaigns of second-wave feminism, a woman's right to choose abortion. In addition, socialist and Marxist feminists challenged the hierarchy and patriarchy of the medical profession. Abortion law had been relaxed in 1967 and campaigns thereafter centred on both resisting the backlash to this reform and widening the scope of the legislation. The campaigns were distinguished by huge marches and demonstrations, coordinated by the National Abortion Campaign (NAC), formed in 1975 to represent around 400 groups.[7] An unremitting response was thus made to the activities of the Society for the Protection of the Unborn Child and Life (Document 20). John Corrie's 1979 Private Member's Bill to limit

abortion rights, introduced when it was feared that the new
Conservative government might back his proposals, was
successfully resisted, partly owing to NAC organisation in local
Labour Parties and trade unions. In particular, there was support
for NAC from white-collar unions such as the National and Local
Government Officers' Organisation, which had a high female
membership.[8] The 1988 Private Member's Bill to restrict abortion,
introduced by David Alton, was also defeated. In 1990, the legal
limit for abortion in normal pregnancies was fixed at 24 weeks.
Campaigns for better information for heterosexual and lesbian
women about HIV and AIDS, originally frequently misrepresented
solely as a gay, male condition, continued to keep issues of sexuality
on the feminist agenda.[9]

The biggest single activity of second-wave feminism was the
Greenham Common protest (Document 21). Greenham Common
was a base for the Royal Air Force and the United States Air Force
(USAF). In 1979: 'NATO decided that 96 USAF ground-launched
cruise missiles would be stationed at the base. Underground silos
would be constructed for this purpose'.[10] In September 1981, a peace
march left Cardiff and reached the base.

Echoing the suffrage protesters at the beginning of the century,
four women chained themselves to the base's fence. A peace camp
was established at the main gate. Although men had participated
in the original march and many mixed groups remained supportive,[11]
the camp became a women-only protest from February 1982. While
some women lived at the base, thousands more, from Britain and
across the world, visited for a few weeks, days or hours. The
December 1982 Embrace the Base demonstration was attended by
30,000 women, who decorated the perimeter fence with feminist
and pacifist emblems and children's toys. At the Nagasaki Day
demonstration of August 1984 women represented the victims of
the nuclear bombs dropped on Japan at the end of the Second World
War by covering their bodies with ashes.[12] Hundreds more were
involved in 'cruise watch', tracking the missile launchers when they
were manoeuvred through the countryside. Although the cruise
missiles were eventually withdrawn, a presence at the camps was
maintained as a peace protest until September 2000. Other camps
had been established at military bases around the country, and local
events such as the Women's International Day for Disarmament in
1983 were widely supported, but 'Greenham' became synonymous
with feminism in the public mind.

Essentialism and Difference

The early emphasis on sisterhood that underlay such protests was challenged by the growing recognition of difference between women. Feminist interest in social policy itself made clear that some women had educational and employment advantages which others lacked (see Chapter 3). Feminist theoreticians were accused of 'essentialism' – theorising from a white, Western perspective – as black and lesbian feminists asserted their claims to equal rights, not least within the feminist movement. Again, this criticism reflected the importance in Britain of American feminism. Essentialism was partly the result of the move into the academy, which meant that feminism was expounded by intellectual women, themselves usually white and Western. It had also been inspired by Simone de Beauvoir's seminal work[13] which had accorded to women a collective identity – 'other' from that of man (Documents 6, 7 and 22). It was from the continuing lesbian challenge, and from the challenge of black American women, that essentialism came to be recognised and developed.

A further problem was that in claiming women were deserving of rights, some feminists had depicted women as special because they were carers and gave birth (Document 8). On the one hand, this 'essentialised' women as reproducers, when the facts of reproduction were very different for black, working-class, lesbian and/or disabled women and on the other it lead to a dilemma – if women were special, they were not equal, they were different. Ruth Lister, then Director of the Child Poverty Action Group, wrote that in practice, women were regarded as different; she thus identified two types of citizen – man warrior and woman carer.[14]

Third-Wave Postmodern Feminism

Black and lesbian feminist challenges were an enrichment of feminism, but contributed to a fragmentation of feminism as a movement which some, particularly those women who had celebrated the sisterhood of the early Women's Liberation Movement, found painful. However, accepting difference between women became one of the tenets of later second-wave feminism. Drawing from the work of French poststructural theorists Jacques Derrida, Jacques Lacan and Michel Foucault, the concept of difference impelled feminism to its third wave (Document 9). Third-wave feminism found accommodations not with political philosophies such as Marxism and socialism, in themselves overarching theories, but with postmodernism. How far feminism and postmodernism may be related has been the subject of debate.[15] Because it denies universalist explanations, postmodernism has been said to defy definition. For some feminists, postmodernism is useful because it offers an appreciation of difference, an exploration of the function of language and the technique of deconstruction. For others, postmodernism is disempowering, endangering women's collective strength and the distinct female voice so recently acquired.[16] Accepting postmodernism entirely makes it difficult to demand collective action premised on shared identities and goals – a position very difficult for holders of traditional Marxist/socialist ideas of class consciousness (Document 10).

Third-Wave Feminist Issues

The second-wave explanation of sexuality as socially constructed no longer held in the third wave, being itself a meta-narrative, or overarching theory. Continuing feminist concern with sexuality was expressed in the third wave by work on difference in sexualities; there was more interest in bisexuality, transsexuality (incorporating transvestism and transgenderism) and intersexed people.[17] Also a focus of interest for gay men and bisexual women, this theorising came under the umbrella heading 'Queer theory'. Issues of sexuality were broadened when male rape was legally recognised by the Criminal Justice and Public Order Act of 1995. In addition, there was continuing concern about the sexual abuse of children, an issue brought into prominence by the Butler-Sloss Inquiry into child abuse in Cleveland in 1987 (see Chapter 3). Easy access to the Internet gave new scope for publishing pornographic representations, including those of children. The Sexual Offences Act of 1997 created a national register of sex offenders.[18] To an extent, feminist concerns about sexual abuse were shared by a wider community. However, while challenging gender stereotypes and associated stereotypes of sexuality in a satisfactorily feminist way, Queer theory left little room for traditional lesbian feminism. To some second-wave feminist thinkers, Queer theory was thus profoundly subversive of feminism. To others, Queer theory was the way forward, a truly postmodern feminism (Document 11).[19]

Feminism developed as a philosophy, an academic discipline and as activity over the last two decades of the twentieth century; the issues discussed were controversial and influenced different feminists at varying times. A fixed chronology cannot be attributed to the demise of second-wave and the arrival of third-wave feminism. Rather, some women maintained the opinions of the early second-wave Women's Liberation Movement into the twenty-first century, while others took a more fragmented, third-wave approach from the 1970s. Sheila Jeffreys is an example of a second-wave feminist who, in the year 2000, restated its typical political lesbianism.[20] Nevertheless, thinking about difference between women, about women's rights to alternative sexualities and about where power resides led feminism to turn full circle, so that at the end of the twentieth century one of the big issues was again that of citizenship (Document 12). The demand for inclusion in the civil state at the beginning of the twentieth century had evolved into the understanding that the 'personal is political'. Feminists now moved towards rethinking the structure of the state, including the reasons for the male, white profile of Western polities, the continued under-representation of women and black and Asian people in central and local governments, the reiteration of family values which did not recognise alternative sexualities, the continued belligerence of nation states.[21] Feminists no longer looked to one political party for achievement of their goals which were, in any case, more diffuse. However, at the end of the century women remained disadvantaged. The next section looks at women's engagement in the late-twentieth-century labour market, where continued discrimination underwrote this disadvantage.

The Labour Market

Labour Market Changes

The persistence and vitality of the feminist movement in the last quarter of the twentieth century was reflected in profound changes in gender relations in the labour market. Legislation on employment rights and sex and race discrimination, enacted in the 1970s and 1980s, was important in giving women a degree of protection (Document 13). Not least, women were able to claim time off for trade union duties, so that their profile in industrial relations was increased (see Chapter 3). The Health and Safety at Work Act 1974, by making safety a concern of the employer and all employees, went some way towards the resolution of a century of feminist debate about whether women should have special protection at work, or whether such measures would decrease their marketability and bargaining power. The European Commission was important in ensuring that

British women benefited from European Union legislation, which extended employment rights to part-time workers.

In addition, extensive changes took place in the labour market itself. The long decline of heavy industry was incremented by the privatising measures of Mrs Thatcher's government and was matched by the rise of the service industry, using female employees. The percentage of women employed grew steadily so that by 1998, in the 25–44 age bracket, where employment rates were highest, 75 per cent of women compared to 93 per cent of men were economically active. Married women in particular increased their employment, 74 per cent being economically active by 1998. It was not unconnected that much of the increase in women's work was in part-time jobs, 44 per cent of women working part-time in 1998, compared to 4 per cent of men.[22]

Women's greater involvement in the labour market was mirrored by a reduction in the wages gap between men and women, the ratio of women's to men's earnings increasing to 80 per cent in 1998, from 72 in 1978.[23] The percentage of equal-pay cases won at employment tribunals steadily increased but remained a small proportion of applications (Document 23). Women's continued segregation into certain sectors of the labour market, the clerical, administrative and service sectors, meant that women remained disadvantaged in terms of pay. However, women steadily won greater access to the upper echelons of the labour force, their representation in the highest sections rising from 5 to 13 per cent between 1975 and 1984, while men's representation rose from 20 to 28 per cent.[24] In 1998, women formed 33 per cent of the management and administration sector and 39 per cent of the professional sector.[25]

Feminist Explanations of Labour Market Changes

Feminists described labour market segregation as vertical or horizontal, vertical segregation describing the division in each occupational category between male and female workers, horizontal sections describing the effect on the overall workforce. As second-wave feminists had been forced to realise, women differ, and the changes affected different women in various ways; in particular, black women had a distinctive experience of the labour market (Document 14). In addition, there were changes according to social status and location. The greatest difference, however, was that of age. Younger women were better educated and had greater expectations of a career and working until retirement age (Document 15).

Understanding women's participation in employment contributed to a rethinking of what constituted work, whether domestic work differed in nature to paid employment, if housework should be waged or whether that would trap women in the home.[26] Reflecting second-wave interest in Marxism, the theory that women constituted a reserve army of labour was propounded. It was seen to be in the capitalist interest to ensure continued, cheap productivity by offsetting the interests of the usual, male labour force against those of the occasional, female labour force. In that way, discipline was maintained by the potential competition for jobs, while women were normally at home, ready to care for and maintain the male workers. Expansion or contraction of production could be easily achieved. A similar theory was that a dual labour market was in operation, the prime, male market having the best pay and conditions and being supported by the secondary, female labour market. These explanations were expanded by recognising that both capitalism and patriarchy were acting to divide the labour market.

During the late 1980s and early 1990s, the segregation of the labour market and the growing preponderance within it of low-paid, female service workers seemed so profound that feminists started to write of the 'feminisation' of the labour force.[27] However, this pattern did not survive into the late 1990s, as young women began to improve their labour market position. The labour market was seen as complex, marked by changing gender relations.[28] Nonetheless, at the end of the twentieth century a difference between men's and women's pay and conditions remained. The persistence of this gender inequality has been seen as the effect of glass walls and/or ceilings, through which women can see the better jobs they are still unable to touch. Employment surveys showed that while skills acquisition had improved for both men and women, the change was greater for men and for full-time workers; employment in part-time jobs excluded many women from the benefits of training and greater responsibility (Document 16).

Conclusion

As there has been substantial progress on many of the issues which have been the subject of women's campaigns, and as life chances have greatly improved for young women compared to women of previous generations, it is sometimes assumed that we live in a post-feminist world. Many young women know little of the aims or vigorous and complex debates of the Women's Movement of the

1970s. Women's Studies courses are being closed down, or merged into other disciplines. Feminists who reclaimed the historical ground are themselves becoming lost from history.

However, continuing debate around the gay, lesbian and bisexual movement, the environment, nuclear disarmament, citizenship and nationality all benefit from past feminist contributions. Third-wave, postmodernist feminism accommodates such a plurality of approach. Second-wave feminism was a construct of the industrial, post-war West, whose personalisation of politics was an important contribution to the democratic process. The alliance made with the Labour movement was successful in returning record numbers of women to parliament (see Chapter 5). Disappointment with progress, that equal pay and prospects have not been achieved, that women remain under-represented in government and at management levels generally, may promote a new wave of feminism, conducted by women whose resources are far superior to those of their forebears.

Documents

SECONDARY SOURCES AND INTERPRETATIONS

1. Elizabeth Fraser, 'Feminist Political Theory' in Stevi Jackson and Jackie Jones (eds), *Contemporary Feminist Theories* (Edinburgh, Edinburgh University Press, 1998), pp.52–3

An important aspect of the contribution of feminism to political theory has been via feminist political practice. Feminism has been a constant feature of modern societies. As a political movement it has engaged with politics in the conventional sense, and has also widened the scope of political action in practically and theoretically significant ways.

First, there are the organised campaigns for particular legislative measures – to secure women the vote, or to give them property rights, or to make abortion legal, or for equal opportunities legislation as regards employment or welfare. These campaigns have often been ignored by conventional political scientists and historians. Where they are attended to, they clearly must count as 'political' in the conventional sense – they are public interventions in the competition for the power to govern. Second, there are organised campaigns for other, non-legislative but important social changes – more women into Parliament and thereby into government, more women into other powerful social positions such as in the professions and education (the campaign for educational institutions, professions and other occupations to be open to women are relevant here, as are such campaigns as those for equal opportunities codes and the like inside organisations such as firms and clubs, women's sections within political parties, and so on). Again, such campaigns count as 'political' in the orthodox sense.

Third, there are many organisations, connected to the pressure for formal social change, but mostly focused on informal change – self-help organisations like the telephone help lines and refuges for women sufferers of violence, or networks of women in particular occupations. Fourth, these organisations and campaigns are supplemented by and merge into cultural organisations and sites for women's organisations and action: publishing collectives, film-makers and theatre groups, shops, cafes and bars...

In feminism in the last thirty years changes in lifestyle, changes in values, changes in the way we relate to friends, colleagues, intimates, sexual partners, spouses and children have been emphasised as supremely important... Cultural activity, inter-personal discussion and self-help have been identified as more important modes of social transformation than the conventional political strategies of organised, public campaigns, at the level of the national or local state, for administrative and legislative change.

The crucial theoretical point which connects with these forms of feminist activism is that *changes within the conventional political realm* and measures taken from within political institutions – legislation and government administration – *will not bring about the kind of social change that really makes a difference to people's lives.* In this, feminism is not so different from a number of other perspectives... But these shared ideas are less important than what distances feminism from these rival social and political theories and traditions.

2. Stevi Jackson, 'Feminist Social Theory' in Stevi Jackson and Jackie Jones (eds), *Contemporary Feminist Theories* (Edinburgh, Edinburgh University Press, 1998), pp.12–13

In the 1970s and early 1980s most feminist theory was addressed to a single, basic question: how can we account for women's sub-ordination? Many feminists looked to Marxism as a means of answering this question – not only those who identified as Marxist or socialist feminists, but also some who identified themselves as radical feminists. Since the women's movement emerged in a period of widespread radical Left activism, feminists were generally familiar with, and often sympathetic to, Marxist ideas. Marxism offered an analysis of oppression as systematic, built into the structure of society. Hence women's subordination could be seen as social in origin, as neither given by nature nor an accidental feature of relations between men and women. Marxism was also a theory of social change, one which held out the promise of a more egalitarian future society. Yet, for all its appeal, Marxist theory could not easily accommodate feminism. Marxism was developed to explain capitalist class relations – the exploitation of the proletariat – and required considerable modification to accommodate gender relations...

Throughout the 1970s and early 1980s, feminists sought in a variety of ways to extend, modify or reformulate Marxist ideas, giving rise to a series of debates on the relationship between capitalism and male domination, often referred to as the patriarchy debates... The differing positions taken on this issue were related to political differences among feminists, particularly on the relationship between women's liberation and class struggle. Many textbooks on feminist theory give the impression that feminists were split into two opposing camps: Marxist or socialist feminists versus radical feminists. In fact the theoretical divisions which emerged in the course of the 1970s were far more complex. Rather than there being a split between two distinct variants of feminism, there was a continuum between those who saw women's subordination as a consequence of capitalism and those who saw it as a consequence of patriarchy, of a system of male domination. Theorists at both ends of the spectrum drew upon Marxism, but in rather different ways: while the more orthodox sought to fit feminist analysis into existing Marxist conceptual frameworks, others experimented with more radical reworkings of Marxism, taking from it only what seemed productive for feminism.

3. Stevi Jackson, 'Feminist Social Theory', in Stevi Jackson and Jackie Jones (eds), *Contemporary Feminist Theories* (Edinburgh, Edinburgh University Press, 1998), pp.16–17

Women's domestic work was itself the subject of much debate... The debate was premised on Capital's need for a constantly replenished labour force. It is largely women who do the work this entails – they cook the meals and wash the shirts necessary to make existing workers ready for each new day and care for the next generation of workers. Marxist feminists initially sought to establish that this work was socially necessary, essential to the functioning of capitalism... The debate became concerned with such issues as whether housework produced 'surplus value', in what sense housework or its products had a value and whether that value was embodied in the labour power of the housewife's husband and realised through his wage...

Yet relations between husbands and wives, particularly inequalities between them, were largely ignored. For most Marxists it was unthinkable that working-class men might be oppressors in their own homes or that 'bourgeois' women might also be oppressed...

From the early 1970s a rather different approach to domestic labour was being developed by French materialist feminists, particularly Christine Delphy. According to Delphy, the peculiarities of housework arise from the social relations within which it is performed. She argues that these relations are patriarchal and within families men systematically exploit and benefit from women's labour within a domestic mode of production... Women's domestic work is undertaken as a personal service to a male head of household. He effectively appropriates her whole person and the labour she embodies, so that the work she does is potentially limitless and depends on his requirements. Hence housework has no fixed job description; it does not directly involve the exchange of a set number of hours or an agreed amount of work for a given return. The maintenance a wife receives is not related to the work she does, but is determined by her husband's income and his generosity. The direct appropriation and non-exchange of women's labour is particularly clear when a wife is also in employment, earning enough to meet her own maintenance costs, but is still expected to do the housework. In this situation she is clearly working for nothing. Delphy argues that within the domestic mode of production men constitute a class of exploiters while women are an exploited class.

4. Linda Nicholson, 'Gynocentrism: Women's Oppression, Women's Identity and Women's Standpoint', in her *The Second Wave: A Reader in Feminist Theory* (London, Routledge, 1997), pp.148-9

This idea that women's oppression was linked to women's sexual relationships with men was beginning to surface in much thinking and writing of the time. The idea received its most theoretically sophisticated articulation in the writings of Catherine MacKinnon. A central claim of MacKinnon's is that sexuality defines gender and represents the key arena of men's domination over women. For MacKinnon, sexuality as we know it, *is* domination. What does it mean to say that sexuality *is* domination? MacKinnon is arguing against a widely held view that sexuality is a neutral domain of pleasure. The feminist appropriation of this latter view claims that this arena of pleasure has often been denied to women and in such denial has existed one source of women's oppression. MacKinnon argues that sexuality, rather than existing as a neutral domain of pleasure, is infused with power. Moreover, this power that constitutes the very dynamic of sexual desire is defined in terms of the masculine/feminine distinction. Thus the very content of masculinity is to sexually desire/have power over women as the content of femininity is to be sexually desired by/subordinated to men. The content of gender and the content of sexuality are identical as expressed in the linkage of the two in the word 'sex'. As MacKinnon argues, it is only by understanding gender, sexuality, and their relationship in such terms that we can make sense of so many aspects of present and many previous societies: the pervasiveness and content of pornography, the similarities in content between what is understood as 'normal' male sexual initiation and sexual harassment, and the similarities in content between what is understood as 'normal' heterosexuality and rape.

In this view, women's identity is constituted by women's position as victim. This does not mean that being a woman entails passivity. Women can negotiate, strategise against, and fight their oppression. But all such actions represent responses to the condition of powerlessness that defines what it means to be a woman. Even lesbianism must be understood within such terms because women's sexuality, like all other aspects of women's existence, is constructed, according to MacKinnon, under conditions of male supremacy.

5. Stevi Jackson and Sue Scott, 'Sexual Skirmishes and Feminist Factions', in *Feminism and Sexuality: A Reader* (Edinburgh, Edinburgh University Press, 1996), pp.13–14

Thus lesbianism was seen by some as a choice any woman could make, as in the slogan 'any woman can'. None the less, there was also a recognition of any constraints which kept women heterosexual. The critique of heterosexuality was seen as an institution through which men appropriated women's bodies and their labour. Romantic attachment to men led only to exploitation. As another popular slogan put it: 'It starts when you sink into his arms and ends with your arms in his sink.' Political lesbianism was thus an escape from and a challenge to patriarchal domination.

Political lesbianism in this sense was most commonly found among those who already held radical feminist views, who saw patriarchy as a system of male dominance. Some of these women became 'separatist' in orientation, rejecting all personal contact and political alliances with men. It was tensions between these radical lesbians and other feminists which, by the end of the 1970s, were to prove particularly disruptive for the WLM. The rifts thus created, alongside other divisions, made a unified women's movement increasingly difficult to sustain. However, there was not a simple split between lesbian and heterosexual women. Many lesbian feminists rejected separatism as a political solution, especially where it implied criticism of those women who remained heterosexual. Those who had been lesbians before the rise of the WLM, so-called 'real lesbians', were often sceptical of the zeal of recent converts, and concerned about the authenticity of their desires. Lesbian socialist feminists, for whom sexuality was a less central political issue, largely remained aloof from disputes about political lesbianism. Lesbian radical feminists were to be found on both sides of the divide, causing acute and painful splits within radical feminism. More positively, the debate this engendered produced a fuller theorisation both of the critique of heterosexuality and of the politics of lesbianism.

6. Ann Garry and Marilyn Pearsall, *Women, Knowledge and Reality: Explorations in Feminist Philosophy* (London, Routledge, 1996), pp.2–3

As feminist philosophers seek to articulate the meaning and implications of differences between women and men, it is important not to obscure or erase differences among women themselves. Unfortunately this has been and continues to be a problem for racism, heterosexism, and other biases exist among feminists, too. For instance, some feminists who are western, white, heterosexual, Christian, middle or upper class (or in any other dominant position) have failed to recognise the ways in which they are privileged at the same time as they are subordinated as women. Incorrectly believing their experiences to be universal, they have over-generalised, spoken on behalf of 'women', and in other ways silenced, ignored and disrespected women different from themselves. The pain caused by these practices and theories has been documented and expressed by many women. Thus, when discussing differences between women, it is important to focus not simply on the impact of differences on feminist theory but also on the impact that ignoring these differences has had on individual women themselves.

The interconnections among gender, race, class, ethnicity, sexual orientation, and other dimensions are truly complex. If the experiences and concerns of women differ so widely, then feminists must ask whether women have enough in common to engage feminist politics or feminist theory. Feminist approaches vary on this topic. Some feminists believe that even the category 'woman' has itself become problematic. Others explore the overlaid, multifaceted identities of women. Feminists who have been marginalised often address issues in terms of identity politics and struggle with priorities on their own terms. Still others search for patterns of similarity amidst the diversity.

7. Heidi Safia Mirza, *Black British Feminism: A Reader* (London, Routledge, 1997), pp.9–11

Just as the political arena witnessed a backlash to the reductionism of identity politics, so too was there a reaction to the reductionism inherent within white feminist theory in the 1980s… However, racial power within the white feminist production of knowledge about gender relations was never problematized. Whiteness was a 'given' social position. Ironically it meant that an epistemology that rests on inclusion and equality was itself excluding and unequitable…

But if the 'woman's' standpoint was embedded in that given, unproblematized space of whiteness – and it was – then how could feminism claim universal legitimacy? Black women's experience was invisible, or if made visible spoken for and constructed through the authoritative, imperial voice of whiteness… The call to recognize difference and diversity in the feminist project was incompatible with the notion of an essential, universal 'woman' subject. The struggle of black women to claim a space within the modernist feminist discourse, and at the same time to engender critical racial reflexivity among white feminists, consumed the black feminist project for more than a decade.

8. Mary Daly, *Gyn/Ecology* (London, The Women's Press, 1978, reprinted 1984), p.355

The rulers of patriarchy – males with power – wage an unceasing war against life itself. Since female energy is essentially biophilic, the female spirit/body is the primary target in this perpetual war of aggression against life. Gyn/Ecology is the re-claiming of life-loving female energy. This claiming of gynergy requires knowing/naming the fact that the State of Patriarchy is the State of War, in which periods of recuperation from and preparation for battle are euphemistically called 'peace'. Furies/Amazons must know the nature and conditions of this State in order to dis-cover and create radical female friendship. Given the fact that we are struggling to emerge from an estranged State, we must understand that the Female Self is The Enemy under fire from the guns of patriarchy. We must struggle to dis-cover this Self as Friend to all that is truly female, igniting the Fire of Female Friendship.

9. Extract from Michèle Barrett, 'The Concept of Difference', *Feminist Review*, 26 (Summer 1987), p.30

In modern feminism a sense of 'difference' as the recognition of diverse social experience has become politically important... So there is now quite a widespread recognition of both class and racism as two major axes of difference between women. In addition, however, the claims of nation, region and ethnicity, as well as age, sexual orientation, disability and religion are being pressed as important and politically salient forms of experiential diversity.

'Difference' used in this sense is a relatively 'commonsensical' term, certainly compared with some of the more elaborated theories... But it is nonetheless very influential. In its treatment of the traditional tension between theory and politics it tends towards what is philosophically regarded as the 'pragmatic' end of the spectrum, relying on experience as a guide to both theory and politics... This charge of essentialism argues that in these writings we find assumptions about women's language, culture and personality that rest on psychic, social and cultural 'separate spheres' for men and women. The essentialism at stake here is an assumed or argued difference between women and men that is held to have very wide repercussions in society generally.

10. Ann Garry and Marilyn Pearsall, *Women, Knowledge and Reality: Explorations in Feminist Philosophy*, pp.3–4

Postmodernists reject the search for underlying truth, certainties and essences. They do not believe it possible to find universal principles that explain the natural and the social world; they reject standard notions of rationality and objectivity and the idea of a stable, knowing self...

Postmodern discourses create the kinds of conceptual spaces that many feminists find appropriate for their intellectual work. For example, a feminist might seek to dismantle the concept of gender or of a right: such concepts have no privileged status in a postmodern context. At the same time that feminism has affinities to postmodernism, there are differences and tensions as well. For postmodernists undermine many of the concepts that feminists themselves continue to use in their theories and practices... For example, in every day life, feminists sometimes find their most promising course of action within the framework of individual rights, for example in a case of job discrimination or sexual harassment.

11. Extract from Clare Farquhar, '"Lesbian" in a Post-Lesbian world? Policing Identity, Sex or Image', *Sexualities*, 3 (2) *Special Issue, Speaking from a Lesbian Position: Opening Up Sexuality Studies* (May 2000), p.220

Does... the dissolution and incorporation of the category 'lesbian' within the category 'queer' represent a strategic step towards the dismantlement, or reproduction, of hegemonic sexual meanings and relations of power...? Has feminism achieved a climate in which women can be 'sexual in a manner utterly different in meaning from either pre-feminist or non-feminist versions demanded by phallocentrically defined female heterosexuality'...? Are we now free to interpret the reemergence of lesbian sexual practices such as 'butch-femme' behaviour or dildo use...? Have lesbian identities become redundant, or indeed counterproductive, to the dissolution of heteropatriarchal power?

Lesbian ambivalence on all of these points is not surprising. The hard-won nature of contemporary lesbian visibility, and the relatively precarious subject position which is arguably occupied by lesbians, as opposed to gay men, means that lesbians have more to lose than most in relinquishing a visible 'lesbian' position before it has fully emerged...

But if women are reluctant to abandon the position lesbian, how do they continue to negotiate this position in a climate where sexual identities are both proliferating and being broken down? What role does sex or sexuality play in their negotiations? And how is this expressed? And what implications do their negotiations have for the negotiation of sexual meanings more widely, both now and in the future?

12. Diane Richardson, 'Claiming Citizenship? Sexuality, Citizenship and Lesbian/Feminist Theory', in *Sexualities*, 3 (2) (May 2000), p.256

Since the 1980s, social movements concerned with 'sexual politics' have increasingly couched their demands in terms of the attainment of citizens' rights, particularly 'lesbian and gay' movements. This has been most evident in the US, but is increasingly dominant elsewhere. The growth in the use of the language of citizenship, in contrast to the language of liberation spoken by social movements of an earlier generation has in a sense, therefore, prompted this examination of the ways in which sexuality intersects with the status of citizenship in modern democracies.

These developments raise a number of important questions for lesbian/feminist theory and practice. At a fundamental level, how are we to interpret this growing interest in and use of the term sexual citizenship. In what ways is sexual citizenship being defined? Is it primarily being used as a gender-neutral or a gender-differentiated concept? What are the consequences of a relative lack of emphasis on gender in the sexual citizenship literature for women, in particular as 'lesbian citizens'. And, in so far as citizenship is defined in terms of rights and duties, what are meant by sexual rights and obligations?

13. Sylvia Walby, *Gender Transformations* (London, Routledge, 1997), pp.38–9

Many discriminatory barriers to women in employment and education have been removed since the 1970s.

These changes have been underpinned by a legal framework for equal opportunities introduced in the 1970s and 1980s. The Equal

Pay legislation, passed in 1970 and implemented in 1975, was important in the narrowing of the wages gap between women and men from 63 per cent of men's hourly earnings in 1970 to 74 per cent in 1977. The legislation has since been regularly strengthened, with the Sex Discrimination Act of 1975, the 1984 Equal Value Amendment which legislated for equal pay for work of equal value, not merely similar work, and in 1994 the extension of many full-time rights to part-time workers.

The passage of this sex equality legislation was due to a number of political factors both domestic and international, including: pressure from organised women trade unionists; a campaign by five trade unions – the National Association of Local Government Officers, The National Union of Teachers, the Civil Service Clerical Association, the Institute of Professional Civil Servants and the Society of Civil Servants (only one of which – the CSCA – was affiliated to the TUC); pressure to ratify the 1951 International Labour Organisation Convention 100 on equal pay; the support of a woman Minister of State, Barbara Castle; and the requirements of the intended membership of the Common Market (now EU) because Article 119 of the Treaty of Rome demanded the equal treatment of women and men in employment-related matters. By the late 1960s and early 1970s when legislation was being considered by the UK Parliament there were no major institutional forces ranged against it. Organised women, the Trades Union Congress, the Confederation of British Industry, the Labour Party and the Conservative Party were all in support of some such legislation.

Further improvements to the legislation were the result of pressure from the European Commission, which took enforcement procedures against the UK Government in the European Court of Justice – for instance to expand the notion of equal pay to cover work of equal value not merely similar work, resulting in the Equal Value Amendment Act in 1984. The UK Government was also forced to provide the same rights to part-time workers as to full-timers as a result of the defeat of the UK Government position in the House of Lords due to the primacy of EU law over UK law in the matter of equal opportunities in employment. Thus in order to understand the legal framework for equal opportunity in employment we need to recognise the importance of not only the UK state, but also the European Union and in particular its Commission...

Equal opportunities policies have been introduced in many companies and many trade unions since the 1970s... They have been encouraged since the 1970s by the CBI, the Equal Opportunities Commission (especially through its 'Equality Exchange'), business-led campaigns such as Opportunity 2000, as well as organised women workers. Companies have innovated with 'family friendly' policies, such as the career break schemes introduced by banks (among other employers) to facilitate women combining careers with raising children... special equal opportunities committees... and forms of 'diversity management' integrated into wider personnel policies.

14. Ann Witz, 'Women at Work' in Diane Richardson and Victoria Robertson (eds), *Introducing Women's Studies* (London, Macmillan, 1993), p.279

Homeworkers are one of the most vulnerable and low-paid groups in the workforce and are often found doing manufacturing, needlework, office and clerical work, childminding and semi-professional work. The Trades Union Congress estimated that there were 390,000 homeworkers in 1981, although it is extremely difficult to gauge the precise number of homeworkers in Britain. The debate about whether or not Black women are dis-proportionately represented amongst their ranks... should alert us to the differences between white women, Asian women and Afro-Caribbean women in Britain, not only in relation to homeworking but also in relation to part-time and full-time employment, and the kinds of jobs done. As regards part-time employment, there are important ethnic differences between women. One study showed that whilst 44 per cent of white women worked part-time, only 29 per cent of Afro-Caribbean women and 16 per cent of Asian women did... And whilst full-time work is associated with better pay and conditions for white women, the same is not true for Black women... Indeed, it has been argued that the emphasis white feminists have placed on part-time work as a determinant of gender inequalities between women's and men's paid work can be seen as ethnocentric... in Britain, Black women are much less likely to be working part-time and appear to be constrained to work full-time; especially West Indian women, who are more likely to be the main or sole breadwinners in a family and to find themselves in poverty. Whereas for white women, rewards, prospects and the quality of work vary greatly between those who work full-time and those who work part-time, the same is not true for Black women.

15. Sylvia Walby, *Gender Transformations* (London, Routledge, 1997), pp.64–5

The massive changes which are taking place in women's employment and education are transforming gender relations. Some younger women are taking up the educational opportunities offered and then using them to gain good jobs. Domestic tasks are less frequently acting as an obstacle to this strategy, in that women are returning to work more rapidly after childbirth, and women are less likely to be married. These changes in education and employment are the leading edge of the change from the private gender regime to the public one.

But these changes do not involve all women. They particularly miss those women who, for reasons including generation, ethnicity, and pregnancy, have not gained educational qualifications. For example, many older women missed the recent expansion of educational opportunities and are much less likely to have qualifications and good jobs (although there are exceptions). Their current choices are constrained by choices made earlier in their lives when private patriarchal relations were more prevalent. Older women are taking up disproportionately the newly restructured lower skilled occupations, especially in services. These are disproportionately part-time, poorly paid forms of employment. This exerts downwards pressure on the availability and conditions of employment for men as well. Further, women in different ethnic communities have different priorities and opportunities which generate different sexual divisions of labour, but recognisable as either of more public or more private form of gender regime. The complex interventions of the state as provider of minimal benefits interact with some household structures so as to discourage some women's employment. Not all young women are doing well, for instance lone parents without employment are likely to be very poor, and women from ethnic minorities are more likely to be unemployed.

Women who are not participating in paid employment with the benefit of educational qualifications are likely to be poor and disadvantaged. We are seeing new forms of polarisation between women. These are based less on the class of their husband and much more on their own education and employment. In practice because of the speed of the changes the more advantaged women are among younger women, the more disadvantaged among the older.

16. Duncan Gallie, 'Skill, Gender and the Quality of Employment', in Rosemary Crompton *et al* (eds), *Changing Forms of Employment: Organisations, Skills and Gender* (London, Routledge, 1996), pp.1, 46–52

The gender gap in skills and responsibility

A comparison of the measures for skill and responsibility for men and women showed that there was a significant gender gap in the early 1990s. Women were more likely to be in jobs where no qualifications were required (39 per cent compared with 30 per cent) and they were less likely to be in jobs requiring at least A Level qualifications (32 per cent compared with 41 per cent). They were also less likely to have experienced an increase in their skills over the previous five years... Whereas 66 per cent of men reported that the skills they used in their work had increased, this was the case for 60 per cent of women. There are similar gender differences with respect to task discretion and responsibility. On the measure of task discretion, women had a score of -0.04, whereas men had a score of 0.04 (a difference statistically significant at the $p<0.05$ level). Similarly, women had benefited less from the growth of responsibility in work, with 61 per cent of women, compared with 70 per cent of men, saying that the responsibility involved in their job had increased.

Women's disadvantage in skill development was evident in all occupational classes other than that of professionals and managers, where they were somewhat more likely to have experienced an increase in skills. The gender gap was particularly marked among technicians/supervisors, manual workers and lower non-manual employees. Women were also less likely to have seen the responsibility in their job increase in all classes, although the difference between sexes was very slight among those in professional/managerial positions and in skilled manual work. In contrast, there was a 15 percentage point difference among those in technical/supervisory grades, a 14 point difference among lower non-manual workers and a 9 point difference among those in semi- and non-skilled manual work. In general men have higher levels of task discretion than women even within specific occupational classes; the only class in which women have higher levels of task discretion than men is that of semi- and non-skilled manual workers.

Change over time in gender differences

While these differences in the experiences of men and women are marked and very consistent, what has been the trend over time?

Have the differences between men and women been decreasing or increasing? The evidence suggests that there was a significant decline over the decade in gender disadvantage with respect to skill but not with respect to task discretion.

To begin with, while there was a rise in the qualifications required for jobs for both sexes, the shift was particularly marked for women... As a result the differential between the proportions of men and women in work without qualification requirements declined from 17 percentage points in 1986 to 9 points in 1992, while the gender gap for jobs requiring degree level qualifications declined from 7 to 4 percentage points...

The trends in the gender gap for training and for on-the-job experience follow a similar pattern... The difference in 1986 in the proportions of men and women who said that they had no training for their type of work was one of 18 percentage points, whereas by 1992 it had been reduced to 10 points. There was a corresponding reduction in the gender differential from 18 to 12 percentage points in the proportions with a year or more training. With respect to on-the-job experience, the gender differential declined from 20 to 13 percentage points in the proportions needing less than a month to be able to do the job well, and from 26 to 19 percentage points in those needing a year or more.

As with the evidence for qualifications, training and on-the-job experience, the data on subjective experiences of skill change indicate that the gender gap is narrowing. In 1986, there was a gap of 11 percentage points in the proportions of men and women who had experienced a skill increase; by 1992, this had diminished to 6 points. The gender gap closed most strikingly at the top and the bottom of the occupational hierarchy: in professional/ managerial jobs on the one hand and in semi- and non-skilled manual jobs on the other. Indeed, while, in 1986, women professionals and managers were less likely to have experienced a skill increase than their male equivalents, in 1992 they were more likely to report upskilling. However, in sharp contrast, in lower non-manual work the relative advantage of men with respect to upskilling had grown greater.

The implications of part-time work

An earlier analysis for the mid-1980s of trends in skill... showed that most of the difference between men's and women's experiences was related to the particularly disadvantageous position of women in part-time work. Women in full-time work were closer to the pattern for male employment than they were to that of female part-timers. Could it be that skill experiences were polarising not along the lines of gender *per se*, but along the line of part-time/full-time work?

Taking first the level of qualifications required for the job, there remained in 1992 a sharp distinction between part-time and full-time workers... Among female part-timers, 56 per cent reported that no qualifications were required of people currently being recruited for their type of work, whereas this was the case for only 27 per cent of female full-timers and 29 per cent of men in full-time work. On the other hand, only 37 per cent of female part-timers said that O Levels were needed, compared with 67 per cent of female full-timers and 63 per cent of male full-timers... Women in full-time work were also closer to men than to women in part-time work on the training and on-the-job experience criteria of skill. It is clear that the main division on all of the skill criteria lies not along gender lines, but between women in full-time and women in part-time work.

However, while the distinction between part-time and full-time work still remains a fundamental one for skill levels, the trend over time has been for the disadvantage of part-time workers to diminish rather than to grow greater. In terms of qualification change, the period saw rather modest changes for men, rather more substantial changes for women in full-time work, but above all quite major changes for women in part-time work... For instance, taking those who reported that no qualifications were required, the proportions dropped by 3 percentage points for men, by 7 percentage points for women in full-time work, and by 14 percentage points for women in part-time work. On the other hand, the increases in the proportions saying O Level equivalent or higher was required were respectively 9, 12 and 15 percentage points.

A similar pattern emerges with respect to training and the on-the-job experience required to do the job well. The proportion of female part-timers who had received no training fell by 19 percentage points between 1986 and 1992, whereas the decrease among women in full-time work was 13 points and among men 8 points. Similarly, the proportion of female part-timers who reported that they needed less than a month of on-the-job experience to do their job well declined by 17 percentage points, whereas that for female full-timers fell by only 2 points and for male full-timers by only one. It should be recognised, however, that the improvement in the position of female part-timers was primarily in the intermediate categories of training and on-the-job experience. They improved their position only very slightly in the category of those who had had a year or more training or required a year or more on-the-job experience.

Finally, if subjective reports of skill increase are considered, it is again clear that the position of female part-time workers has improved relative to that of full-time workers since the mid-1980s … while both full-timers and part-timers were more likely to have experienced an increase in their skills in 1992 compared with 1986, the change was considerably greater among part-timers. The proportion reporting a skill increase was 12 percentage points higher among male full-timers, 11 points higher among female full-timers, but 20 points higher among female part-timers.

PRIMARY EVIDENCE AND INFORMATION

17. 'Studying Ourselves', *Spare Rib*, 93 (April 1980), pp.50–53

For the past five years feminists in Edinburgh have run a Women's Studies course through the Department of Extra Mural Studies of the University. In practice it owes its beginnings and continued existence to one particular woman working in the extra mural department who has encouraged us and invited us back year after year. It is advertised with the other day and evening classes run by the department in a prospectus which is quite widely distributed in the city…

The enrolment fee for the course is now £4.20 per term which we think is prohibitive for some women, and it seems likely too that the title 'University' puts some women off. This has made us question the wisdom of running the course through an official body. We have agreed that the department publicity opens it up to women who would not otherwise find and come to women's liberation meetings and that the neutral territory helps in the same way, so we feel that the advantages outweigh the disadvantages at the moment. Since it is an official class it cannot be closed to men but men generally do not come so this has not been major problem.

It is our choice to run the course as a group and we're only able to get one tutor's fee for the sessions. Since this is such a small amount when shared out between us we usually put the money into women's campaigns and activities.

Originally a women's studies group at the University was invited to run the course. They did it for one year and then handed it on to another group. Now each year the course is run by a different group of women, who come together specifically for this purpose. Some of these women are professional teachers but it's always a mixed group and we see it as important that women with different backgrounds and experience work together, sharing skills. It has become an acknowledged responsibility of the women's movement in Edinburgh to make sure that there are women to run the course each year. Some women return for a second year on the collective and most years there is someone on the collective who first joined the course as a student.

The women running the course work as a collective, jointly taking responsibility for planning the course, producing material, preparing talks and inviting speakers. Each year the group is different, so there is a different approach, although certain features remain constant. All the women are feminists but the orientation of their feminism can be very different and in their work on the collective these differences can be productive both in personal terms and in the context of the course.

We make conscious efforts to keep the atmosphere in the class informal and to involve the women who come as students in the structuring and planning of the sessions. We pull the tables and chairs out of their serried ranks and put them in a circle; we provide tea and coffee and often go to the pub together after the class.

As feminists I think we see the importance of breaking down the framework of conventional teaching and learning, stressing that in women's studies all women are experts because of their experience as women. With a group rather than an individual running the class it is much easier to recognise the reality of us learning together, and to avoid the absurdity of an 'expert' on women teaching other 'inexpert' women. This is demonstrated practically during the year when 'students' take on the responsibility themselves of planning and preparing parts of the course. In women's studies the way in which we learn is a vital part of what we learn.

18. *Feminist Review, Special Issue: Socialist Feminism 'Out of the Blue'*, 23 (Summer 1986), pp.4–5

The changes that have taken place in national, socialist and feminist politics have been one of the recurring themes in the constant assessment and reassessment of priorities which the politics of the last decade have demanded. Currently some of us are very conscious that socialist-feminism is regarded by many as a dead political perspective, and a label that was attached to a particular current in the women's liberation movement of the 1970s. We are also conscious of a generation gap in feminism. The women involved in the formative period of socialist-feminism in Britain were nearly all highly educated, white and middle class, their policies indebted to the 1960s student revolt and its legacies. Younger feminists' formative experiences are of chronic unemployment, a massive dismantling of public services and provision, and a more right-wing, embattled and confrontational political culture. In this history gross social divisions have been given new and painful meaning.

19. Greater London Council Equal Opportunities Group, *Challenging Heterosexism in the Workplace* (London, GLC, 1986), p.31

Again the misinformation in relation to this is largely the mass media's responsibility. Very few gay men actually contract AIDS; drug users who use infected needles and those who use blood products are also at risk of getting the disease. Further, AIDS cannot be passed through ordinary social contact, such as drinking from someone else's teacup or shaking hands. The AIDS scare ignores the fact that there are heterosexually linked diseases which kill, like cervical cancer in women. The idea of linking disease with an oppressed group is not new and has been used in the past to stir up hatred against a particular race or class.

This is not to say that AIDS should not be taken seriously by the health services, and funding provided to treat it. Both heterosexual people and gay people should also be given accurate information on causes and prevention. Lesbians are the group least at risk of getting AIDS unless they fall into one of the other categories as well, or unless they use infected sperm for artificial insemination.

20. 'October 28', *Spare Rib*, 89 (December 1979)

Susan Hemmings was there... This is the demonstration we won't easily forget, the one which won't fade into a blur of sore feet, sore throats, and the steely gaze of the bus conductor as you try to get the banner poles up the stairs... This time, the sheer size of it, acres of people, streams of banners, all in one place at one time to support abortion rights, marked both feminist and trade union histories. It was a hard-won success, to which every women there had in some measure contributed. For the women in the National Abortion Campaign planning committees and in the Trade Union Women's Advisory Committee it was the culmination of years of negotiation, persuasion, and hard organising slog.

Such a crucial meeting point between the women's and the labour movement could not be expected to pass completely smoothly. Our aims are by no means entirely unified, and there are misrepresentations and mistrust between us that make a strained alliance. Women whose main area of struggle has been their union know how difficult it is to persuade men that women count and should have a say, especially on their own issues. While it was amazing to see so many men from the labour movement on the march, the feeling of 'At Last!' had also to contain the sentiment 'and about time too'.

Rumblings of discontent began first about the visible leadership of the march – a row of men, with one or two women, followed by a mixed contingent; then about the attitude of male TUC stewards towards the all-women contingent – not even planned for originally, and then placed fifth of the seven parts of the march! What had started as a handful of women who'd been trying all week to phone NAC and the TUC to discuss the proposed marching order, suddenly burst into a spontaneous act by 300, all differing in their politics but united by the provocative stewarding, and the belief that abortion is basically about women, and women should lead. So with the march now more or less assembled, they took off for the front.

The *Spare Rib* banner was one of the few to join the London Women's Liberation banner in front of the march, and it got there in a mixture of spontaneity and confusion. Some of us were looking after the banner and selling the magazine at the side of the park when we saw what seemed like a vast mass of women streaming over towards us, and assembled with them. The rest of the collective members were in the main all-women contingent or selling at other points and did not know, like the mass of the women there, what was happening.

Some who were furious at the outset changed their minds and supported the action, others when they thought more about it were distressed both by the take over and the *Spare Rib* banner being a part of it. For those who decided to stay, it was Len Murray's attempts to use the police to send us off separately that forged a link between us and women who had originally come to the front. And by this time 200 more women had joined us.

Now the collective was scattered throughout the march with our banner at the front, when we'd previously promised readers they could look out for it and rally under it if they wanted. Some might say this vividly reflects our collective practice – politically all over the place! It certainly illustrated some of the dilemmas of the day – perhaps a microcosm of the confusions and frustrations that many women felt.

It was clear to me that the new front of the march contained women from all sorts of groups and political commitments. I expected at the time that the papers and TV were likely to lump us together as loony libbers (but in fact we were pleasantly surprised by what they did say). I didn't expect that reaction, though, from other women. Mixed in with serious criticisms of taking unplanned action and seeming to ignore other women's considered decisions, have been comments grouping us all together as irresponsible wreckers and an un-representative vocal minority. I'm not often swayed by the 'vocal minority' argument, since I know that changes are often (not always) made by little loud groups – such as women in the trade unions who pressed for this march so hard over the years. Of course, it is just about possible to say that by the very act of going to the front we *became* instantly politically infantile, but that doesn't seem like a very satisfactory analysis of what made 500 women change their minds about where they would march that day. NAC and TUC organisers have to reflect on what part they too might have played in bringing the conflict about. If there had been a group of trade union women at the head, everyone would have been satisfied. A shared explanation rather than a fight, is what we need.

There was further trouble when the march ended at Trafalgar Square. Where the speakers were assembling there were only TUC slogans displayed ('Keep It Legal, Keep It Safe', 'Defend the 1967 Act' – not that abortion *is* all that legal now). There was pressure to take a women's liberation banner up, too. After scuffles and three women arrested, heckling broke out. The speakers were very distressed by the noise, especially those two women who had less experience of mass public speaking. The general agreements, subsequently, have been that it is unsisterly to heckle women speaking on shared issues, whatever the circumstances; and that women's slogans such as 'A Woman's Right to Choose', 'Free Contraception and Abortion', 'No Forced Sterilisation', could and should have been prominent.

We have discussed the day, and the issues, at great length in *Spare Rib*. By taking the banner to the front none of us wanted to make a gesture placing ourselves at the forefront of the movement, alienating masses of women or destroying the work of other sisters. Not all women *did* respond that way to our action. But when you make spontaneous gestures (or carefully planned ones) you have to take *all* reactions into account when you assess what you've done. We all agree on the need to make alliances with sympathetic organisations, and to work together with women in the unions. We have disagreements, as we always do, about how to go about that.

The dust is still settling. To me the central area of argument still seems to be between those women saying that solidarity and publicity are politically crucial at this time – why did you threaten it with your thoughtless act? And other women asking – how can you put the matter of women's autonomy aside over an issue like abortion? How could the march have been planned that way in the first place? Between the two positions we can see important questions for us all to resolve.

21. Beth Junor, *Greenham Women's Peace Camp: A History of Non-Violent Resistance, 1984–1995* (Working Press, 1995), (i) p.15; (ii) p.29; (iii) p.45

(i) January 1st, 1984: Sarah Hipperson
I was determined to start the year of 1984 on Greenham Common.

I had been in London, recovering from a water only fast in Holloway Women's Prison which had lasted from November 1st until December 1st, 1983. The fast was never intended to be a 'Hunger Strike' – it was an offering, as so many offerings were made by other women to bring about a change of heart and mind. On the 14th of November I had listened on my radio to the first of the consignment of 96 ground launched cruise missiles arriving by plane over the heads of the women waiting to blockade the roads... I remember thinking, 'Now the real work starts – we will have the missiles removed; it will take ten years, but it will be done.' The quality of commitment was there and women were prepared to live in an entirely different way from their previous experiences. It was exhilarating to come to the realisation that this disparate group of women could come together for the purpose of taking on the greatest military power in the world, with the strongest belief that they had the right to do so, and set about doing so with absolute determination.

Once out, I was desperate to get back to the camp, but I knew living on the Common needed more strength than I had at the time. I'd lost 2½ stone of body weight.

(ii) July 1984: Mary Millington – A large number of women had taken part in the early morning fence-cutting action on the North side of Greenham, but only a chosen minority of us were arrested and charged. The Metropolitan Police, who had been drafted in to practice techniques they would use on miners pickets, were using horrendously violent crowd control tactics, isolating individuals and then attacking them in groups of 6. Sarah Green, holding a two-week old baby Jay, and deliberately keeping well away from the fence, was one of those attacked in this way.

There were 14 women in court, including 3 of us who had 'confessed' after failing to be arrested, but there were 18 pairs of boltcutters exhibited by the prosecution. Had some of us been using 2 pairs at once?! The fact was that the police had learned by now that the prisons could not cope with a lot of us at once, but they had not yet learned to keep the damage calculation down to below the Crown Court level.

We caused chaos in Reading Crown Court. At first they searched us every morning on our arrival, in spite of the fact that we were all on bail. Some women insisted on stripping to avoid being touched by the prison officers, which caused such embarrassment to the court that the searches were discontinued...

(iii) April 30th – May 5th 1985: Mary Millington – After it became clear that 'melting into the countryside' (which was what the military said cruise missiles would do!) actually meant having war-game exercises on Salisbury Plain, an idea began to grow in some of our minds: Salisbury Plain should be reclaimed by non-violent women...

The following day we mustered... After a long meeting, it was the strong wills of Katrina, Sarah Green and Missy which got us all over a barbed wire fence and on to military land. Only a handful of arrests were made. The MoD police were quite inadequate in numbers to prevent our passage, and firing on the ranges had to be stopped as we tramped through on our Reclaiming path down the Centre Range Road.

Katrina – We were facing certainly over fifty MoD Police who were determined we weren't going to go on. What we did was, instead of going through them we went around them: over a barbed wire fence, around them, onto the Range and then straight down the road. They went berserk. They were running around shouting at us, 'Don't you know there's live firing!' although it was a clear road and we had some distance to go before we would get to the point where they were shelling.

The police were trying to stop women and they didn't succeed...

22. *Feminist Review: Special Issue, Socialist Feminism 'Out of the Blue'*, 23 (Summer 1986), p.6

Much feminist writing today is heavily influenced by forms of 'essentialism' in which the idea or assumption that really women are such and such, while men are something else, is central. This surfaces in many forms, in the idea of 'women's language', 'women's culture', 'women-centred values', 'women's morality' and so on. It is, moreover, by far the most popular version of feminism currently available, both within feminism and within society more generally. This form of feminist consciousness has its origins in the invisibility and silencing of women which is the day-to-day creation and re-creation of their powerlessness. When we insist, as socialist-feminists, on the importance for sexual politics of the content and dynamics of gendered qualities and attributes, we simultaneously, and equally, insist that these are not some defining core of men and women but have been created by particular societies. As masculinity and femininity are social creations so feminists should be critical of the specific versions of these identities that are formed and reinforced in contemporary society. So too socialist-feminists emphasise that among the sources of the significant forms of these gendered identities is the class nature of society.

23. http://www.eoc.org.uk/Valuing Women/html/ body_srmsdast.html, Employment Tribunal Statistics

EMPLOYMENT TRIBUNAL STATISTICS
EQUAL PAY CASES ONLY FROM 1976 TO 1998

Year	Total no. applications	Total heard	Withdrawn	Won	Settled	Dismissed	Disposed of otherwise
1976	1742	709	927	213	106	496	
1977	751	363	332	91	56	272	
1978	343	80	234	24	33	56	
1979	263	78	156	13	29	65	
1980	91	26	55	4	10	22	
1981	54	27	18	6	9	21	
1982	39	13	18	2	8	11	
1983	35	15	15	9	5	6	
1984	70	24	31	11	15	13	
1985*	302	64	148	37	84	27	6
1986	517	161	282	44	71	117	3
1987	1043	24	750	7	89	17	180
1988	813	63	350	14	95	49	305
1989	397	55	210	33	64	22	68
1990	508	35	246	10	64	25	163
1991	227	81	100	5	45	76	1
1992	240	55	83	21	102	34	0
1993	780	43	685	19	50	24	2
1994	418	25	286	8	98	17	9
1995	694	82	456	36	128	46	28
1996	no figures available						
1997	1483	91	1069	18	253	73	70
1998	1530	316	650	7	517	309	47
Total	12344	2430	7101	632	1931	1798	882

*from the end of 1985 the figures were calculated by financial year rather than by calendar year.

Notes

1. Stevi Jackson and Sue Scott, 'Sexual Skirmishes and Feminist Factions', in *Feminism and Sexuality: A Reader* (Edinburgh, Edinburgh University Press, 1996), fn.43, p.29.

2. Leeds Revolutionary Feminists, 'Political Lesbianism: The Case against Heterosexuality', in *Love Your Enemy: The Debate between Heterosexual Feminism and Political Lesbianism* (London, Onlywoman Press, 1981).

3. Jackson and Scott, 'Sexual Skirmishes and Feminist Factions', p.13.

4. Sue Jackson, 'Networking Women: A History of Ideas, Issues and Developments in Women's Studies in Britain', in *Women's Studies International Forum*, 23 (1) (2000); Fiona Montgomery and Christine Collette, *Into the Melting Pot: Teaching Women's Studies in the New Millennium* (Aldershot, Ashgate, 1997).

5. Editorial, *Feminist Review, Special Issue: Socialist Feminism 'Out of the Blue'*, 23 (Summer 1986), p.4. This sort of debate was also apparent in *History Workshop*.

6. Ruth Henig and Simon Henig, *Women and Political Power: Europe since 1945* (London, Routledge, 2001), pp.36–7; Sue Bruley, *Women in Britain since 1900* (London, Macmillan, 1999), pp.152–3.

7. Henig and Henig, *Women and Political Power*, p.36.

8. Joni Lovenduski, 'Parliament, Pressure Groups, Networks and the Women's Movement', in Joni Lovenduski and Joyce Outshoorn (eds), *The New Politics of Abortion* (London, Sage, 1986), p.60.

9. Tamsin Wilton, 'Desire and Politics of Representation: Issues for Lesbian and Heterosexual Women', in Hilary Hinds *et al* (eds), *Working Out: Directions for Women's Studies* (Brighton, Falmer Press, 1992); Lesley Hall, *Sex, Gender and Social Change in Britain since 1880* (London, Macmillan, 2000) pp.186–193.

10. Beth Junor, *Greenham Common Women's Peace Camp: A History of Non-Violent Resistance* (London, Working Press, 1995), p.x.

11. This includes National Union of Mineworkers' groups in the 1984/5 miners strike; see Chapter 3.

12. Bruley, *Women in Britain since 1900*, p.154.

13. Simone de Beauvoir, *The Second Sex* (London, Jonathan Cape, 1953).

14. Ruth Lister, '"She Has Other Duties": Women, Citizenship and Social Policy', in Sally Baldwin and Jane Falkingham (eds), *Social Security and Social Change: New Challenges to the Beveridge Model* (Hemel Hempstead, Harvester Wheatsheaf, 1994).

15. Diane Elam, *Feminism and Deconstruction: Ms. En Abyme* (London, Routledge, 1994).

16. Linda Nicholson, *Feminism/Postmodernism* (London, Routledge, 1990).

17. Debbie Cameron, 'Body Shopping', *Trouble and Strife*, 41 (Summer 2000).

18. Hall, *Sex, Gender and Social Change in Britain since 1880*, pp.186–193.

19. Sheila Jeffreys, 'Bisexual Politics: A Superior Form of Feminism?',

Women's Studies International Forum, 22 (3) (1999); Merl Storr, 'Postmodern Bisexuality', *Sexualities*, 2 (3) (1999); *Sexualities*, 2 (4) (1999), special issue on Queer theory.

20. Jeffreys, 'Bisexual Politics', *passim*.
21. Ruth Lister, *Citizenship: Feminist Perspectives* (London, Routledge, 1998).
22. Equal Opportunities Commission, *Facts about Men and Women in Great Britain, 1999* (EOC, 1999), pp.7–8, 12.
23. *Ibid.*, p.12.
24. Sylvia Walby, *Gender Transformations* (London, Routledge, 1997), pp.34–35.
25. Equal Opportunities Commission, *Facts about Men and Women*, p.8.
26. Rosemary Crompton, Duncan Gallie and Kate Purcell, *Changing Faces of Employment: Organisations, Skills and Gender* (London, Routledge, 1996), p.2.
27. Jane Jenson *et al*, *Feminisation of the Labour Force: Paradoxes and Promises* (London, Polity Press, 1994), *passim*.
28. Sylvia Walby, *Gender Transformations* (London, Routledge, 1997).

Chapter 9

Ethnicity and Racial Equality

Introduction

While Britain in 1979 benefited from a richly diverse society, methods of combating the racism, discrimination and disadvantage that affected ethnic minority groupings had yet to be developed. Ethnic minority workers were disadvantaged in the labour market (see Chapter 3), discriminated against in housing, education and social policy, and under-represented in trade unions and political life. In response, ethnic minority groups organised, Community Relations Councils strengthened their profile and equal opportunities policies were adopted. Studies aimed to improve policymakers' and the majority group's understanding of Britain's multiracial society. This chapter will, first, examine the situation in 1979; second, consider steps taken towards racial equality and, third, consider what progress had been achieved by the later 1990s.

Racism in Britain, 1979–81

Referring to a series of studies by the Policy Studies Institute in the 1960s and 1970s, the sociologist John Rex wrote that in housing, employment, education and urban planning 'immigrant minorities from Asia, Africa, and the West Indies have suffered disadvantage due to racial discrimination'.[1] Racial attacks on housing estates were documented by the London Race and Housing Forum's 1981 report.[2] Asian people were 50 times more likely, and West Indian people 30 times more likely, to be the victims of racially motivated attacks than were white people.

In addition, racist groups such as the National Front and the British Movement carried out attacks on black and Asian people (Document 17). The National Front, whose journal *Spearhead* notoriously questioned the extent of the holocaust of Jewish people in Nazi Germany, was formed in 1967 and aimed to stop immigration and start repatriation of people of African and Asian descent. There was a lack of confidence in the way racial attacks were policed, and in policing generally in the black and Asian communities. Riot shields had been first used on the British mainland when ethnic minority groups and the broad left resisted National Front marches, for instance in Lewisham, South London (Document 18). At a demonstration in Southall in April 1979, Blair Peach was killed and allegations were made that a member of the Special Patrol Groups, set up to police sensitive areas, was implicated in his death. In January 1981, a fire at the Albany, a club in South London frequented by community and broad left groups, killed 13 West Indians. Arson was suspected but a full investigation into the fire did not even begin until 2001. Ron Ramdin, one of the first historians to document black people's experiences in Britain, wrote that racist perceptions meant that 'Black youths had become a social problem'.[3] In this context, the 1981 Criminal Attempts Act, which replaced the 1824 Vagrancy Laws, creating a new offence of 'vehicle interference' and allowing police the power to stop and search potential offenders on suspicion – the 'Sus' laws – was highly controversial. A disproportionate number of black people were arrested under the Act. The Community Relations Commission warned of the resentment of young black people while the Institute of Race Relations complained that Judges' Rules on questioning suspects were being disregarded.[4]

Following restrictive Commonwealth Immigration Acts of 1962, 1968 and 1971, the 1981 Nationality Act fed the phobias of racist organisations by creating three tiers of British citizenship; holders of British Overseas Citizenship and Citizens of Dependent Territories were denied the automatic right to enter and reside in Britain. Ethnic minority groups thus seemed, on the one hand, to be denied the full protection of the state whilst, on the other, the citizenship rights of those not born in Britain was challenged. Part of the resistance to this double jeopardy was the proclamation of a 'Black' identity, in which the term 'Black' signified unity in struggle rather than skin colour.

While the African, Caribbean and Asian populations of multi-racial Britain were divided by language, religion, national origins and cultural practices, they nevertheless shared a common history of colonial oppression, common description as 'Commonwealth immigrants' and similar discriminatory treatment as the victims of race hatred, housing discrimination and social and political exclusion.[5]

There were cultural, as well as political expressions of this commonality, including Rastafarianism (see below), pirate radio stations and 'raregroove' music, 'an eclectic mix of black musical genres', itself influenced by the American Black Power Movement.[6]

Common identification assisted the development of groups such as the Black Trade Unionists Solidarity Movement (see Chapter 3) and the Organisation of Women of Asian and African Descent (OWAAD). Initially, OWAAD had an Africanist orientation, aiming to unite African women wherever they resided, but soon came to focus on the empowerment of all black women in Britain, regardless of their origin. Campaigns included health issues such as the recognition of sickle-cell anaemia, discrimination against black women in the mental health services, discriminatory fertility treatment, as well as trials on black women of the controversial contraceptive drug Depo Provera. OWAAD challenged white feminists for failing to take into account black women's experiences.[7] OWAAD remained active until 1982. Still extant is the group Southall Black Sisters, formed in 1979 in response to heavy policing, which challenged the virginity testing of women immigrants (an outcome of immigration regulations; virginity was 'proof' of the unmarried status of fiancées allowed to enter Britain). In the Liverpool 8 district of Toxteth, a defence group was formed which called for the dismissal of the Chief Constable, Kenneth Oxford. Black groups – Liverpool Black Sisters, Liverpool Somali Community, Merseyside Nigerian Association, Amandudu women's refuge, the Elimu Wa Name project – and Liverpool Trades Council had protested harassment under the 'Sus' laws.[8]

1980 and 1981 Riots and the Scarman Report

Harassment, discrimination and the unemployment which affected black and white young people were all factors in a series of 29 urban riots across Britain in 1980 and 1981. The major riots were in Bristol, in April 1980, followed by Brixton in April 1981 and Liverpool and Southall in July 1981. Whereas the Bristol riot was reported as a 'race riot', where black youths challenged white police, later riots were perceived rather as demonstrations of disaffection in which white youths participated. Black activists, however, emphasised that the riots were a response to endemic racism and discrimination.[9]

A Commission of Inquiry under Lord Scarman was appointed to investigate the riots in Brixton, where £10 million of damage was caused, but was viewed with suspicion in the black community (Documents 1, 19). Scarman reported that there were two views on the cause of the Brixton 'disorders': that they were a response to long-term oppressive policing or a protest to draw attention to the grievances of a deprived community. The Inquiry looked into both the immediate disorders and their underlying causes, taking evidence from the police, the local council and Community Relations Council and community groups. Poor housing and the lack of employment or leisure facilities were held to be contributory factors, plus the lack of extended family networks in a community distinguished by its youth. Underachievement in education led to poor employment prospects: 'the young black person makes his life on the streets and in the seedy commercially run clubs of Brixton'. Scarman's opinion was that, the potential for violence thus in place, what began as a confrontation with police spread into a riot, unpremeditated but possibly maintained by outside agitators. He condemned the racist prejudice of a few police officers, while maintaining that the Metropolitan Police itself was not a racist organisation. Scarman's recommendations included the appointment of more black police officers, improved police training, an independent element in the police complaints procedure; rationalisation of the 'Sus' laws; a review of the role of Community Relations Councils; and improved urban planning. In addition, he recommended that racist marches should be banned under the existing 1936 Public Order Act, but this should be amended to require advanced notification and to allow specific marches to be banned.[10]

Equal Opportunities and Multiculturalism

The riots and the Scarman Report alerted policymakers to the need for action against discrimination. Urban aid programmes were funded and diverted some resources to local groups, although social and cultural projects tended to benefit rather than those with a political profile.[11] While ethnic groupings' own organisations developed, what is sometimes referred to as 'the race relations industry' proliferated. Whereas the early 1980s had witnessed the identification of a black community, attention turned towards multiculturalism. At heart, this meant that policy changed from the assimilation of groups into the mainstream white community, to a celebration of Britain's multiracial society, but the way forward was far from clear. John Rex wrote: 'a new goal has become widely accepted in British race relations, namely that of a multi-cultural society, but that the meaning of this term remains remarkably obscure'; the result would be 'a society in which people are not equally but differently treated', although he doubted whether this could be achieved in Britain.[12]

The Swann Report

An important milestone was the 1985 publication of the Swann Report into 'the Education of Children from Ethnic Minority Groups' (Document 20). Set up in 1979 in response to under-achievement among West Indian children in schools, the Swann Committee found that West Indian children underachieved compared to white children, while Asian children, except Bangladeshis, did not. The committee had no truck with criticisms of its failure to test IQ but instead laid the blame on the 'climate of racism' in Britain and took the stance that the problem to be addressed was the education of all children for life in a multicultural Britain. Multiculturalism should thus permeate all schoolwork; the first priority should be learning English, although Britain's linguistic diversity should also be recognised and catered for by the wider community. Religious education should be non-denominational and undogmatic, schools undertaking religious education and communities religious instruction. The under-representation of teachers from ethnic minority groups should be addressed. The report also identified institutional racism: 'the way in which a range of long established systems, practices and procedures in education and the wider society, conceived to meet the demands of a homo-genous society, fail to take account of multi-racial Britain and ignore or work against the interests of ethnic minority communities'.[13]

The Equal Opportunities Industry

The continuing racism and disadvantage which the Swann Report noted was the concern of local authorities, given the duty of promoting equality by the Race Relations Act 1976. Local authorities were thus important in developing equal opportunities policies. The greater numbers of councillors elected from ethnic minorities during the 1980s assisted this process.[14] The Greater London Council followed particularly imaginative policies. However, there were a number of philosophical and practical difficulties. An equal opportunities policy is essentially an assimilationist one, rather than the pluralist approach adopted by the Swann Report. Moreover, the GLC and other radical authorities were belatedly accepting the identification of a black community in struggle, and giving that struggle their support, while simultaneously attempting to recognise the differences and specific needs of a diverse multiracial community. In addition, gender, sexuality, age and disability were component parts of the equal opportunities agenda and resources were scarce. Juggling resources from the centre, authorities did not share power with the various groups. Moreover each group tended to be represented not through a democratic process, but by fairly arbitrary methods of selection (Documents 2, 3).

In its 1989 publication *New Partnership for Racial Equality*, the statutory Council for Racial Equality (CRE, which itself began life as the Community Relations Commission) wrote of the necessity for a nationally coordinated policy. To illustrate their participation in the *Partnership* project and their own commitment to anti-racism in the face of continued racist attacks, the National Association of Community Relations Councils, a non-statutory body founded in 1972, which represented Community Relations Councils and other groups throughout Britain, changed its name in 1989 to the National Association of Racial Equality Councils. Local groups became Racial Equality Councils, subordinating all other activity to combating racism and appointing full-time, professional staff.[15]

Celebrating Diversity

Despite continued racism, during the 1980s the use of 'black' as an umbrella term for ethnic groupings became less acceptable. It seemed to prioritise the agenda of the African and Afro-Caribbean group and to be unduly influenced by American perceptions of African origins. Rather, the anti-racism struggle was pursued by asserting the different experiences and identities of African, Caribbean and Asian Britons (Document 4) and of European, Chinese and other ethnic groups.

Some of these groups, for instance the largely London-based Cypriot community, managed to overcome racial disadvantage without abandoning their culture (Document 5). Floya Anthias, however, brought up in a Greek Cypriot community, commented that while the older population maintained the language, religion and mores of their country of origin and its division into Greek and Turkish causes, the younger generation tended to share their common Cypriot identity and identified with the interests of other black groups: 'They are more concerned with stressing the commonality of experience in a racist society'.[16] The long-established Chinese community was reinforced first by refugees from oppression in 1989, following the massacre of protesters in Tiananmen Square and then by relatively wealthy immigrants able to benefit from the 1990 legislation allowing the entry of 80,000 people from Britain's former territory of Hong Kong. Immigrants from Malaya, Taiwan, Singapore and Vietnam added to the Chinese population in Britain.[17]

While they were still subject to the racist abuse which white-skinned groups partly escaped, some Asians also succeeded in acquiring wealth and stability, despite occasional militant championship of traditional values (Document 6). Ramindar Singh wrote that in the Sikh community in Bradford the tendency of the first immigrants to discard their turbans and cut their hair was reversed by the younger generation who identified more strongly as Sikh: 'Racial discrimination and racial tension in Britain tend to enforce ethnic differences'.[18] Iqbal Wahhab described Muslims as 'disproportionately represented at both ends of the social scale', un/ semi-skilled and professional. While dispersed in separate communities, 'Punjabis are predominant in Birmingham, Mirpuris in Bradford, Gujeratis in Leicester and Sylhetis in East London', Muslims shared the same religious needs, time off work for prayer and recognition of religious festivals and mores by employers and education authorities.[19] Mosques were built as Muslims turned more towards Islam in response to continued racism (Document 7). The controversy over Salman Rushdie's novel *The Satanic Verses*, denounced by Muslim religious leaders, helped to unite the disparate Muslim groups (Documents 6, 8).

One group, the Rastafarians, of whom Lord Scarman had commented: 'their faith and their aspirations, deserve more sympathy than they get from the British people'[20] continued to celebrate African origins and a pan-African identity. Lord Scarman's opinion was that black youths took on merely the outward appearance and interests (dreadlocks and red, green and black Tam, reggae music and Jamaican patois) of 'the deeply religious, essentially humble and sad' Rastafarian.[21] He condemned cannabis smoking. Dr EE Cashmore, however, described 'The Journey to Jah' rather differently: disadvantaged black youths first sought solace in adopting a Rasta appearance and then came to understand the faith (Document 9). Rastas sought 'liberation before repatriation' to an African homeland, but their pan-Africanism and openness to all who identified as black in the struggle against racism denied them status in law as a separate racial group.

The 1991 Census

In 1991, for the first time, the census of the British population attempted to achieve a complete picture of Britain's multiracial population. This was a controversial measure, which had been strongly opposed by ethnic minority groups a decade before. The census used four basic groups – White, Black, Asian, Other – but asked those who did not identify as 'White' to choose from a number of categories, thus implying that 'White' was the non-problematic majority option. The census authorities worked on the understanding that 'ethnic group is what people categorise themselves as belonging to in answering the question' which reopened the debate on black identification and caused particular problems for people of mixed ethnic origin. Three million people were finally identified as belonging to ethnic minority groupings, 5.5 percent of the total population of 54.9 million, with Asians replacing Afro-Caribbeans as the majority within those groups. The census tables provided information on ethnic origin (Documents 10, 11). Ron Ramdin has noted the phenomenon that the demographic profiles of ethnic minority groups differ by age and is generally youthful (Document 12).

Progress?

What made the 1991 census so controversial was the continuance of racism in Britain. Despite the Housing Act of 1985, which gave local authorities powers against tenants engaged in racial harassment, and the 1986 Public Order Act, which made it an offence to use racially abusive language and/or threatening or insulting behaviour, the CRE's 1987 report *Living in Terror* found that racial attacks, harassment and graffiti were growing, following a survey of 142 local authorities with a 75 per cent response rate. Indeed, 80 percent of respondents reported racial harassment an issue and 77 percent that it was a serious problem. Records were not consistently kept and under-reporting was suspected.[22] A mere 38 percent of housing departments had policies to counter racial harassment and only 70 percent of those who had a policy kept records. Reported cases of racial harassment in the Metropolitan Police District increased by 350 per cent from 1989 to 1999. Estimated racist attacks in Britain were around 20,000 a year, 40,000 people were victims of property damage, 23,000 of racist abuse, with a quarter of a million people suffering some kind of racial harassment. Three-fifths of attacks were by a complete stranger.[23] Southall Black Sisters protested against these attacks (Document 13) and also campaigned to free Asian women convicted of the 'murder' of violent husbands. Sarah Thornton, a white woman convicted in these circumstances, won remission of sentence in 1991 and Southall Black Sisters allied with feminist groups, Women's Institutes and Townswomen's Guilds to secure the release of Kiranjit Ahluwalia following her 1989 murder conviction.[24]

Discrimination in social policy also continued to disadvantage Britain's ethnic minorities (see Chapter 2). Unemployment rates were 7 per cent for white but 13 per cent for ethnic minority groups from 1988 to 1990. Pakistani and Bangladeshi households remained likely to face poverty, rates of homeownership were lower amongst ethnic minority groups and primary health care still needed improving. Young people from ethnic minority groups were able to minimise disadvantage by overcoming, to an extent, the educational problems identified by the Swann Report, so that Indian and African-Asian men were more likely to achieve a degree qualification than white men. Older black people, however, faced greater difficulties, low-paid jobs throughout their working lives in Britain meaning that pension provision was poor. Many black elders had been involved in struggles against racism and over rights of residence.[25] The 1988 Immigration Act made the situation worse by making access to social security provision more problematic and by depriving people of the right to bring their families to Britain (Document 21).

The Murder of Stephen Lawrence

In 1993, the murder of Stephen Lawrence, compounded by the mishandling of the subsequent investigation, was evidence of continuing racism in Britain. Sir William Macpherson, who conducted the enquiry set up by the newly-elected Labour government in 1997, which aimed to draw lessons for future investigations of racially motivated crimes, reported that Stephen Lawrence's murder 'was simply and solely and unequivocally motivated by racism' and that the fact no-one was convicted 'is an affront both to the Lawrence family and to the community at large'

(Document 22).[26] A failed private prosecution by the Lawrence family in 1996, in the face of police inadequacies, meant that three young men acquitted could not be retried. The 1997 Inquiry concluded that Stephen Lawrence was 'unlawfully killed in a racist attack by five white youths'. The many criticisms of the police investigation were first dealt with by the Police Complaints Committee. Doreen Lawrence, Stephen's mother, gave evidence to the Inquiry of the black community's lack of faith in the police. Duwayne Brooks, Stephen's companion at the time of the murder and at first the only witness interviewed, was treated as a hostile interviewee. Evidence was not gathered at the scene of the crime. The Inquiry's recommendations echoed those of Lord Scarman in 1981: that priority be given to increasing confidence in the police, that racist incidents should be better recorded and dealt with, that more ethnic minority police should be recruited (Document 23).

Extensive press reporting followed Stephen Lawrence's death; he was one of those young men for whom education had seemed a way of escaping disadvantage. Concern was shown across the spectrum of the usual political orientation; for instance, the traditionalist *Daily Mail* was to the fore in demanding an inquiry. Most disorienting, to those portions of society which had believed the events of Bristol and Brixton to have been overcome by the efforts of the equal opportunities 'industry' and greater general tolerance of multiculturalism, were Sir William Macpherson's conclusions that there was evidence of 'a sub-culture of obsessive violence, fuelled by racist prejudice and hatred against black people' and that the Metropolitan Police Service, and other police services and institutions countrywide, were institutionally racist (Document 14). Lord Scarman had not detected institutional racism; the Swann Report had provided a definition which Macpherson extended:

> The collective failure of an organisation to provide an appropriate and professional service to people because of their colour, culture or ethnic origin. It can be seen or detected in processes, attitudes and behaviour which might amount to discrimination through unwitting prejudice, ignorance, thoughtlessness and racist stereotyping which disadvantages ethnic minority people.[27]

Conclusion

The charge of institutional racism was a controversial one which undermined perceptions of 'English' fair play (Document 14). It added to unease about the nature of nationalism and citizenship in

Britain when devolution in Scotland and Wales and relationships with Europe featured largely on the political agenda (see Document 19 in Chapter 6). Fears that Britain might have gone full circle back to the 1981 summer of rioting were raised by the riots in the North of England in the summer and autumn of 2001.[28] What action should be taken against asylum seekers was also a feature of the election. Multiculturalism had appeared to offer the hope of progress, but was a concept whose achievement, by equal opportunities policies, was beset by inherent difficulties; as John Rex had warned, the problem was not so much ensuring equality but recognising difference. Ethnic minority communities themselves had moved from the commonality of 'black' identification to the celebration of diversity. Ron Ramdin, noting that ethnic minorities more often partnered the white majority, that a British identity was more often claimed than a Caribbean or Afro-Caribbean identity by young people, that it had been possible for disadvantage in life chances to be overcome, particularly in the Asian community, was hopeful that black and Asian people could 'reimage' a Britain where identities were 'vibrant and changing'.[29] There seemed to be some progress, in that four black and five Asian MPs were elected in 1997. Then, 66 minority ethnic candidates stood in the 2001 election and twelve black and Asian MPs were returned. Of these, Keith Vaz had an unhappy time as a junior minister in the 1997 government, facing charges of corruption; finally, Vaz returned to the parliamentary backbenches. Both minor events like the reportage on Keith Vaz and the more serious issues around Stephen Lawrence's murder led some to perceive that little progress has been made in eradicating racism. At the heart of this failure lies an unspoken monoculturalism: 'To be black and British is to be unnamed in official discourse. The construction of a national British identity is built upon a notion of a racial belonging, upon a hegemonic white ethnicity that never speaks its presence' (Documents 15, 16).[30]

Documents

SECONDARY SOURCES AND INTERPRETATIONS

1. Ron Ramdin, *The Making of the Black Working Class in Britain* (Aldershot, Wildwood House, 1987), pp.454–5

During these riots the police resorted to 'dispensing justice on the streets, to arbitrary arrests and in some cases mass arrest'. By

Tuesday 14 July, according to the press, 1000 people had been arrested. This figure, according to the Home Office, had risen to 3000 by 30 August 1981. After the 'riots', committees were set up to defend and campaign for those arrested, and to expose the official version of events. In Brixton, the black community organisations were head by the Brixton Defence Campaign.

The BDC called for a total boycott of the state's inquiry into the Brixton Uprising of 10–13 April 1981, set up under Lord Scarman's chairmanship, with the terms of reference: 'To inquire urgently into the serious disorders in Brixton on 10–12 April and to report, with the power to make recommendations.'

The BDC argued that there was no escaping the fact that the Scarman inquiry (particularly Phase I) 'very seriously prejudices the legal position and therefore endangers the liberty of all defendants yet to be tried'. The three main arguments against this Phase were firstly, that Scarman himself had positively to agree that Phase I will 'prejudice the rights to fair trial of those who have yet to come before the courts'; secondly, the question that must be asked was: what were the 'immediate causes' into which Scarman was going to investigate so urgently in Phase I. (They argued that the immediate causes of what happened in Brixton were already well understood); and thirdly, instead of looking at the real 'immediate cause' of the uprising, they feared that Scarman would 'give subtle legitimacy to the totally racist view (so dramatically put by Margaret Thatcher) that the Brixton uprising was simply a confrontation between, on the one hand, fundamentally blameless forces of law and order and, on the other, mainly black criminals!'

Thus, the BDC was satisfied that Lord Scarman was disposed to be used by the state to provide it with a basis for re-writing the Riot Act and to provide justification for dramatically increasing repressiveness in policing methods which were already massively racist, lawless and brutal as well as substantially uncontrolled. Why, the BDC asked, was there no response by the state to the repeated requests for a public inquiry into police brutality and malpractice during the previous five years.

On Phase II of the Scarman inquiry, it argued that for the black community there were no benefits to be derived for three reasons. Firstly, it was not aware that Scarman had any expertise in the field of social policy and was not satisfied that even were he to have both the necessary expertise and sympathy that these would be sufficient, given the other factors which apply. Secondly, that there were no good reasons to hold that ignorance on the part of the state was a major cause/force determining the present direction of its policies in the field of housing, employment, education, etc. Thirdly, that the BDC was satisfied particularly that where the uncontrolled policing methods used against them were concerned, the state had no basis for even claiming to be ignorant. 'A mountain of evidence', the Campaign argued, had been 'submitted and ignored'.

2. Harriet Cain and Nira Yuval-Davis, 'The "Equal Opportunities Community" and the Anti-Racist struggle', *Critical Social Policy*, 29, 10 (2) (Autumn 1990), pp.7–8

Metropolitan Labour Authorities showed their commitment to Equal Opportunities by either setting up specialised units, or placing representatives in local government departments to ensure the implementation of Equal Opportunities, in terms of their own specialisms e.g. race, gender, sexuality or disability. Committee structures were reorganised along the same lines and grants became distributed on the basis of what was to become known as 'Positive Action'.

In 1983 a Community Affairs Department was established in the local council of the SE London borough where we worked. Its official aim was, as it was publicised in the local press, was [sic] to be 'a powerful new people's committee... with the objectives of trying to reach a situation where the council is seen to be accessible and acceptable to all'.

In practice, like many other similar units which flourished in the 80s, the 'community affairs' department incorporated specialist workers in the areas of race, gender, disability, welfare rights, police liaison and grants to local projects.

A similar approach was adopted in the establishment of an 'alternative community training centre' which was established during this period by a consortium of local statutory and voluntary organisations and which, over a period of time, had input from both the GLC and GLTB and the local council, who to all intents and purposes had the same aims and political philosophy. In one of the centre's original policy documents its objectives were outlined as 'It was necessary to be clear and sensitive to race, disability, sex and class difference, an image which would hopefully be reflected by centre staff.'

Given the shortage of places in an area where unemployment was abundant, places on the courses were actually offered only to people who could 'prove' that in addition to class disadvantage they also had a least one other 'Equal Ops' category – e.g. were black, lesbian, single parent or disabled. In other words, people who would have had greater difficulty in gaining access to more traditional training.

The training centre was built round the principles of Equal Opportunities and Popular Planning, and the assumption that given funding, the 'true' objectives of blacks, lesbians, disabled and gays would not only be the same, but would result in a joint platform. However, these groups are arbitrarily defined, with any commonality of interests being assumed.

Moreover, the criteria around which these groups were being defined were not mutually exclusive. This created much competition, bitterness and infighting amongst the groups. For instance, a fierce conflict broke out in the local Council as to who could lay most claim to a black woman (who was to be funded by section 11) – the Race or the Women's Unit. Ultimately they were forced to bid against each other, and consequently the bitterness continued.

Sometimes struggles developed in several organisations we observed, between black caucuses and women's caucuses. In addition, spokespersons from the Afro-Caribbean groups often resented Asian religious groups getting funds from the council, feeling at a disadvantage in speaking on behalf of a smaller and less cohesive group. They considered Asians to be getting more of the available resources precisely because they had so many different religious and cultural practices. As a result of this debate the Asians and Afro-Caribbeans became even more entrenched in their own exclusivity.

The dynamics of these struggles are necessarily very complex. What is fundamental here, however, is that having to compete within the hierarchy of oppressions for one's bread and butter does little to ease the tensions, especially if the underlying ideological assumption of the overall political strategy within which they developed, is of unity, if not oneness.

3. Ramindar Singh, *The Sikh Community in Bradford* (Faculty of Contemporary Studies, Bradford College, April 1980)

During recent years some noticeable changes have taken place in the attitude of migrants. Many people have become conscious of their status within the community here. One way of enhancing social status within the community is to obtain an official position within an ethnic organisation because this normally provides recognition in the wider community too. Thus the number of potential candidates for offices in these organisations has greatly increased.

The old leaders of the community are relatively more successful in their personal achievement. They hold good jobs or own their own businesses, live in good houses and enjoy a good standard of living. Examining carefully the case of the Sikh leaders in Bradford one would conclude that their personal achievements are due to their higher educational qualifications, enterprising efforts, occupational mobility, hard work and longer stay in this country. Some members of the community tend to relate the personal success of these leaders to the positions they have held or hold within the ethnic organisation. Obviously, wider contacts within the community at large are helpful to any migrant wishing to establish himself in his new home, but one could grossly overstate the gains which ethnic minority leaders have made because of their official positions in community organisations... The relative prosperity of leaders have developed feelings of keen competition for recognition and status within the community and have led to a certain amount of jealousy as well.

4. Julia Sudbury, '(Re)constructing Multiracial Blackness: Women's Activism, Difference and Collective Identity in Britain', *Ethnic and Racial Studies*, 24 (1) (January 2001), p.42 [htttp://www.tandf.co.uk]

While early organising attempted to obscure and police differences between women in the name of 'black unity', by the late 1980s more differentiated definitions of black womanhood began to emerge. This can be seen, in part, as a result of regional differences which were becoming increasingly evident as black women in Liverpool, Birmingham and Manchester began forming organisations and giving voice to their unique perspectives. The experiences of black women from outside London varied from those in the capital in a number of ways. Firstly, they had not benefited from the large-scale allocation of grants under the Greater London Council which had a policy of funding black, women's and gay and lesbian organisations in the mid 1980s. Thus, regional organisations had had to develop survival strategies which did not rely on state funding or support from local authorities. Secondly, they lived in much smaller black communities and as a result had less access to political power and elected representation. Finally, they had developed notions of black womanhood which melded British regional accents and experiences with African, Caribbean or Asian culture forms...

Black women interviewees from Liverpool therefore identified as LBBs (Liverpool Born Blacks) and identified the struggle against southern hegemony as part of their social agenda. Similarly, women from Edinburgh had some allegiances to Scottish nationalist ideologies which emphasised the injustice of rule from a London-based parliament. Regional black women were therefore less wedded to consultation with the state and felt that their priorities, strategies and regional identities had been marginalised by London-based black women. The assertion of regional agency took the form of a critique of national groups for their 'London-centricity' and was a profound challenge to essentialising discourses on black women.

5. Robin Oakley, *Changing Patterns of Distribution of Cypriot Settlement: Research Papers in Ethnic Relations no. 5* (Centre for Research in Ethnic Relations, ERSC, 1987), pp.18–19

Housing patterns such as these suggested that Cypriots have been able to exercise a relative degree of choice in housing matters as compared with other minority ethnic groups. Of course Cypriots have like other groups been affected by a number of general changes in housing patterns in inner-city areas, such as the decline in private rented housing, Council redevelopment, and the process of gentrification. The latter may have particularly affected Cypriots insofar as they were initially concentrated in the boroughs of Camden and Islington – two inner London boroughs which have been especially subject to this process. On the other hand, surveys of racial discrimination have indicated very little experience of discrimination among Cypriots, just as for other white minority groups. A number of Cypriot estate agents have been well-established in north London for two decades or more, thus mediating Cypriot access for the housing market. These factors together with increased self-employment and general material advancement have enabled many Cypriots to realise cultural aspirations for higher quality owner-occupied housing, and to do so in proximity to their fellow-Cypriots and to ethnic services and employment.

6. Ron Ramdin, *Reimaging Britain: 500 Years of Black and Asian History* (London, Pluto, 1999), p.302

In the mid-1980s, Asian cornershops, clothing stores and chemists continued to proliferate, and an Asian middle class emerged, many of them house-owners. On council housing estates, however, there was an increase in racial tension, as Asians were terrorised by persistent racial harassment, ranging from threatening letters, excrement daubed against doors and walls, to physical and verbal abuse. In some cases, their homes were petrol-bombed while they slept, too often with fatal results. Their fear of harassment in certain areas such as Tower Hamlets in London, grew by the minute.

The majority of Asians (over 70 per cent of them home-owners), however, lived in relative security. Indeed the economic profile of some Asians in Britain by the end of the 1980s was impressive. According to the *Sunday Times* there were an estimated 200 Asian millionaires, compared with 1,800 millionaires in Britain as a whole. If this suggests Conservative Party links, that would be more or less correct, for by the early 1980s, the Anglo-Asian Society of the Conservative Party, was ten times bigger than the party's Anglo-West Indian Society. In this decade, while there was a mood of militancy among young Sikhs, many of whom had also adopted a more conservative attitude evident in styles of dress and a return to traditional values, many of the followers of Islam not only reacted strongly to Indian-born author Salman Rushdie's novel *The Satanic Verses*, but also maintained a high profile during the controversy arising from it.

7. Daniele Joly, *Making a Place for Islam in British Society: Muslims in Birmingham, Research Papers in Ethnic Relations no. 4* (Centre for Research in Ethnic Relations, ERSC, 1987), pp.9–10

Muslim leaders have expressed their concern for the development of Islam in Britain, where it is subject to the menace of an alien environment. They portray Western society as meaningless, aimless, rootless, characterised by vandalism, crime, juvenile delinquency, the collapse of marriages and psychiatric disorder. They postulate that Islam can provide an alternative lifestyle in Europe: Islam is presented as an ideological movement confronted with the ideology of the West and of capitalist secular society. Whereas the latter is said by Muslims to have lost its moral signposts, they claim that Islam proposes a sense of purpose and holds high its moral precepts advocating truthfulness, justice, equality, obedience to one's parents. Islam is said to liberate man from 'Western'-like materialism, egoism and money-grabbing corruption. To the overriding selfish individualism of the West, is contrasted the Muslim collective responsibility, the correct appreciation of accountability to family, society, fellow Muslims, of the employer to the employee and vice-versa. To the 'Western decadent promiscuity' between men and women, sexual education at school, the mixing of sexes in all areas of life including school, the wearing of revealing feminine clothes, is opposed the modesty of Muslim women, the well-regulated interactions between men and women, in which Islam allows both for their spiritual and material needs. Moreover Islam is often presented by Muslims as the religion of measure and moderation, striking the right balance between the excesses of capitalism (extreme individualism) and communism (extreme collectivism). Islam is said to permit individual initiatives (in art, business, science) without the loss of collective responsibility.

8. Iqbal Wahhab, *Muslims in Britain: Profile of a Community* (London, Runnymede Trust, 1989), pp.19–20

In the past two decades which have made up the major part of the Muslim presence in Britain, the Islamic agenda had by and large gone ignored. Little effort had previously been made by the Muslims themselves to link up their local campaigns on a wider national scale. One of the major reasons for this has always been that, although they share the same Islamic faith, they also have major divisions among themselves, not least the Pakistani/Bangladeshi divide. Also, the limited resources and know-how available meant that for many it was as much as they could manage to maintain local pressure, let alone define a national agenda.

Moreover, the attitude of both national and local government has been typified by an incapability to address itself to the new, multi-faith, multi-cultural Britain. Inability to allow religious integration to operate has now led to the Muslim withdrawal from various state institutions, only to go away and create their own, most visibly in the field of education.

The Salman Rushdie affair has provided the first real national melting pot for Muslim activity. From the unprecedented levels of protest that the book engendered, Muslim leaders have now learned a number of important lessons: how to harness a particular mood and politically act upon it; how to attract media attention; how to seek influence over the decision-making process.

The press and politicians are now aware of their ignorance of Muslim needs, though many still do not act upon that ignorance in a positive manner. The language they use of extremism, fanaticism and fundamentalism conjures up images of savagery, barbarism and unBritishness. But, following their initial hysteria against the book-burnings that took place, a calmer, more dispassionate view of Muslims is beginning to form. Indeed, just as the Rushdie protests began to die down, the *Daily Mail* ran a series of centre-spread articles on Muslims in Britain under the banner title, 'The New Traditionalists'. One such article opened thus: 'Their world is traditionally, predominantly masculine. They work 14 hours a day, demand deference from their children, and adhere to a strict moral code. They are the New Traditionalist, Muslims who personify so much of what was once thought "typically British"'.

It is ironic in the extreme that a novel which allegedly blasphemes their faith has brought Muslims in Britain to the brink of recognition – not just for what they want, but for what they are and what they do.

9. EE Cashmore, 'Journey to Jah', in *The Rastafarians* (London, Minority Rights Group Report no. 64, 1984), pp.6–7

There is a complex of reasons behind the enormous upsurge of interest in rastafarian ideas and images in the late 1970s and 1980s, the growth of the movement is attributable to the material conditions of black youths which rendered them suggestible to new ideas and in turn exposed them to rasta beliefs... Coupled with this was the increasingly widespread availability of rastafarian messages through the medium of reggae music generally and work of Marley in particular. It was a powerful combination and one which set many thousands of youths along what I have called 'the journey to jah' (jah being the rastas' term for god). This involved a series of sometimes spontaneous (sometimes organised) reasoning sessions at which literally any topic could be discussed and debated at length. In this way, rasta themes and ideas were circulated around young blacks. Reasoning was a type of liturgical experience through which the neophytes became aware of the rastafarian doctrine. And while these reasoning sessions were occurring in the seventies in virtually every major British city, parallel processes were at work elsewhere in the world...

[B]lack youths who involved themselves in the rastafarian movement felt not so much excluded as totally dislocated from the main spheres of society. They felt they had been systematically denied education that benefited them or jobs that had any prospect of a future. As unemployment amongst youth mounted, blacks were the worst hit; the plausibility of rasta beliefs strengthened with every successive round of black school-leavers joining the unemployment queues. In particular, the concept of Babylon gained credence amongst young blacks; here was an analytical instrument with which the individual could dissect society and lay bare its component parts. It enabled him or her to understand why racism existed, why they were continual victims of social injustices and why their deprivation would not last much longer. The theory of Babylon contained almost wondrous explanatory power and it is worth appreciating...

By 1980 the rastafarian presence was established; disillusioned at a society they believed, quite plausibly, denied them opportunities and discriminated against them, blacks found in the movement a coherent theory that offered not only an explanation of their present circumstances, but an historical interpretation of why this was so, plus a vision of the future in which those circumstances could be transformed. Also, in rasta, young blacks found a source of ancestry and, therefore, the basis for a collective black identify. In the words of rasta musician Peter Tosh, 'Don't care where you come from, as long as you're a black man, you're an African' ('Africa', ATV Music, 1977).

10. Equal Opportunities Committee, *Ethnic Minority Women in the Labour Market, Analysis of the 1991 Census* (EOC, 1991), pp. 6–11, omitting tables pp.7 & 9

The ethnic group data from the 1991 Census is based on a four-fold division of the population into 'white', 'black', 'Asian' and 'other' (which includes Chinese). The LBS, like the printed reports, breaks these categories down farther into ten groups; 'White', 'Black-Caribbean', 'Black-African', 'Black-Other', 'Indian', 'Pakistani', 'Bangladeshi', 'Chinese', 'Other Asian', and 'Other-other'. In addition, persons born on the island of Ireland are identified as a separate category (though they are also counted in the totals for their ethnic group).

Only ten out of the Census tables contain information on ethnic groups, most being in the 'hundred per cent' section of the Census data... Two... useful tables... enable the comparison of 1991 Census data with 1981 Census data. Census table 7 lists the countries of birth of residents of an area, while Census table 50 details the age structure of persons resident in a household, cross-tabulated by the country of birth of the household head. This later table provides the equivalent information to that used in 1981 to estimate the magnitude of the ethnic minority population of an area. In the Local Base Statistics, most tables use the full ten-fold classification of ethnic groups to present information. However, in the Small Area Statistics a cruder four-fold division of the population into 'White', 'Black', 'South Asian' and 'Chinese and other' is used, except for SAS table 6, which provides basis demographic data for the ten-fold classification...

The amount of data related to the labour market is extremely limited for minority ethnic groups. Census table 6 provides data on the age and gender structure of individual ethnic groups, while Census table 9 contains the only information on economic activity, disaggregated by gender. The two tables in the 'ten per cent' part of the Census, tables 85 and 93, contain valuable information on qualifications and social class, but this is not disaggregated by gender. More seriously, this Census data provides no information at all on the occupation, industry of employment, hours worked or travel-to-work behaviour of people from minority ethnic groups. This information is available at the national scale in the *Country of Birth and Ethnic Group* report published by OPCS in January 1994...

Ethnic status was one of a number of new questions asked on the 1991 Census form; the others included whether a member of a household was suffering from a limiting long-term illness, the presence of central heating and the number of hours worked per week. Previous Censuses had yielded estimates of the number of people in Britain from minority ethnic groups, but these had been based on the responses to the question on country of birth. Plans to include a question on ethnic group in the 1981 Census had to be abandoned largely due to opposition from minority ethnic groups to the collection of information on ethnic origin, led by the Afro-Caribbean community. The number of people from minority ethnic groups in Great Britain in 1981 was estimated at 2.2 million, being the number of people living in households headed by a person born in the New Commonwealth or Pakistan. However, these estimates were somewhat unsatisfactory, since they did not include household heads from minority ethnic groups born in the UK or non-white persons living in households headed by a UK-born person, while including white people born in the New Commonwealth and their families.

With the continued growth of the UK-born population in minority ethnic groups, the need for definitive information on the ethnic composition of the British population had become pressing.

A successful test of the question on ethnic group in 1989 resulted in the decision being made to include it in the 1991 Census. The information on ethnic groups yielded by the 1991 Census is based around the concept that '*ethnic group is what people categorise themselves as belonging to in answering the question*', rather than being based on a formal definition of ethnicity (and therefore the categories used in the ethnic group question can be problematical). The design of the question drew upon the experience of OPCS in testing the abortive ethnic group question for the 1981 Census and in collecting ethnic group information in the Labour Force Survey and General Household Survey, together with the advice of bodies such as the Home Office and the Commission for Racial Equality.

The 1991 Census form asked respondents to identify their ethnic identity from a series of seven pre-coded alternatives – White, Black-Caribbean, Black-African, Indian, Pakistani, Bangladeshi and Chinese – and to describe their ethnic group if they ticked either of the two 'other' categories. In the case of household members descended from more than one ethnic group, the person completing the form was directed to either tick the box corresponding to the group to which the person considered that the individual belonged or tick an 'other' box and describe their ancestry in the space provided. In the 1989 Census Test 98 per cent of answers consisted of a single tick of one of the main categories. The Census Offices drew up a set of rules for coding the remaining 2 per cent of responses, based on the information provided in the write-in answers from which 28 common responses were identified... This strategy was adopted in preference to the mixed ethnic group categories used by the Labour Force Survey, since it was felt that the latter did not provide a sufficiently mutually exclusive categorisation of ethnic origin. It is worth discussing the composition of the ethnic categories used by the Census in greater detail... the 'White' group includes all 'European' ethnic types; individuals are also allocated to this category where the 'any other ethnic' box is ticked, unless a non-white mixed origin is specified. The 'Black-Caribbean' group contains Black people who determine their ethnicity in terms of origin in the West Indies or Guyana; the 'Black-African' group covers those who identify their ethnicity in terms of Africa south of the Sahara. The three South Asian ethnic categories similarly contain Asian people who identify themselves with an origin in a particular country. In contrast, the 'Chinese' group contains those who identify with an ethnic group which may have more than one national origin...

The 'Other Asian' category outnumbers the Chinese and Bangladeshis, comprising 196.7 thousand people in 1991. It includes Sri Lankans, East African Asians and Indo-Caribbeans. It also includes other Asian ethnic origins, including the Vietnamese, Philippinos, Japanese, etc. Unfortunately, these individual national origins, which may be of particular importance for local areas, are not accessible through the ethnic group coding frame, though they can be indicated by information on country of birth...

The ethnic group classification was specifically devised to reduce the proportion of 'other' answers in published tables. Despite this, these groups are still relatively large; the 1991 Census allocated 178.8 thousand people to the 'Black-Other' category and 290.1 thousand people to the 'Other-other' category. It is therefore important to understand the composition of these categories. 'Black-Others' includes those for whom the 'Black-Other' box was ticked, but excludes those for which this box was ticked and an Asian or mixed white and Asian descent was written in. This is done because of the tendency identified by the Census Offices for some Asian people to tick the 'Black-Other' box, in contradiction to the intentions of the classification. It is likely that the large size of this ethnic group and its youthful character is strongly influenced by the inclusion of Black people for whom 'British' was written in... most of these probably being the UK-born children of people identified as of West Indian or African origin. Indeed, one motivation for including this category was the preference of many West Indian parents for recording their children as being 'British' rather than of Caribbean ethnic origin. The category also includes children of mixed Black and White parentage.

The 'Other-other' group covers all remaining categories, and includes North Africans (e.g. Egyptians and Moroccans), Arabs and Iranians, who are aggregated together in the ethnic group coding frame... This category also includes persons of mixed White and Asian ethnic origin while those of mixed Black origin are allocated to 'Black-Others' (which also contains most people of mixed Black/ White origin) and those of mixed Asian origin are allocated to 'Other-Asians'. This category also receives those people identifying themselves as 'British', whether or not they specify an ethnic minority and those who give 'other answers' (e.g. answers such as 'Scouser'); it therefore probably also includes persons who object to providing ethnic group information. Clearly, the grouping is heterogeneous, and will comprise a quite different ethnic mix in different localities. It forms a significant proportion of all ethnic minorities in some of the longest established areas of settlement of ethnic groups, such as Cardiff, Liverpool and Southampton. All are port cities in which the minority population comes from highly diverse origins and has had a long history of intermarriage. Some critics have criticised the use of ethnic classifications in themselves, arguing that the use of the ethnic group as the object of study, rather than the problem of discrimination, treats ethnic minorities as a 'problem'. However, even if it is accepted that ethnic classification is necessary for the monitoring of the circumstances of ethnic minorities, specific criticisms can be made of the Census approach.

The categories adopted in the classification are a mixture of racial, national and ethnic classifications. Thus, while 'White' and 'Black' are pseudo-racial categories, referring to skin colour, Indian, Pakistani and Bangladeshi are all legal nationalities and 'Chinese' is at one and the same time a nationality, an ethnic description and a linguistic group.

Ethnic classifications used in many official data collection exercises have been criticised for excessive aggregation. Many surveys and ethnic monitoring exercises simply adopt broad categories such as 'Black' or 'Asian', which do not permit the diversity of experience of ethnic groups covered by the category to be examined. The OPCS classification avoids the worst pitfalls of this approach, since it disaggregates the Black and Asian categories. However, the categories are still broad and many important constituents of some of the larger categories are not distinguished.

New forms of ethnic differentiation and identities are constantly coming to prominence in British society and ethnic classifications continually lag behind in their recognition of ethnic identification. The lack of a true ethnic classification becomes increasingly serious as it means that official statistics ignore differences in religion, ethnic origin within nation and language which have a significant bearing upon the differential experience of minority ethnic communities. For example while Pakistanis and Bangladeshis are known to be more economically disadvantaged than other South Asian ethnic groups, economic differentials exist between Muslims and practitioners of other religions amongst Indian people and also between sects of Islam. Ethnic group differences are particularly pertinent from the perspective of provision of health and social welfare, due to the need for the recognition of cultural sensitivities in providing these services. The growing integration of Europe also increases the need for more detailed knowledge of the ethnic composition of the white population, in order to monitor policies such as freedom of movement of labour, quite apart from the need for statistics to recognise the growing ethnic consciousness of many 'White' groups (for example the Irish).

Attempts to establish discrete ethnic categories are made increasingly difficult by the growing numbers of people who cross ethnic boundaries. The Census Offices recognise the problem that the classification may not properly allocate some ethnic groups to the main categories, while possibly failing to describe some ethnic groups in ways consistent with their own self perception. There is also the question of how appropriate static ethnic categories are in the context of changing and overlapping ethnic group boundaries, and the size of heterogeneity of the 'other' categories discussed above.

11. Jayne O Ifekwunigwe, 'Diaspora's Daughters, Africa's Orphans? Lineage, Authenticity and "Mixed Race" Identity', in Heidi Safia Mirza (ed.), *Black British Feminism: A Reader* (London, Routledge, 1997), pp.128–9

At the moment, countless terms abound to describe 'mixed' people and usually reflect the prevailing political and social attitudes regarding racial and ethnic pluralism. As part of a constantly expanding inventory there are: 'mixed race', 'mixed parentage', 'mixed heritage', 'mixed blood', 'mixed racial descent', 'mixed descent', 'mixed origins', 'mixed ethnicity', 'multiethnic', 'dual heritage', 'multiracial', 'biracial', 'inter-racial', 'creole', 'mestizo', or 'mestiza' to the more derogatory and colloquial 'half caste', 'mulatto' or 'mulatta', 'half blood', 'half breed', 'hybrid', 'zebra', 'Heinz 57' and the list goes on. In England, currently the most popular terms appear to be 'mixed parentage' and 'dual heritage'. Tizard and Phoenix, the authors of *Black, White or Mixed Race?* (1993) define those of 'mixed parentage' as 'people with one White parent and one Black parent of African or Afro-Caribbean descent' (1993: 6). Although an improvement on 'mixed race' which legitimates and reifies the sociocultural construct 'race', the term 'mixed parentage' fails in its presumption that the 'mixing' is first generation. Anthropologist Michael Banton has attempted to popularise the implicitly ambiguous 'mixed origins' which could describe any individual with a diverse background – i.e. English and Scottish – and not solely individuals who stem from a mixture of so-called different races. 'Dual heritage' pinpoints the convergence of different cultures and ethnicities; however, the fact that it is de-racialised also broadens it potential relevance.

A complicating matter is the concomitant lack of consensus in Britain over who is Black, which has become an essentialised political term lacking both dynamism and fluidity and frequently confused with nationality... The Census classification system clearly embodies this rigid fixity of terminology. The first time the government Census attempted to calculate the number of non-White people in Britain was 1991. Out of a total British population of 54.9 million people, just over 3 million or 5.5 per cent were then designated as ethnic minorities. The major 'ethnic' subheadings of the Census are Black-Caribbean, African, or Other; Asian-Indian, Pakistani, Bangladeshi, or Other; Chinese; and Other. This classification system is flawed in its conflation of race, ethnicity and nationality and discriminatory in its homogenisation of peoples from continental Africa and the Caribbean. This categorisation scheme is most problematic when accounting for the ethnic origins of people of so-called mixed or multiple ethnicities, wherein there are two significant and interlocking factors at work. First, the prevailing and inconsistent social and political stance that anyone who does not look White is seen as Black impinges on identity construction for many multiethnic *métis(se)* people. Second, in specific temporal, spatial, and sociocultural contexts, self-identification for this group may or may not coincide with the aforementioned classification. They often negotiate several different identities depending on 'where they are' both physically and psychologically and with whom they are interacting... However, both Anne Wilson's study of mixed race children (1987) and my own research... on *métis(se)* adults and identity formation coincide with Okamura's notion of an ethnic identification which is by nature operationally situational (1981). In other words, on the night of the Census, for simplicity's sake, an individual may have reported themselves as Black-Caribbean (of which there are 500,000) when in fact they have one White English parent. In another context, that same individual could just as adamantly identify or be identified as *métis(se)* or at times even White.

12. Ron Ramdin, *Reimaging Britain: 500 Years of Black and Asian History* (London, Pluto, 1999), pp.309–10

One of the striking differences identified in the 1990s is the age difference among the more recent ethnic minority migrants. It is significant that all the minority groups had a larger number of children and fewer elderly people than the white population. Pakistanis and Bangladeshis were among the leaders in this respect.

In terms of age distribution, 40 per cent of all South Asians (Indians, African Asians, Pakistanis, Bangladeshis) were under 16 in 1982. This figure fell to 35 per cent in 1994, when Caribbeans and Asians showed a 'small increase' in the numbers of elderly people. While the vast majority of children in each of the ethnic groups are British-born, only among the Bangladeshis was there a very significant number of children who were not, and very few non-white elderly people had been born in Britain.

There were important differences among those of working age born in Britain: Caribbeans being just over half, between a quarter and a third of Indians and Pakistanis, and only an estimated one-seventh of African Asians, Bangladeshis and Chinese.

In just over a decade since the last survey, the proportion of members of minority groups born in Britain had increased, the largest shift appearing among African Asians, the smallest among Indians. Bearing in mind that a fairly large number of ethnic minority adults (especially from the Caribbean) were also born in Britain, 'new births are increasingly into the second British-born generation'. And among the younger children in the five years before 1994, the greater was the likelihood that their parents were also British-born. As the latest research noted: 'a sixth of Pakistani and Bangladeshi babies, a quarter of Indian and African Asian babies, and three-quarters of Caribbean babies had at least one British-born non-white parent'. Thus, the migrants can be regarded as first generation, while their grand-children can be described as the third generation.

Much has changed over the past 30 years and family structures have been influenced by a number of factors, including economic, ethnical, moral, social and political influences.

The patterns which Caribbean and Asian people have in-corporated since they came to Britain reflect both their traditional values and those of the adopted country. Because their migration took place within the life-span of many of them, it characterised their age-structure as a group.

Caribbean and South Asian family structures differ from their white counterparts, but not in the same way. As the most recent survey noted the 'most striking' feature is that of negligible interest in long-standing relationships, especially in formal marriage. For all age groups, men and women from this group were the least likely of all the ethnic minority groups to be married, and most likely to be either separated or divorced. Yet, their unconventional partnering patterns indicated a direction which is being adopted by many whites too. Of those who were married or lived as married, as many as half of the British-born Caribbean men and one-third of women chose a white partner. Caribbean women have children at any early age, and almost a third of Caribbean families with children were unmarried mothers, as much as 'five times the proportion among whites'.

13. Pragna Patel, 'Third Wave Feminism and Black Women's Activism', in Heidi Safia Mirza (ed.), *Black British Feminism: A Reader* (London, Routledge, 1997), pp.256–7

What follows is an attempt to locate these struggles by retracing some of the campaigns of Southall Black Sisters (SBS) and our sister organisation, Brent Asian Women's Refuge. Our struggles have, out of necessity, arisen from the routine experiences of many Asian, African, Caribbean and other women who come to these centres with stories of violence, persecution, imprisonment, poverty and homelessness experienced at the hands of their husbands, families and/or the state. In attempting to meet the challenges they pose in their demands for justice for themselves and for women generally, we have had to organise autonomously. But we have always endeavoured to situate our practice within wider anti-racist and socialist movements, involving alliances and coalitions within and across the minority and majority divides. This has not always been easy, but it is the only way we know in which new and empowering politics can be forged.

By organising in women's groups and refuges, many of us have fought for autonomous spaces and for the right for our own voices to be heard in order to break free from the patriarchal stranglehold of the family. In the process we have also had to challenge the attitudes of the wider society, as well as the theory and practice of social policy and legislation which seeks to restrict our freedom to make informed choices about our lives. Our organisations and our practice are critical in unmasking the failures, not only of our communities and the state and wider society, but perhaps more tellingly, of so-called multi-culturalist and anti-racist policies.

Throughout our campaigns on domestic violence, whilst countering racist stereotypes about the 'problematic' nature of

South Asian families, SBS has sought to highlight not only the familiar economic and legal obstacles faced by all women struggling to live free of abuse, but also the particular plight of Asian women; language barriers, racism, and the specific role of culture and religion which can be used to sanction their subordinate role and to circumscribe their responses. Culture and religion in all societies act to confer legitimacy upon gender inequalities, but these cultural constraints affect some women more than others in communities where 'culture' carries the burden of protecting minority identities in the face of external hostility. We have had to formulate demands and strategies which recognise the plurality of our experiences, without suppressing anything for the sake of political expediency. Alliances have been crucial in this, not only in gaining wider support, but also in breaking down mutual suspicion and stereotypes and to ensure that some rights are not gained at the expense of others.

We began our protests in the early 1980s over the murder of Mrs Dhillon and her three daughters by her husband who burnt them to death. In 1984 we took to the streets in response to the death of Krishna Sharma, who committed suicide as a result of her husband's assaults. Organising with other women in very public ways, through demonstrations and pickets, we broke the silence of the community. Until that point there has been not a single voice of protest from either progressive or conservative elements within the community. The women who led the demonstrations had themselves fled their own families in Southall, but returned to join us with scarves wrapped around their faces so that they might escape recognition. We demanded and won the support of many white women in the wider feminist movement, although initially they were hesitant in offering support for fear of being labelled 'racist'! One of our slogans – 'self defence is no offence' – was appropriated from the anti-racist 'street fighting' traditions, but ironically it has now become the much quoted slogan of the wider women's movement against male violence in Britain. The form of our protests drew directly from the varied and positive feminist traditions of the Indian sub-continent. We picketed directly outside Krishna Sharma's house, turning accepted notions of honour and shame on their heads. It is the perpetrators of violence, we shouted, who should be shamed and disrobed of their honour by the rest of the community, not the women who are forced to submit. Another slogan – 'black women's tradition, struggle not submission' – was first coined on this demonstration, and that, too, has been adapted to become the rallying cry of feminists against male violence in this country.

14. Arun Kundnani, 'Stumbling on: Race, Class and England', *Race and Class*, 41 (4) (2000), pp.8–9

Certain elements of the Stephen Lawrence case has an obvious appeal for the traditional *Mail* reader. Here was a young student from a respectable family, with ambitions to become an architect, whose life was cut short by a violent gang of thugs. Despite a weight of evidence against the five, they remained at large and, furthermore, when they had appeared in court, they had sneered and mocked its authority. Stephen's parents, Doreen and Neville, were forceful and articulate in expressing their frustration with the criminal justice system. Editor Paul Dacre had previously employed Neville as a painter and decorator at his Kent home and so the newspaper already had a connection with the family. This was potentially a classic *Mail* law and order story. The only difference this time was that the victim was black and the murderers were motivated by racism.

The Lawrence case offered an opportunity for the *Mail* to continue its same 'get tough' stance on law and order, while also recognising that a black student could be a victim of crime. It is not so much that the earlier stereotyping of blacks as criminals had been rejected; rather, the power of the Stephen Lawrence story for the *Mail* rested precisely on its being an exception. In this way, the Stephen Lawrence story was fitted into a *Daily Mail* mould and middle England was, for a time, carried into the streets of Eltham.

What the readers discovered there shocked them. After twenty years of reading about how the English had become 'foreigners in their own country', it came as a surprise to learn that a young black man's life could be so casually lost, with so little response from the police. But, beyond the disturbing facts of the murder itself and the subsequent incompetence of the police, there was nothing in the *Mail*'s reports which could be said to actually call into question the middle-England world view. So, throughout the period when the *Mail* was running its Lawrence campaign, it was also running inflammatory articles on asylum-seekers – in spite of the risk of racial violence which such stories incite. It was never thought that there might be a contradiction.

That the public inquiry, which the *Mail* had campaigned for, would eventually report that the police were 'institutionally racist' – a phrase that is anathema to the *Mail* – was beyond the newspaper's control. Macpherson's acceptance that the police were institutionally racist owed everything to the efforts of family-based campaigns which had struggled for years to raise the issues of racial violence and police indifference.

15. Arun Kundnani, 'Stumbling on: Race, Class and England', *Race and Class*, 41 (4) (2000), pp.1–2

Today, we are told that we have moved on from the monoculturalism of the Thatcher years to a new, inclusive, Blairite multiculturalism. Britain has learnt to live without its imperialist fantasies, to be 'at ease' with its diversity and 'tolerant' of difference. The talk of 'swamping' and of cricket tests has been replaced by the regular appearance of the prime minister's wife, sari-clad, at celebrations of Asian business success. A meritocratic system of social mobility providing equality of opportunity, if not actual equality, will allow those ethnic groups with the requisite 'entrepreneurial' skills to progress out of the ghetto...

This is the official view. It would be easy to argue that this vaunted inclusiveness only amounts to a few superficial changes on the level of presentation, while beneath the cosmetic surface, the old warts remain. Yet to see Thatcherite nationalism as preserved intact within the Blairite political vision, albeit more effectively camouflaged, would be to underestimate and evade the more worrying reconfigurations which are actually taking place.

16. Heidi Safia Mirza (ed.), *Black British Feminism: A Reader* (London, Routledge, 1997), p.3

To be black and British is to be unnamed in official discourse. The construction of a national British identity is built upon a notion of a racial belonging, upon a hegemonic white ethnicity that never speaks its presence. We are told that you can be either one or the other, black or British, but not both. But we live here, many are born here, all 3 million of us 'ethnic minority' people, as we are collectively called in the official Census surveys... What defines us as Pacific, Asian, Eastern, African, Caribbean, Latina, Native, and 'mixed race' 'others' is not our imposed 'minority status', but our self-defining presence as people of the postcolonial diaspora. At only 5.5 per cent of the population we still stand out, we are visibly different and that is what makes us 'black'.

Thus being 'black' in Britain is about a state of 'becoming' (racialised); a process of consciousness, when colour becomes the defining factor about who you are. Located through your 'otherness' a 'conscious coalition' emerges: a self-consciously constructed space where identity is not inscribed by a natural identification but a political kinship. Now living submerged in whiteness, physical difference becomes a defining issue, a signifier, a mark of whether or not you belong. Thus to be black in Britain is to share a common structural location; a racial location.

PRIMARY EVIDENCE AND INFORMATION

17. *Education For All: The Report of a Committee of Inquiry into the Education of Children from Ethnic Minority Groups* (London, HMSO, 1985, Cmnd. 9453), p.31

Racial Attacks – A considerable amount of attention has been devoted over recent years to the issue of racial attacks culminating in the publication, in 1981, of a report by a Home Office Study Group ('Racial Attacks' – Report of a Home Office Study, November 1981) investigating this situation. The Group offered the following vivid portrait of the situation which they found:

> The views expressed by ethnic minority representatives about racial attacks reflected a general feeling of fear and apprehension for the future. In all the places we visited, we were given accounts of racial violence, abuse and harassment... Assaults, jostling in the streets, abusive remarks, broken windows, slogans daubed on walls – these were among the less serious kinds of racial harassment which many members of the ethnic minorities (particularly Asians) experience, sometimes on repeated occasions. The fact that they are interleaved with far more serious racially-motivated offences (murders, serious assaults, systematic attacks by gangs on people's homes at night) increases the feeling of fear experienced by the ethnic minorities. It was clear to us that the Asian community widely believes that it is the object of a campaign of unremitting racial harassment which it fears will grow worse in the future. In many places we were told that Asian families were too frightened to leave their homes at night or to visit the main shopping centre in town at weekends when gangs of young skinheads regularly congregate. Even in places where comparatively few racial incidents have occurred,

the awareness of what is happening in other parts of the country induces a widespread apprehension that the climate locally is likely to deteriorate and that more serious incidents are likely in the future. In some places there was a sense of uncomplaining acceptance among some Asians to manifestations of racial violence: the problem was thought to be so widespread that they regarded it a little more than an unwelcome feature of contemporary British life.

18. Christine Trebett, *All Lewisham Council Against Racism and Fascism, Report to West Lewisham Labour Party*, 24 August 1980

An emergency ALCARAF meeting was held on 18 April to discuss the proposed National Front march through Lewisham and our response.

Notice was taken that the Anti-Nazi League were assembling at Lewisham Town Hall at 1.00pm and it was decided to maximise support against the National Front by calling ALCARAF supporters to a rally in the same area; to distinguish this as a static rally, the time was set at 12.30 and it was intended to use the car park. It was felt that the massive police presence expected would make it impossible to stop the National Front marching.

Permission to use the car park having been refused, the rally was held outside Eros House. Anti-Nazi League demonstrators joined the rally and there were speakers from Lewisham Council and the Trades Council. Hundreds of local men and women, black and white, came out to demonstrate against the National Front.

Police were present in enormous numbers and prevented the counter-demonstrators reaching the National Front by sealing all routes to their march and threatening arrest to those who tried to break through; counter-demonstrators in Brockley Rise were lined up against the wall and people leaving the local public house were prevented from going home. At about 4.00pm the National Front were diverted into the Catford stations and the counter-demonstrators started to march towards Lewisham. The police lost control and started to run along the main road, driving vans fast along both sides of the carriageway; the police then formed up and drove back the demonstrators, kicking and knocking down any who resisted and making arrests. The police were particularly violent towards the women demonstrators.

19. *The Brixton Disorders, 10–12 April 1981: Report of an Inquiry by the Rt. Hon. The Lord Scarman, OBE* (London, HMSO, 1981, Cmnd. 8427), p.1

A The submission – 1.1 On 14 April 1981, pursuant to Section 32 of the Police Act 1964, you appointed me to hold a local inquiry into certain matters connected with the policing of the Brixton area of South London. The terms of reference were: 'to inquire urgently into the serious disorder in Brixton on 10–12 April 1981 and to report, with the power to make recommendations'. I now submit my report.

B The two basic problems – 1.2 During the weekend of 10–12 April (Friday, Saturday and Sunday) the British people watched with horror and incredulity an instant audio-visual presentation on their television sets of scenes of violence and disorder in their capital city, the like of which had not previously been seen in this century in Britain. In the centre of Brixton, a few hundred young people – most, but not all of them, black – attacked the police on the streets with stones, bricks, iron bars and petrol bombs, demonstrating to millions of their fellow citizens the fragile basis of the Queen's peace. The petrol bomb was now used for the first time on the streets of Britain (the idea, no doubt, copied from the disturbances in Northern Ireland). These young people, by their criminal behaviour – for such, whatever their grievances or frustrations, it was – brought about a temporary collapse of law and order in the centre of an inner suburb of London.

1.3 The disturbances were at their worst on the Saturday evening. For some hours the police could do no more than contain them. When the police, heavily reinforced, eventually restored order in the afflicted area, the toll of human injury and property damage was such that one observer described the scene as comparable with the aftermath of an air-raid. Fortunately no one was killed: but on that Saturday evening 279 policemen were injured, 45 members of the public are known to have been injured (the number is almost certainly greater), a large number of police and other vehicles were damaged or destroyed (some by fire), and 28 buildings were damaged or destroyed by fire. Further, the commitment of all available police to the task of quelling the riot and dispersing the rioters provided the opportunity, which many seized, of widespread looting in the shopping centre of Brixton.

20. *Education for All: The Report of the Committee of Inquiry*
into the Education of Children from Ethnic Minority Groups
(London, HMSO, 1985, Cmnd. 9453), p.7

It is essential, we feel, to acknowledge the reality of the multi-racial context in which we all now live, to recognise the positive benefits and opportunities which this offers all of us and to seek to build together a society which both values the diversity within it, whilst united by the cohesive force of the common aims, attributes and values which we all share. In advocating the development of our society along ethnically pluralist lines we are conscious that Britain can in principle be seen as already pluralist in other respects, for example in terms of the regional variations and various cultural groupings which are readily accepted as part of the overall British 'way of life'. We are not therefore seeking a radically different social structure, but rather looking for an extension of this existing pluralism to embrace ethnic minority communities. We realise that some people when faced with our aim of a more genuinely pluralist society may challenge this as in some way seeking to undermine an ill-defined and nebulous concept of 'true Britishness'. The identity of our society however represents an amalgam of all the various forces which have been and indeed are still at work within it and the many influences which have impinged upon it from outside. Thus to seek to represent 'being British' as something long established and immutable fails to acknowledge that the concept is in fact dynamic and ever changing, adapting and absorbing new ideas and influences. As put in evidence to us:

> Britain has always been a multi-cultural society. Over four centuries of Empire and Commonwealth it has become a multi-racial society. This process is irreversible – a legacy of British history.

And, as the Home Secretary himself has asserted (Speech at the Hindu Cultural Centre and temple, Bradford, on 22 July 1983):

> It is no longer appropriate to speak of the ethnic minorities in this country as immigrants. Already almost half of Britain's population whose origins lie in the New Commonwealth or Pakistan were born here. Many more were brought up in this country and, for practical purposes, know no other. Britain is their home. They belong here; they are here to stay and to play their part in the life of their country.

21. National Association of Community Relations Councils, *Annual Report 1988–9*, Dr Nasim Hasnie, Chair, *Immigration and Nationality Sub-Committee Report*

The 1988 Immigration Act has deprived black people long settled here of their right to bring their families to join them and has removed certain rights of appeal against deportation.

Enforcement of the Immigration Laws has in practice denied many people the rights they are supposed to enjoy in a civilised society. In particular, family reunion has become increasingly difficult. Fiancé(e)s, husbands and wives from the Indian Sub Continent now face the almost impossible task of convincing the Immigration Officers that the purpose of their marriage is not Immigration. Children continue to be separated from their parents because Immigration Officers say they are not 'related as claimed'. Genetic finger printing may be helpful to establish relationships, but it is not fair to charge the oppressed for the cost of the test.

Recent changes to the Social Security System and the Health Service have sanctioned questioning of claimants about their Immigration Status. In other areas, such as housing and education, there is evidence of links between the welfare state and the Immigration Service.

As 1992 approaches and the Single European Act comes into force, NACRC needs to work in concert with other groups to insure that: there are no more racist barriers; there is no internal Immigration Control; everyone should enjoy the same family unity. All should enjoy full civic, employment, welfare and political rights, including the right of abode and citizenship, to help organisations and free associations and the right to vote. Migrant workers and refugees should have full access to jobs, training, union membership, housing, welfare benefits and equal pay for work of equal value. Immigrants should not be treated as criminals.

There should be a genuine amnesty for those who may have been in breach of immigration laws, but are now living and working as law abiding citizens. Immigration procedures should be fair to all and there should be rights to legal representation. Refugees, once given asylum, should have the same rights as other immigrants. There should be no policy of encouraging or compelling new nationals to leave the UK.

22. *The Stephen Lawrence Inquiry: Report of an Inquiry by Sir William Macpherson of Cluny* (London, The Stationery Office, 1999, Cmnd. 4261 -1), pp.1–2

1.1 Descriptions of the murder of Stephen Lawrence have been given in thousands of newspapers and television programmes since his horrific death on 22 April 1993. The whole incident which led to his murder probably lasted no more than 15–20 seconds...

1.2 Stephen Lawrence had been with his friend Duwayne Brooks during the afternoon of 22 April. They were on their way home when they came at around 22.30 to the bus stop in Well Hall Road with which we are all now so familiar. Stephen went to see if a bus was coming, and reached a position almost in the centre of the mouth of Dickson Road. Mr. Brooks was part of the way between Dickson Road and the roundabout when he saw the group of five or six white youths who were responsible for Stephen's death on the opposite side of the road.

1.3 Mr Brooks called out to ask if Stephen saw the bus coming. One of the youths must have heard something said, since he called out *'what, what nigger?'* With that the group came quickly across the road and literally engulfed Stephen. During this time one or more of the group stabbed Stephen twice. One witness thought that Mr Brooks was also attacked in the actual physical assault, but it appears from his own evidence that he was a little distance away from the group when the killing actually took place. He then turned and ran and called out to Stephen to run and to follow him.

1.4 Three eye witnesses were at the bus stop. Joseph Shepherd knew Stephen. He boarded a bus which came to the stop probably as Stephen fell. He went straight to Mr & Mrs Lawrence's house and told them of the attack. Alexandra Marie also boarded the bus. She was seen later, and gave all the help she could. Royston Westbook also boarded the bus. It was he who believed that Mr Brooks had also been physically attacked. None of these witnesses was able later to identify any of the suspects. All of them said that the attack was sudden and short.

1.5 The group of white murderers then disappeared down Dickson Road. We refer to them as a group of murderers because that is exactly what they were; young men bent on violence of this sort rarely act on their own. They are cowards and need the support of at least a small group in order to bolster their actions. There is little doubt that all of them would have been held to be responsible for the murder had they been in court together with viable evidence against them. This murder has the hallmarks of a joint enterprise.

1.6 Mr. Brooks ran across the road in the direction of Shooters Hill, and he was followed by his friend Stephen Lawrence, who managed somehow to get to his feet and to run over 100 yards to the point where he fell. That place is now marked with a granite memorial stone set into the pavement.

1.7 Stephen had been stabbed to a depth of about five inches on both sides of the front of his body to the chest and arm. Both stab wounds severed axillary arteries, and blood must literally have been pumping out of and into his body as he ran up the road to join his friend. In the words of Dr. Shepherd, the pathologist, '*It is surprising that he managed to get 130 yards with all the injuries he had, but also the fact that the deep penetrating wound of the right side caused the upper lobe to partially collapse his lung. It is therefore a testimony to Stephen's physical fitness that he was able to run the distance he did before collapsing*'.

1.8 No great quantities of blood marked the scene of the attack or the track taken by Stephen because he wore five layers of clothing. But when he fell he was bleeding freely, and nearly all of the witnesses who saw him lying there speak of a substantial quantity of blood. There are variations in their description of the amount and location of the blood. The probability is that the blood came out in front of his body as he lay by chance in the position described which appeared to many witnesses to be the 'recovery' position. His head looked to the left into the roadway and his left arm was up.

1.9 The medical evidence indicates that Stephen was dead before he was removed by the ambulance men some time later. The amount of blood which had been lost would have made it probable that Stephen died where he fell on the pavement, and probably within a short time of his fall.

1.10 What followed has ultimately led to this public Inquiry. Little did those around Stephen, the police officers, or indeed the public, expect that five years on this Inquiry would deal with every detail of what occurred from the moment of Stephen's death until the hearings at Hannibal House, where this Inquiry has taken place.

1.11 Stephen Lawrence's murder was simply and solely and unequivocally motivated by racism. It was the deepest tragedy for his family. It was an affront to society, and especially to the local black community in Greenwich.

1.12 Nobody has been convicted of this awful crime. That also is an affront both to the Lawrence family and the community at large.

23. *The Stephen Lawrence Inquiry*, pp.327–8

We recommend:
OPENNESS, ACCOUNTABILITY AND THE RESTORATION OF CONFIDENCE
1 That a Ministerial Priority be established for all Police Services: '*To increase trust and confidence in policing amongst minority ethnic communities*'.
2 The process of implementing, monitoring and assessing the Ministerial Priority should include Performance Indicators in relation to:

(i) the existence and application of strategies for the prevention, recording, investigation and prosecution of racist incidents;

(ii) measures to encourage reporting of racist incidents;

(iii) the number of recorded racist incidents and related detection levels;

(iv) the degree of multi-agency co-operation and information exchange;

(v) achieving equal satisfaction levels across all ethnic groups in public satisfaction surveys;

(vi) the adequacy of provision and training of family and witness/victim liaison officers;

(vii) the nature, extent and achievement of racism awareness training;

(viii) the policy directives governing stop and search procedures and their outcomes;

(ix) levels of recruitment, retention and progression of minority ethnic recruits; and

(x) levels of complaint of racist behaviour or attitude and their outcomes.

The overall aim being the elimination of racist prejudice and disadvantage and the demonstration of fairness in all aspects of policing.
3 That Her Majesty's Inspectors of Constabulary (HMIC) be granted full and unfettered powers and duties to inspect all parts of Police Services including the Metropolitan Police Service.
4 That in order to restore public confidence an inspection by HMIC of the Metropolitan Police Service be conducted forthwith. The

inspection to include examination of current undetected HOLMES based murders and Reviews into such cases.

5 That principles and standards similar to those of the Office for Standards in Education (OFSTED) be applied to inspections of Police Services, in order to improve standards of achievement and quality of policing through regular inspection, public reporting, and informed independent advice.

6 That proposals as to the formation of the Metropolitan Police Authority be reconsidered, with a view to bringing its functions and powers fully into line with those which apply to other Police Services, including the power to appoint all Chief Officers of the Metropolitan Police Service.

7 That the Home Secretary and Police Authorities should seek to ensure that the membership of police authorities reflects so far as possible the cultural and ethnic mix of the communities which those authorities serve.

8 That HMIC shall be empowered to recruit and to use lay inspectors in order to conduct examination and inspection of Police Services particularly in connection with performance in the area of investigation of racist crime.

9 That a Freedom of Information Act should apply to all areas of policing, both operational and administrative, subject only to the 'substantial harm' test for withholding disclosure.

10 That Investigating Officers' reports resulting from public complaints should not attract Public Interest Immunity as a class. They should be disclosed to complainants, subject only to the 'substantial harm' test for withholding disclosure.

11 That the full force of the Race Relations legislation should apply to all policy officers, and that Chief Officers of Police should be made vicariously liable for the acts and omissions of their officers relevant to that legislation.

Notes

1. John Rex, *The Concept of a Multicultural Society: Centre for Research in Ethnic Relations, Occasional Papers in Ethnic Relations* (Coventry, University of Warwick, 1985), p.2.
2. *Racial Harassment on Local Housing Estates* (Council for Racial Equality, 1981).
3. Ron Ramdin, *The Making of the Black Working Class in Britain* (Aldershot, Wildwood House, 1987), p.458.

4. *Ibid.*, p.432.
5. Julia Sudbury, '(Re)constructing multi-racial blackness: women's activism, difference and collective identity in Britain', *Ethnic and Racial Studies* 24 (1) (January 2001).
6. Bibi Bakare-Yusuf, 'Raregrooves and Raregroovers: A Matter of Taste, Difference and Identity', in Heidi Safia Mirza (ed.), *Black British Feminism: A Reader* (London, Routledge, 1997), p.84. See also Ron Ramdin, *Reimaging Britain: 500 Years of Black and Asian History* (London, Pluto, 1999), fusion music, Bhayra and Jungle, p.378.
7. See Chapter 8 for the black feminists' challenge, and Valerie Amos and Prathibdia Parmar, 'Challenging Imperial Feminism', in Heidi Safia Mirza (ed.), *Black British Feminism* (1997), pp.56–8.
8. For these groups, see Merseyside Community Relations Council *Annual Report* 1988–89.
9. Ramdin, *The Making of the Black Working Class in Britain*, pp.457–507; Darcus Howe, *Darcus Howe on Black Sections in the Labour Party* (Race Today Publications, 1985), *passim.*
10. *The Brixton Disorders, 10–12 April 1981: Report of An Inquiry by the Right Honourable the Lord Scarman O.B.E., November 1981* (London, HMSO, Cmnd 8472), *passim,* cited, pp.10–11.
11. Harriet Cain and Nira Yuval-Davis, 'The "Equal Opportunities Community" and the Anti-Racist Struggle', *Critical Social Policy*, 29, 10 (2) (Autumn 1990), pp.14–15.
12. Rex, *The Concept of a Multicultural Society*, pp.2–3, 16.
13. *Education for All: The Report of the Committee of Inquiry into the Education of Children from Ethnic Minority Groups* (London, HMSO,1985, Cmnd. 9453), *passim,* p.28.
14. Ramdin, *Reimaging Britain*, p.301.
15. National Association of Community Relations Councils, *Annual Reports,* 1988–9, 1989–90.
16. Floya Anthias, *Ethnicity, Class, Gender and Migration* (Aldershot, Avebury, 1992), p.131.
17. Yui Min Chan and Christine Chan, 'The Chinese in Britain', *New Community*, 23 (1) (1997).
18. Ramindar Singh, *The Sikh Community in Bradford* (Faculty of Contemporary Studies, Bradford College, April 1980), pp.23–24. The Swann Report had also noted 'there are growing signs within some ethnic minority communities of a trend towards a separatist philosophy'; see *Education for All*, p.6.
19. Iqbal Wahhab, *Muslims in Britain: Profile of a Community* (London, Runnymede Trust, 1989), pp.7, 11.
20. Scarman Report, or *The Brixton Disorder*, p.44.
21. *Ibid.*; Ramdin, *The Making of the Black Working Class in Britain*, pp.458–62.
22. Council for Racial Equality, *Living in Terror: A Report on Racial Violence and Harassment in Housing* (CRE, 1987).

23. Ramdin, *Reimaging Britain*, p.332.
24. Pragna Patel, 'Third Wave Feminism and Black Women's Activism', in Heidi Safia Mirza (ed.), *Black British Feminism*, p.258.
25. Nina Patel, *A 'Race' Against Time? Social Service Provision for Black Elders* (Runnymede Trust, 1990), *passim*; Ramdin, *Reimaging Britain*, pp.231, 313–331.
26. http://www.official-documents.co.uk/document/cm/4262.htm
27. Report of an Inquiry by Sir William Macpherson of Cluny (London, the Stationery Office, 1999), Cmnd. 4262–1, p.28.
28. *Home Office Independent Review Team's Community Cohesion Report, Oldham Independent Review Report , Burnley Taskforce Report, Bradford Race Review Report*, 11 December 2001.
29. Ramdin, *Reimaging Britain*, pp.334–7.
30. Mirza (ed.), *Black British Feminism*, p.3.

Chapter 10

Northern Ireland

Introduction

The religious conflict in Northern Ireland, with its consequent political and social problems for the Catholic and Protestant communities, has been a prominent issue in British politics since the revival of religious and social unrest in the late 1960s and early 1970s. The Catholic minority had then reasserted its claim to the civil rights that were being denied it by the Protestant majority and through violence, perpetrated by the Irish Republican Army (IRA) and various offshoots such as the Provisional IRA, kept the issues of civil rights and the reunification of Northern Ireland with the rest of Ireland at the forefront of British politics. As a result all the British prime ministers of the last 21 years of the twentieth century – Margaret Thatcher (Anglo-Irish Agreement of 1985), John Major (Downing Street Declaration of 15 December 1993) and Tony Blair (Good Friday Belfast Agreement of 10 April 1998) – have attempted to broker some type of compromise which would end the religious conflict and paramilitary violence that has occurred between the those wanting the reunification of Ireland (largely Catholics) and those wishing to maintain the union with Britain (largely Protestants). It has been a goal fraught with difficulties, with two religions and political groups whose objectives are almost diametrically opposed, and has revolved around various discussions and responses to power-sharing, the devolution of powers from

Westminster to Northern Ireland, and North-South (of Ireland) cooperation. The failure of both sides of the religious divide to agree, for more than a temporary period, on various aspects of these arrangements has meant that the attempts to create and sustain an Assembly for Northern Ireland, bringing all parties of the religious divide together, has faced, and continues to face, almost insuperable difficulties. Thus the means by which successive British governments have sought to divorce themselves from the politics of Northern Ireland – the creation of permanent and successfully working Assembly – has not yet emerged.

Conflict and Civil Rights, 1979–82

Following the protests of the Catholic minority population against civil and social disadvantage, direct rule had been imposed on Northern Ireland in 1972 and was maintained, despite the wish of successive British governments to distance themselves from politics in the province (Document 1). Representation of Northern Ireland at Westminster was limited to 12 MPs; the British Conservative and Unionist Party, despite its name, had little to gain from maintaining an expensive and problematic presence in Northern Ireland, while the Labour Party was content to let the Social and Democratic Labour Party (SDLP) organise the mainstream left. The perceptions of the Unionist parties – Ulster Unionists, Democratic Unionists and Alliance – that they were British citizens, underwrote the continuance of British rule, which was objected to by the nationalist SDLP and by Sinn Fein.

Rule was enforced both by the Royal Ulster Constabulary (RUC) and, because of the latter's inefficiencies and prejudices, the British army. The 1969 Criminal Law (Northern Ireland) Act had determined that soldiers could use 'such force as is reasonable', a phrase whose ambiguity led to its being tested on the ground; judicial treatment of soldiers who killed civilians has not always been consistent.[1] Surveillance was increased, while emergency legislation allowed arrest without trial, trial without jury and with relaxed rules of evidence.

The fine detail of these events is not relevant here. Nevertheless, it is clear that the rising level of violence in 1971, most particularly the four nights of rioting by the Catholic community in Londonderry at the beginning of July 1971, led to an influx of British soldiers as direct rule was imposed, with the abandonment of the Stormont government (the Northern Ireland parliament, formed in 1920, which found a permanent home at Stormont from 1934). Soon afterwards, several attempts were made to introduce power sharing and the White Paper *Northern Ireland Constitutional Proposals*, published in March 1973, suggested the need to create an assembly, with an executive committee composed of Catholics as well as Protestants, and the development of North-South cooperation in recognition of the 'Irish Dimension' of British politics. Such an arrangement led to elections and the formation of the Northern Ireland Assembly in June 1973. However, the Assembly was prorogued and then dissolved in March 1975. Violence and bombing in Northern Ireland and mainland Britain, the opposition of Ian Paisley's Democratic Unionist Party (DUP, a Protestant party) against the talks at Sunningdale, Berkshire, to establish North-South cooperation, and the decision of the Ulster Workers' Council, a new organisation of loyalist workers, to call a general strike in Northern Ireland on 15 May 1974, conflated to make the continuation of the Northern Ireland Assembly impossible. From 1975 until 1979, Britain's Labour government looked on hopelessly as the conflict of the two religious communities led to car bombings, deaths and ever-greater sectarianism. Direct rule continued and the Catholic community increasingly complained of the loss of human rights, the Diplock Courts, in which one judge dealt with terrorist cases, and arrests conducted by the police.

Allegations of torture by the police were investigated by Amnesty International in 1977 and substantial evidence of maltreatment was found in 78 cases examined. Indeed, the Bennett Report in 1979 confirmed that the injuries had been inflicted during police detention.[2]

By 1979, the protest against direct rule and the army presence had reached crisis point, culminating in massive demonstrations. Both the Dublin government and the Catholic Primate, Archbishop O'Fiach, had called for Britain's withdrawal the previous year. The prominent Conservative Airey Neave, who favoured strict security measures, was killed by an Irish National Liberation Army bomb in the House of Commons car park in March 1979. Margaret Thatcher, an admirer of Neave who had a fine military service record, became Prime Minister at the head of the Conservative government elected in May 1979. That August, Lord Mountbatten, cousin of the Queen, was assassinated and 18 soldiers were killed. A constitutional conference was called which, while supporting a continued British presence, indicated an intention to move forward to a political solution to the Northern Ireland 'troubles'. Both the government and the Labour opposition were prepared to countenance some form of limited devolution. On its part, Dublin was beginning to call for an all-Ireland solution to the problems of the minority Northern nationalist community.

Unionist parties split into those in favour of and those opposed to devolution. Ian Paisley, whose policy was to preserve Northern Ireland as a Protestant stronghold, became leader of the anti-devolution Democratic Unionist Party (DUP) in 1979: 'the DUP had a major advantage in its cohesion. Unlike other Loyalist parties, it spoke with a single, clear voice: that of Ian Paisley.'[3] The DUP built up its organisation and expanded its strength thereafter. The same year, John Hume replaced Gerry Fitt as leader of the SDLP, which, like Sinn Fein, did not abate its nationalism. The Irish Republican Army (IRA), long dormant until the 1960s, was reorganised in 1979 with a Northern leadership and small, well-armed operational groups which aimed to create 'no go' areas outside RUC control. The activities of the IRA and of the breakaway Provisional IRA (PIRA), plus the constitutional politics of Sinn Fein, gave rise to the appellation of Republican tactics as 'the armalite and the ballot box'.[4] In turn, the success of Republican tactics meant renewed loyalist effort: 'Increased weight at the Republican end calls for increased weight at the loyalist end'.[5]

The Dirt and Hunger Strikes

In 1980, a series of protests about prison conditions and the 1976 removal of special-category status began which became the focal point of Northern Ireland politics. Those prisoners sentenced before 1976 and specially categorised retained their status and were held separately. The loss of this status meant reduced exercise and handicraft time, stoppage of political papers and films, and for male prisoners, the end of the right to wear their own clothes. In Armagh jail, the only women's prison in Northern Ireland, built in the eighteenth century, women began a work strike and lost privileges and remissions. As this escalated, 83 women denied washing and toilet facilities began a 'dirt' strike in February 1980 (Document 2). Feminist groups had managed to campaign across the political divide, for instance in 1978 successfully winning the release from prison of Noreen Winchester, sentenced to 12 years for the murder of her father who had repeatedly raped her and her sister. Feminists had split on the issue of whether to put demands to the British, or to wait for an independent Ireland to legislate for women, and were further divided on the issue of support for the striking women prisoners. The Northern Ireland Women's Rights Movement was opposed to political prisoner status on the grounds that it legitimised the armed struggle.[6] However, a big demonstration picketed Armagh jail on International Women's Day in 1979. Two members of the group Women Against Imperialism were arrested and joined the strike.

In the Maze (Long Kesh) prison, male political prisoners denied special status demanded the right to refuse prison work and uniform, free association and the right to organise, and entitlement to full remission of sentence. They began a hunger strike in October 1980, joined by three women at Armagh. This was called off in December as promises to ameliorate conditions were given. When no concessions were forthcoming, a rolling programme of hunger strikes began in 1981. Bobby Sands, the first to begin his fast, was elected to parliament at a by-election but died on 5 May 1981. International condemnations of British failure to avert the death of Sands included those from America, Dublin and the Polish Solidarity Movement. An estimated 90,000 people attended his funeral. Street riots during the protest led to the deaths of 101 people including 21 RUC officers and 15 soldiers.[7] The hunger strike ended after a further ten deaths (the last man dying on 20 August 1981); relatives increasingly gave consent to intervention when prisoners went into coma and the right for prisoners to wear their own clothes had been won.[8]

The effects of the hunger strike were far-reaching. Extensive press coverage, including the historical context and outlining the Republican position, brought Northern Ireland politics to the mainland.[9] Republican leaders supported the fast once it was underway and secret negotiations were held between Sinn Fein and the prisoners, the IRA and the government; the Sinn Fein negotiations were revealed by the current affairs coverage.[10] When the strike was over, the government met the strikers' demands. The government had tactically recognised the importance of Republican leaders in maintaining law and order and Sinn Fein thereafter consistently won between ten and 15 per cent of the vote at elections. Republican emotions were heightened by the sacrifice of Sands and PIRA benefited from increased support. Thus both the armalite and the ballot box tactics of the Republicans were strengthened. Moreover, the economic disadvantages of the province which underlay Republican grievances were increased as investment was diminished; ICI, Grundig, Michelin and Gallaher all closed large plants.[11]

The hunger strike was also important in winning Labour Party support for a united Ireland. The Labour Party had not discussed Ireland at its annual conference since 1974, until a short debate took place in 1979. Thereafter the grass roots Labour Committee on Ireland was formed (1980) and the National Executive Study Group on Northern Ireland. Despite trade union caution about dividing their Northern Ireland membership, the Labour Party protested against interrogation techniques and prison conditions, asking for trade-union rates of pay for prison work, although Labour's demands fell short of restoring special-category status. After Bobby Sands' death, there was growing grassroots and backbench condemnation of the Labour leadership's support for the government position and at its 1981 conference Labour changed its policy to 'the unification of Ireland by agreement and consent' (Document 3).

In Search of a Solution from 1982

The period from 1982 was marked by a series of measures that attempted to find the basis for a solution to the problems of Northern Ireland. The policies of the Thatcher government on the mainland, in minimising government intervention and encouraging the private sector, were not followed in Northern Ireland. The economy differed; while private sector investment remained weak, the provision of grants and subsidies obscured the distinction between private and public spheres. Gross domestic product grew slowly from 1979, but gross national product failed to increase. While the manufacturing sector grew, jobs in manufacturing diminished, leading to severe unemployment and emigration in the later 1980s. As with the rest of the United Kingdom, the service sector grew, employing 66 per cent of the labour force by 1988.[12] Discrimination against Catholic workers, who were twice as likely to be unemployed as Protestant workers, led to fair employment legislation. Poverty led to dependency on the social security system. The public housing sector remained sizeable and the 1986 legislation, which provided for agencies to take possession of tenancies, was inapplicable in Northern Ireland where housing estates were divided into Republican and Loyalist communities. Local authorities in Northern Ireland had little power and thus faced fewer challenges from the government while running the gamut of sectarian politics; in 1986, for example, a Sinn Fein councillor was elected Chair of Omagh District Council, prompting the Unionists to boycott council meetings. Similarly, trade-union power to organise did not face the same checks as were imposed on the mainland, in view of the need for stability. In the face of these problems, Paisley's DUP was as much opposed to privatisation measures as the SDLP.[13]

The policies of repression, however, continued. In 1982, a new method began to be used, the gathering of uncorroborated evidence from a converted paramilitary 'supergrass'. Deputy Chief Constable Stalker of Greater Manchester led an enquiry into the deaths of three unarmed republicans but his report was never published: 'Stalker probed too deeply and was suspended in bizarre circumstances'.[14] Procedures first used in Northern Ireland were exported to the mainland, for instance use of CS gas and plastic bullets to dispel demonstrations and strip-searching of remand and convicted prisoners on journeys to and from jail; strip-searching was used particularly on women remand prisoners: 'one woman held on supergrass evidence was strip-searched 240 times!' (See Chapter 8, Document 21).[15] Paramilitary activity in the face of such measures included the bombing of the Conservative Party conference hotel at Brighton in 1984, when Mrs Thatcher escaped unhurt but other victims included the wife of cabinet minister Norman Tebbitt, who was severely injured.

Political attempts at a solution, however, continued. James Prior, when Secretary of State for Northern Ireland in 1982, produced a white paper for a programme of 'rolling devolution', creating a 78-member consultative assembly, by the Northern Ireland Act of 1982, to which it was envisaged power would eventually be transferred. Unionist and Alliance parties participated in the Assembly, although both the SDLP and Sinn Fein boycotted it. The following year, an Anglo-Irish Ministerial Council was created, with an executive body to promote social, cultural and political exchanges. Meanwhile, John Hume, leader of the SDLP, initiated the New Ireland Forum to find a peaceful way to achieve Irish unity. This reported in 1984, recommending an all-island state but noting other possibilities (Document 4).[16] In 1984, the Kilbrandon Report recommended 'cooperative devolution'. The following year, the Consultative Assembly recommended power-sharing between Britain and Northern Ireland. While seemingly unimpressed with much of this activity, Mrs Thatcher empowered talks between senior civil servants from Westminster and Dublin. Their proposals led to the 1985 Anglo-Irish Agreement.

The Anglo-Irish Agreement, 1985

The Anglo-Irish Agreement provided Dublin with a role in finding a solution to the problems of Northern Ireland by establishing an Intergovernmental Conference with a secretariat in Belfast, staffed by civil servants from both Westminster and Dublin (Document 9). Despite the declaration in the Agreement that the wishes of the majority in the North would be respected, the Agreement was perceived as betrayal by the Unionists. Indeed, it was an attempt to establish communication and widen the basis of discussion which went beyond the rhetoric of the Conservative government and, in regard to Mrs Thatcher, has been seen as 'an interesting example of her capacity occasionally to transcend her own prejudices and instincts'.[17] The Catholic minority was to be encouraged to be involved in policing and the security services, and Article 1 of the Agreement stated that if the wishes of the majority were for a united Ireland, the UK and Dublin governments would give support: 'this publicly established for the first time that whilst the British were willing to retain Northern Ireland as long as it wanted them, they were also prepared to leave'.[18] Thus the paramilitary position that the British government had to be forced to quit was undermined (Documents 5, 9).

The period before the implementation of the Agreement in 1986 was marked by unrest in both Unionist and Republican communities; the route of the Orange Order parade through Republican Portadown brought protests and at the St Patrick's Day parade soldiers clashed with young men. All 15 Unionists resigned their Westminster seats in protest at the Agreement, and at the subsequent by-elections on 23 January 1986, the Unionist vote against the Agreement was 43.9 per cent, while Catholic approval was 54 per cent.[19] There had been 500 arrests following 'supergrass' information by December 1985; however, by the next December the system had become discredited by the high number of convictions overturned on appeal.[20] Finally, there was a Unionist 'Day of Action' against the Consultative Assembly on 3 March 1986. In the face of such Protestant opposition, it was dissolved.

To provide a counter to the Agreement, the Ulster Defence Association's Political Research Group produced 'Common Sense', a document which argued for a permanent solution of devolution and power-sharing and was welcomed by the DUP in its 1987 report An End to Drift. At Enniskillen on 8 November 1987 a tragic reminder of the need for progress was given when 11 civilians were killed by an IRA bomb at a Remembrance Day service. A new Public Order Act was introduced in 1987. However, the 'ballot box' approach of the nationalists was gaining weight; Sinn Fein, while commemorating events such as the 1981 hunger strike and the 1916 Easter Rising, was building republicanism into a mass movement. For its part, the SDLP kept clear of the demonstrations and parades that marked Loyalist and Republican politics.[21] John Hume and Gerry Adams of Sinn Fein were meeting by 1988. In the face of such moves on the Republican side, the Unionists participated the following year in talks under the aegis of the Agreement started by Peter Brookes, then Secretary of State.

'Armalite' tactics, PIRA (Provisional IRA) activity from 1987 and Loyalist from 1989, were rather stimulated than subsumed by the growing constitutional campaigns. Ian Gow, Conservative MP, was killed in 1990. PIRA brought its campaign to the mainland with a mortar attack on Downing Street (7 February 1991) and bombs in the City of London (1992), Warrington (March 1993, when two small boys were killed in the shopping centre) and Heathrow Airport (1994). Damages to the City of London amounted to over a £1 billion, while bombs on commercial premises in Northern Ireland led to compensation claims of £102 million.[22] In turn, this escalation of violence had the effect of stimulating the constitutional procedure. Following John Hume's frequently iterated suggestion, talks were in three phases, within Northern Ireland first, second between North and South Ireland, third between Britain and Ireland. Talks in Northern Ireland started in June, broke down in July 1991, and were renewed in April 1992, John Major having succeeded Margaret Thatcher as Prime Minister in 1990. The Ulster Unionists were relatively more powerful after the 1992 election, the Conservative government having a majority of merely 21 seats. However, despite their opposition to talks including Dublin, phases two and three of the talks began in 1992, Unionists travelling to Dublin to participate. At the end of this round in November 1992, although no concrete proposals had been agreed, progress in discussion had been made.[23] Four main fractures were identified in Northern Ireland: national identities, religious groups, cultural traditions and social and economic discrimination suffered by the Catholic minority.[24]

Declaration and Ceasefire

John Major brought new energy to the constitutional process of solution-seeking by promoting the 15 December 1993 Downing Street Declaration, signed by the British and Irish governments. This stated that Britain had 'no selfish strategic or economic interests in Northern Ireland'[25] and went a step further than the Anglo-Irish Agreement in that it aimed to win support across Northern Ireland's communities for constitutional change. The Unionist community was angered, although only the DUP abandoned the talks. For the Republican community, there was finally a prospect of real progress. The SDLP was winning support for its constitutionalist position. Sinn Fein, having to meet this challenge while containing paramilitary activity, could not afford to stand aloof; in 1992 it had produced *Towards a Lasting Peace in Northern Ireland*, in which some recognition was given to the British mediating role. The British had kept PIRA informed of the progress of the talks and secret negotiations between the British government and PIRA had been held since 1993. On 31 August 1994, PIRA announced a ceasefire. This lasted for only about 18 months, and its end was marked by the explosion of a bomb at Canary Wharf in London on 4 February 1996, causing the deaths of two people, the injury of over 100 and a cost of £85 million. It was followed by other actions, most notably the explosion of a bomb in the middle of Manchester on Saturday 15 June 1996. Nevertheless, the Protestant paramilitaries, who were suspicious of the secret talks, announced their own ceasefire on 13 October 1996 when they were assured that the people of Northern Ireland would not be forced into a United Ireland.

Towards 'The Good Friday Agreement' of 10 April 1998, and Beyond

Despite the suspicions of both the Protestant and Catholic communities, it is clear that some progress was being made. A change of government in Ireland led to new discussions with the British government and the production of *Framework for the Future*. This proposed a new Northern Ireland assembly of 90 members elected by proportional representation, to be chaired by a directly-elected panel of three people, with an all-party committee to oversee the Northern Ireland departments. The two main aims of the document were to involve the Catholics in the government of

Northern Ireland and develop a North-South body and institutions. Although rejected by the Unionists, the publication did represent a shift by the Irish government which was now prepared to accept that Northern Ireland would only become part of an all-Ireland government with the consent of the majority of the electorate in the North. In turn, John Major, the British Prime Minister, promised a referendum would take place on any changes to the Northern Ireland constitution.

The Unionist rejection of the *Frameworks* document prompted the resignation of James Molyneaux, the Ulster Unionist party leader, and his replacement by David Trimble did not, at first, suggest any change in policy. However, in November 1995, the United States President, Bill Clinton, visited both Northern Ireland and the Irish Republic in an attempt to promote the peace process. There was rapturous support for his efforts and out of them emerged an international body, chaired by the former US Senator George Mitchell, to deal with the decommissioning of weapons and the creation of the framework for all-party talks. The Mitchell Report was accepted by the British government and published on 24 January 1996. It suggested that the decommissioning of weapons should take place at the same time as all-party talks were held and not before, as the British government had previously insisted, nor after, as Sinn Fein and the Irish Catholics had suggested. It encouraged talks as being the peaceful and democratic means of achieving peace in Northern Ireland. Unfortunately, the difficulties that still existed were revealed, in dramatic form, with the end of the PIRA ceasefire in February 1996.

It was at this juncture that Tony Blair and the Labour Party won the 1 May 1997 UK general election with a landslide majority. At first it looked as though this victory would not bring about much change in the pace of moves towards peace in Northern Ireland. Indeed, Sinn Fein, the main political party of the Catholics and a body regarded as the political wing of the IRA, won 17 per cent of the Northern Ireland vote and, despite winning two seats in Parliament, continued to refuse to send its members to Westminster. The SDLP with 24 per cent of the vote and three seats did not seem to have inched forward. However, a second IRA ceasefire was declared in July 1997 and the Prime Minister encouraged a more intensive round of all-party discussions through Mo Mowlam, his new Secretary of State for Northern Ireland. In the wake of these, in September 1997, an Independent International Commission of

Decommissioning (of weapons) was set up by the Irish and British governments and chaired by General John de Chastelain.

The Catholic interest in the talks was encouraged further by two events. The first was the announcement by Tony Blair, to the House of Commons on 29 January 1998, that there would be an inquest into the Bloody Sunday events of 30 January 1972, when British soldiers shot dead 13 and wounded 15 unarmed civilians. The (Saville) Inquiry formally opened on 3 April 1998. It was to examine evidence which the Widgery Inquiry of 1972 had not examined and test whether or not the Widgery Inquiry's suggestion that the British soldiers had been shot at first was accurate (Document 8). The second was the holding of a St Patrick's Day parade in 1998, the first major parade ever allowed in Belfast City Centre. Supported partly by the Belfast City Council, and devoid of banners and military bands, this parade represented a landmark in Irish politics by extending the nationalists' rights to march at a time when there were increasing pressures to curtail and control the routes of the Orange parades.[26]

In a tense and fragile atmosphere of compromise, the all-party talks, which always seemed on the point of collapse, were taken a stage further by Tony Blair's 'Good Friday Agreement' of 10 April 1998. All parties to this agreement were supposed to attempt to achieve the decommissioning of paramilitary weapons within two years of a referendum being held (in both Northern Ireland and the Irish Republic) and to work with the Independent International Commission, to be chaired by Chris Patten, the ex-Governor of Hong Kong and a leading Conservative politician. The Agreement accepted the need to form a Northern Ireland Assembly, of 108 members, which would take over the running of the province and operate through a multi-party executive. There was to be a British-Irish Council, which would bring in representatives of the devolved governments of Scotland and Wales. In addition, the Irish Republic was to amend its constitution in order to accept that Northern Ireland would remain part of the United Kingdom until the majority wished otherwise whereupon the British government would organise the procedures to form a united Ireland. The Agreement also paved the way for an improved climate of trust in the justice system that was already operating in Northern Ireland (Document 7).

The Northern Ireland Elections Act was passed in 1998 and, on 22 May 1998, 80.9 per cent of the Northern Ireland electorate took part in a referendum on the 'Good Friday Agreement'. This saw an independent, non-party 'Yes' campaign and a 'No' campaign by Ian Paisley's DUP and the UKUP (Document 6). Nevertheless, the vote was 71.1 per cent in favour and 28.8 per cent against. In the Irish Republic there was a 55.5 per cent turnout with 94.3 per cent in favour and 5.6 per cent against. With this acceptance of the Agreement, the new Northern Ireland Assembly of 108 members was elected on 25 June 1998, with the Ulster Unionists (28 seats) the SDLP (24), the Democratic Unionists (20) and Sinn Fein (18) emerging as the largest parties. Arrangements also began for an accelerated programme for the release of paramilitary prisoners, under a strict licensing system as from July 1998.

The formation of a viable and working assembly for Northern Ireland was never going to be easy. David Trimble became First Minister and Seamus Mallon, of the SDLP, became his Deputy when the Northern Ireland Assembly met on 1 July 1998. However, Trimble maintained that the Unionists would not allow Sinn Fein representatives to take up their seats on the Executive until IRA weapons were decommissioned. In response, Sinn Fein suggested that it could not force the IRA on this issue and that de-commissioning was not in the Agreement. As a result, at Easter 1999 the new cross-party Executive was still not in place and the British and Irish prime ministers produced the Hillsborough Declaration calling for the IRA to put a token quantity of weapons 'beyond use'. Sinn Fein rejected this proposal. In May 1999, the British and Irish prime ministers called for a cross-party executive to be formed and for the IRA to begin decommissioning arms thereafter. This was rejected by the Unionists.

The problem was that there was still deep distrust between the two sides, fuelled by the continuation of hostilities and atrocities. Indeed, on 16 March 1999 Mrs Rosemary Nelson, who had defended many IRA suspects, was assassinated when her car was booby-trapped. Also, in August 1999, the Continuing IRA, a splinter group, carried out an attack in Omagh which resulted in the deaths of 29 people.

By the end of 1999, however, it looked as though moves to form an assembly would speed up. Peter Mandelson became Northern Ireland Secretary on 11 October 1999, and George Mitchell continued to broker agreements between the various parties, resulting in conciliatory remarks by the Ulster Unionists and Sinn Fein on 16 November, and by the IRA on 17 November. Shortly afterwards the power-sharing Executive came into existence and the IRA appointed a representative to meet General de Chatelain to discuss de-commissioning. Finally, the Ulster Unionist Council met on 27 November 1999 and voted, by 480 votes to 349, to accept the latest agreement, warning, however, that the Agreement might end if the IRA had not begun to decommission its arms by February 2000. Since then, the Northern Ireland Assembly has had a chequered history, given the very slow rate of the decommissioning of arms, and it was suspended in 2001 as a result of Unionist protest at the failure of decommissioning, although it has since been reformed.

Conclusion

There is no doubt that substantial progress has been made, over the last 20 years, towards bringing peace and representative government in Northern Ireland. The violence between the Catholic and Protestant communities has lessened since the late 1990s, as the various paramilitary groups have largely accepted the need to maintain the ceasefire. Also, in the mid-1990s, the acceptance by the Irish government, in its constitution, that a united Ireland would only occur with the support of a majority in Northern Ireland has also helped allay some of the fears of Unionists in what was a fundamental shift of positions. The formation of a multi-party executive in the Northern Ireland Assembly has also forced politicians of all political persuasions to attempt to work together as Catholics, as well as Protestants, increasingly exercise their democratic rights. There have also been changes in the framing and operation of policing and justice in Northern Ireland, resulting from the Good Friday Agreement, which encouraged the increasing observation of the rule of law (Document 7). In sum, there is now a level of cooperation and understanding which has not been seen for years, although there still remain political shoals in the way of a permanent peaceful political arrangement, mainly in the form of the decommissioning of arms. Whether the current situation lasts and improves remains to be seen.

Documents

SECONDARY SOURCES AND INTERPRETATIONS

1. Peter Catterall and Sean McDougall (eds), *The Northern Ireland Question in British Politics* (London, Macmillan, 1996), p.6

They are instead saddled with the unpleasant ultimate responsibility for the rule of law in a territory where no state form commands the allegiance of all communities. This responsibility is based on the wish of the majority to remain part of the United Kingdom, and was exercised at first at arm's length through the majority itself in the form of the unionist state. The collapsing legitimacy of the unionist state (and the virtual collapse of the RUC) in the early 1970s meant, however, that subsequently it had to be discharged more directly. Faced with the choice of allowing a discredited state to take control of the military or of becoming involved, British Ministers, reluctant as always, chose to end Stormont and impose direct rule in Northern Ireland.

This changed the circumstances in which British policy operated and brought the topic of Northern Ireland more clearly into the ambit of British politics. The thrust of policy remained, however, to externalise the problem from British politics.

2. Christine Loughran, 'Armagh and Feminist Strategy: Campaigns around Republican Women Prisoners in Armagh Jail, *Feminist Review, Special Issue: Socialist Feminism 'Out of the Blue'*, 23 (Summer 1986), (a) p.60, (b), pp.64–5

(a) By Easter 1978 the Governor wished to break their protest. He imposed a twenty-one-hour lock-up, reduced visits to one per month and the women lost all privileges and remission. In May 1978 male warders were used to baton charge remand prisoners on protest. But it was on 7 February 1980 that the women's protest escalated into a 'no wash' protest, similar to the dirt strike in the H Blocks. While queuing for an unusually appetising meal, the women prisoners were attacked by warders, who also searched and stripped their cells. This was on the pretext of looking for black skirts and berets, part of a Cumman na mBann (women's branch of the IRA) uniform which would have been used on Easter parade in the prison in defiance of the authorities and as a most potent symbol of their political status. As a punishment the warden locked the women out of toilet and washing facilities and they were refused exercise. The Armagh women were therefore forced on to the dirt strike, which they used to highlight the deteriorating conditions inside the prison. Altogether this no wash protest conducted by some thirty women continued for thirteen months. This period saw the most activity by feminists in outside protest groups...

(b) Nell McCafferty writing in the Irish Times (1980) argued that the 'menstrual blood on the walls of Armagh prison smells to high heaven. Shall we (feminists) turn our noses up?' She graphically described the dirt strike and how it affected the health of prisoners who, after 200 days without toilet or washing facilities, were lying 'amid their own excreta and blood'. The choice facing feminists on the matter of Armagh jail is clear-cut, she argued: 'we can ignore these women or we can express our concern about them. Since the suffering of women anywhere, whether self-inflicted or not, cannot be ignored by feminists, then we have a responsibility to respond. The issue then is the nature of our response.'

In replies to Nell McCafferty in the next days, some feminists argued that the Republican Movement was 'male dominated' with a 'male-defined ideology' and that feminists should rather be concerned with the victims of violence: the Armagh women therefore could not be supported. The 'no wash' protesters replied, stating that not taking up the issue was blinding feminists to the true issue as they saw only their Republican politics:

> It is our belief that not only is our plight a feminist issue, but a very fundamental social and human issue. It is a feminist issue in so far as we are women, even though we are treated like criminals. It is a feminist issue when the network of this jail is completely geared to male domination. The Governor, the Assistant Governor and the doctor are all males. We are subject to physical and mental abuse from male screws who patrol our wing daily, continually peeping into our cells ... If this is not a feminist issue then we feel that the word feminist needs to be redefined to suit these people who feel that 'feminist' applies to a certain section of women rather than encompassing women everywhere regardless of politically held views. (No Wash Protesters, 1980)

Women Against Imperialism (WAI), a small group of Republican and anti-imperialist left-wing women based in Belfast and Derry, organised the first pickets on Armagh attended by feminists. They highlighted the conditions and humiliations which the women suffered and gained support in Ireland, Britain and abroad. Sexual abuse, both in interrogation and while the women were held in the prison, was emphasised. They stressed the denial of medical care and sanitary protection, the petty controls and beatings by male warders. They linked this to the fact that for women the dirty protest against withdrawal of status caused serious menstrual problems and infections.

3. Martin O'Donnell, 'The Impact of the 1981 H Block Hunger Strike on the British Labour Party', *Irish Political Studies*, 14 (1999), pp.74–5

[T]he hunger strikes, and the subsequent electoral successes for Sinn Féin, were to awaken many in the Labour movement to the reality of catholic working class support for the Provisionals. It was not just the enhancing of the sentimental support for Irish nationalism and for the ideal of a united Ireland following the death of each hunger striker, but the show of popular support for Bobby Sands through the ballot box in the Fermanagh/South Tyrone by-election which had the greatest impact on attitudes. Although on polling day Don Concannon had warned that 'a vote for Mr Sands is a vote of approval for the La Mon massacre, the murder of Lord Mountbatten at Warrenpoint [sic] and all the other senseless murders' (House of Commons Debates, Vol. 2 Col. 1101, 9 April 1981), the fact that so many voters had ignored such pleas and given Sands such a sizeable endorsement led to a major rethink throughout the Labour movement. The historic impact on Labour thinking is probably best summed up by the *Labour Weekly* editorial which followed the by-election, but was written before Sands' death: 'Northern Ireland is at long last seen as a political question, by both politicians and the public' (*Labour Weekly*, 24 April 1981). This curious statement (which begs the question, what is considered a political question if not the Northern Ireland problem?) is an indication of how the by-election altered Labour's decade old view of the Provisionals as a small group of terrorists in much the same mould as the Red Army Faction in Germany, the Red Brigades in Italy, or as Tom Pendry described them two years earlier, 'not a bona fide political movement' but 'a small, dedicated group of fanatics'. For so long the lack of empathy with the Provisionals was due to the fact that unlike the Labour movement they did not present themselves to the electorate in order to gain a mandate. They did not sit on local councils, they did not work within the community, they did not work with the trade unions in the workplace and they insisted on using violence not just against the security forces but against elected political opponents. The hunger strikes by contrast, were an example of non-violent passive resistance which led even Dick Barry to reflect, after his visit to the dying Sands, for what political cause would he starve himself to death? (Barry, D. Interview, March 1996)

4. Brendan O'Duffy, 'The Price of Containment: Deaths and Debate on Northern Ireland in the House of Commons, 1968–94', in Peter Catterall and Sean McDougall (eds), *The Northern Ireland Question in British Politics* (London, Macmillan, 1996), p.120

[I]t should have been no surprise that rolling devolution failed to lead to any agreed form of power-sharing. Both the SDLP and Sinn Fein contested the election for the new Assembly in October 1982, but both declared that they would abstain from participation in the Assembly. Without the participation of the intended opposition the Assembly merely acted as a forum for Unionist politicians to denounce the activities of the British-Irish Inter-Governmental Council where the external political process was gaining momentum.

The inter-governmental approach took precedence over the internal approach for three primary reasons. First, the successive failures of the Constitutional Conference and the following devolution Assembly suggested that neither continuing violence nor the related economic crisis were sufficient to induce significant compromise among local leaders. Secondly, the threat of Sinn Fein's challenge to the SDLP was turned into an opportunity by John Hume to create a united constitutional nationalist position on political progress. The report of the New Ireland Forum was published in May 1984 and while its proposed options (a unitary state, a federal state and joint authority) were all rejected by Thatcher, the report was approved by both houses of Congress in the US and praised (though not endorsed) by Ronald Reagan. The Forum Report contributed directly to the inter-governmental process because it presented a semblance of unity among the constitutional nationalist parties which could be used to deliver a compromise agreement.

Finally, the escalating threat of violence was demonstrated by the attempt on Thatcher's life in the bombing of the Grand Hotel in Brighton during the Conservative Party Conference in October 1984. Before the bombing a seven-ton shipment of arms from America was seized aboard the *Marita Ann* off the coast of Kerry. The shipment was an indication that the PIRA was preparing for a 'long war'. These factors all contributed to the momentum for an agreement between London and Dublin which would contribute at a minimum, to cooperation on security, and more hopefully to a new momentum for a form of devolved government based on power-sharing and an institutional Irish Dimension.

5. Peter Catterall and Sean McDougall (eds), *The Northern Ireland Question in British Politics* (London, Macmillan, 1996), p.9

But all this has done is to make publicly ever clearer what has always been implicit; that the status of Northern Ireland as part of the United Kingdom rests upon the wishes of the majority of its population. What the Anglo-Irish Agreement and subsequent declarations have made explicit is that this is now the only basis for this status. But they have also made clear that this status will only change if the view of the majority changes.

As John Hume told Sinn Féin's leader, Gerry Adams, during their first series of talks, the problem was not that the United Kingdom was attacking or coercing the nationalist community, it was the legitimate opposition of the unionists to being themselves coerced. Earlier in his career Adams, in contrast, had been a great articulator of the traditional republican view that it was the British who were the problem and who had to be forcibly ejected. Although he was the principal architect of the 'armalite and ballot box' strategy which added a political dimension to the republican campaign during and after the hunger strikes, he remained wedded to these old certainties. The development of British declaratory policy in 1985 and after was, however, to undermine, and designed to undermine, such beliefs. Adams – who saw himself as the patient teacher of Irish history – was himself slow to learn, and it took several shifts in policy in the Republic before he began to question his diagnosis of the Northern Ireland problem. When the subsequent PIRA ceasefire announcement came on 31 August 1994 he claimed, as he had to, that the campaign had been worth it. Its main tangible achievement, however, had only been to make explicit in British

policy what had always been implicit, what had been clear, if only
he had listened, in his clandestine talks with the British
Government in 1972. Was it *really* worth so many deaths?

For it was not British policy that was the problem, nor was Britain's
expulsion the solution. This could only be arrived at by agreement
between the two communities of Northern Ireland itself, agreement
which the two Governments have sought to foster since 1985 by
explicitly distancing themselves from the communities' irreconcilable
national claims. This is in keeping with long-term British policy. So
far that policy has failed. If it should ever succeed, however, it will
also fulfil another constant of British policy, which is to marginalise
as far as possible the place of Northern Ireland in British politics.

6. Sydney Elliott, 'The Referendum Question and Assembly Elections in Northern Ireland', *Irish Political Studies*, 14 (1999), pp.138–9

The NI (Elections) Bill comprised nine sections and one Schedule.
The first section provided for the establishment of an Assembly
comprising 108 members, six elected from each parliamentary
constituency, to take part in preparations for the implementation
of the Belfast Agreement. It enabled the Secretary of State to refer
matters arising from the Agreement and other matters to the
Assembly. It provided for an Assembly of 108 members from the
parliamentary constituencies with each returning six members. The
second section set 25 June as the day of election; the franchise was
the same as for district council elections and enabled residents who
were nationals of other EU countries to vote, if registered. (Citizens
of the Republic of Ireland, Commonwealth countries and other UK
parliamentary electors could also vote if registered in a constituency.) The method of voting was the single transferable vote
method of proportional representation. The section also gave
extensive power to the Secretary of State to make orders covering
any matter on the initial election, including the register and deposits
for candidates. Section three enabled the Secretary of State to make
provision for the filling of vacancies through by-elections or
substitution. Section four set the rules for disqualification to the
NI High Court of Justice. Sections six to nine were general
provisions relating to orders, finance commencement and short title.
The commencement of the Act was dependent on the outcome of
the referendum on the Agreement on 22 May. The schedule gave

the Secretary of State extensive powers over the timing and place of meetings of the Assembly, the regulation of proceedings by standing orders, the appointment of an initial presiding officer and a deputy, the provision of premises, staff and facilities and the provision of salaries and allowances to members who had taken their seats in the prescribed manner. The powers given to the Secretary of State were criticised during the debate, in part because no finite time limits were placed on their exercise.

PRIMARY EVIDENCE AND INFORMATION

7. David Harkness, *Ireland in the Twentieth Century: Divided Island* (London, Macmillan, 1998), pp.168–9

Reaffirming their commitment to a society in Northern Ireland in which all may live in peace, free from discrimination and intolerance, and with the opportunity for both communities to participate fully in the structures and processes of government; Have accordingly agreed as follows:

A
STATUS OF NORTHERN IRELAND
ARTICLE 1
The two Governments
(a) affirm that any change in the status of Northern Ireland would only come about with the consent of a majority of the people of Northern Ireland;
(b) recognise that the present wish of a majority of the people of Northern Ireland is for no change in the status of Northern Ireland;
(c) declare that, if in the future a majority of the people of Northern Ireland clearly wish for and formally consent to the establishment of a united Ireland, they will introduce and support in the respective Parliaments legislation to give effect to that wish.

B
THE INTERGOVERNMENTAL CONFERENCE
ARTICLE 2
(a) There is hereby established, within the framework of the Anglo-Irish Intergovenmental Council set up after the meeting between the two Heads of Government on 6 November 1981, an Intergovernmental Conference (hereinafter referred to as 'the Conference'), concerned with Northern Ireland and with

relations between the two parts of the island of Ireland, to deal, as set out in this Agreement, on a regular basis with

    (i)   political matters;

    (ii) security and related matters;

    (iii) legal matters, including the administration of justice;

    (iv) the promotion of cross-Border co-operation.

(b) The United Kingdom Government accept that the Irish Government will put forward views and proposals on matters relating to Northern Ireland within the field of activity of the Conference in so far as those matters are not the responsibility of a devolved administration in Northern Ireland. In the interest of promoting peace and stability, determined efforts shall be made through the Conference to resolve any differences. The Conference will be mainly concerned with Northern Ireland; but some of the matters under consideration will involve co-operative action in both parts of the island of Ireland, and possibly also in Great Britain. Some of the proposals considered in respect of Northern Ireland may also be found to have application by the Irish Government. There is no derogation from the sovereignty of either the Irish Government or the United Kingdom Government, and each retains responsibility for the decisions and administration of government within its own jurisdiction.

ARTICLE 3

The Conference shall meet at ministerial or official level, as required. The business of the Conference will thus receive attention at the highest level. Regular and frequent ministerial meetings shall be held; and in particular special meetings shall be convened at the request of either side...

8. Dermot P Walsh, *Bloody Sunday and the Rule of Law in Northern Ireland* (London, Macmillan, 2000), pp.283–4, 305

[pp.283–4] In the light of the Good Friday Peace Agreement it would appear that efforts are finally being made to lay the foundations for the restoration of the rule of law and justice in Northern Ireland. For the present, the emergency legislation and much of the security apparatus remains in place. Nevertheless the prolonged cease-fire by the dominant paramilitary organisations, coupled with progress on the political front, have created an environment in which the impact of the emergency legislation and security apparatus is considerably reduced.

[p.305] *A political settlement*

Unquestionably a political settlement, such as that reached in the Good Friday Peace Agreement, is essential if the cycle of terrorist violence and state oppression is to be broken permanently in Northern Ireland. Indeed it is significant that the agreement directly addresses many of the political, economic and social grievances which have been alienating the nationalist community from the province of Northern Ireland since its establishment in 1921. Under the terms of the agreement, for example, nationalists are effectively guaranteed an opportunity to participate in all-Ireland bodies for the implementation, on an all-Ireland basis of certain executive responsibilities of mutual interest to both governments in the island. Equally, the agreement provides for the development of new social and economic policies to address, *inter alia* the problems of a divided society, social exclusion, a strengthening of fair employment legislation, the progressive elimination of the differential in unemployment rates between the two communities and action to support the development and use of the Irish language.

While all these measures are undoubtedly essential to combat the sources of alienation and promote the development of an inclusive society in Northern Ireland, a vital pre-requisite for the success of the agreement itself is the restoration of nationalist confidence in the rule of law. The very fact that a second inquiry into Bloody Sunday has been established will, of course, make an important contribution to this end.

9. Kelly Totten and Nathalie Collomb-Robert, *The Northern Ireland Question: Towards a 21st Century Solution?* (Sheffield, Sheffield Hallam University Press and produced for the Politics Association, Manchester, 2001), p.106

In January 1998 Tony Blair made a statement to the House of Commons announcing an inquest into Bloody Sunday; its terms of reference would be to inquire into:

'... the events on Sunday, 30 January 1972 which led to loss if life in connection with the procession in Londonderry on that day, taking account of any new information relevant to the events of that day.'

The Bloody Sunday (or Saville) Inquiry opened on 3 April 1998, chaired by Lord Saville of Newdigate and assisted by Sir Edward Somers, a former judge of the Court of Appeal of New Zealand,

and Justice William Hoyt, Chief Justice of the Canadian Province of New Brunswick. Evidence would be received in a number of ways. The Inquiry has the power to require persons to give evidence or produce documents and to seek expert advice. Already evidence has been received from a variety of people including civilians, clergy, media, soldiers, RUC, politicians and government officials.

Much controversy has already surrounded the inquiry:

* Following a preliminary meeting in April 1999, Lord Saville announced that the inquiry would not automatically provide a guarantee of immunity from prosecution to every person giving evidence to the inquiry. Immunity would instead be granted on a case-by-case basis, based upon an assessment of risk to each witness' personal safety. This decision was later overturned by the High Court in London who concluded that the anonymity of soldiers giving evidence to the Bloody Sunday inquiry should be protected...

* In February 2000 it was revealed that two guns used by the British army on Bloody Sunday had been destroy(ed) even though they were to be safeguarded for use as evidence.

* A British security document made the controversial claim that Sinn Fein Minister, Martin McGuinness, had fired at British soldiers during the events of Bloody Sunday (April 2001).

Although the inquiry is not due to report until late 2001 at the earliest, any conclusion is likely to provoke further controversy surrounding the events in Londonderry.

Notes

1. Tony Geraghty, *The Irish War: The Military History of Domestic Conflict* (London, HarperCollins, 1998), p.101.
2. *Ibid.*, pp.74–5; David Reed, *Ireland: The Key to the British Revolution* (London, Larkin Publications, 1984), pp.255–278.
3. Steve Bruce, *God Save Ulster: The Religion and Politics of Paisleyism* (Oxford, Oxford University Press, 1986), p.107.
4. Geraghty, *The Irish War*, p.77; Brendan O'Duffy, 'The Price of Containment: Deaths and Debate on Northern Ireland in the House of Commons, 1968–94', in Peter Catterall and Sean McDougall (eds), *The Northern Ireland Question in British Politics* (London, Macmillan, 1996), p.119.
5. Bruce, *God Save Ulster*, p.118.
6. Margaret Ward, 'The Women's Movement in the North of Ireland: Twenty Years On', in Sean Hutton and Patrick Stewart (eds), *Ireland's Histories: Aspects of State, Society and Ideology* (London, Routledge, 1991), pp.154, 156, *passim*.

7. Reed, *Ireland*, pp.318–50; Geraghty, *The Irish War*, p.99.
8. Michael von Tangen Page, 'The Inter-relationship of the Press and Politicians during the 1981 Hunger Strike at the Maze Prison', in Peter Catterall and Sean McDougall (eds), *The Northern Ireland Question in British Politics*, p.164.
9. *Ibid.*, *passim*, and Howard Smith, 'BBC Current Affairs Coverage of the 1981 Hunger Strike', in Catterall and McDougall, *The Northern Ireland Question*.
10. Reed, *Ireland*, p.348; Geraghty, *The Irish War*, p.100.
11. Liam Kennedy, *The Modern Industrialisation of Ireland, 1940–1988* (Dundalgon Press, 1989), p.28.
12. *Ibid.*, pp.9–54.
13. Frank Gaffikin and Mike Morrisey, *Northern Ireland: The Thatcher Years* (London, Zed Books, 1990), pp.92–105. For Omagh, see Bruce, *God Save Ulster*, p.119.
14. Geraghty, *The Irish War*, pp.101–2.
15. Christine Loughran, 'Armagh and Feminist Strategy: Campaigns around Republican Women Prisoners in Armagh Jail', *Feminist Review, Special Issue: Socialist Feminism 'Out of the Blue'* 23 (Summer 1986), p.61.
16. David Harkness, *Ireland in the Twentieth Century: Divided Island* (London, Macmillan, 1996), p.106.
17. Gaffikin and Morrisey, *Northern Ireland*, p.205.
18. Catterall and McDougall (eds), *The Northern Ireland Question in British Politics*, p.7.
19. W Harvey Cox, 'From Hillsborough to Downing Street – and After', in Catterall and McDougall (eds), *The Northern Ireland Question and British Politics*, pp.184–5.
20. Geraghty, *The Irish War*, p.101.
21. Neil Jarman and Dominic Bryan, *From Riots to Rights: Nationalist Parades in the North of Ireland* (Belfast, Centre for the Study of Conflict, University of Ulster, 1998), pp.69, 72.
22. O'Duffy, 'The Price of Containment', p.122.
23. Cox, 'From Hillsborough to Downing Street – and After', pp.186–190.
24. *Ibid.*, p.198.
25. Catterall and McDougall (eds), *The Northern Ireland Question in British Politics*, p.5.
26. Jarman and Bryan, *From Riots to Rights*, pp.71–7.

Bibliography

This section lists a few of the many books and articles relevant to each chapter. Some extracts from these articles and books are included in this volume.

Chapter 1: Thatcher, Thatcher's Britain and Thatcherism: Government and Conservative Politics, 1979–2002

Brendan Evans, *Thatcherism and British Politics, 1975–1999* (Stroud, Sutton, 1999)

Nigel Lawson, *The View from No. 10: Memoirs of a Tory Radical* (London, Corgi Books, 1991)

Anthony Seldon, *Major, A Political Life* (London, Weidenfeld and Nicolson, 1997)

Margaret Thatcher, *The Downing Street Years* (London, Harper Collins, 1993)

Hugo Young, *One of Us: A biography of Margaret Thatcher* (London, Macmillan, 1988)

Chapter 2: The Welfare State: 1979–2002

Equal Opportunities Commission, *Women and Men in Britain: The Lifecycle of Inequality* (Manchester, EOC, 2001)

David Gladstone, *The Twentieth Century Welfare State* (London, Macmillan, 1999)

Caroline Glendinning and Jane Millar (eds), *Women and Poverty in Britain* (Brighton, Harvester Wheatsheaf, 1987)

Keith Laybourn, *The Evolution of British Social Policy and the Welfare State, 1800–1993* (Keele, Keele and Edinburgh University Presses, 1995)

Robin M Page and Richard Silburn (eds), *British Social Welfare in the Twentieth Century* (London, Macmillan, 1999)

Sarah Payne, *Women, Health and Poverty: An Introduction* (Brighton, Harvester Wheatsheaf, 1991)

Chapter 3: The Attack upon Trade Unionism: 1979–2002

Keith Laybourn, *A History of British Trade Unionism c. 1770–1990* (Stroud, Sutton, 1992)

Ron Ramdin, *The Making of the Black Working Class in Britain* (Aldershot, Wildwood House, 1987)

Richard Taylor, *The Future of Trade Unions* (London, Andre Deutsch, 1994)

Sylvia Walby, *Gender Transformations* (London, Routledge, 1997)

Chapter 4: The Fall of the 'Old' and the Rise of 'New' Labour

Brian Brivati and Richard Heffernan (eds), *The Labour Party: A Centenary History* (London, Macmillan, 2000)

Darcus Howe, *Darcus Howe on Black Sections in the Labour Party* (London, Race Today Publications, 1985)

Kevin Jefferys (ed.), *Leading Labour: From Keir Hardie to Tony Blair* (London, I.B.Tauris, 1999)

Keith Laybourn, *A Century of Labour: A History of the Labour Party* (Stroud, Sutton, 2000)

Peter Mandelson and Roger Liddle, *The Blair Revolution: Can New Labour Deliver?* (London, Faber and Faber, 1996)

Andrew Thorpe, *A History of the British Labour Party* (London, Palgrave, 2001 edition)

Chapter 5: The Social Democratic Party, the Liberals and the Liberal Democrats

Alan Beith, *The Case for the Liberal Party & The Alliance* (London, Longman, 1983)

Chris Cook, *A Short History of the Liberal Party, 1900–1992* (London, Macmillan, 1993)

Make the Difference: The Liberal Democrat Manifesto 1997 (London, Liberal Democrats, 1997)

Geoffrey Lee Williams and Alan Lee Williams, *Labour's Decline and the Social Democrats' Fall* (London, Macmillan, 1989)

Chapter 6: The Rise of Nationalism in Scotland and Wales

Alice Brown, 'Women and Politics in Scotland', *Parliamentary Affairs*, 49 (1) (1996)

Michael Keating and Arthur Midwinter, *The Government of Scotland* (Edinburgh, Mainstream, 1983)

Laura McAllister, 'The Welsh Devolution Referendum: Definitely, Maybe?', *Parliamentary Affairs*, 51 (2) (April 1998), p.82

Catriona MM MacDonald (ed.), *Unionist Scotland, 1800–1997* (Edinburgh, John Donald, 1998)

Kenneth O Morgan, *Rebirth of a Nation, 1880–1980* (Oxford, Oxford University Press, University of Wales Press, 1981)

Kenyon Wright, *The People Say Yes: The Making of Scotland's Parliament* (Argyll, Argyll Publishing, 1997)

Chapter 7: Eurocommunism, the End of the Cold War and the Collapse of the Communist Party of Great Britain

John Callaghan, *Socialism in Britain* (Oxford, Blackwell, 1990)

Keith Laybourn and Dylan Murphy, *Under the Red Flag: A History of Communism in Britain* (Stroud, Sutton, 1999)

Willie Thompson, *The Good Old Cause: British Communism, 1920–1991* (London, Pluto Press, 1992)

Chapter 8: Feminist Debates and the Changing Position of Women in British Society

Sally Baldwin and Jane Falkingham (eds), *Social Security and Social Change: New Challenges to the Beveridge Model* (Hemel Hempstead, Harvester Wheatsheaf, 1994)

Rosemary Crompton, *et al.* (eds), *Changing Form of Employment Organisations, Skills and Gender* (London, Routledge, 1996)

Equal Opportunities Commission, *Facts about Men and Women in Great Britain, 1999* (Manchester, EOC, 1999)

Stevi Jackson and Jackie Jones (eds), *Contemporary Feminist Theories* (Edinburgh, Edinburgh University Press, 1998)

Ruth Lister, *Citizenship: Feminist Perspectives* (London, Routledge, 1998)

Chapter 9: Ethnicity and Racial Equality

Education For All: The Report of a Committee of Inquiry into the Education of Children from Ethnic Minority Groups (London, HMSO, 1985, Cmnd. 9453)

Iqbal Wahhab, *Muslims in Britain: Profile of a Community* (London, Runnymede Trust, 1989)

Heidi Safia Mirza (ed.), *Black British Feminism: A Reader* (London, Routledge, 1997)

Ron Ramdin, *The Making of the Black Working Class in Britain* (Aldershot, Wildwood, 1987)

The Stephen Lawrence Inquiry: Report of an Inquiry by Sir William Macpherson of Cluny (London, The Stationery Office, 1999)

Chapter 10: Northern Ireland

Steven Bruce, *God Save Ulster: The Religion and Politics of Paisleyism* (Oxford, Oxford University Press, 1986)

Peter Catterall and Sean McDougall (eds), *The Northern Ireland Question in British Politics* (London, Macmillan, 1996)

Sydney Elliott, 'The Referendum Question and Assembly Elections in Northern Ireland', *Irish Political Studies*, 14 (1999)

Frank Gaffikin and Mike Morrisey, *Northern Ireland: The Thatcher Years* (London, Zed Books, 1990)

David Harkness, *Ireland in the Twentieth Century: Divided Island* (London, Macmillan, 1998)

Martin O'Donnell, 'The Impact of the 1981 H Block Hunger Strike on the British Labour Party', *Irish Political Studies*, 14 (1999)

Dermot P Walsh, *Bloody Sunday and the Rule of Law in Northern Ireland* (London, Macmillan, 2000)

Index